Blue Flag

story and art by
KAITO

6

CHAPTER 34

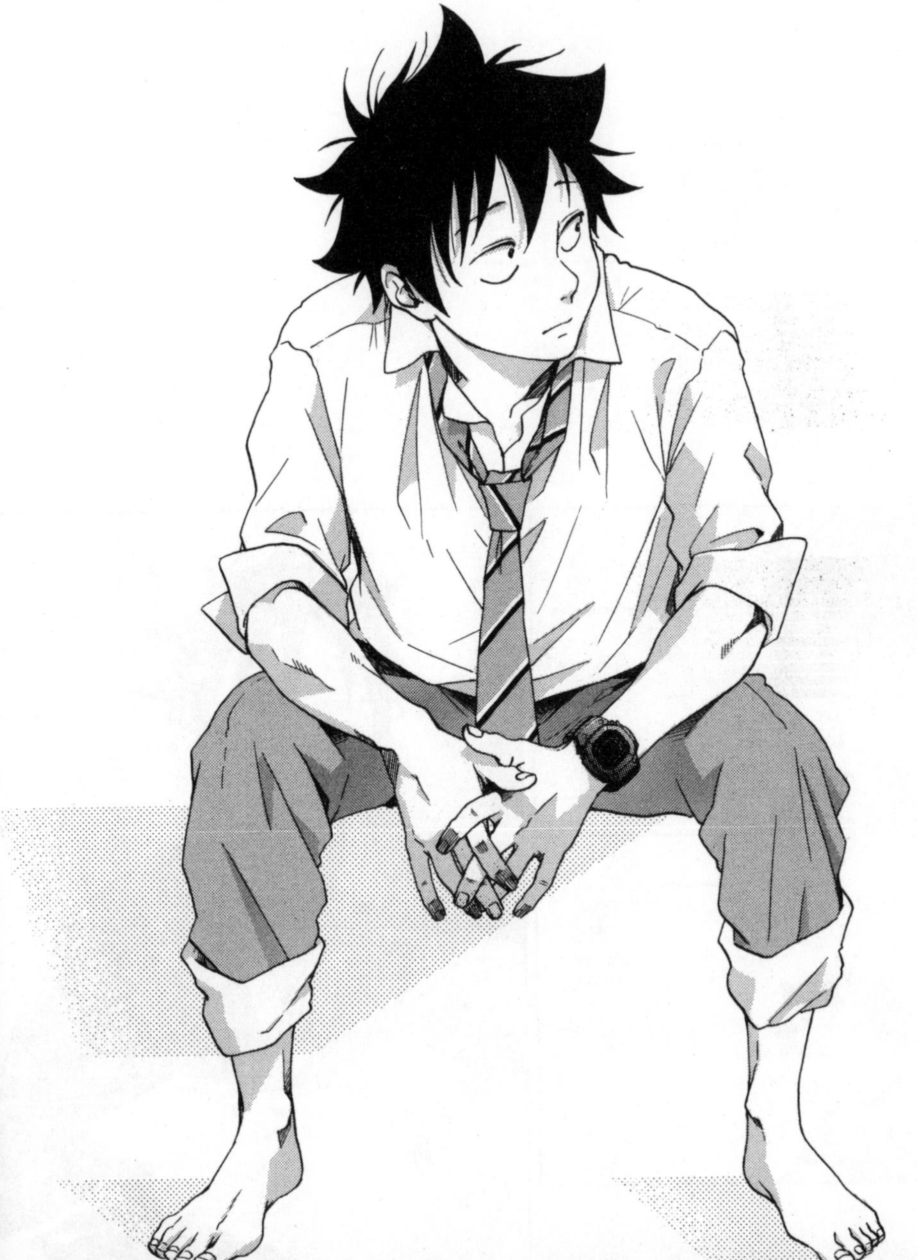

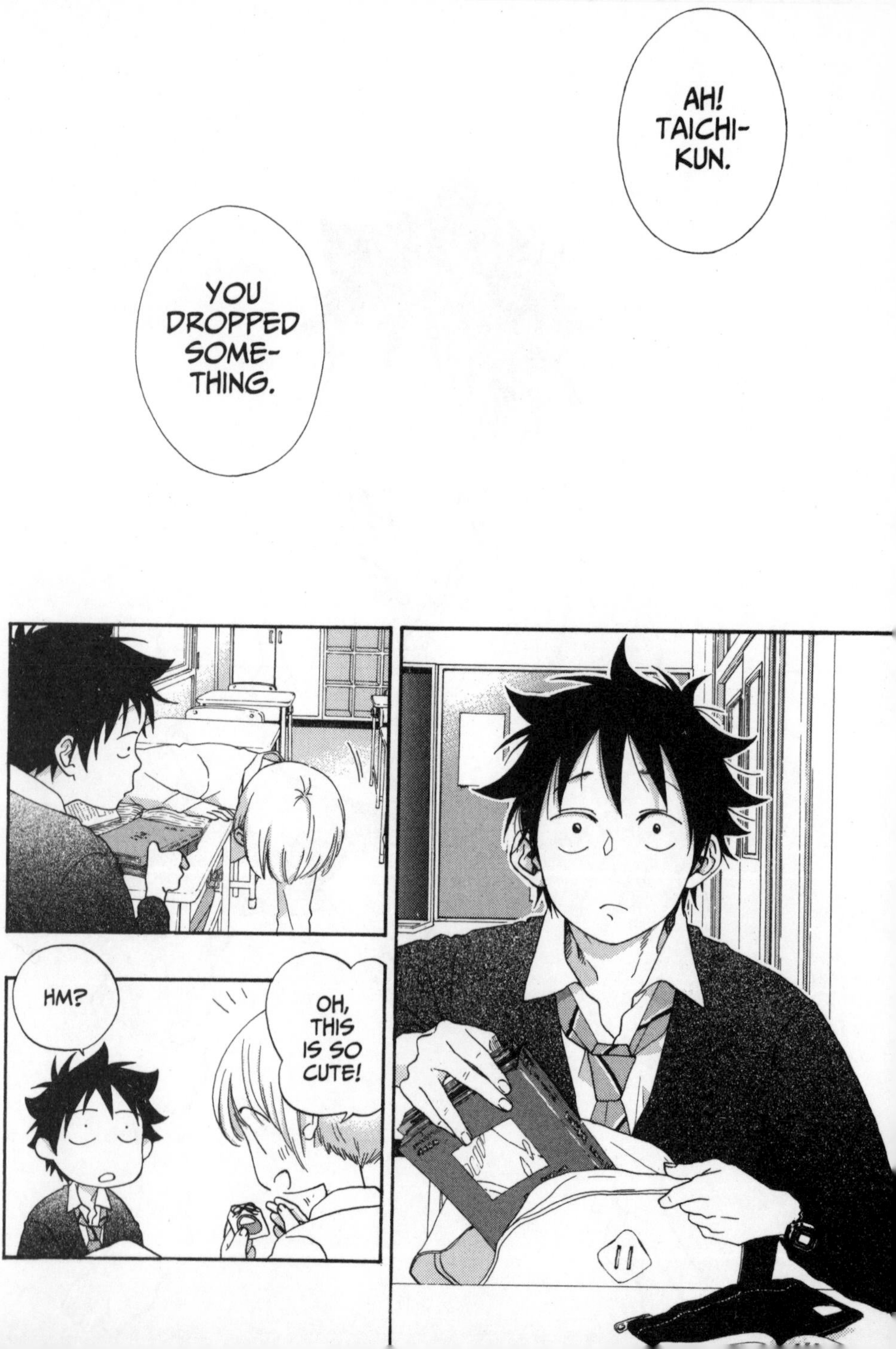
AH! TAICHI-KUN.
YOU DROPPED SOME-THING.
OH, THIS IS SO CUTE!
HM?

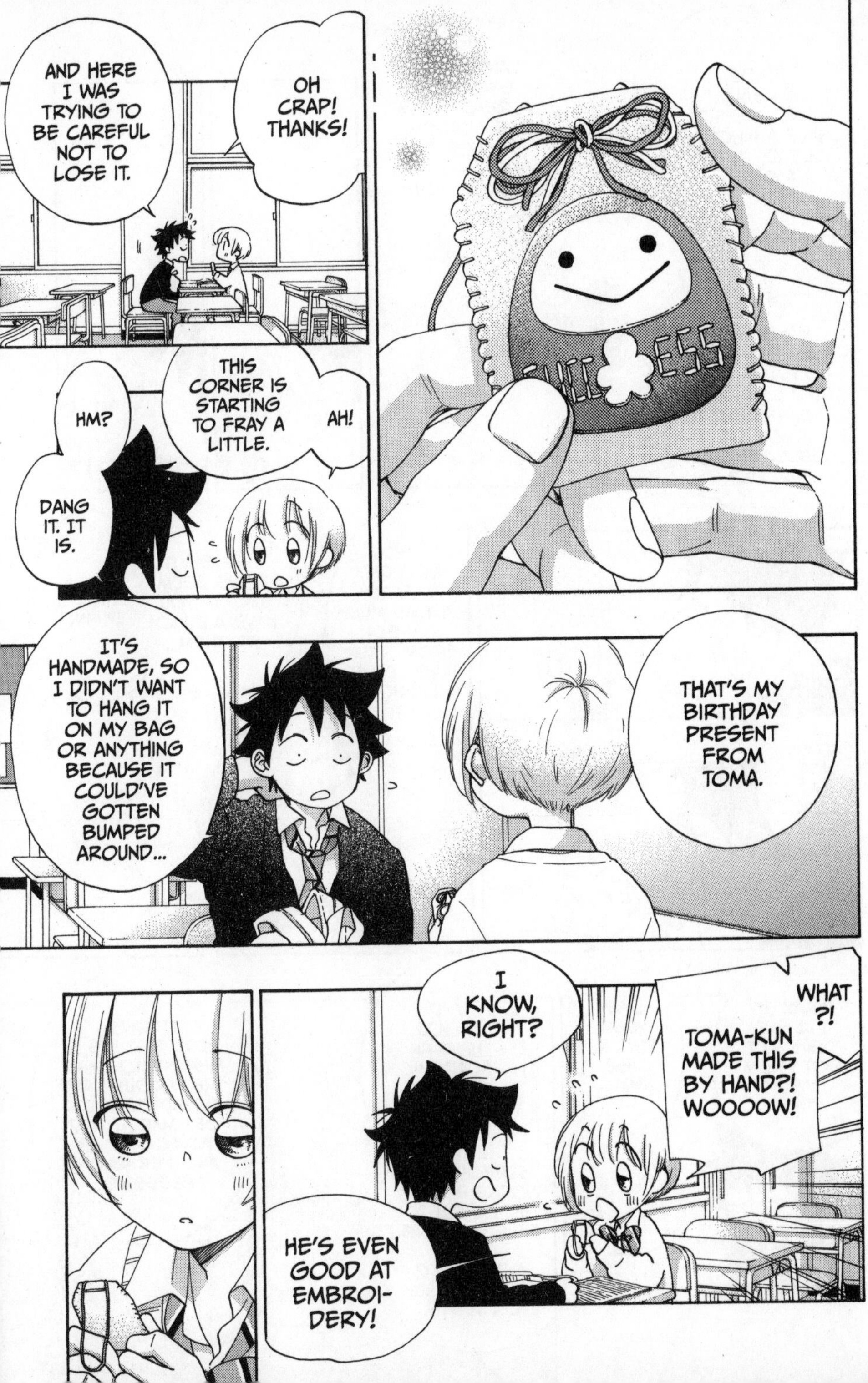
OH CRAP! THANKS!
AND HERE I WAS TRYING TO BE CAREFUL NOT TO LOSE IT.
THIS CORNER IS STARTING TO FRAY A LITTLE.
AH!
HM?
DANG IT. IT IS.
THAT'S MY BIRTHDAY PRESENT FROM TOMA.
IT'S HANDMADE, SO I DIDN'T WANT TO HANG IT ON MY BAG OR ANYTHING BECAUSE IT COULD'VE GOTTEN BUMPED AROUND...
WHAT?!
TOMA-KUN MADE THIS BY HAND?! WOOOOW!
I KNOW, RIGHT?
HE'S EVEN GOOD AT EMBROIDERY!

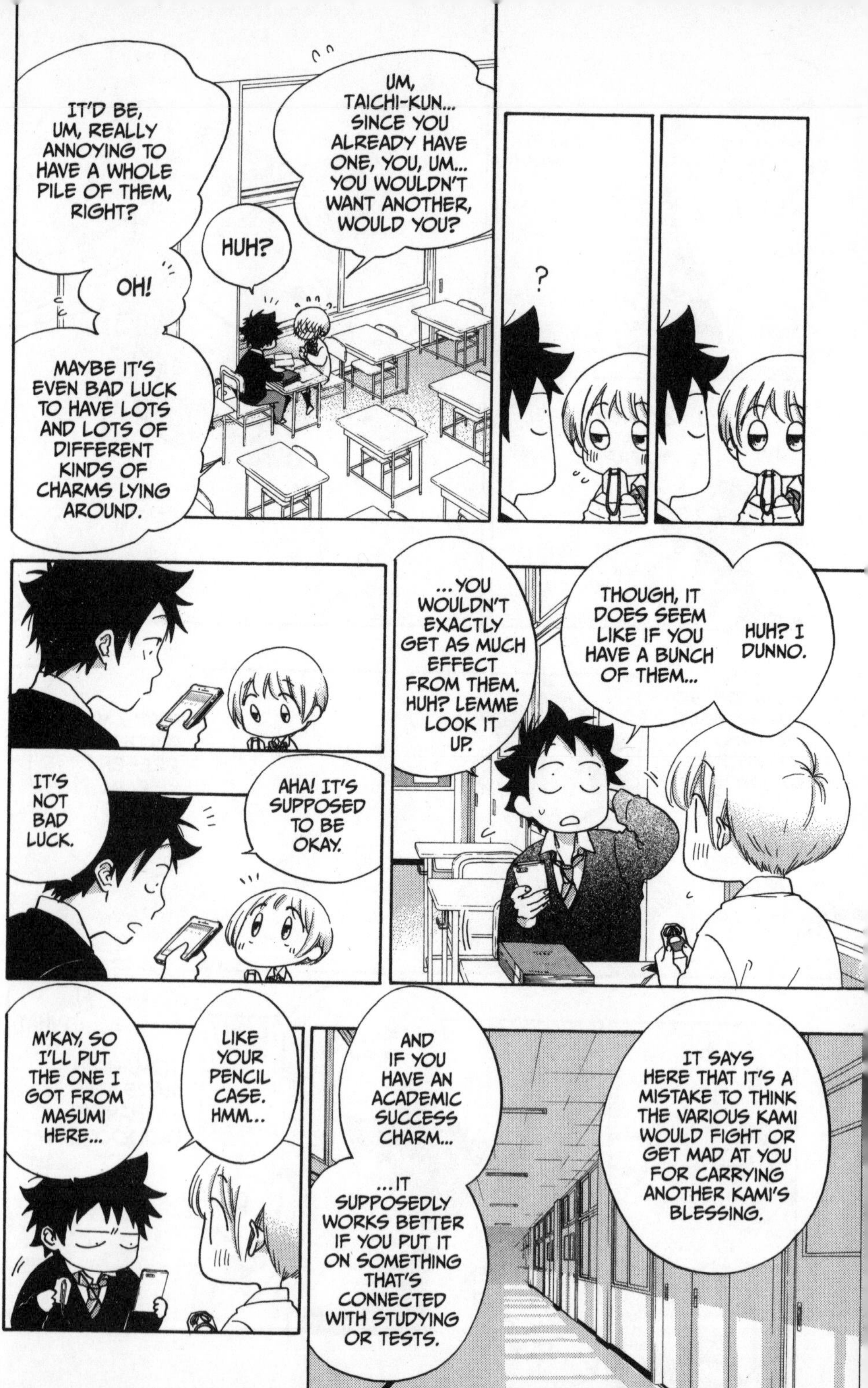
?
UM, TAICHI-KUN... SINCE YOU ALREADY HAVE ONE, YOU, UM... YOU WOULDN'T WANT ANOTHER, WOULD YOU?
HUH?
IT'D BE, UM, REALLY ANNOYING TO HAVE A WHOLE PILE OF THEM, RIGHT?
OH!
MAYBE IT'S EVEN BAD LUCK TO HAVE LOTS AND LOTS OF DIFFERENT KINDS OF CHARMS LYING AROUND.
HUH? I DUNNO.
THOUGH, IT DOES SEEM LIKE IF YOU HAVE A BUNCH OF THEM...
...YOU WOULDN'T EXACTLY GET AS MUCH EFFECT FROM THEM. HUH? LEMME LOOK IT UP.
AHA! IT'S SUPPOSED TO BE OKAY.
IT'S NOT BAD LUCK.
IT SAYS HERE THAT IT'S A MISTAKE TO THINK THE VARIOUS KAMI WOULD FIGHT OR GET MAD AT YOU FOR CARRYING ANOTHER KAMI'S BLESSING.
AND IF YOU HAVE AN ACADEMIC SUCCESS CHARM...
...IT SUPPOSEDLY WORKS BETTER IF YOU PUT IT ON SOMETHING THAT'S CONNECTED WITH STUDYING OR TESTS.
LIKE YOUR PENCIL CASE. HMM...
M'KAY, SO I'LL PUT THE ONE I GOT FROM MASUMI HERE...

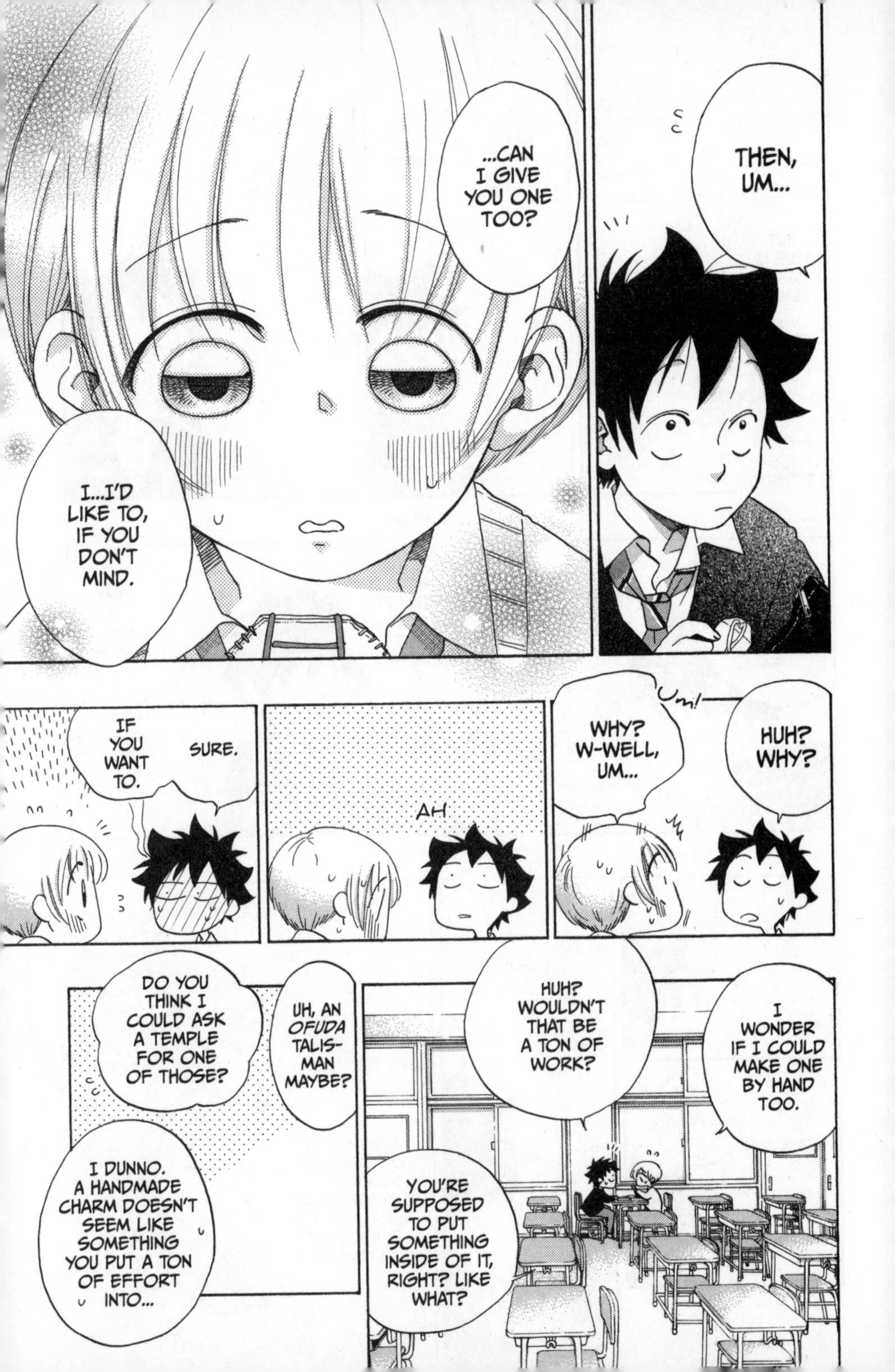
THEN, UM...
...CAN I GIVE YOU ONE TOO?
I...I'D LIKE TO, IF YOU DON'T MIND.
HUH? WHY?
Um!
WHY? W-WELL, UM...
AH
SURE.
IF YOU WANT TO.
I WONDER IF I COULD MAKE ONE BY HAND TOO.
HUH? WOULDN'T THAT BE A TON OF WORK?
YOU'RE SUPPOSED TO PUT SOMETHING INSIDE OF IT, RIGHT? LIKE WHAT?
UH, AN *OFUDA* TALISMAN MAYBE?
DO YOU THINK I COULD ASK A TEMPLE FOR ONE OF THOSE?
I DUNNO. A HANDMADE CHARM DOESN'T SEEM LIKE SOMETHING YOU PUT A TON OF EFFORT INTO...

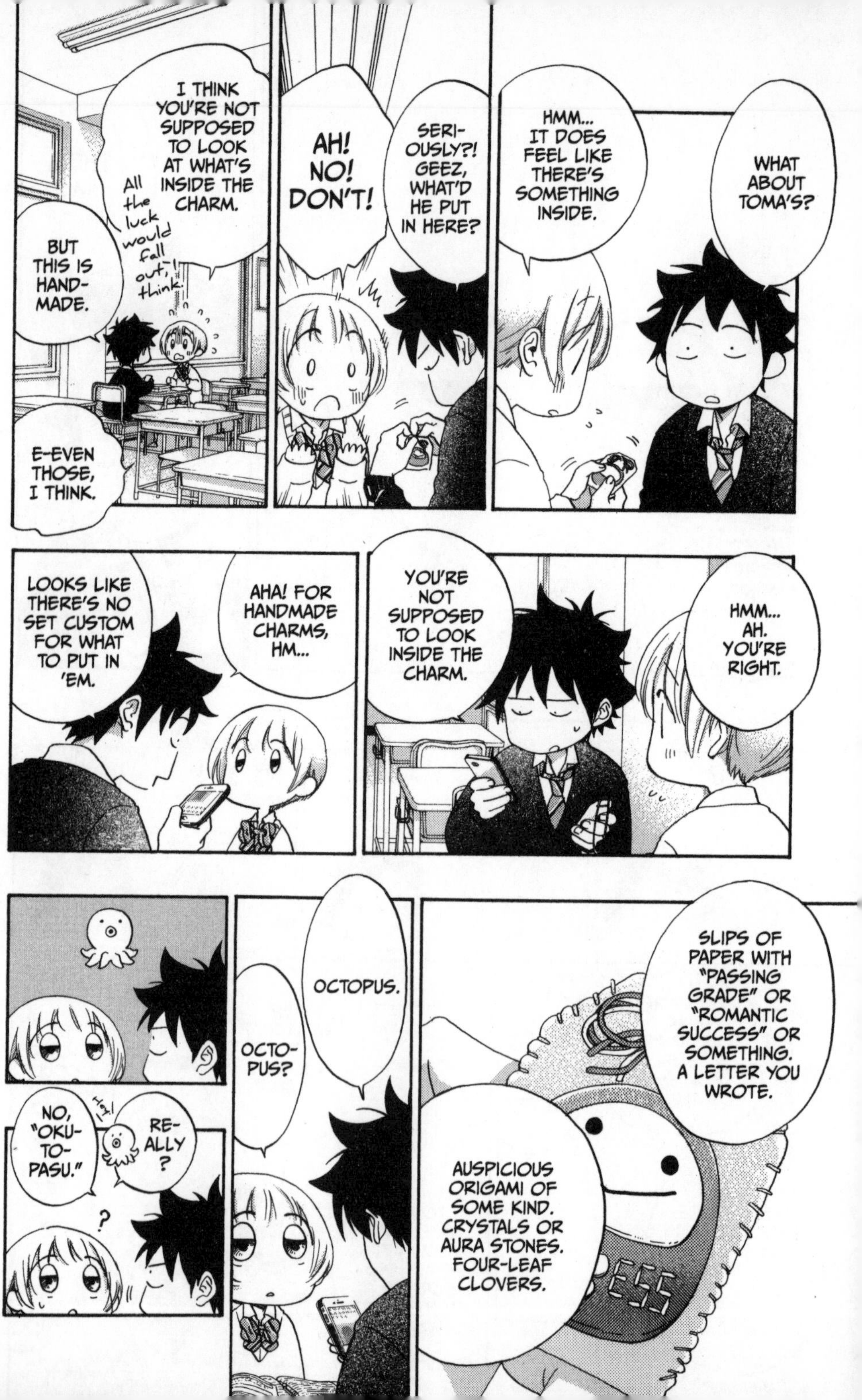
WHAT ABOUT TOMA'S?
HMM... IT DOES FEEL LIKE THERE'S SOMETHING INSIDE.
SERI-OUSLY?! GEEZ, WHAT'D HE PUT IN HERE?
AH! NO! DON'T!
I THINK YOU'RE NOT SUPPOSED TO LOOK AT WHAT'S INSIDE THE CHARM.
All the luck would fall out, I think.
BUT THIS IS HAND-MADE.
E-EVEN THOSE, I THINK.
HMM... AH. YOU'RE RIGHT.
YOU'RE NOT SUPPOSED TO LOOK INSIDE THE CHARM.
AHA! FOR HANDMADE CHARMS, HM...
LOOKS LIKE THERE'S NO SET CUSTOM FOR WHAT TO PUT IN 'EM.
SLIPS OF PAPER WITH "PASSING GRADE" OR "ROMANTIC SUCCESS" OR SOMETHING. A LETTER YOU WROTE.
AUSPICIOUS ORIGAMI OF SOME KIND. CRYSTALS OR AURA STONES. FOUR-LEAF CLOVERS.
OCTOPUS.
OCTO-PUS?
NO, "OKU-TO-PASU."
RE-ALLY?

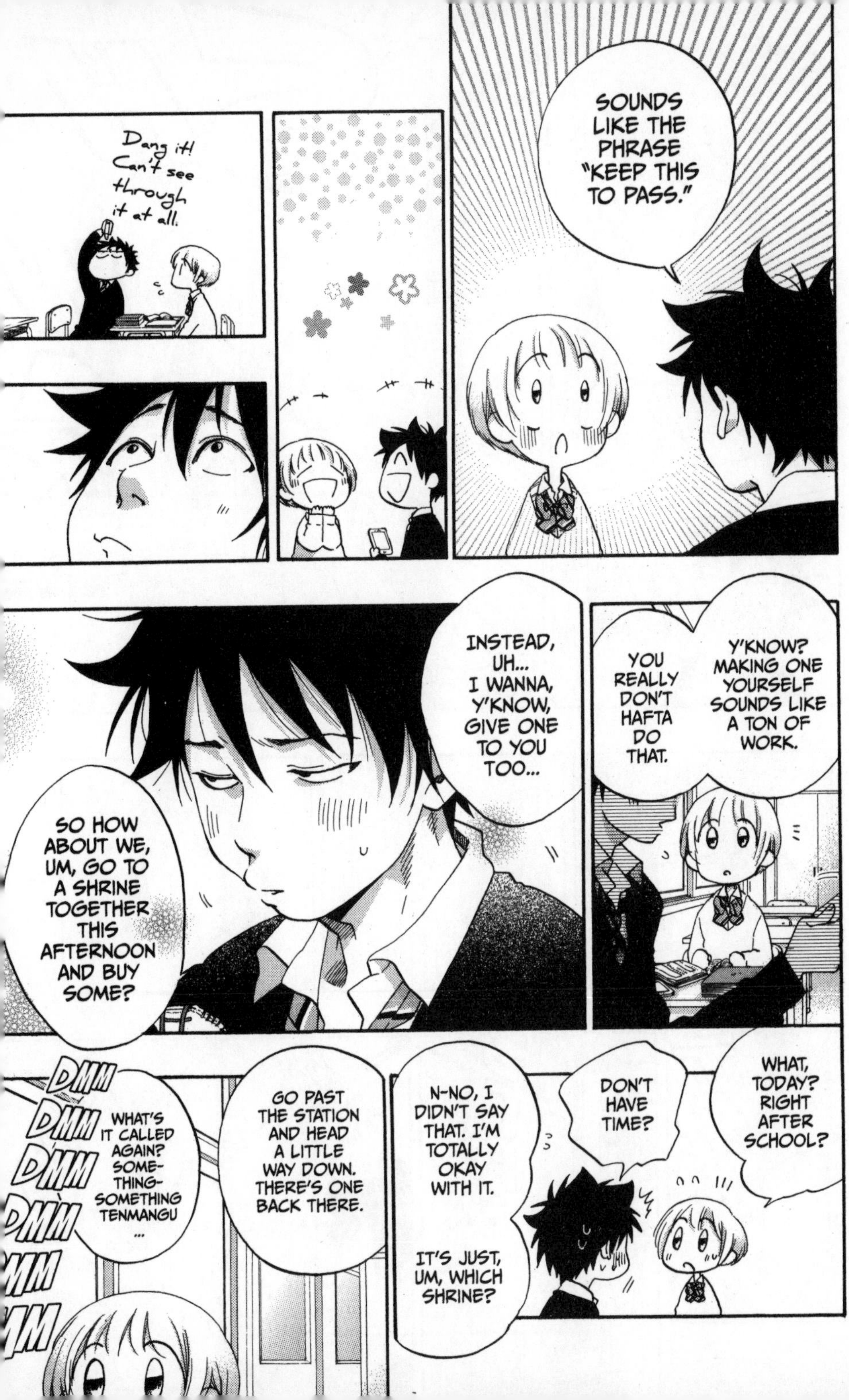
SOUNDS LIKE THE PHRASE "KEEP THIS TO PASS."
Dang it! Can't see through it at all.
Y'KNOW? MAKING ONE YOURSELF SOUNDS LIKE A TON OF WORK.
YOU REALLY DON'T HAFTA DO THAT.
INSTEAD, UH... I WANNA, Y'KNOW, GIVE ONE TO YOU TOO...
SO HOW ABOUT WE, UM, GO TO A SHRINE TOGETHER THIS AFTERNOON AND BUY SOME?
WHAT, TODAY? RIGHT AFTER SCHOOL?
DON'T HAVE TIME?
N-NO, I DIDN'T SAY THAT. I'M TOTALLY OKAY WITH IT.
IT'S JUST, UM, WHICH SHRINE?
GO PAST THE STATION AND HEAD A LITTLE WAY DOWN. THERE'S ONE BACK THERE.
WHAT'S IT CALLED AGAIN? SOME-THING-SOMETHING TENMANGU ...
DMM DMM DMM DMM MM MM

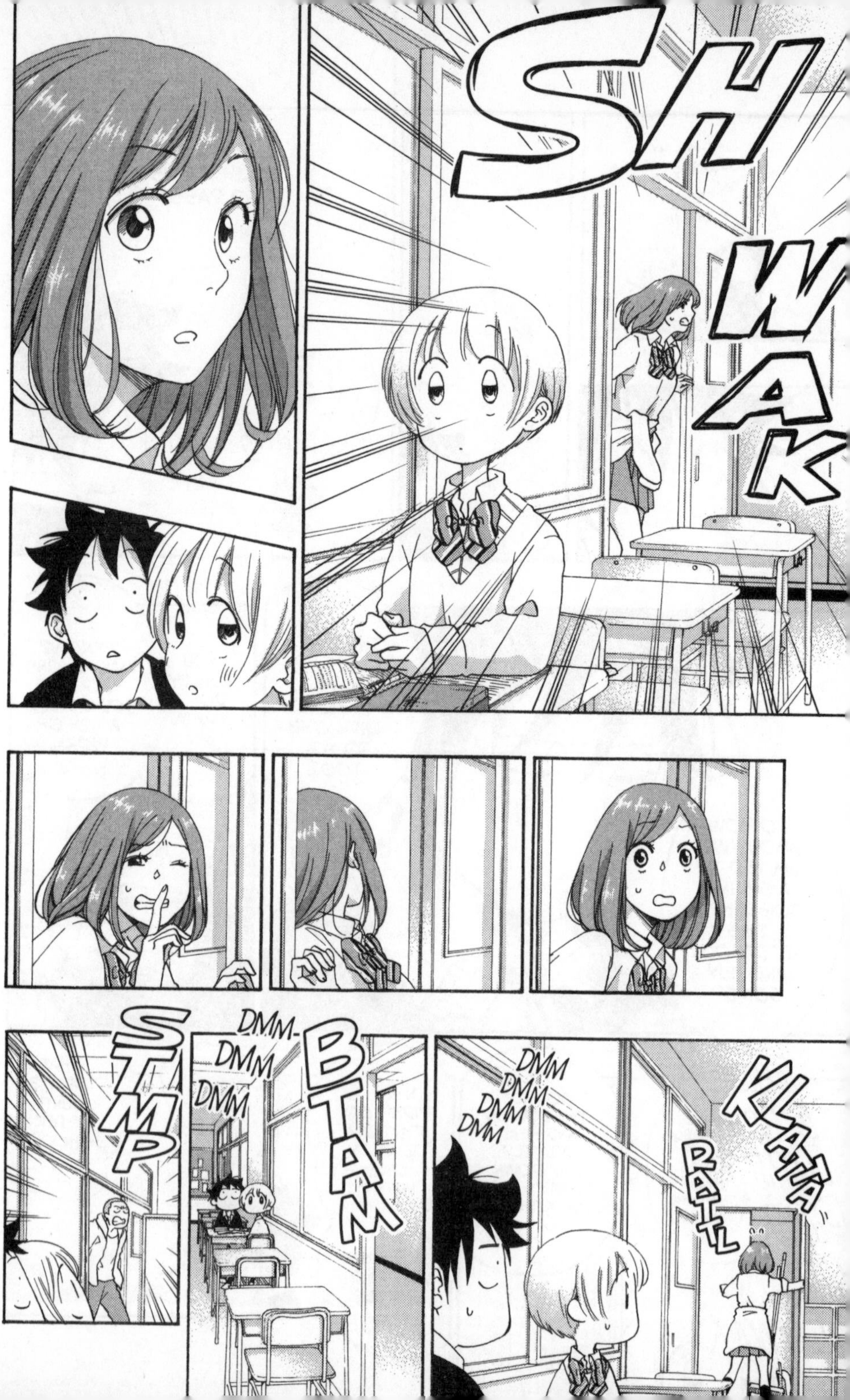
SHWAK
KLATA
RATTL
DMM
DMM
DMM
DMM
BTAM
DMM-
DMM
DMM
STMP

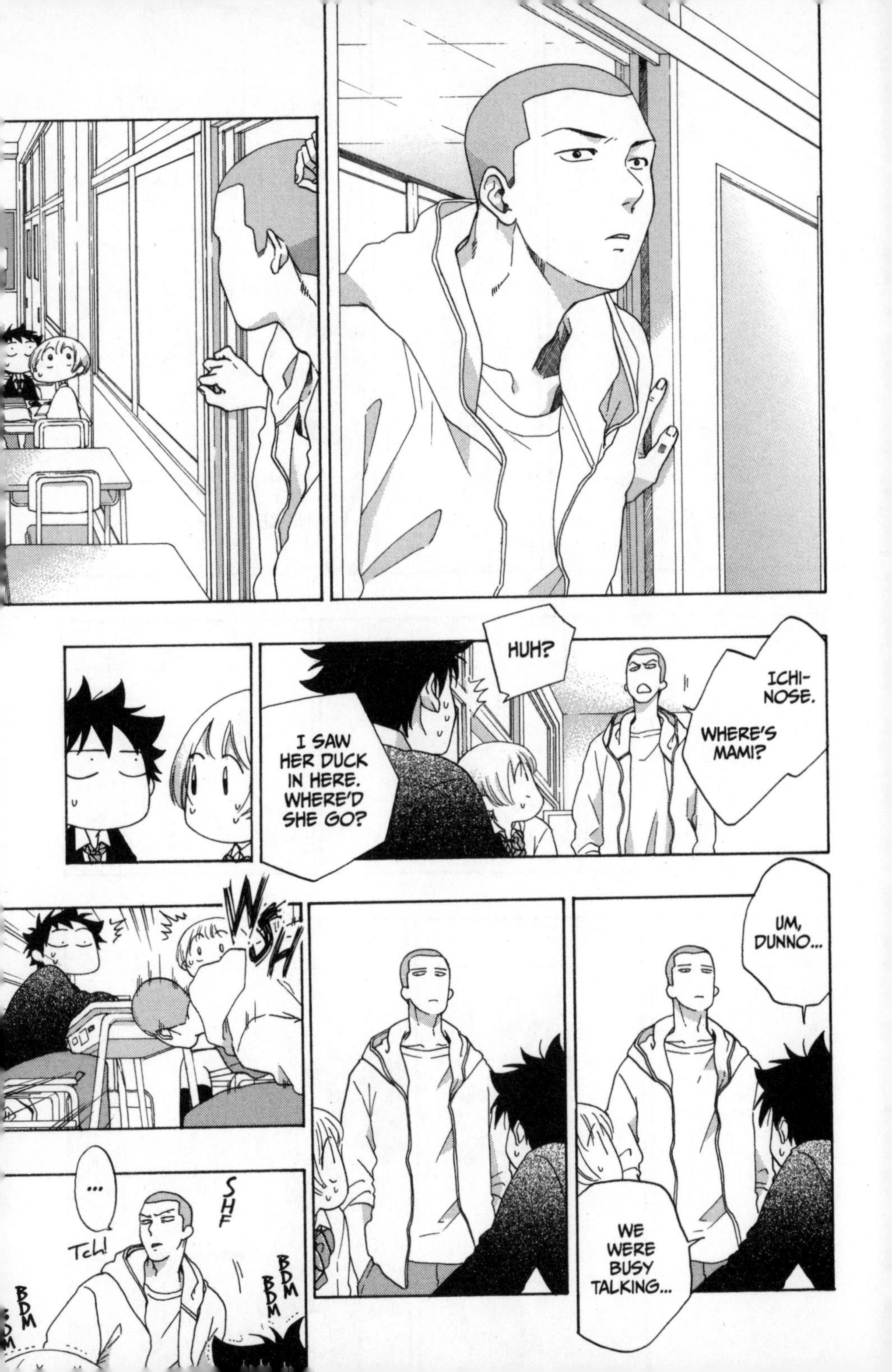

ICHI-NOSE.
WHERE'S MAMI?
HUH?
I SAW HER DUCK IN HERE. WHERE'D SHE GO?
UM, DUNNO...
WE WERE BUSY TALKING...
WSH
...
SHF
TCH!
BDM BDM
BDM

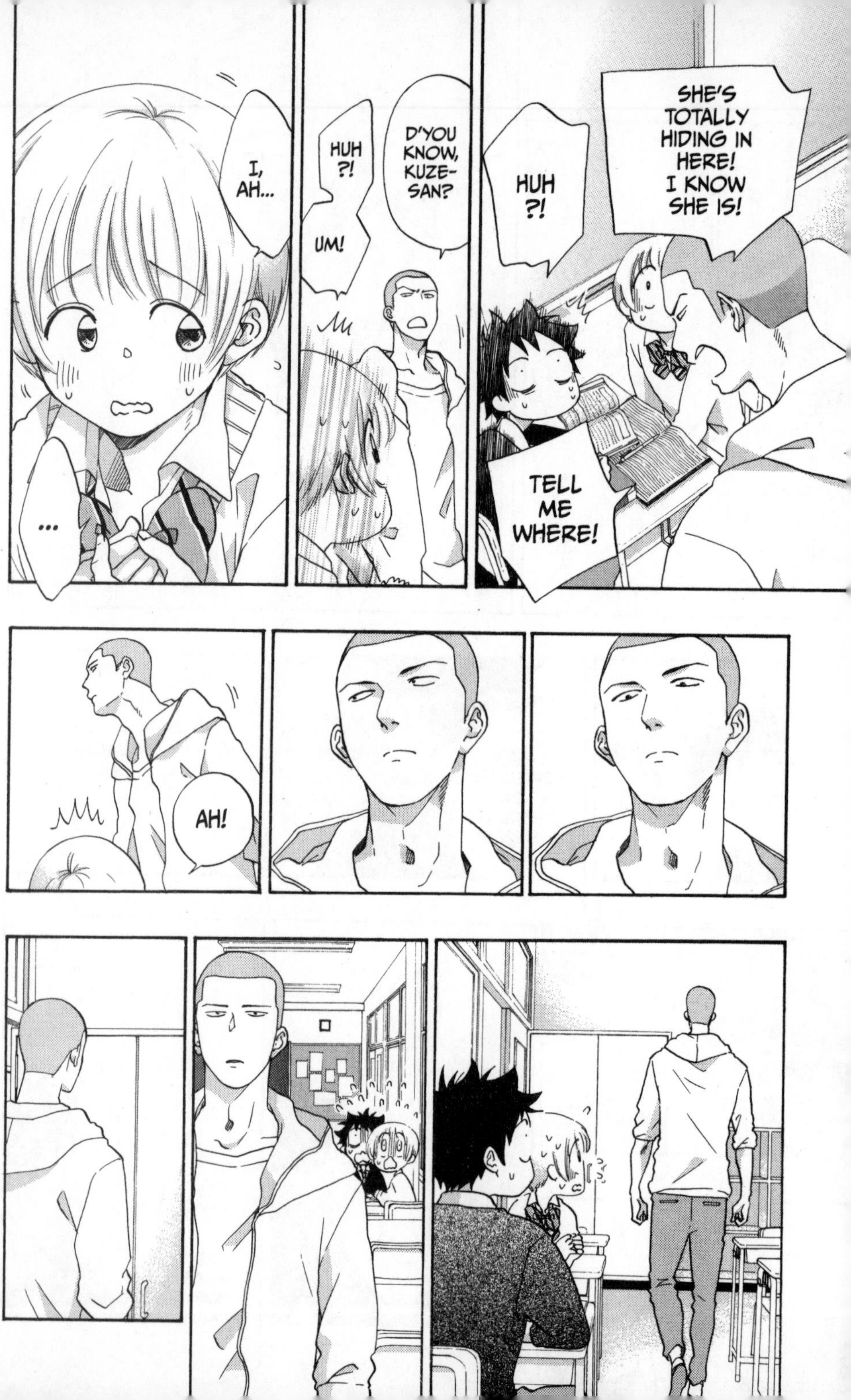
SHE'S TOTALLY HIDING IN HERE! I KNOW SHE IS!
HUH ?!
TELL ME WHERE!
D'YOU KNOW, KUZE-SAN?
HUH ?!
UM!
I, AH...
...
AH!

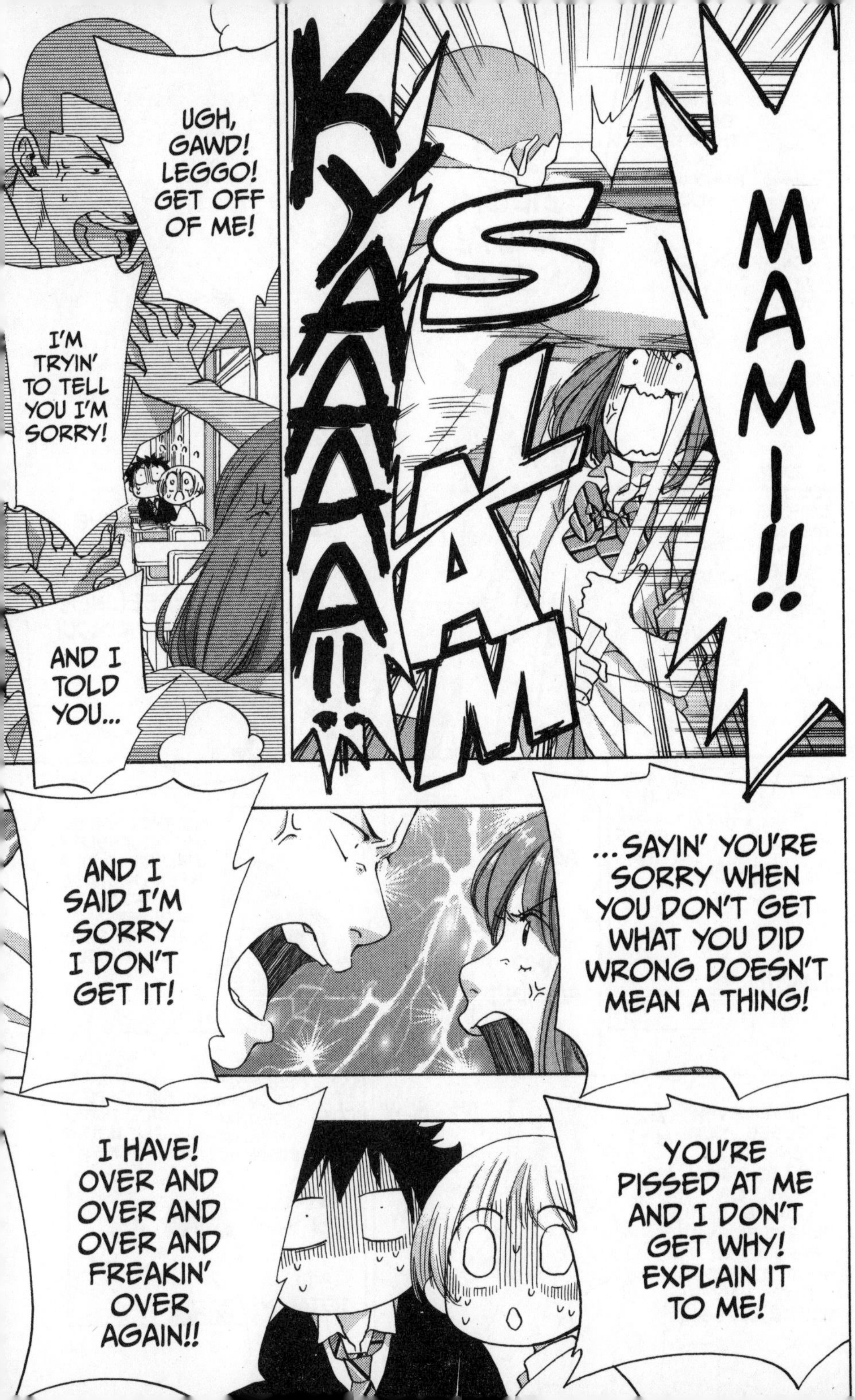
MAMI!!
SLAM
KYAAAA!!
UGH, GAWD! LEGGO! GET OFF OF ME!
I'M TRYIN' TO TELL YOU I'M SORRY!
AND I TOLD YOU...
...SAYIN' YOU'RE SORRY WHEN YOU DON'T GET WHAT YOU DID WRONG DOESN'T MEAN A THING!
AND I SAID I'M SORRY I DON'T GET IT!
YOU'RE PISSED AT ME AND I DON'T GET WHY! EXPLAIN IT TO ME!
I HAVE! OVER AND OVER AND OVER AND FREAKIN' OVER AGAIN!!

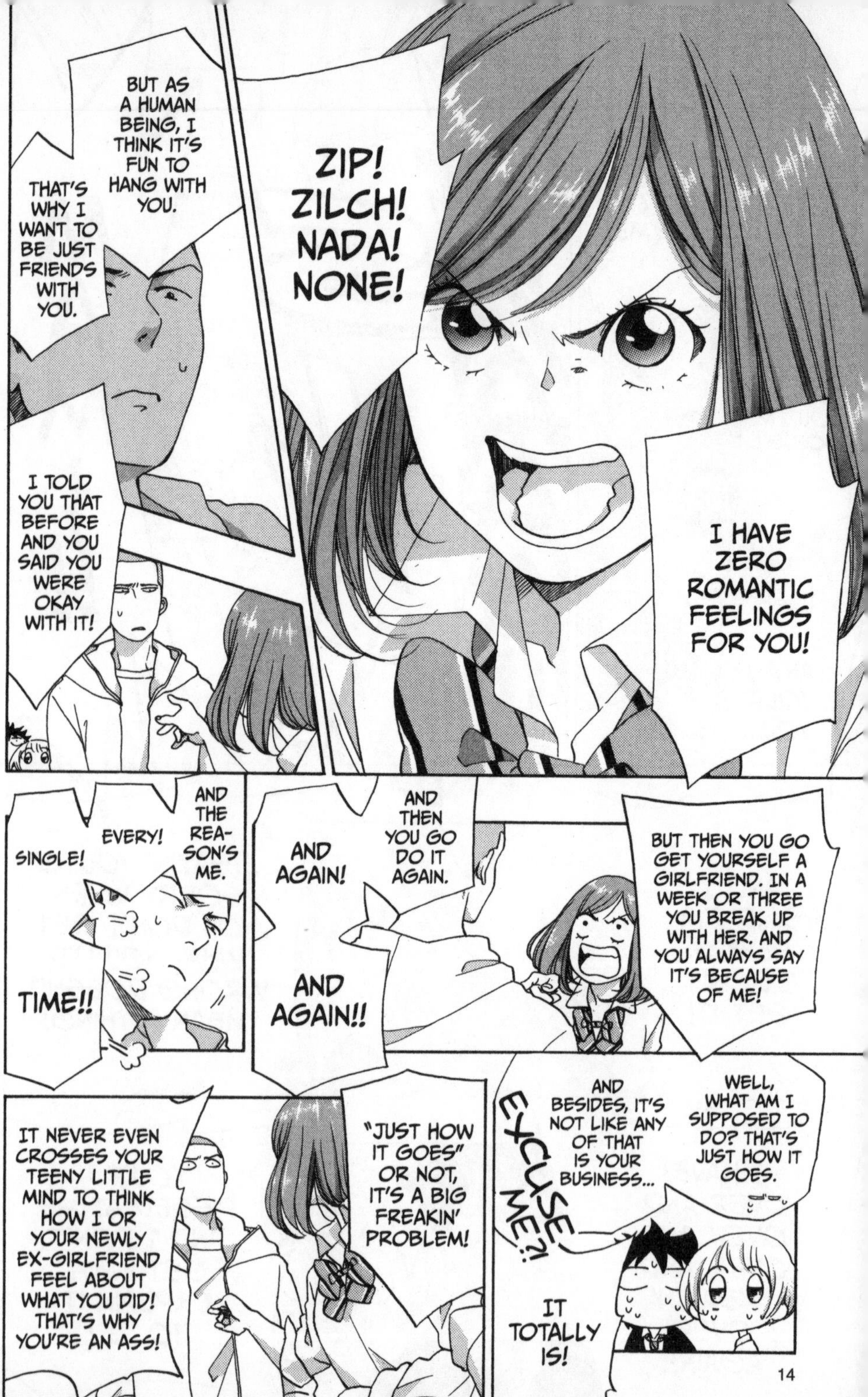
I HAVE ZERO ROMANTIC FEELINGS FOR YOU!
ZIP! ZILCH! NADA! NONE!
BUT AS A HUMAN BEING, I THINK IT'S FUN TO HANG WITH YOU.
THAT'S WHY I WANT TO BE JUST FRIENDS WITH YOU.
I TOLD YOU THAT BEFORE AND YOU SAID YOU WERE OKAY WITH IT!
BUT THEN YOU GO GET YOURSELF A GIRLFRIEND. IN A WEEK OR THREE YOU BREAK UP WITH HER. AND YOU ALWAYS SAY IT'S BECAUSE OF ME!
AND THEN YOU GO DO IT AGAIN.
AND AGAIN!
AND AGAIN!!
AND THE REA-SON'S ME.
EVERY!
SINGLE!
TIME!!
WELL, WHAT AM I SUPPOSED TO DO? THAT'S JUST HOW IT GOES.
AND BESIDES, IT'S NOT LIKE ANY OF THAT IS YOUR BUSINESS...
EXCUSE ME?!
IT TOTALLY IS!
"JUST HOW IT GOES" OR NOT, IT'S A BIG FREAKIN' PROBLEM!
IT NEVER EVEN CROSSES YOUR TEENY LITTLE MIND TO THINK HOW I OR YOUR NEWLY EX-GIRLFRIEND FEEL ABOUT WHAT YOU DID! THAT'S WHY YOU'RE AN ASS!

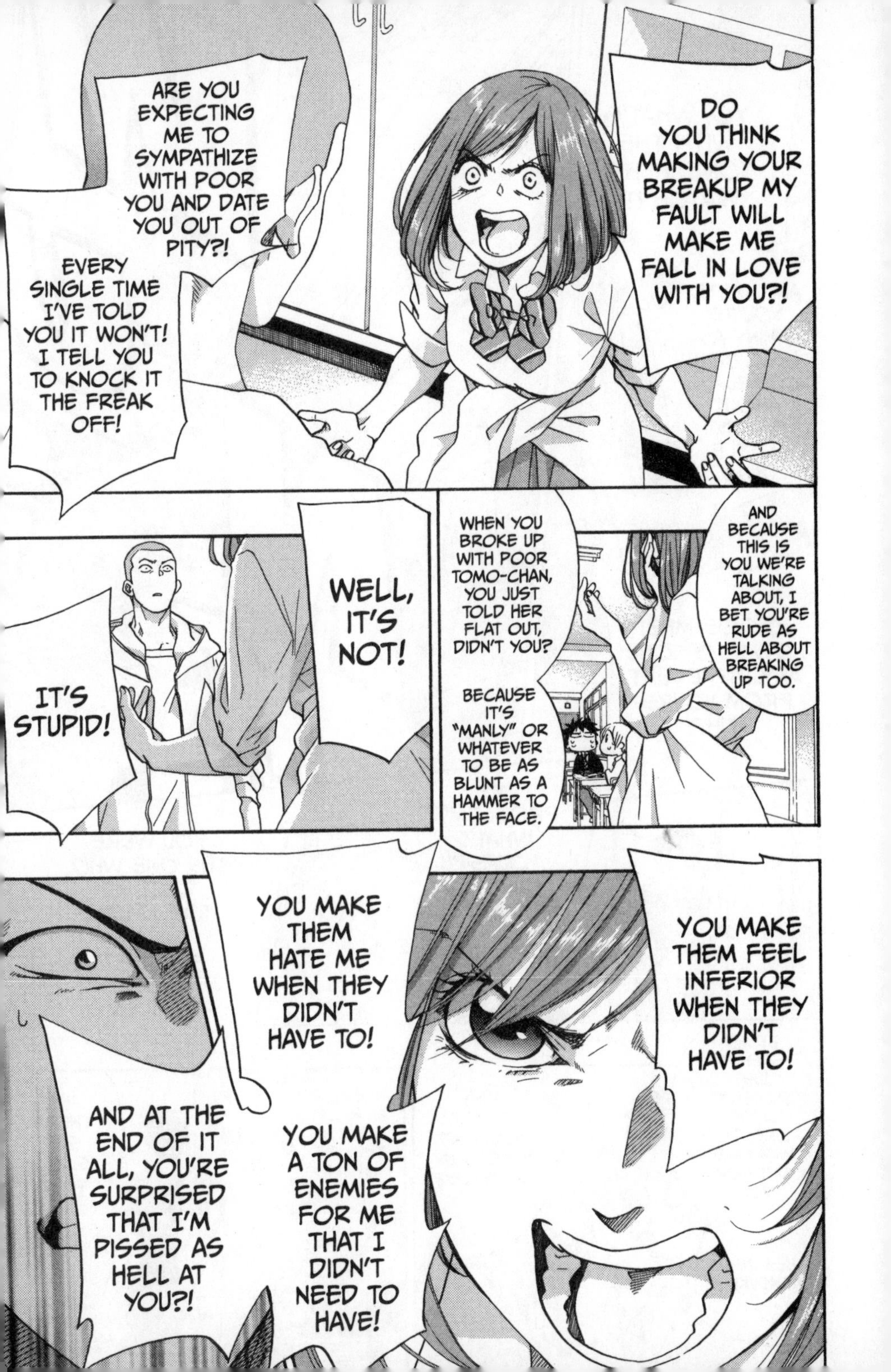
DO YOU THINK MAKING YOUR BREAKUP MY FAULT WILL MAKE ME FALL IN LOVE WITH YOU?!
ARE YOU EXPECTING ME TO SYMPATHIZE WITH POOR YOU AND DATE YOU OUT OF PITY?!
EVERY SINGLE TIME I'VE TOLD YOU IT WON'T! I TELL YOU TO KNOCK IT THE FREAK OFF!
AND BECAUSE THIS IS YOU WE'RE TALKING ABOUT, I BET YOU'RE RUDE AS HELL ABOUT BREAKING UP TOO.
WHEN YOU BROKE UP WITH POOR TOMO-CHAN, YOU JUST TOLD HER FLAT OUT, DIDN'T YOU?
BECAUSE IT'S "MANLY" OR WHATEVER TO BE AS BLUNT AS A HAMMER TO THE FACE.
WELL, IT'S NOT!
IT'S STUPID!
YOU MAKE THEM FEEL INFERIOR WHEN THEY DIDN'T HAVE TO!
YOU MAKE THEM HATE ME WHEN THEY DIDN'T HAVE TO!
YOU MAKE A TON OF ENEMIES FOR ME THAT I DIDN'T NEED TO HAVE!
AND AT THE END OF IT ALL, YOU'RE SURPRISED THAT I'M PISSED AS HELL AT YOU?!

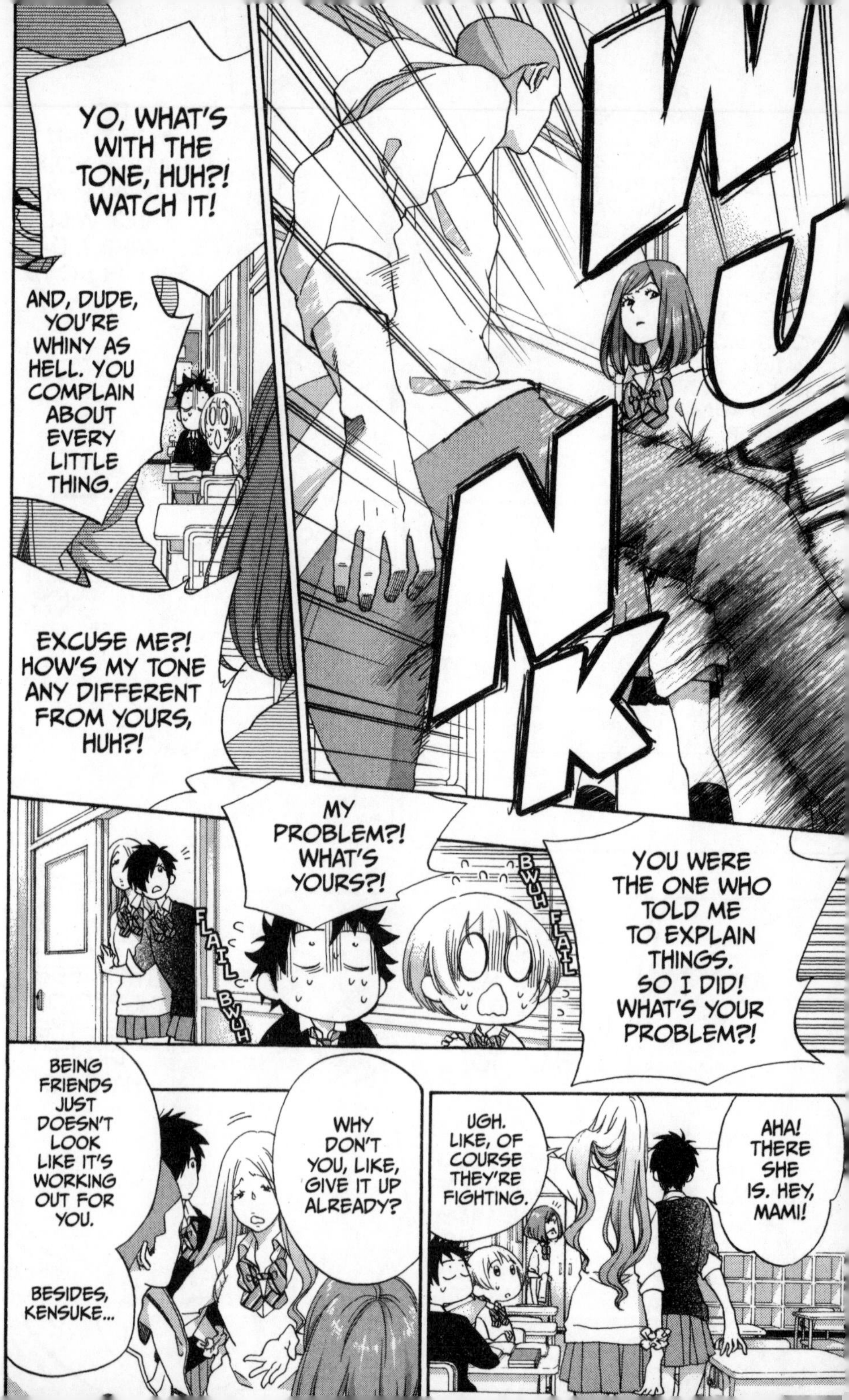
WHUNK
YO, WHAT'S WITH THE TONE, HUH?! WATCH IT!
AND, DUDE, YOU'RE WHINY AS HELL. YOU COMPLAIN ABOUT EVERY LITTLE THING.
EXCUSE ME?! HOW'S MY TONE ANY DIFFERENT FROM YOURS, HUH?!
YOU WERE THE ONE WHO TOLD ME TO EXPLAIN THINGS. SO I DID! WHAT'S YOUR PROBLEM?!
MY PROBLEM?! WHAT'S YOURS?!
BWUH FLAIL
FLAIL BWUH
AHA! THERE SHE IS. HEY, MAMI!
UGH. LIKE, OF COURSE THEY'RE FIGHTING.
WHY DON'T YOU, LIKE, GIVE IT UP ALREADY?
BEING FRIENDS JUST DOESN'T LOOK LIKE IT'S WORKING OUT FOR YOU.
BESIDES, KENSUKE...

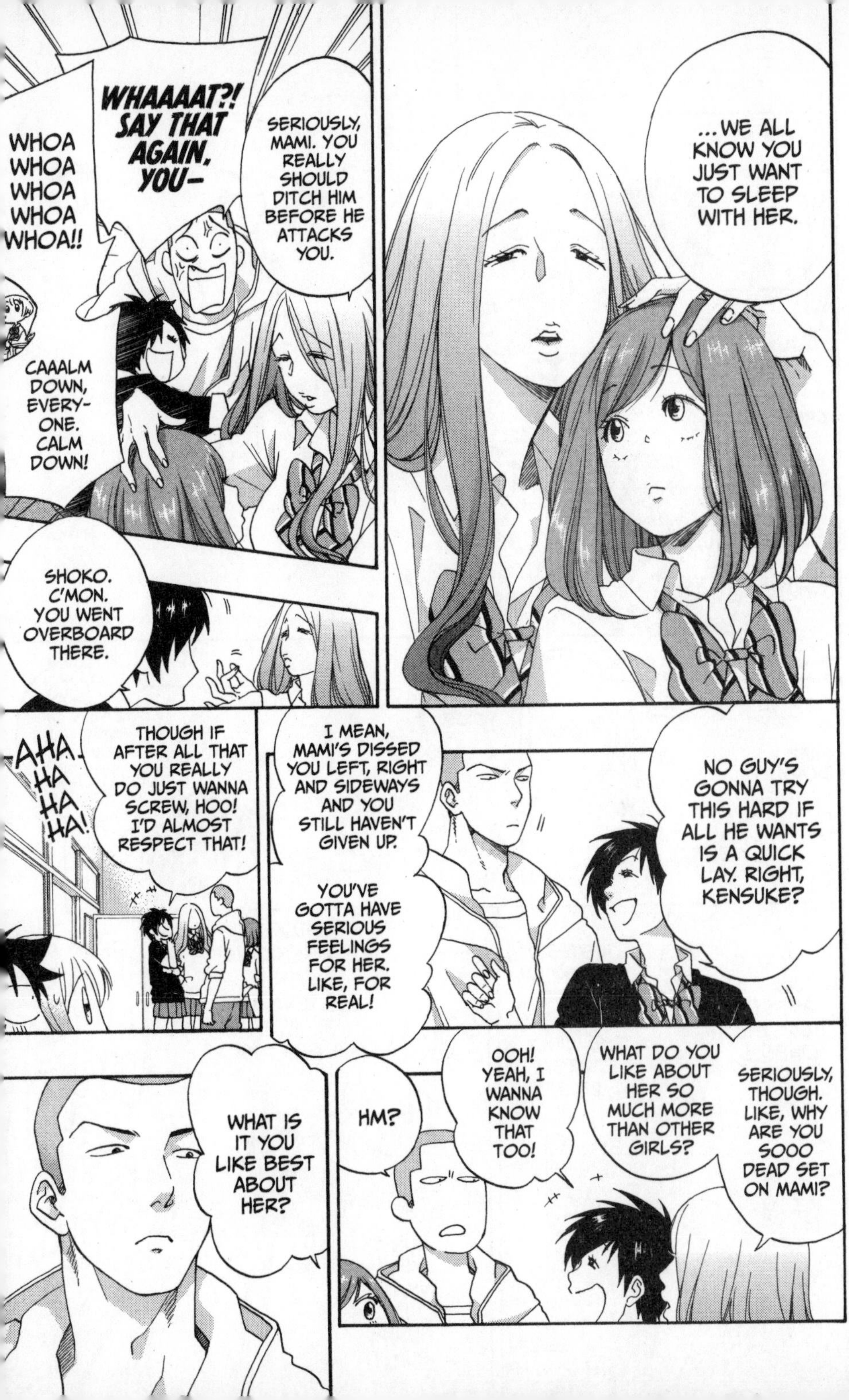
...WE ALL KNOW YOU JUST WANT TO SLEEP WITH HER.
SERIOUSLY, MAMI. YOU REALLY SHOULD DITCH HIM BEFORE HE ATTACKS YOU.
WHAAAAT?! SAY THAT AGAIN, YOU—
WHOA WHOA WHOA WHOA WHOA!!
CAAALM DOWN, EVERY-ONE. CALM DOWN!
SHOKO. C'MON. YOU WENT OVERBOARD THERE.
NO GUY'S GONNA TRY THIS HARD IF ALL HE WANTS IS A QUICK LAY. RIGHT, KENSUKE?
I MEAN, MAMI'S DISSED YOU LEFT, RIGHT AND SIDEWAYS AND YOU STILL HAVEN'T GIVEN UP.
YOU'VE GOTTA HAVE SERIOUS FEELINGS FOR HER. LIKE, FOR REAL!
THOUGH IF AFTER ALL THAT YOU REALLY DO JUST WANNA SCREW, HOO! I'D ALMOST RESPECT THAT!
AHAHAHAHA!
SERIOUSLY, THOUGH. LIKE, WHY ARE YOU SOOO DEAD SET ON MAMI?
WHAT DO YOU LIKE ABOUT HER SO MUCH MORE THAN OTHER GIRLS?
OOH! YEAH, I WANNA KNOW THAT TOO!
HM?
WHAT IS IT YOU LIKE BEST ABOUT HER?

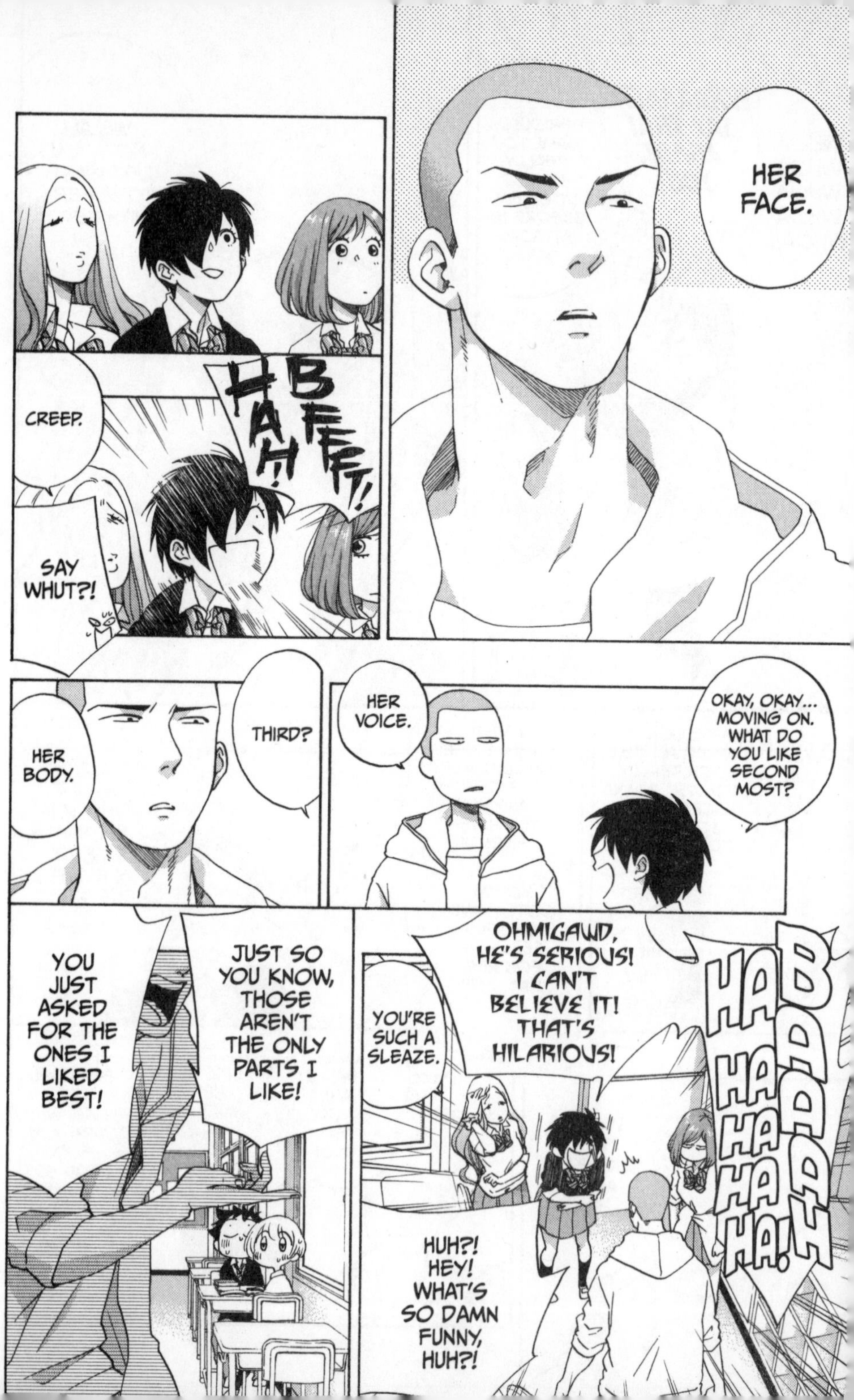
HER FACE.
BFFFT!!
HAH!
CREEP.
SAY WHUT?!
OKAY, OKAY... MOVING ON. WHAT DO YOU LIKE SECOND MOST?
HER VOICE.
THIRD?
HER BODY.
HA HA HA HA HA!
OHMIGAWD, HE'S SERIOUS! I CAN'T BELIEVE IT! THAT'S HILARIOUS!
YOU'RE SUCH A SLEAZE.
HUH?! HEY! WHAT'S SO DAMN FUNNY, HUH?!
JUST SO YOU KNOW, THOSE AREN'T THE ONLY PARTS I LIKE!
YOU JUST ASKED FOR THE ONES I LIKED BEST!

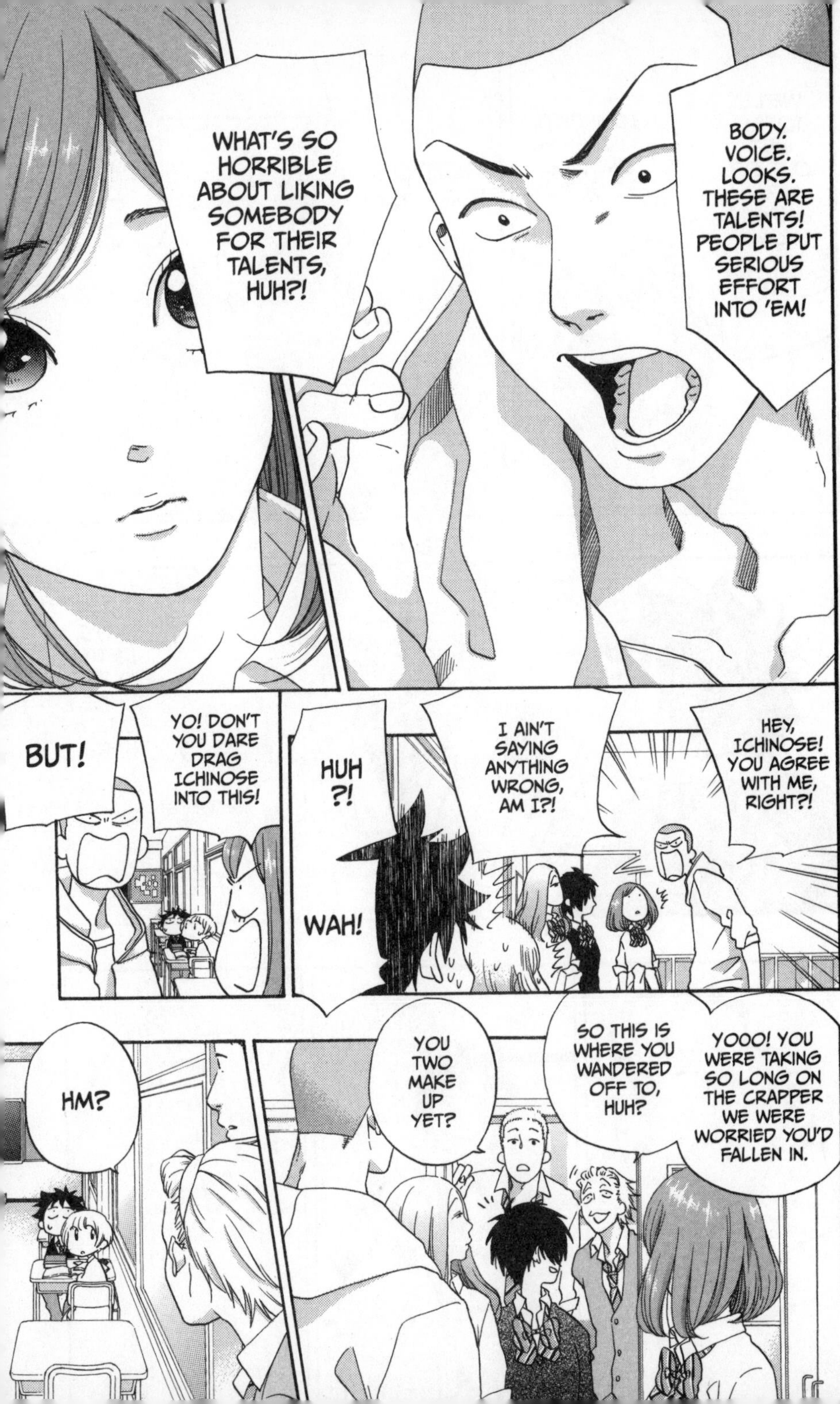
BODY. VOICE. LOOKS. THESE ARE TALENTS! PEOPLE PUT SERIOUS EFFORT INTO 'EM!
WHAT'S SO HORRIBLE ABOUT LIKING SOMEBODY FOR THEIR TALENTS, HUH?!
HEY, ICHINOSE! YOU AGREE WITH ME, RIGHT?!
I AIN'T SAYING ANYTHING WRONG, AM I?!
HUH ?!
WAH!
YO! DON'T YOU DARE DRAG ICHINOSE INTO THIS!
BUT!
YOOO! YOU WERE TAKING SO LONG ON THE CRAPPER WE WERE WORRIED YOU'D FALLEN IN.
SO THIS IS WHERE YOU WANDERED OFF TO, HUH?
YOU TWO MAKE UP YET?
HM?

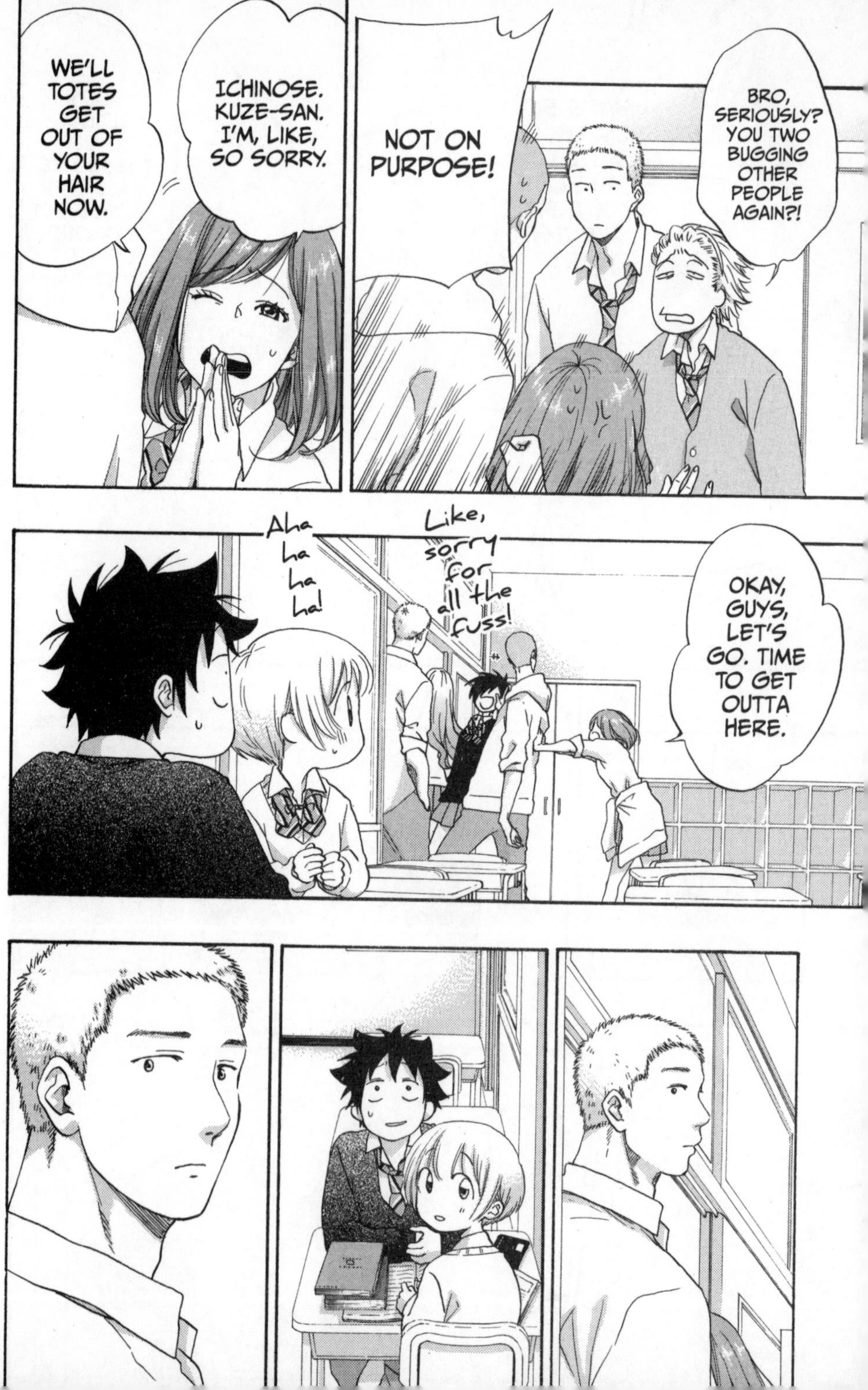
BRO, SERIOUSLY? YOU TWO BUGGING OTHER PEOPLE AGAIN?!
NOT ON PURPOSE!
ICHINOSE. KUZE-SAN. I'M, LIKE, SO SORRY.
WE'LL TOTES GET OUT OF YOUR HAIR NOW.
OKAY, GUYS, LET'S GO. TIME TO GET OUTTA HERE.
Like, sorry for all the fuss!
Aha ha ha ha!

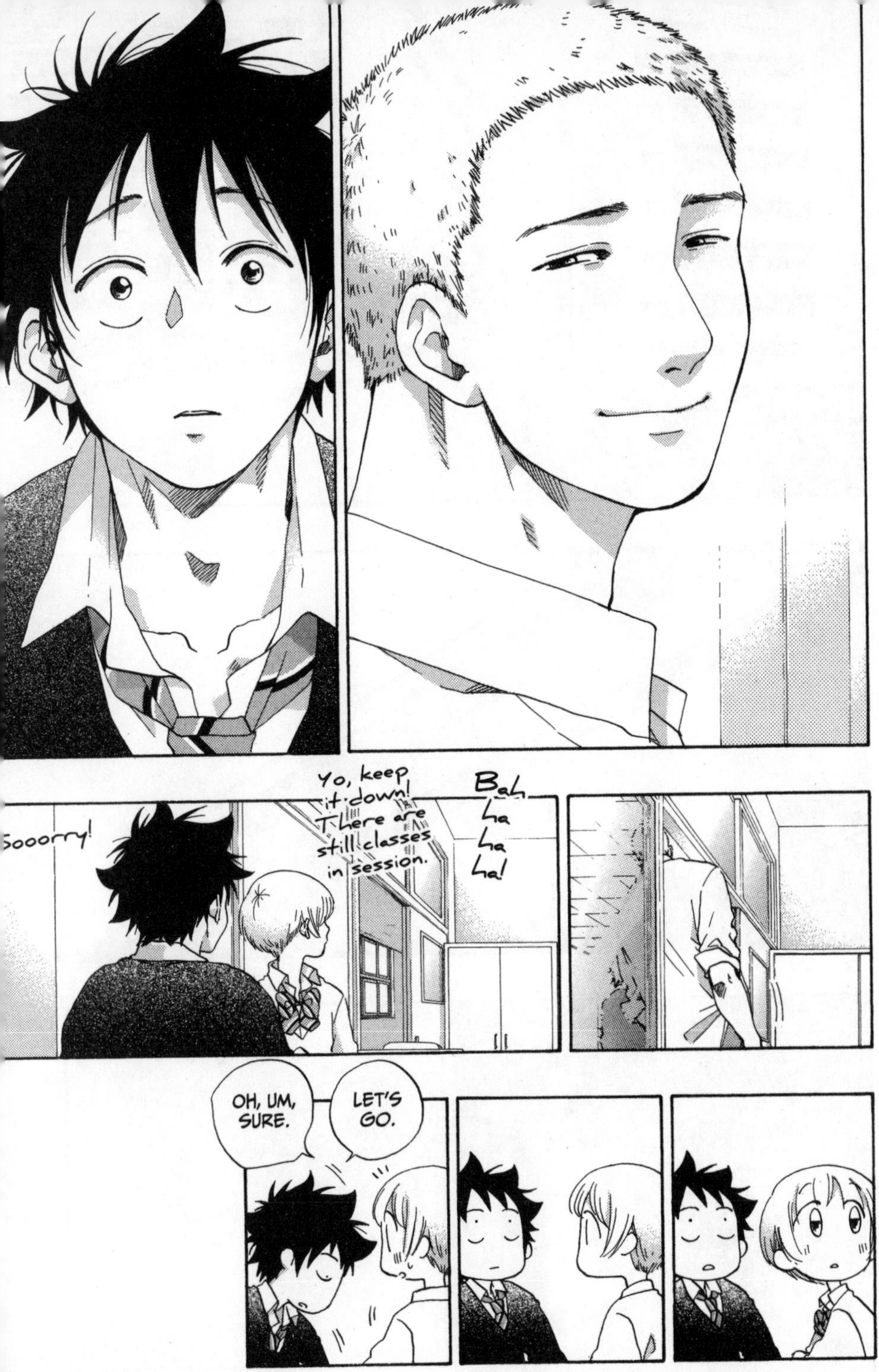
Bah ha ha ha!
Yo, keep it down! There are still classes in session.
Sooorry!
LET'S GO.
OH, UM, SURE.

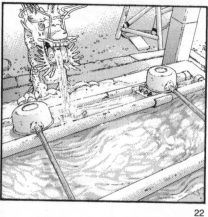

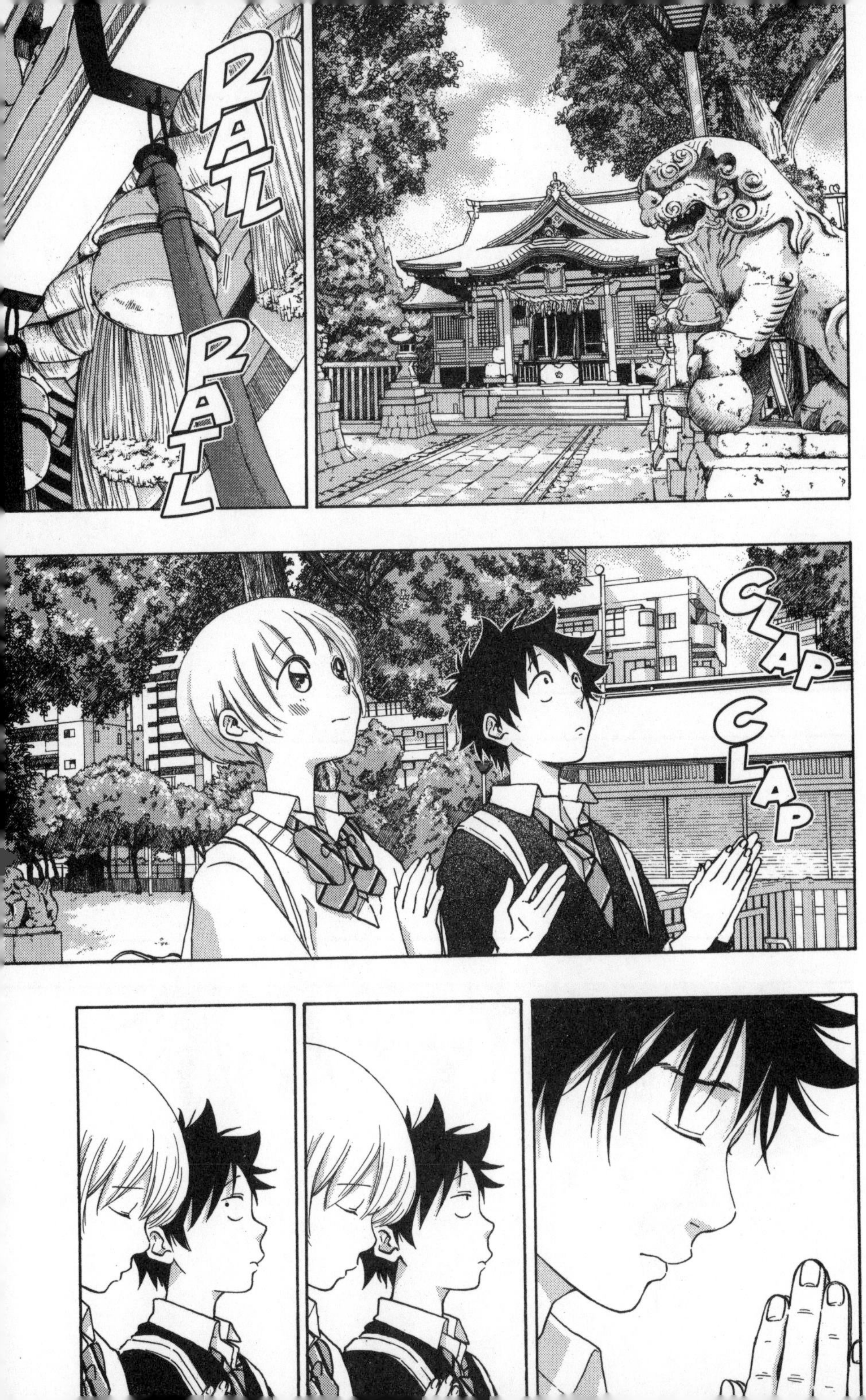
RATL
RATL
CLAP
CLAP

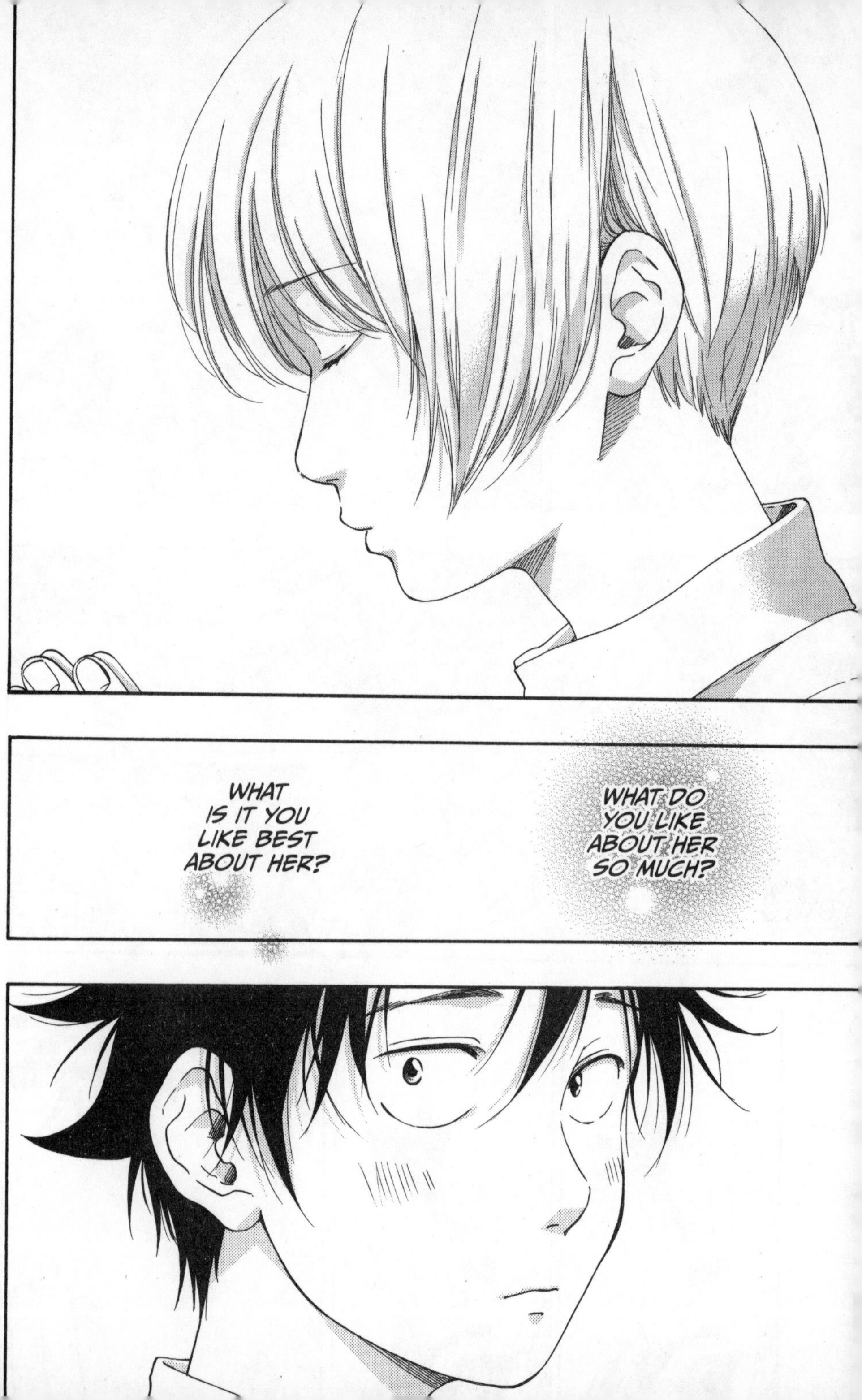
WHAT DO YOU LIKE ABOUT HER SO MUCH?
WHAT IS IT YOU LIKE BEST ABOUT HER?

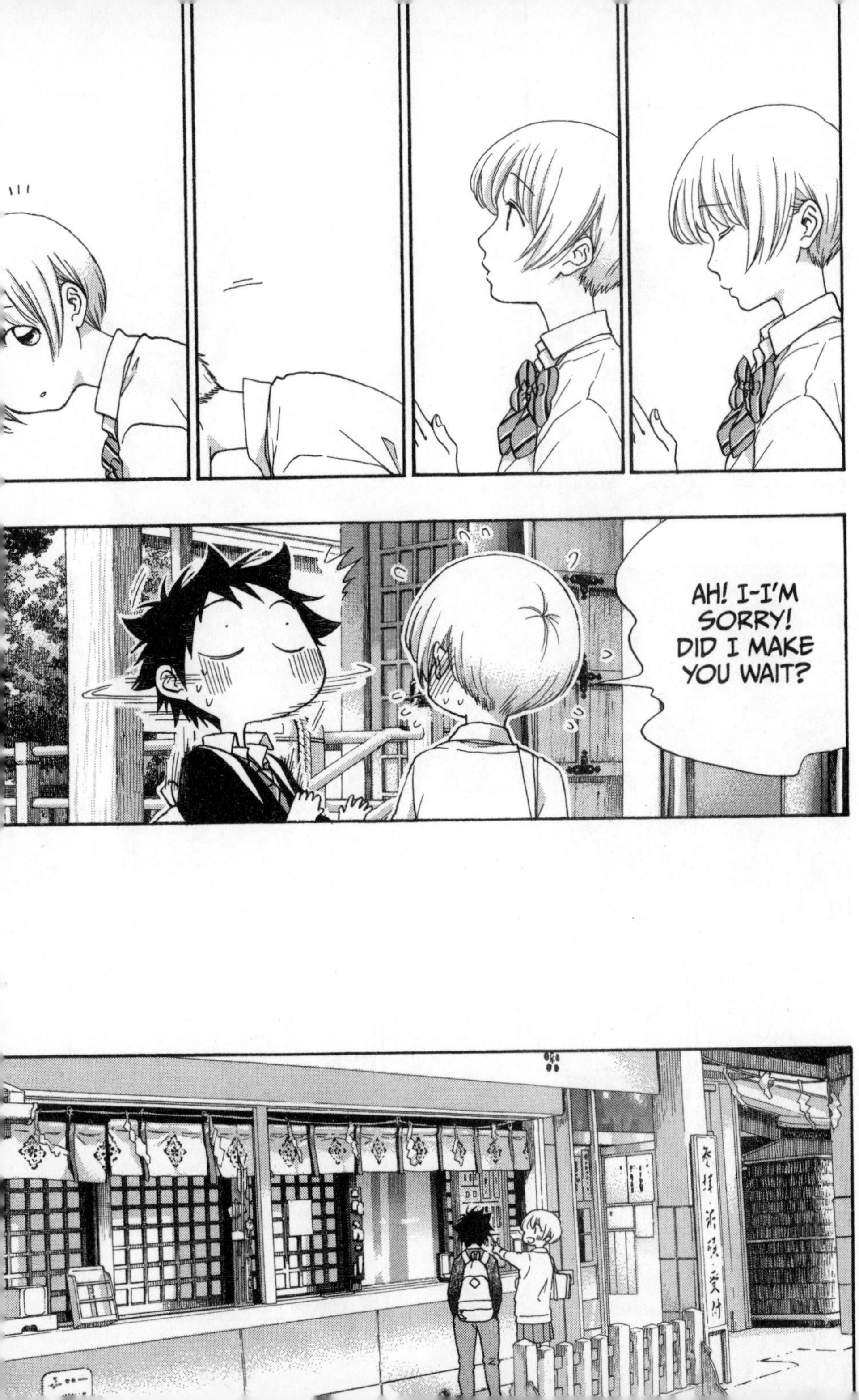
AH! I-I'M SORRY! DID I MAKE YOU WAIT?

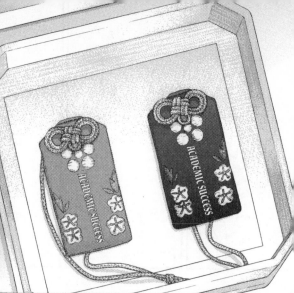

ACADEMIC SUCCESS

ACADEMIC SUCCESS

TENMANGU

Here!

I PUT EXTRA LUCK IN IT.

Hmmmmm!

26

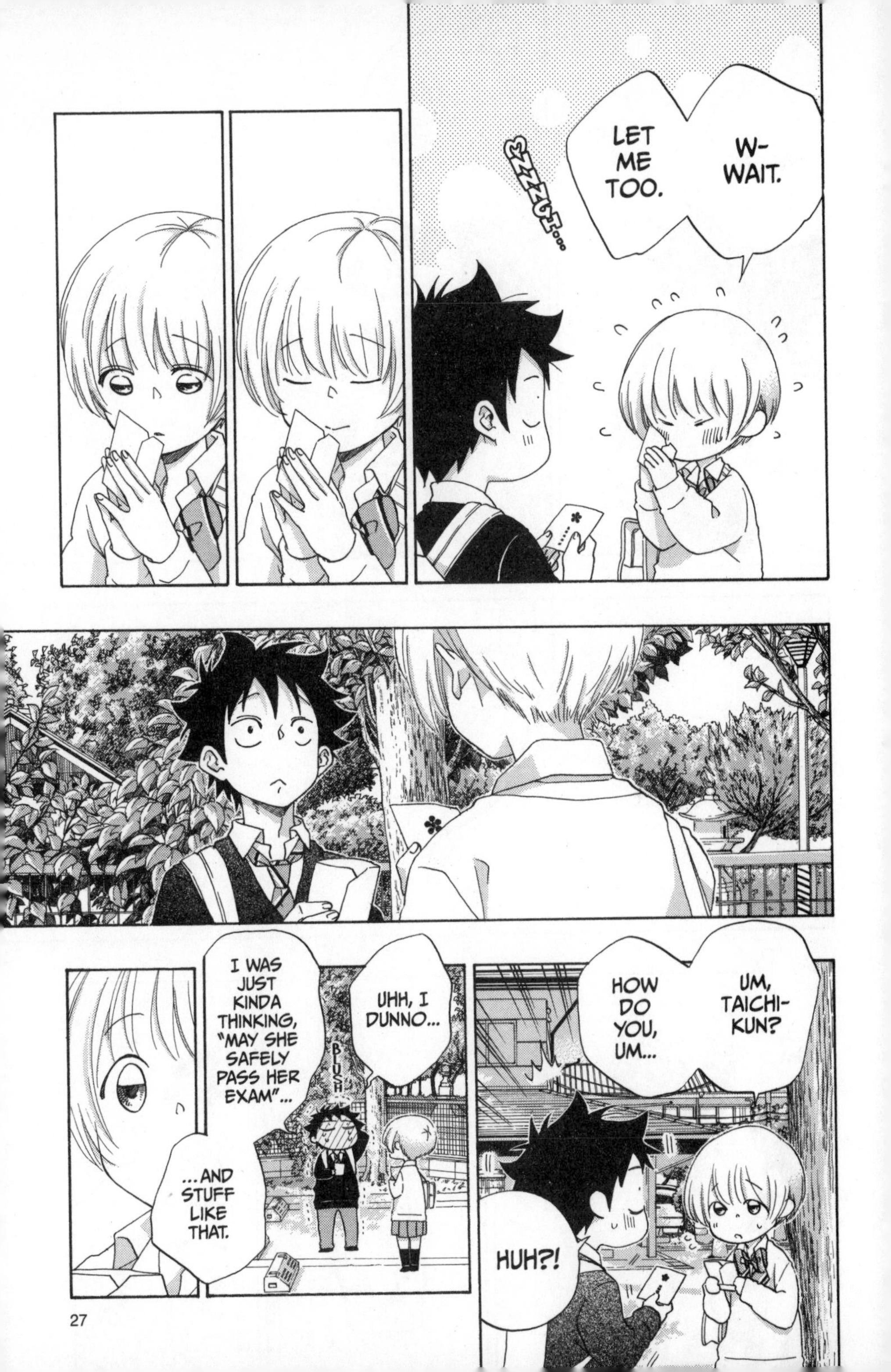
W-
WAIT.
LET ME TOO.
SNNGH...
UM, TAICHI-KUN?
HOW DO YOU, UM...
HUH?!
UHH, I DUNNO...
I WAS JUST KINDA THINKING, "MAY SHE SAFELY PASS HER EXAM"...
BLUSH
...AND STUFF LIKE THAT.

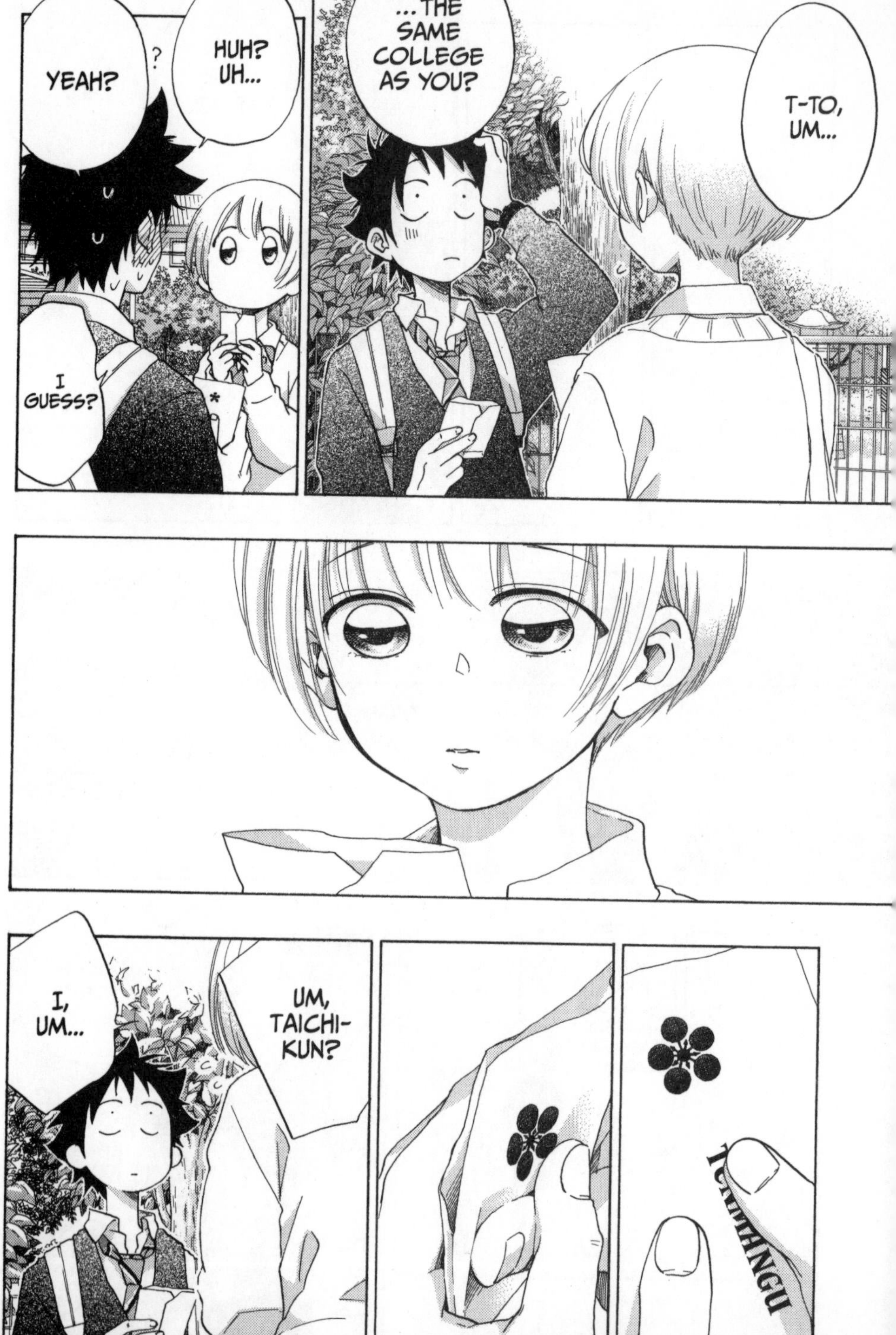
T-TO, UM...
...THE SAME COLLEGE AS YOU?
HUH? UH...
?
YEAH?
I GUESS?
TENMANGU
UM, TAICHI-KUN?
I, UM...

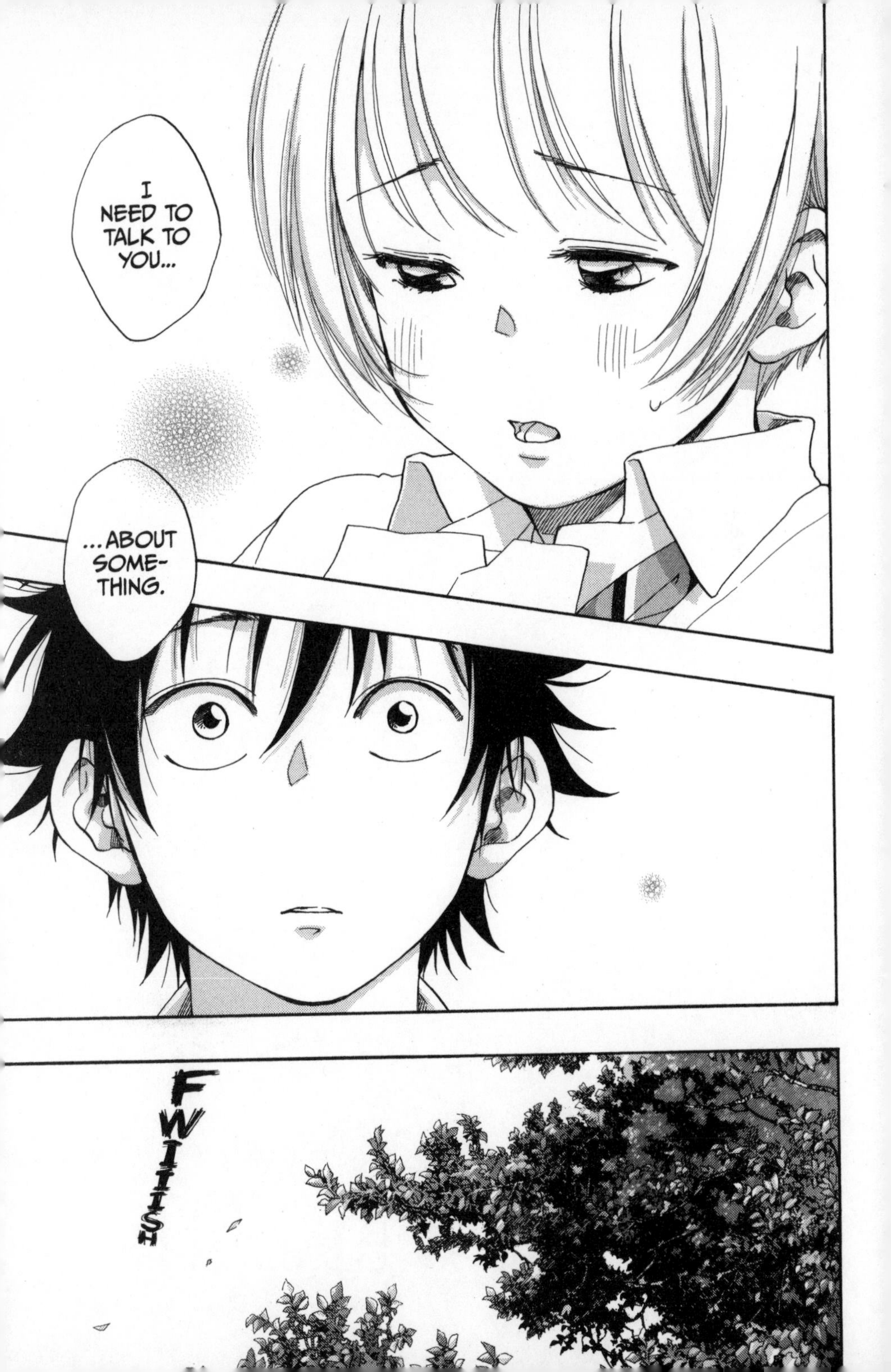
I NEED TO TALK TO YOU...
...ABOUT SOME-THING.
FWITTISH

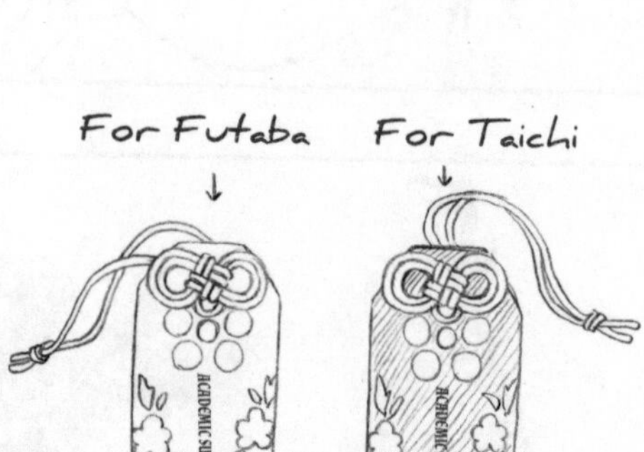
For Futaba
For Taichi
ACADEMIC SUCCESS
ACADEMIC SUCCESS
Crimson
Dark blue

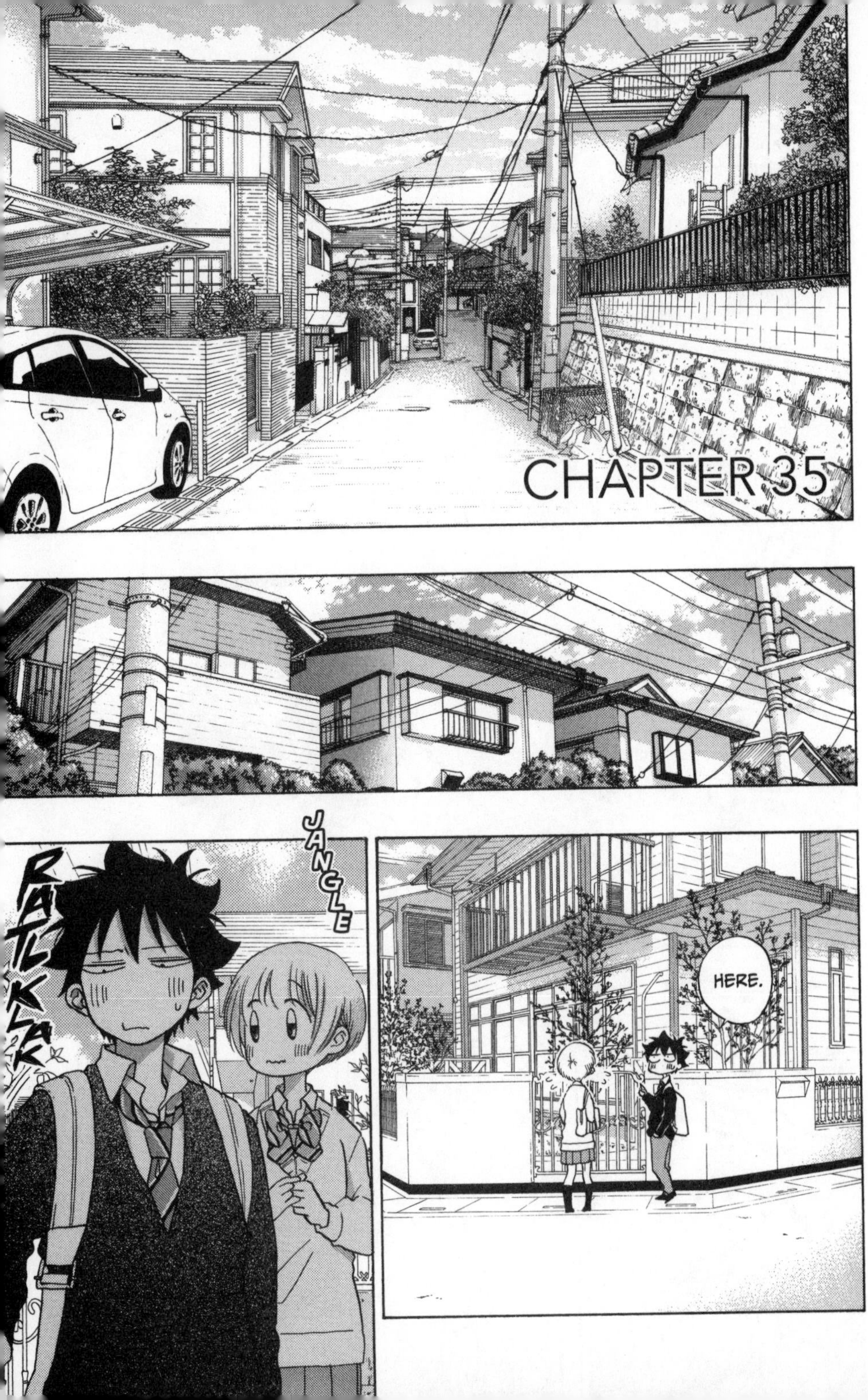
CHAPTER 35
HERE.
JANGLE
RATLKLAK

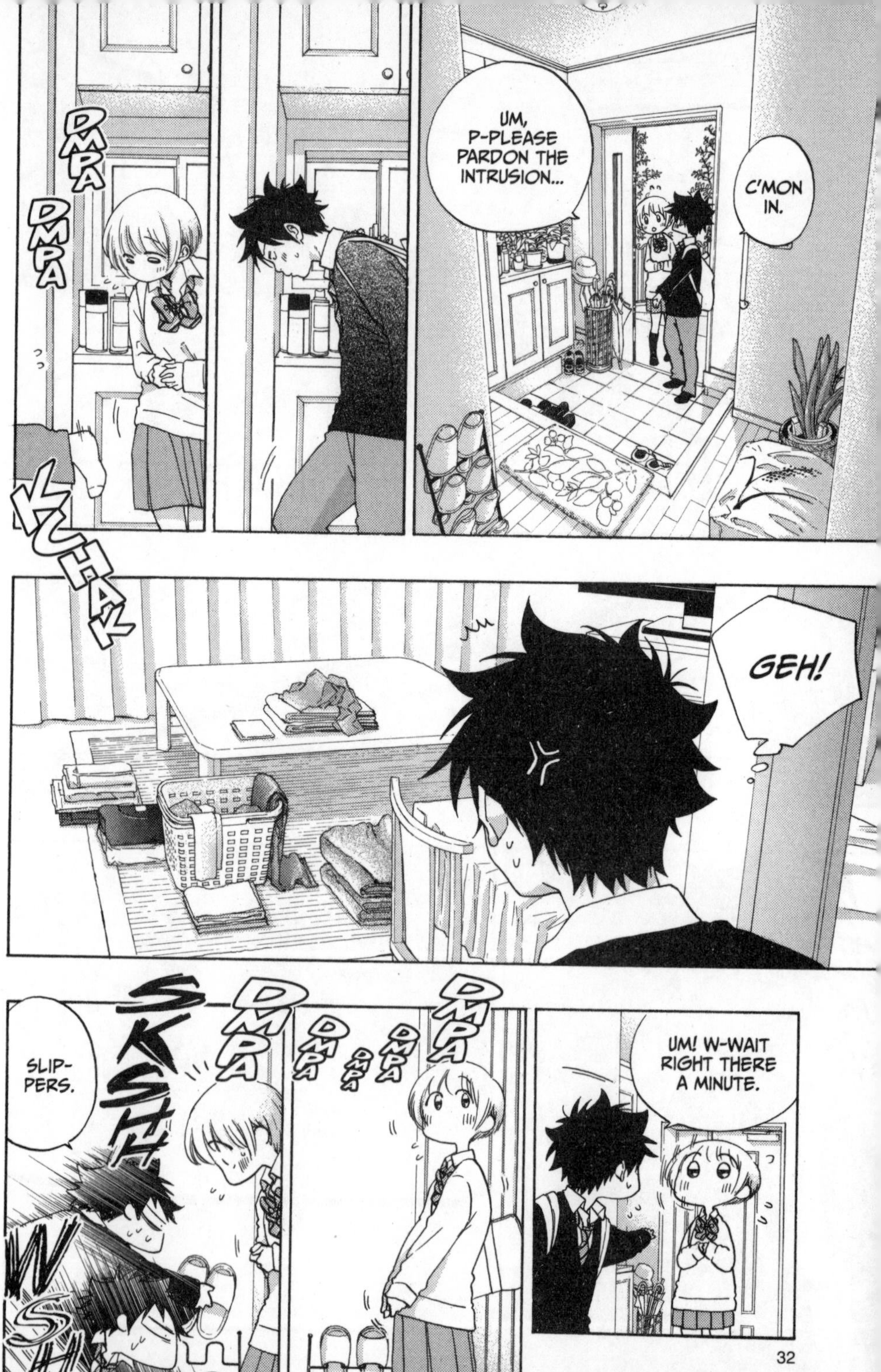
C'MON IN.
UM, P-PLEASE PARDON THE INTRUSION...
DMPA DMPA
KUHAK
GEH!
UM! W-WAIT RIGHT THERE A MINUTE.
DMPA
DMPA DMPA DMPA
DMPA
SKSHH
SLIP-PERS.
WSHH

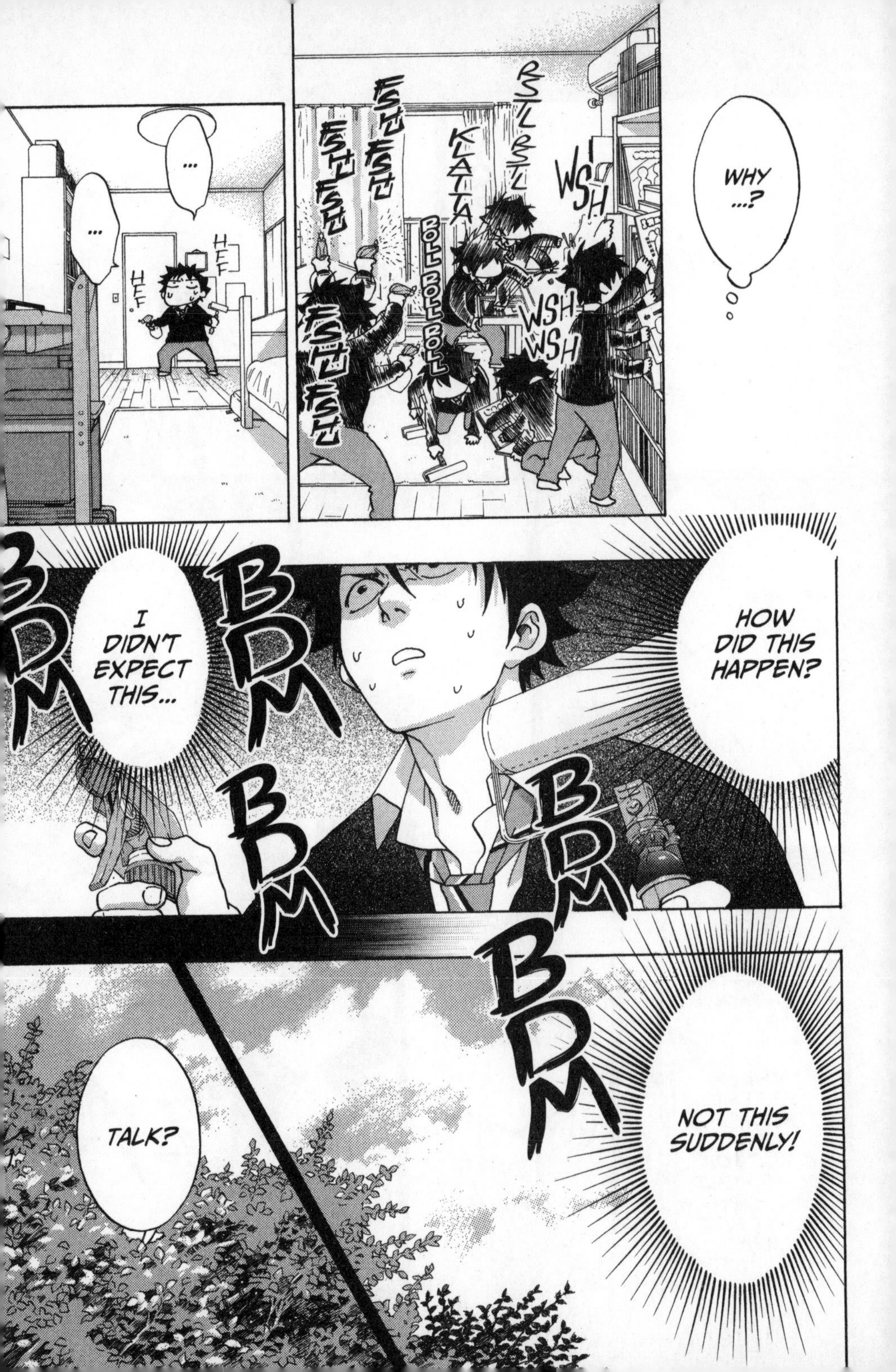
WHY ...?
RSTL RSTL
KLATTA
WSH
WSH WSH
FSHU FSHU
FSHU FSHU
FSHU FSHU FSHU
ROLL ROLL ROLL
...
...
HEF HEF
HOW DID THIS HAPPEN?
BDM BDM
I DIDN'T EXPECT THIS...
BDM BDM
BDM BDM
NOT THIS SUDDENLY!
BDM
TALK?

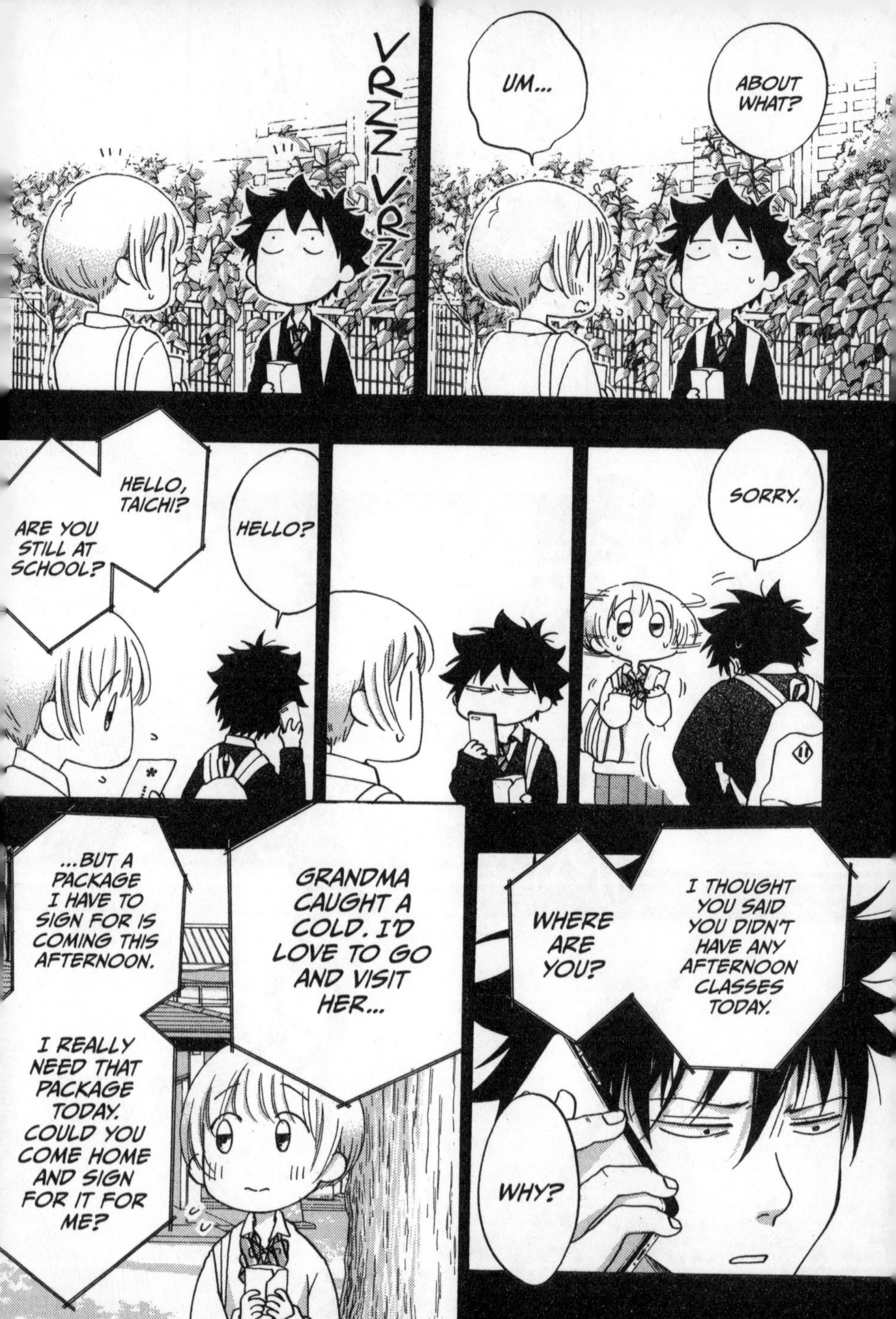
ABOUT WHAT?
UM...
VRZZ VRZZ
SORRY.
HELLO?
HELLO, TAICHI?
ARE YOU STILL AT SCHOOL?
I THOUGHT YOU SAID YOU DIDN'T HAVE ANY AFTERNOON CLASSES TODAY.
WHERE ARE YOU?
WHY?
GRANDMA CAUGHT A COLD. I'D LOVE TO GO AND VISIT HER...
...BUT A PACKAGE I HAVE TO SIGN FOR IS COMING THIS AFTERNOON.
I REALLY NEED THAT PACKAGE TODAY. COULD YOU COME HOME AND SIGN FOR IT FOR ME?

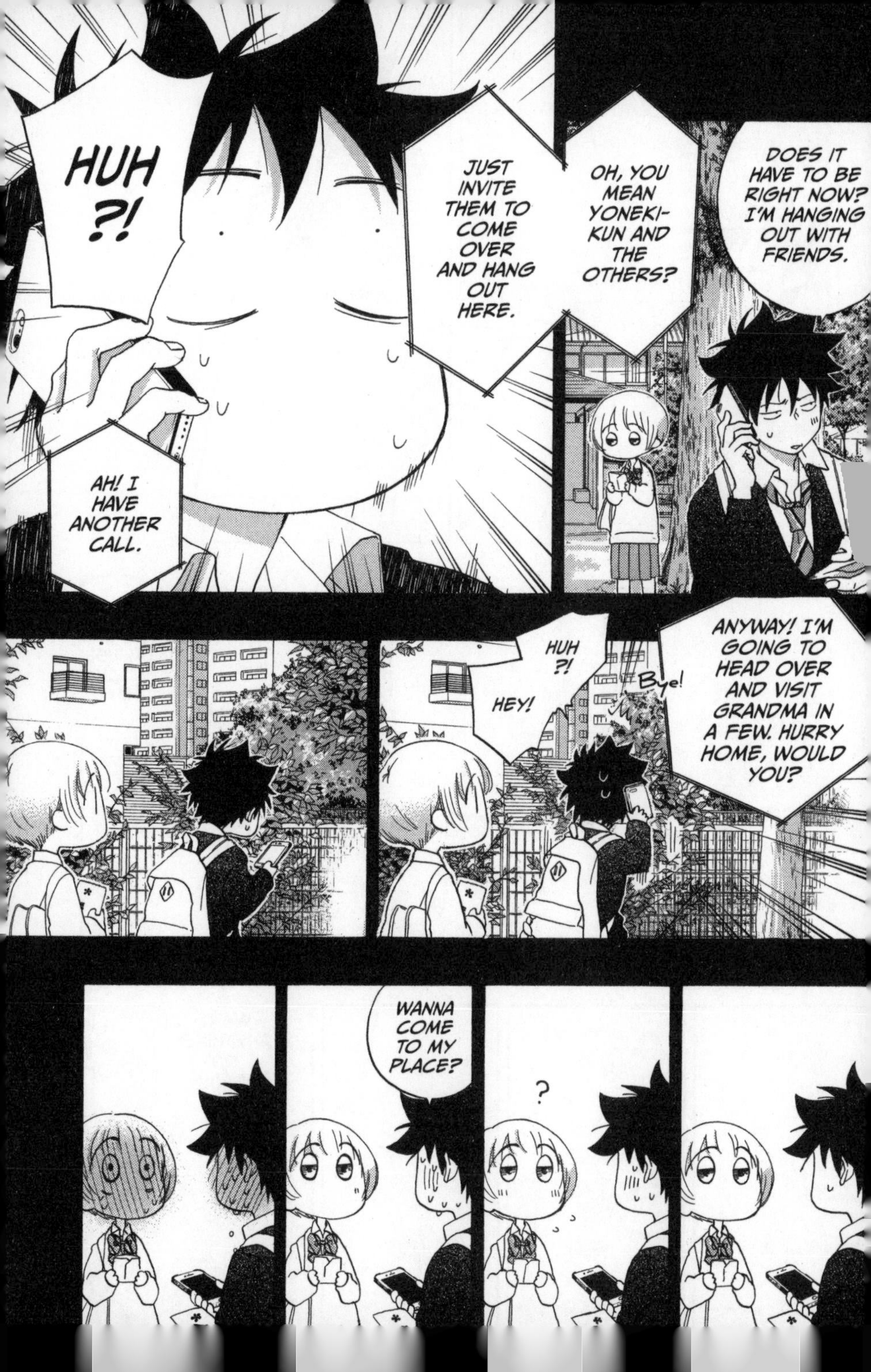
DOES IT HAVE TO BE RIGHT NOW? I'M HANGING OUT WITH FRIENDS.
OH, YOU MEAN YONEKI-KUN AND THE OTHERS?
JUST INVITE THEM TO COME OVER AND HANG OUT HERE.
HUH ?!
AH! I HAVE ANOTHER CALL.
ANYWAY! I'M GOING TO HEAD OVER AND VISIT GRANDMA IN A FEW. HURRY HOME, WOULD YOU?
Bye!
HUH ?!
HEY!
?
WANNA COME TO MY PLACE?

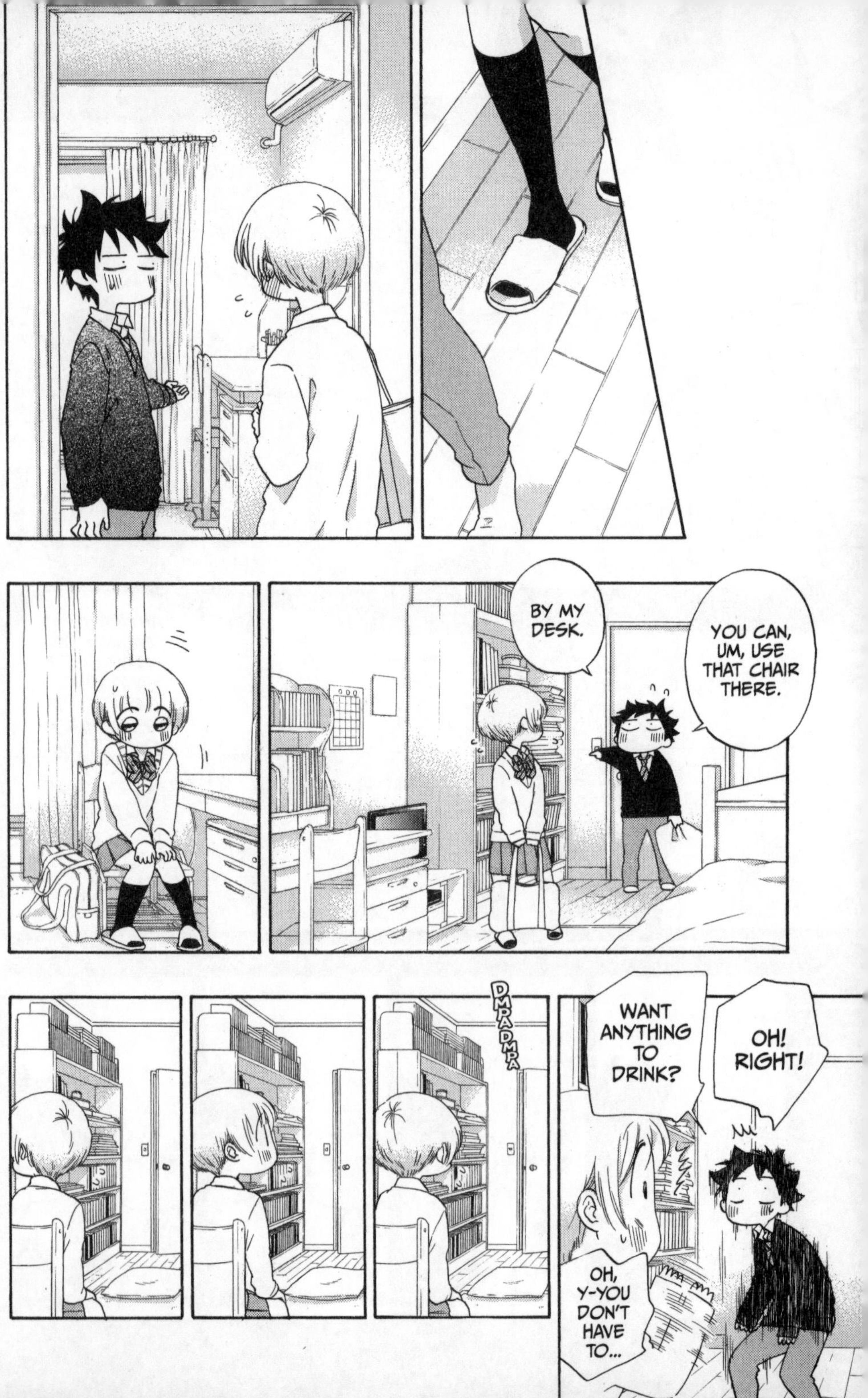
YOU CAN, UM, USE THAT CHAIR THERE.
BY MY DESK.
OH! RIGHT!
WANT ANYTHING TO DRINK?
OH, Y-YOU DON'T HAVE TO...
DMPA DMPA

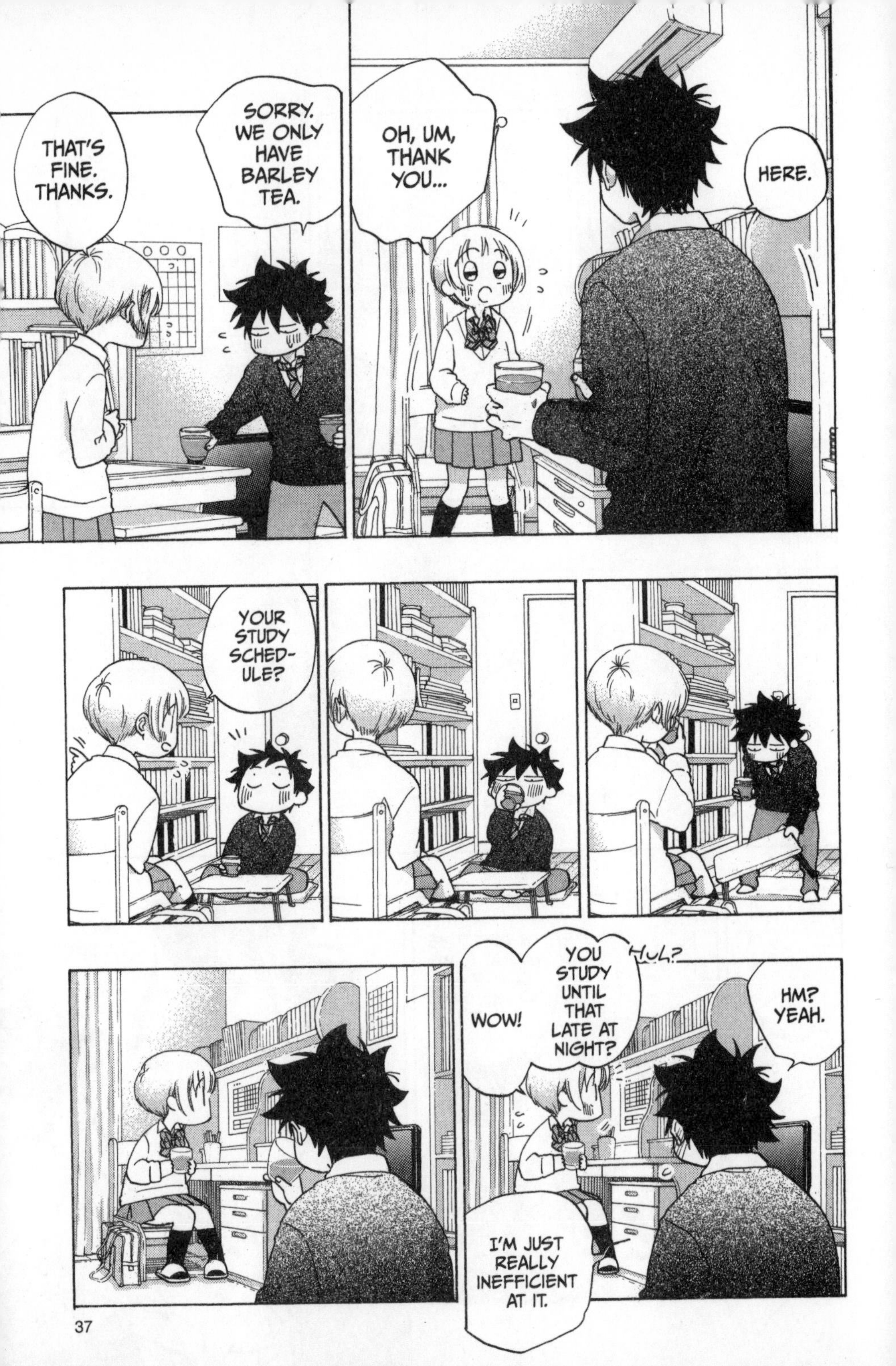
HERE.
OH, UM, THANK YOU...
SORRY. WE ONLY HAVE BARLEY TEA.
THAT'S FINE. THANKS.
YOUR STUDY SCHED-ULE?
HM? YEAH.
HUH?
YOU STUDY UNTIL THAT LATE AT NIGHT?
WOW!
I'M JUST REALLY INEFFICIENT AT IT.

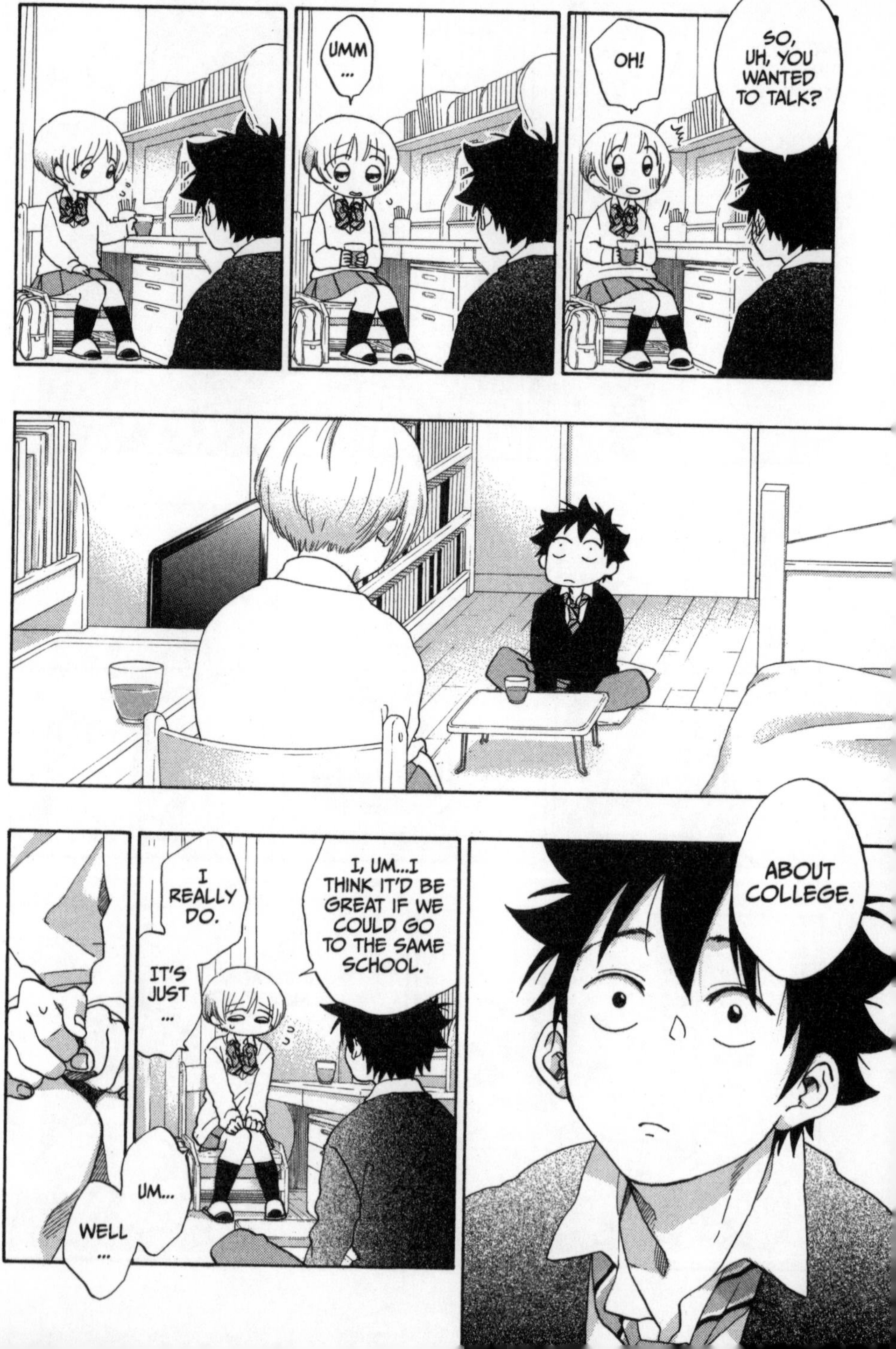

SO, UH, YOU WANTED TO TALK?
OH!
UMM ...
ABOUT COLLEGE.
I, UM...I THINK IT'D BE GREAT IF WE COULD GO TO THE SAME SCHOOL.
I REALLY DO.
IT'S JUST ...
UM...
WELL ...

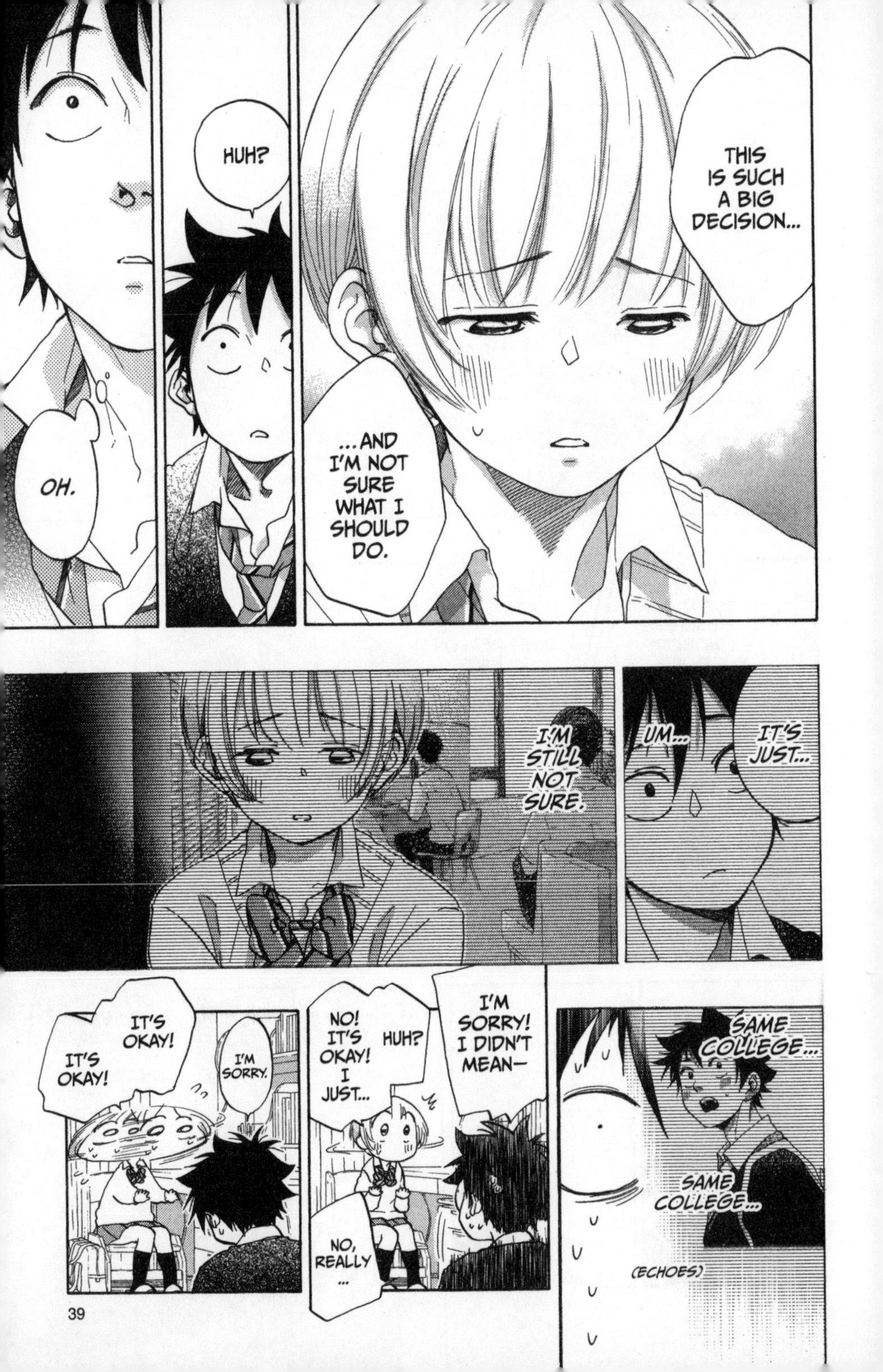
THIS IS SUCH A BIG DECISION...
...AND I'M NOT SURE WHAT I SHOULD DO.
HUH?
OH.
IT'S JUST...
UM...
I'M STILL NOT SURE.
SAME COLLEGE...
SAME COLLEGE...
(ECHOES)
I'M SORRY! I DIDN'T MEAN—
HUH?
NO! IT'S OKAY! I JUST...
NO, REALLY ...
I'M SORRY.
IT'S OKAY!
IT'S OKAY!

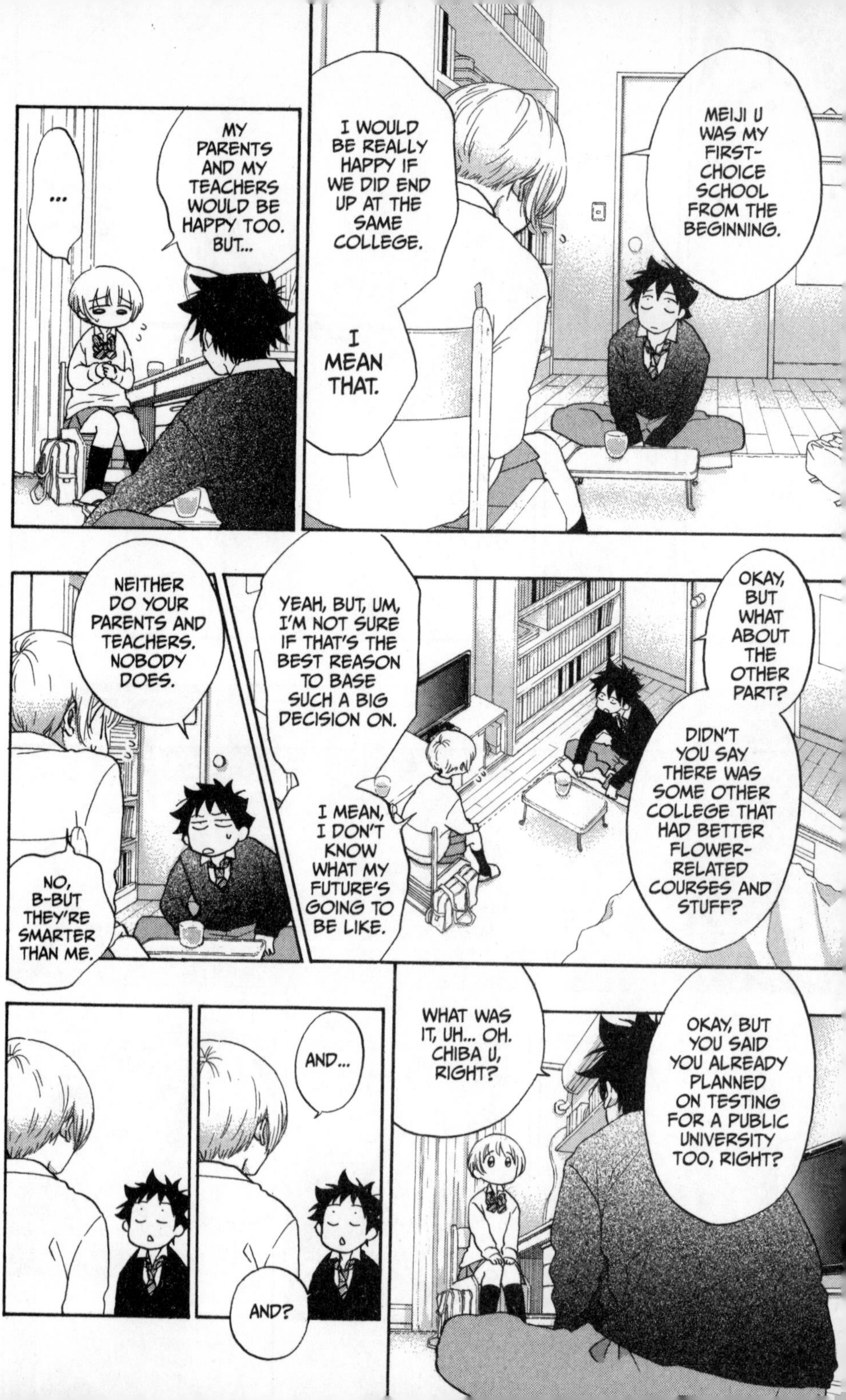
MEIJI U WAS MY FIRST-CHOICE SCHOOL FROM THE BEGINNING.
I WOULD BE REALLY HAPPY IF WE DID END UP AT THE SAME COLLEGE.
I MEAN THAT.
MY PARENTS AND MY TEACHERS WOULD BE HAPPY TOO. BUT...
...
OKAY, BUT WHAT ABOUT THE OTHER PART?
DIDN'T YOU SAY THERE WAS SOME OTHER COLLEGE THAT HAD BETTER FLOWER-RELATED COURSES AND STUFF?
YEAH, BUT, UM, I'M NOT SURE IF THAT'S THE BEST REASON TO BASE SUCH A BIG DECISION ON.
I MEAN, I DON'T KNOW WHAT MY FUTURE'S GOING TO BE LIKE.
NEITHER DO YOUR PARENTS AND TEACHERS. NOBODY DOES.
NO, B-BUT THEY'RE SMARTER THAN ME.
OKAY, BUT YOU SAID YOU ALREADY PLANNED ON TESTING FOR A PUBLIC UNIVERSITY TOO, RIGHT?
WHAT WAS IT, UH... OH. CHIBA U, RIGHT?
AND...
AND?

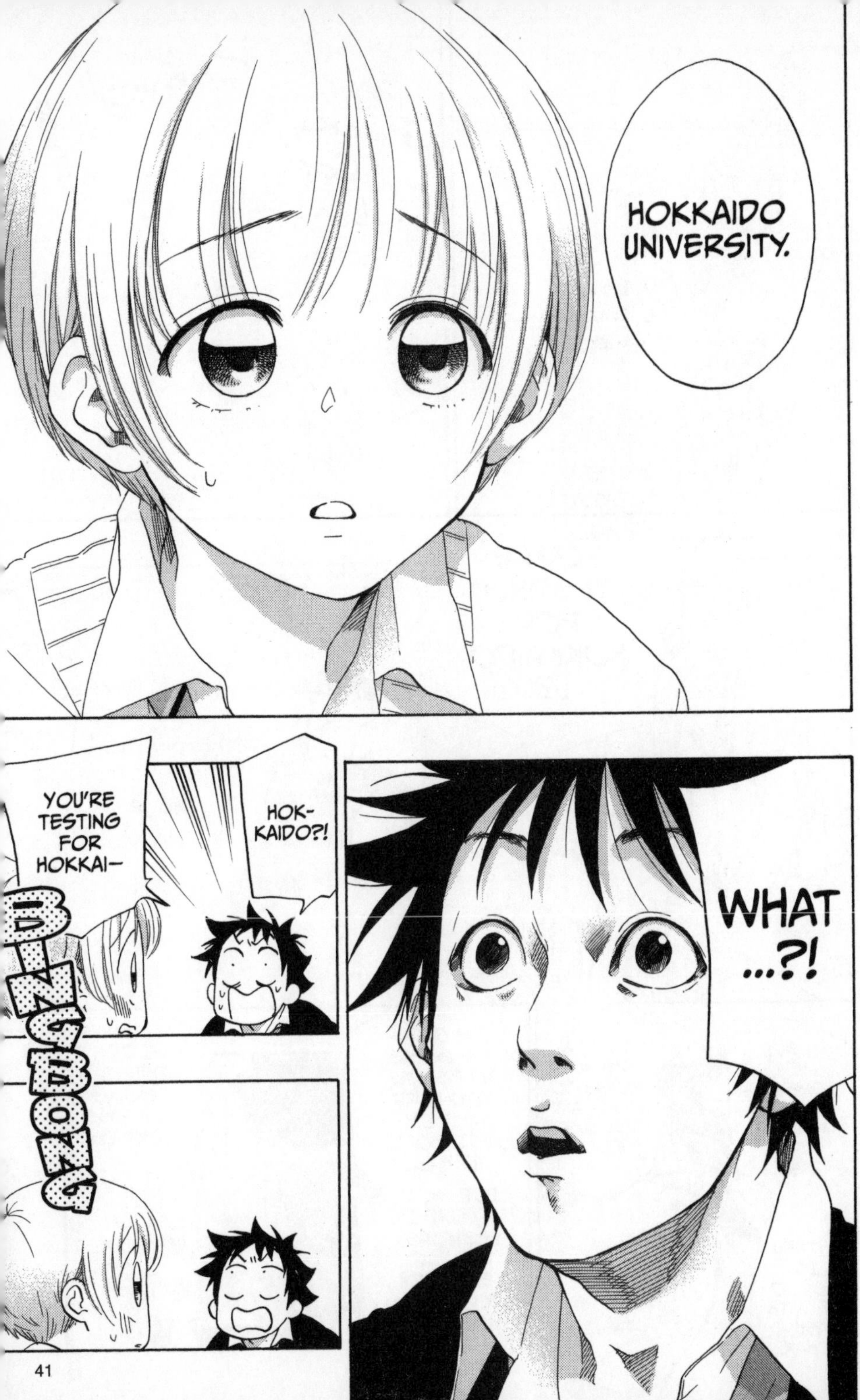
HOKKAIDO UNIVERSITY.
WHAT ...?!
HOK-KAIDO?!
YOU'RE TESTING FOR HOKKAI—
DINGDONG

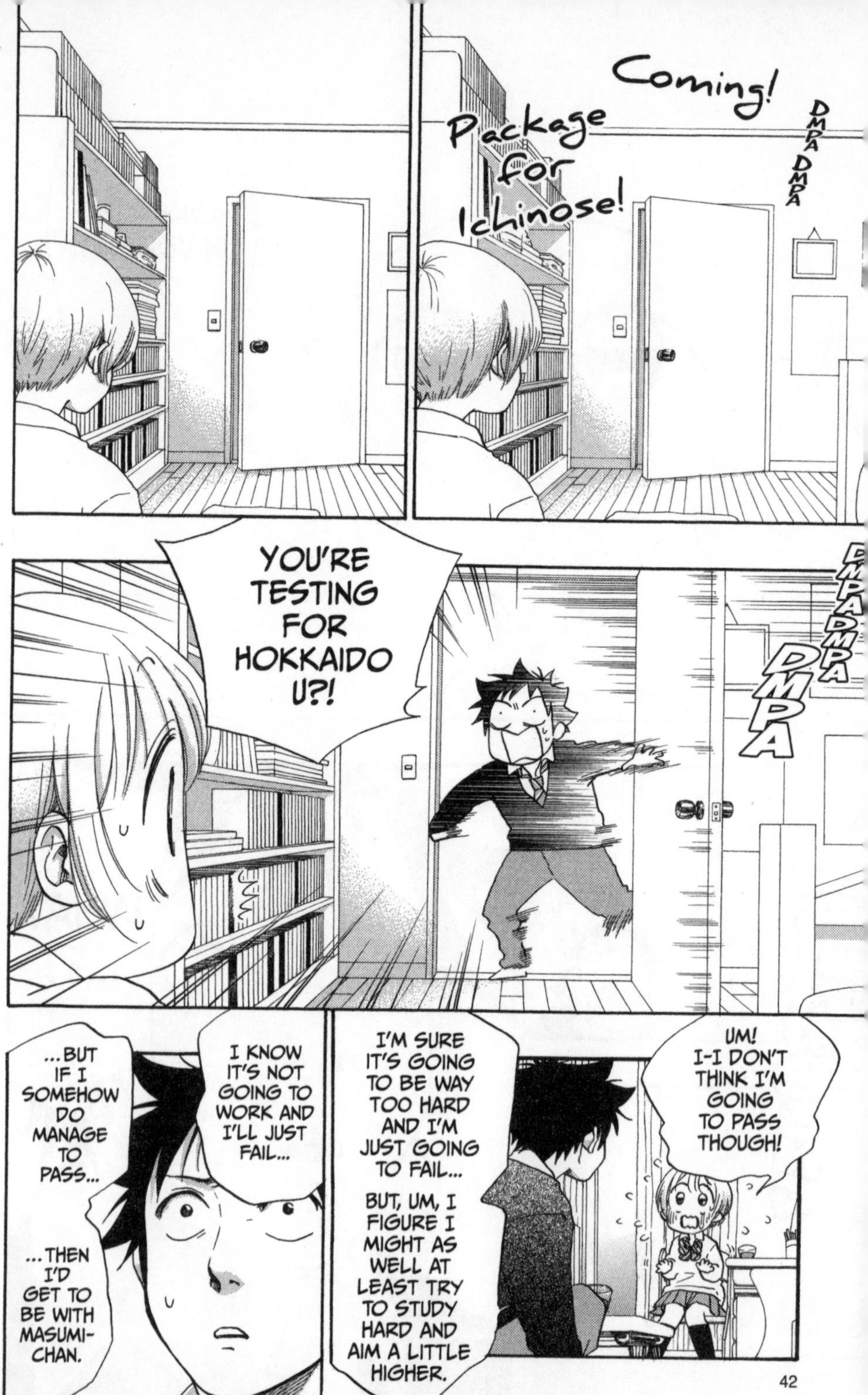
Coming!
DMPA DMPA
Package for Ichinose!
DMPADMPADMPA
DMPA
YOU'RE TESTING FOR HOKKAIDO U?!
UM! I-I DON'T THINK I'M GOING TO PASS THOUGH!
I'M SURE IT'S GOING TO BE WAY TOO HARD AND I'M JUST GOING TO FAIL...
BUT, UM, I FIGURE I MIGHT AS WELL AT LEAST TRY TO STUDY HARD AND AIM A LITTLE HIGHER.
I KNOW IT'S NOT GOING TO WORK AND I'LL JUST FAIL...
...BUT IF I SOMEHOW DO MANAGE TO PASS...
...THEN I'D GET TO BE WITH MASUMI-CHAN.

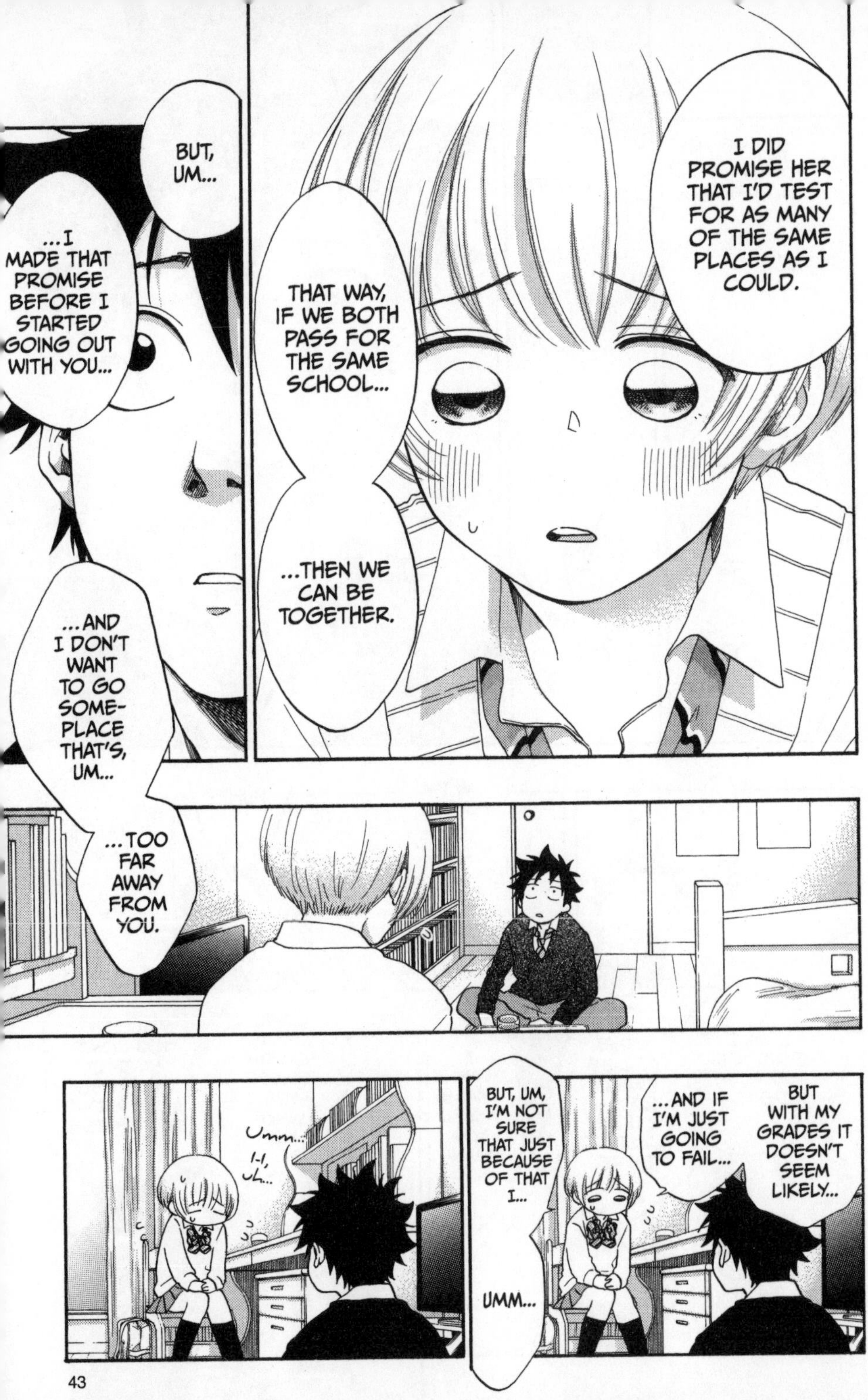
I DID PROMISE HER THAT I'D TEST FOR AS MANY OF THE SAME PLACES AS I COULD.
THAT WAY, IF WE BOTH PASS FOR THE SAME SCHOOL...
...THEN WE CAN BE TOGETHER.
BUT, UM...
...I MADE THAT PROMISE BEFORE I STARTED GOING OUT WITH YOU...
...AND I DON'T WANT TO GO SOME-PLACE THAT'S, UM...
...TOO FAR AWAY FROM YOU.
BUT WITH MY GRADES IT DOESN'T SEEM LIKELY...
...AND IF I'M JUST GOING TO FAIL...
BUT, UM, I'M NOT SURE THAT JUST BECAUSE OF THAT I...
UMM...
Umm...
I-I, uh...

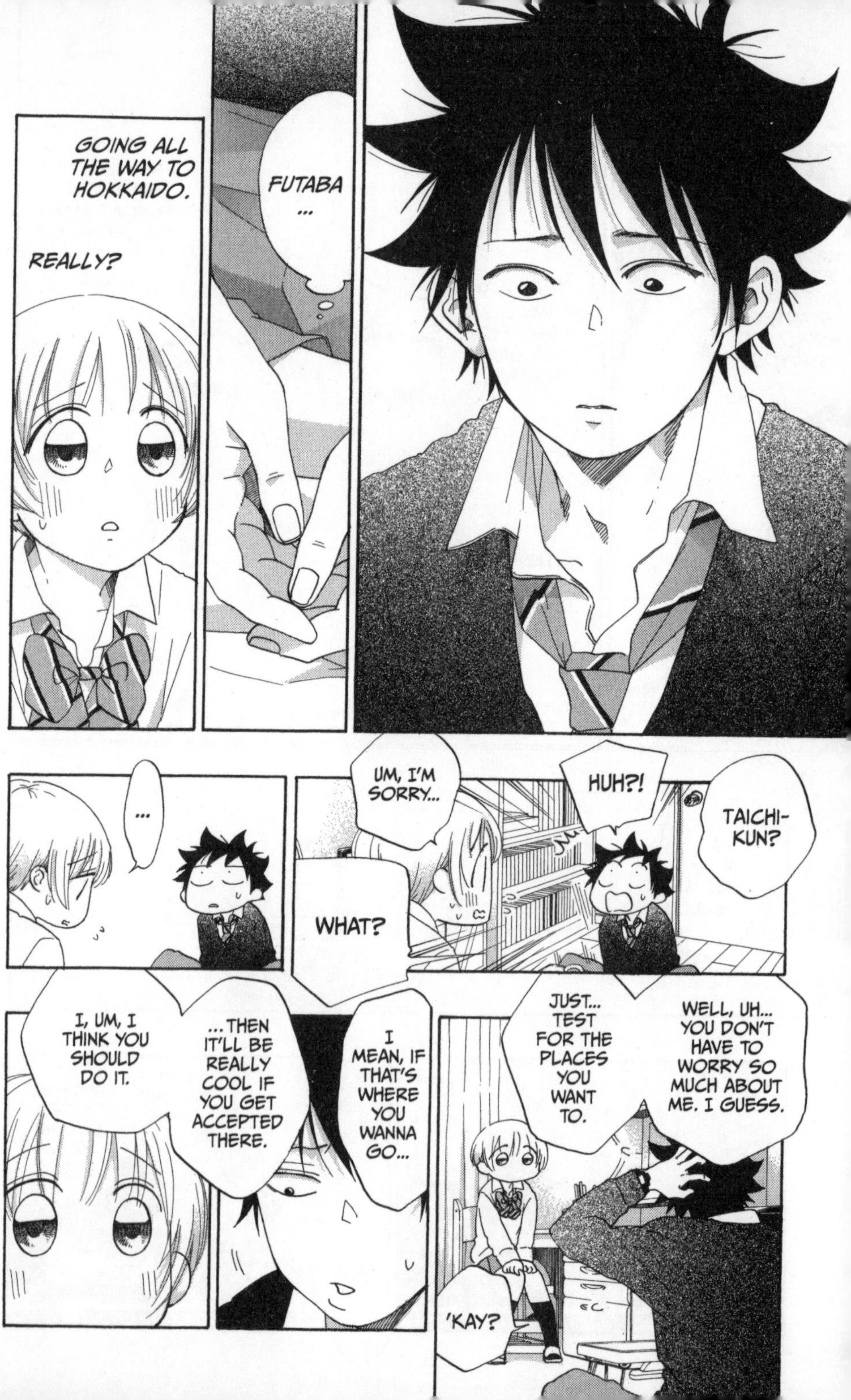
FUTABA ...
GOING ALL THE WAY TO HOKKAIDO.
REALLY?
TAICHI-KUN?
HUH?!
UM, I'M SORRY...
WHAT?
...
WELL, UH... YOU DON'T HAVE TO WORRY SO MUCH ABOUT ME. I GUESS.
JUST... TEST FOR THE PLACES YOU WANT TO.
'KAY?
I MEAN, IF THAT'S WHERE YOU WANNA GO...
...THEN IT'LL BE REALLY COOL IF YOU GET ACCEPTED THERE.
I, UM, I THINK YOU SHOULD DO IT.

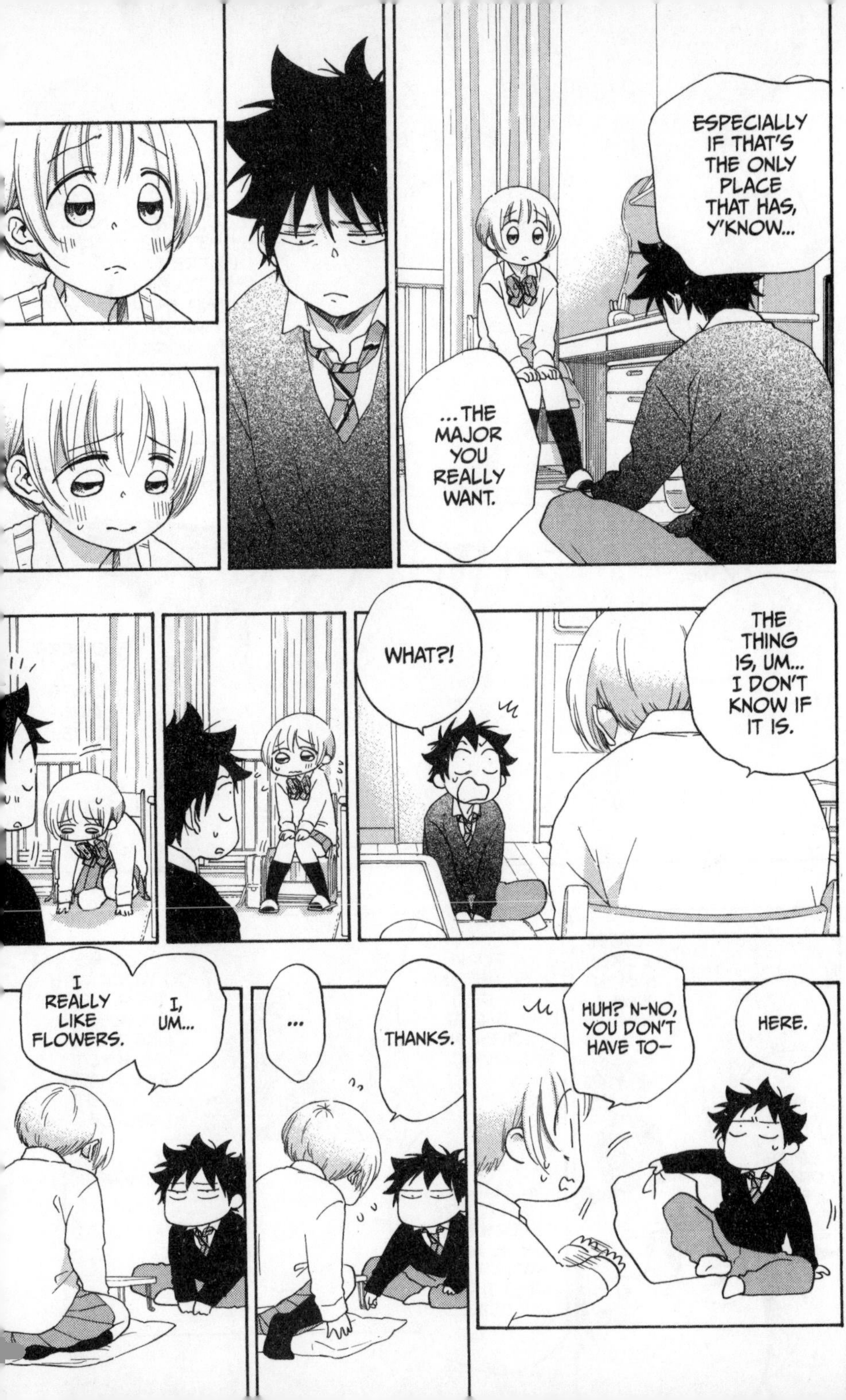
ESPECIALLY IF THAT'S THE ONLY PLACE THAT HAS, Y'KNOW...
...THE MAJOR YOU REALLY WANT.
THE THING IS, UM... I DON'T KNOW IF IT IS.
WHAT?!
HERE.
HUH? N-NO, YOU DON'T HAVE TO—
THANKS.
...
I, UM...
I REALLY LIKE FLOWERS.

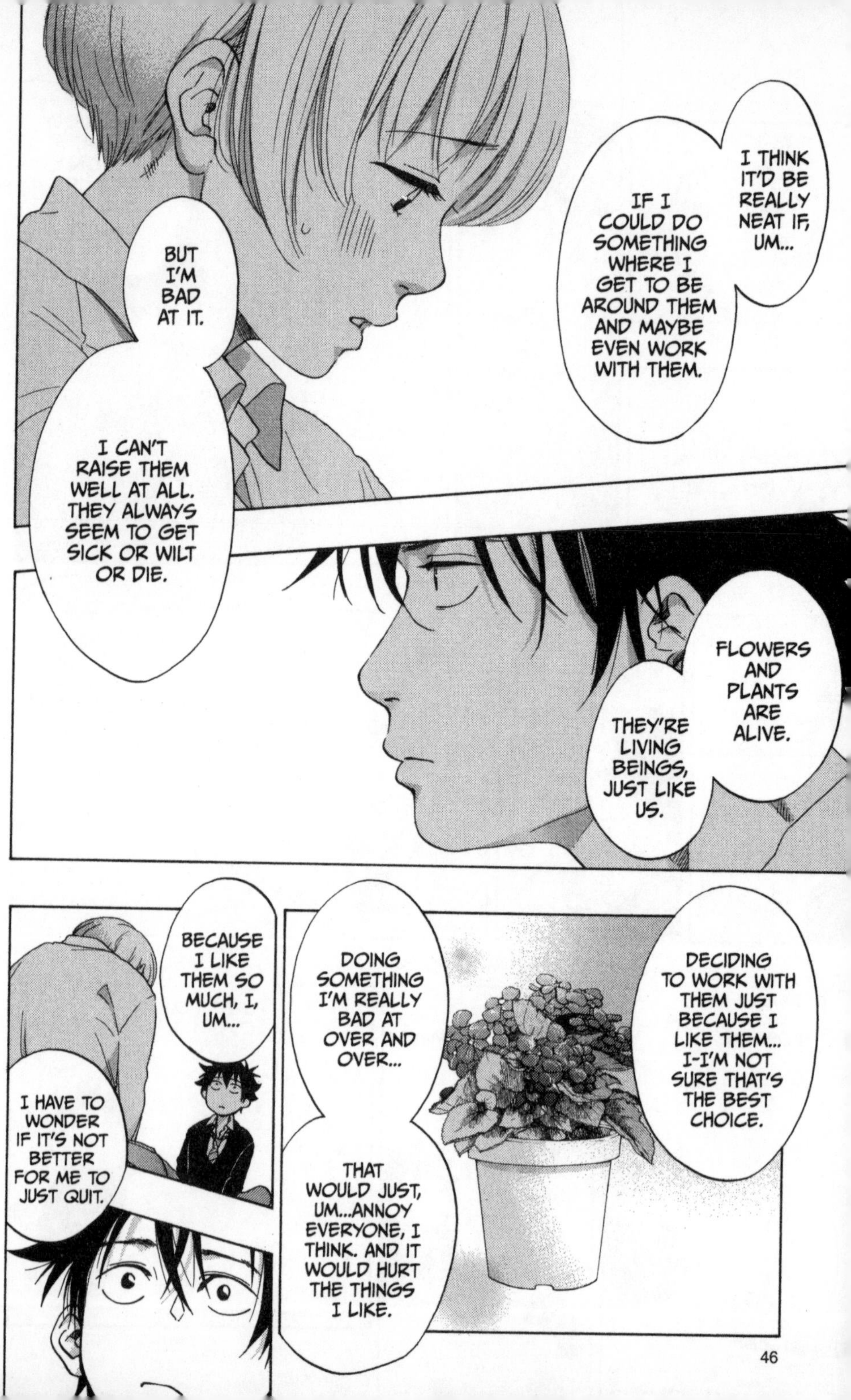
I THINK IT'D BE REALLY NEAT IF, UM...
IF I COULD DO SOMETHING WHERE I GET TO BE AROUND THEM AND MAYBE EVEN WORK WITH THEM.
BUT I'M BAD AT IT.
I CAN'T RAISE THEM WELL AT ALL. THEY ALWAYS SEEM TO GET SICK OR WILT OR DIE.
FLOWERS AND PLANTS ARE ALIVE.
THEY'RE LIVING BEINGS, JUST LIKE US.
DECIDING TO WORK WITH THEM JUST BECAUSE I LIKE THEM... I-I'M NOT SURE THAT'S THE BEST CHOICE.
DOING SOMETHING I'M REALLY BAD AT OVER AND OVER...
THAT WOULD JUST, UM...ANNOY EVERYONE, I THINK. AND IT WOULD HURT THE THINGS I LIKE.
BECAUSE I LIKE THEM SO MUCH, I, UM...
I HAVE TO WONDER IF IT'S NOT BETTER FOR ME TO JUST QUIT.

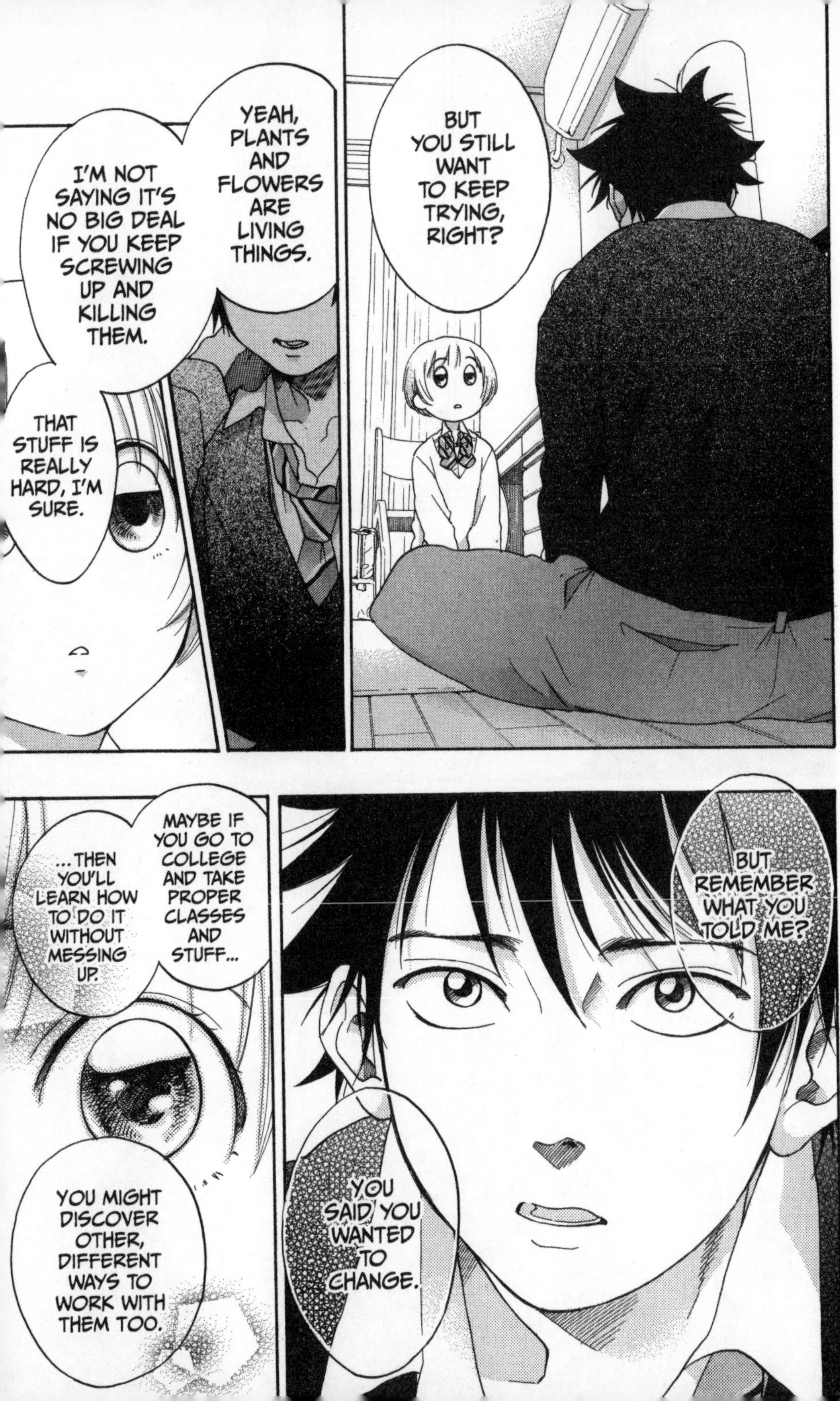
BUT YOU STILL WANT TO KEEP TRYING, RIGHT?
YEAH, PLANTS AND FLOWERS ARE LIVING THINGS.
I'M NOT SAYING IT'S NO BIG DEAL IF YOU KEEP SCREWING UP AND KILLING THEM.
THAT STUFF IS REALLY HARD, I'M SURE.
BUT REMEMBER WHAT YOU TOLD ME?
YOU SAID YOU WANTED TO CHANGE.
MAYBE IF YOU GO TO COLLEGE AND TAKE PROPER CLASSES AND STUFF...
...THEN YOU'LL LEARN HOW TO DO IT WITHOUT MESSING UP.
YOU MIGHT DISCOVER OTHER, DIFFERENT WAYS TO WORK WITH THEM TOO.

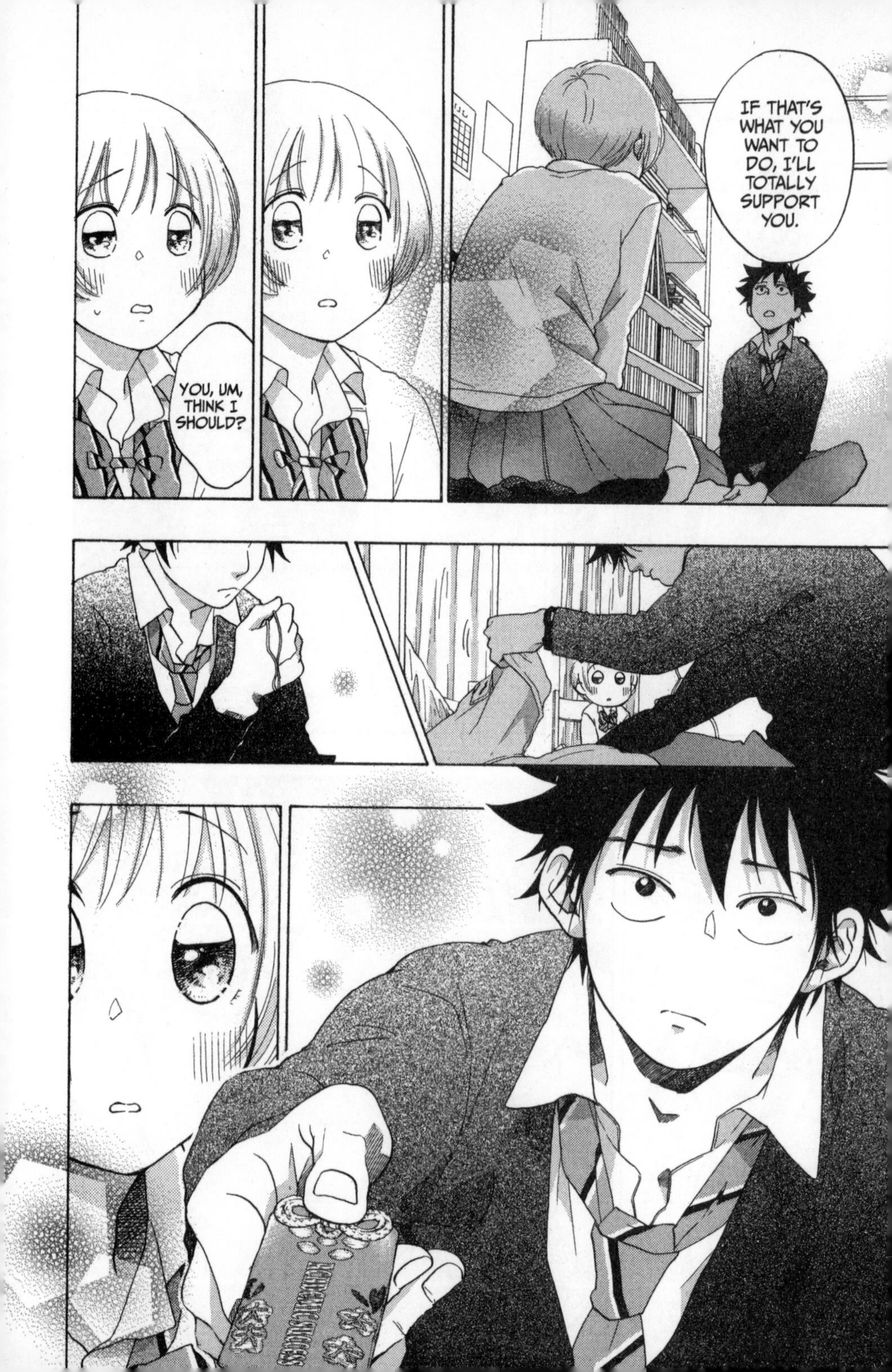
IF THAT'S WHAT YOU WANT TO DO, I'LL TOTALLY SUPPORT YOU.
YOU, UM, THINK I SHOULD?

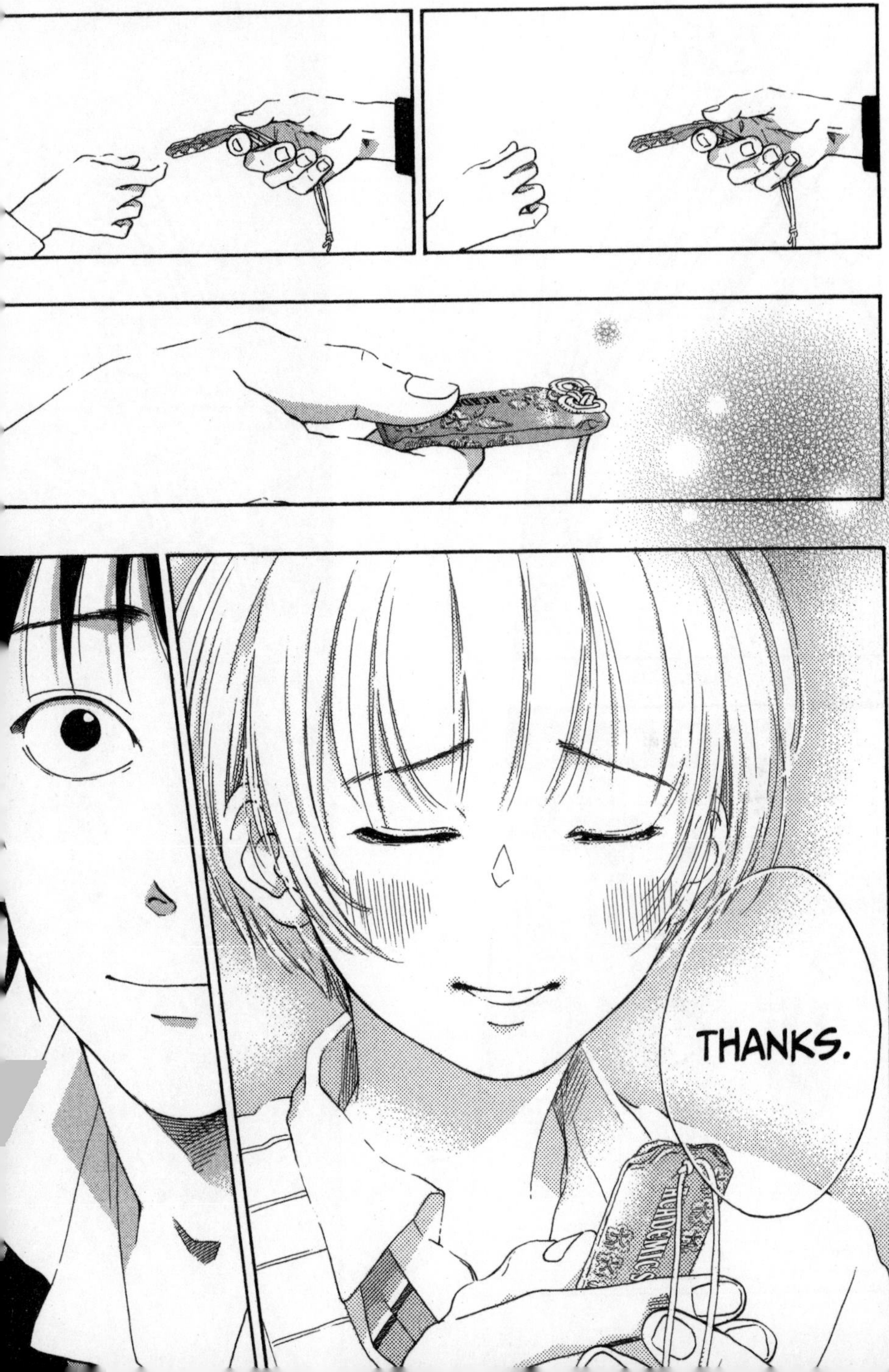
THANKS.

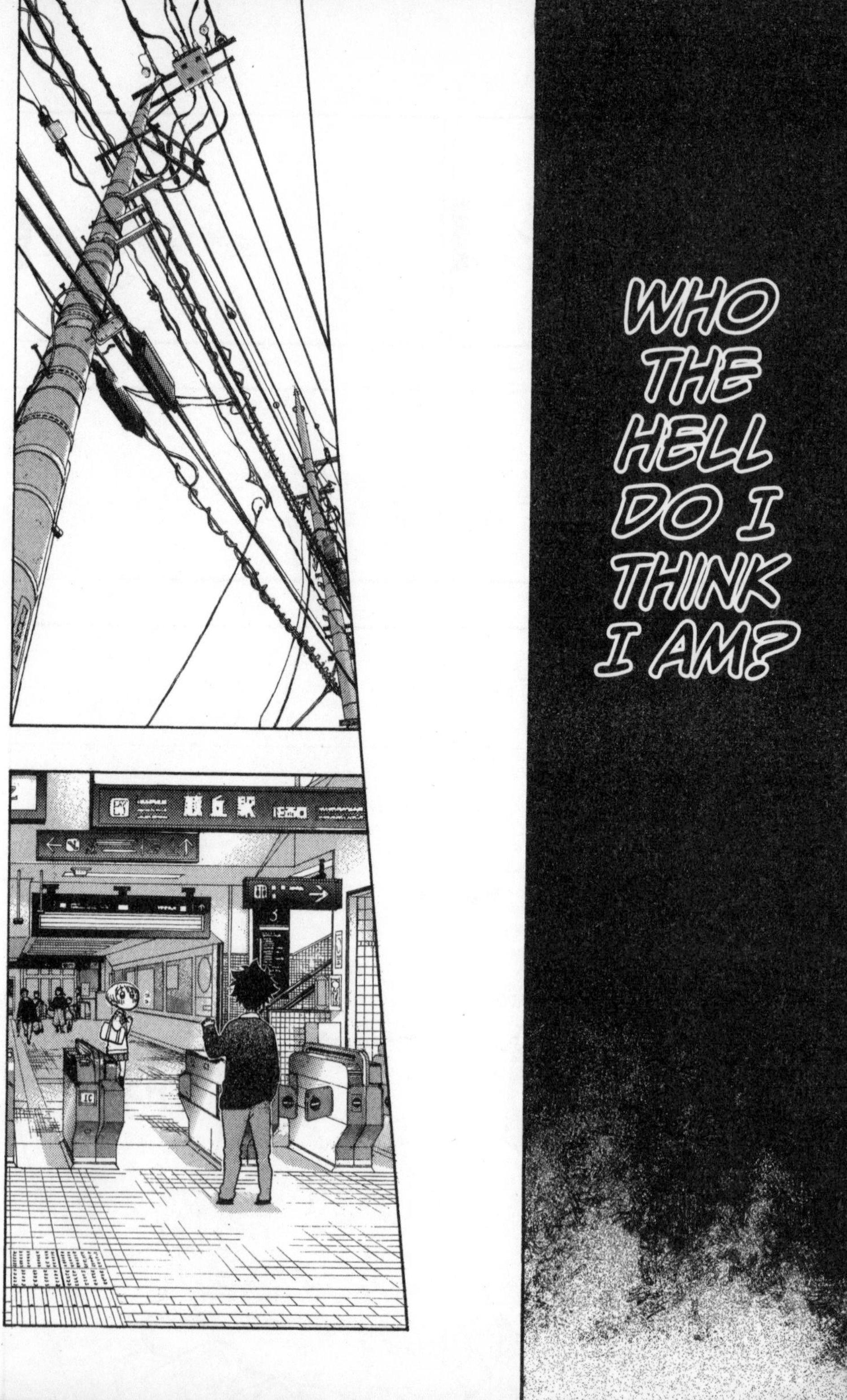
WHO THE HELL DO I THINK I AM?

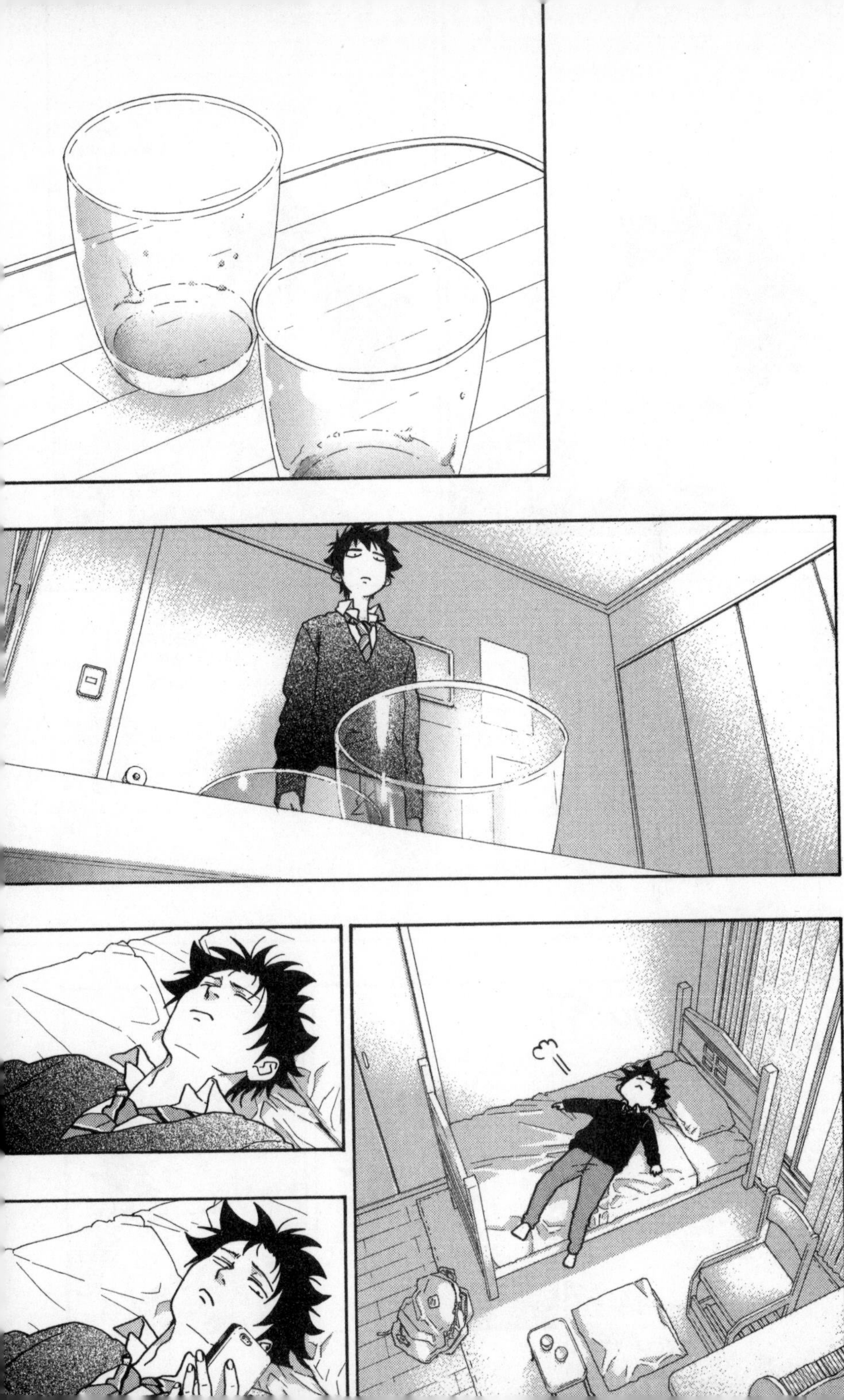

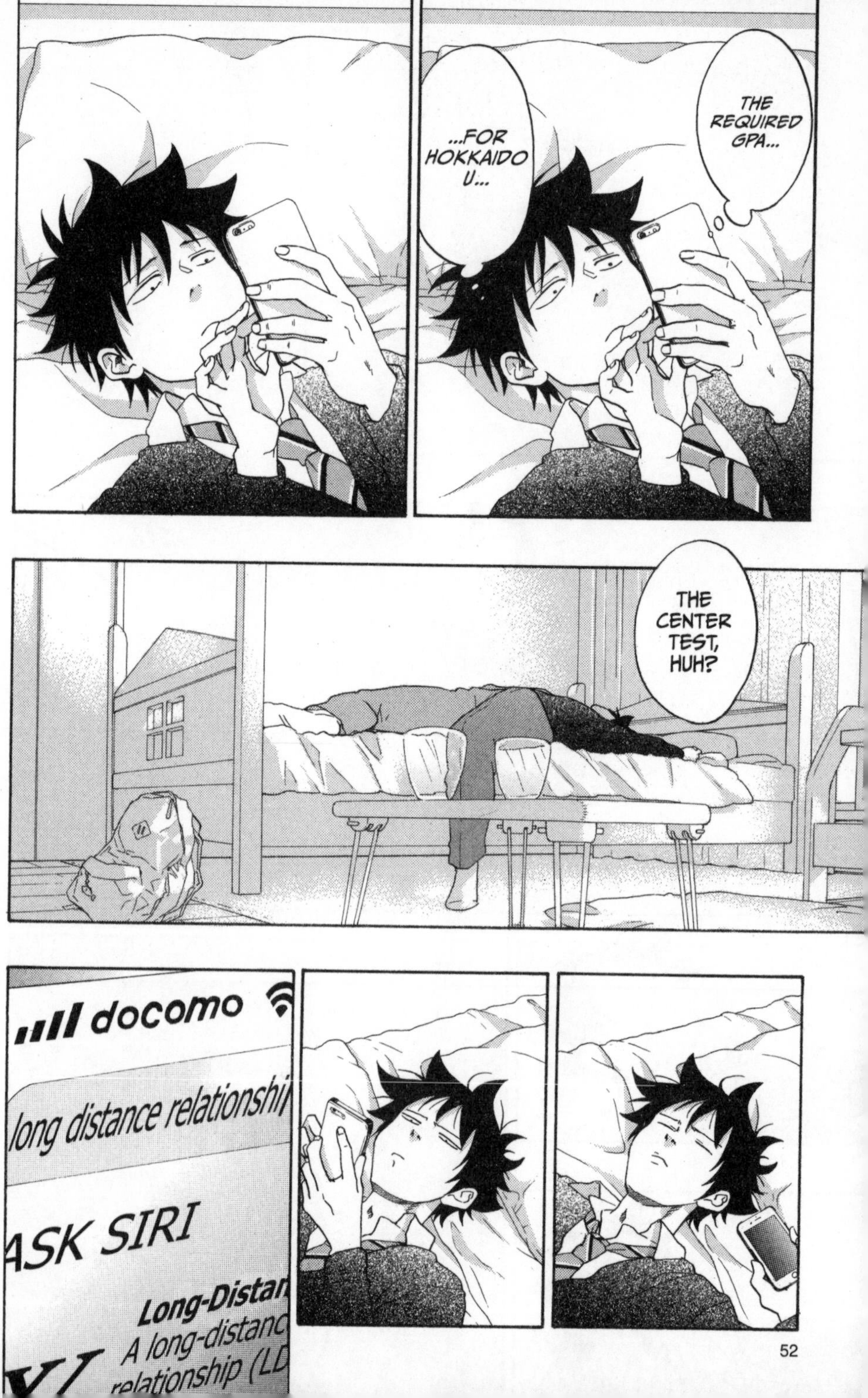
THE REQUIRED GPA...
...FOR HOKKAIDO U...
THE CENTER TEST, HUH?
docomo
long distance relationshi
ASK SIRI
Long-Distan
A long-distanc
relationship (LD

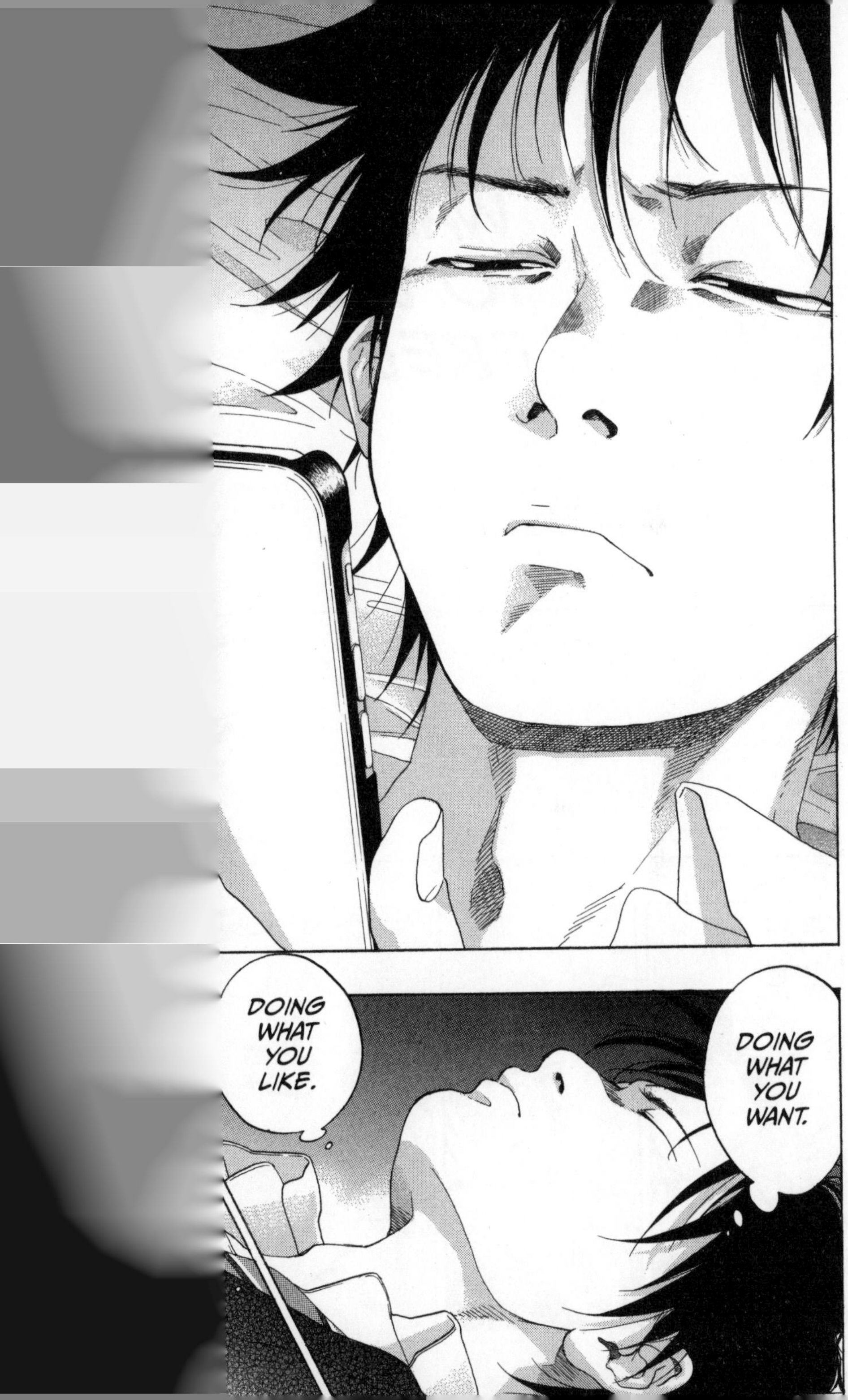
DOING WHAT YOU WANT.
DOING WHAT YOU LIKE.

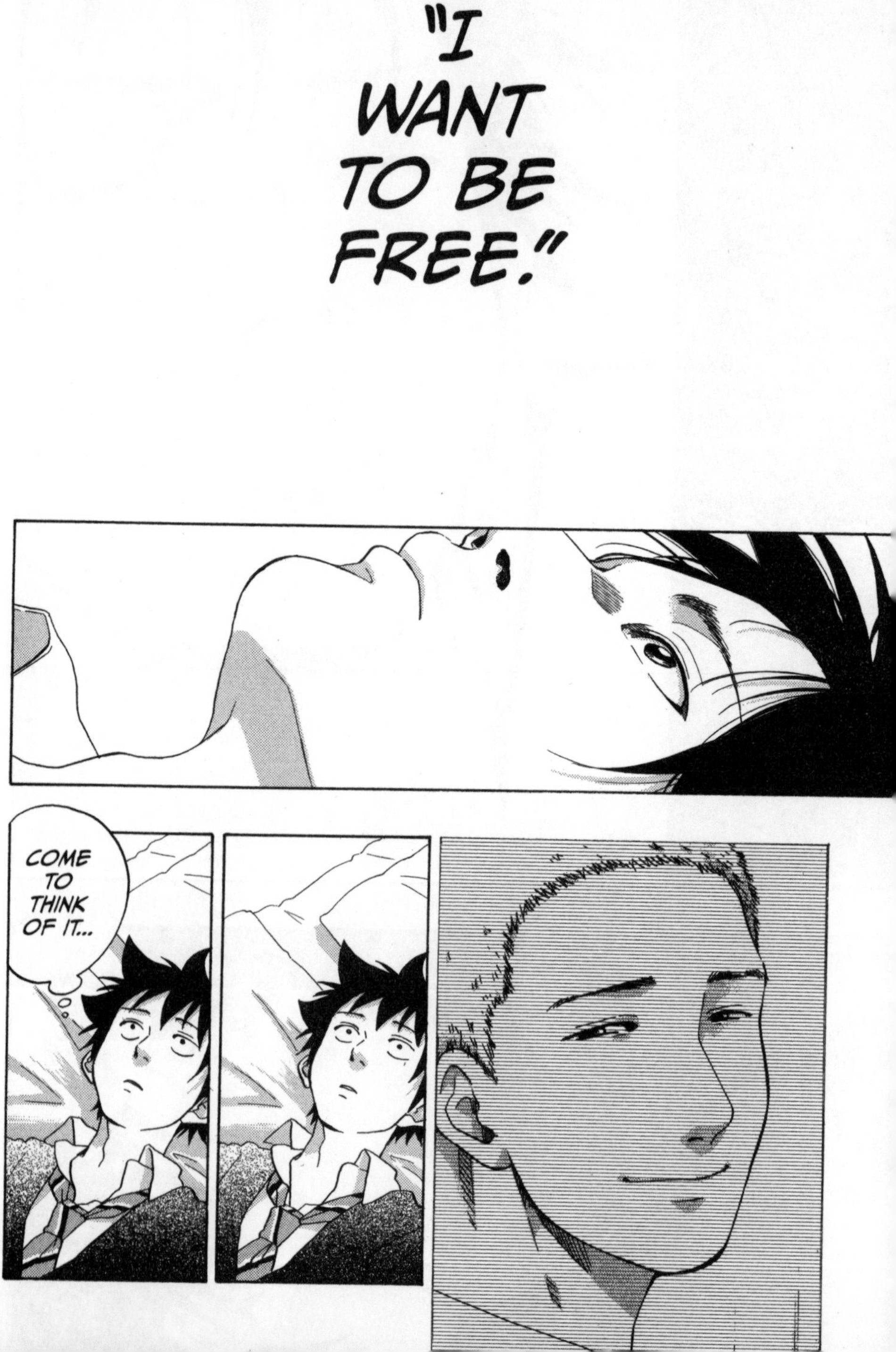
"I WANT TO BE FREE."
COME TO THINK OF IT...

...WHAT'S HE GOING TO DO?

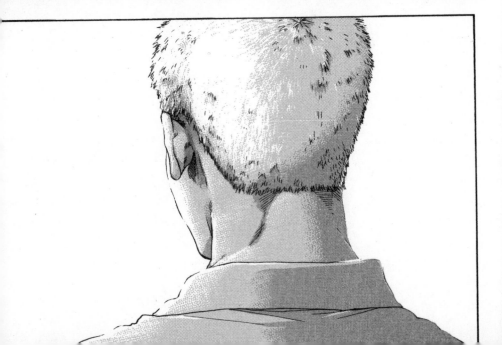

Taichi's homeroom teacher. Whenever he gets page time, everyone always mentions how cool he looks.

Hm?

What?

CHAPTER 36

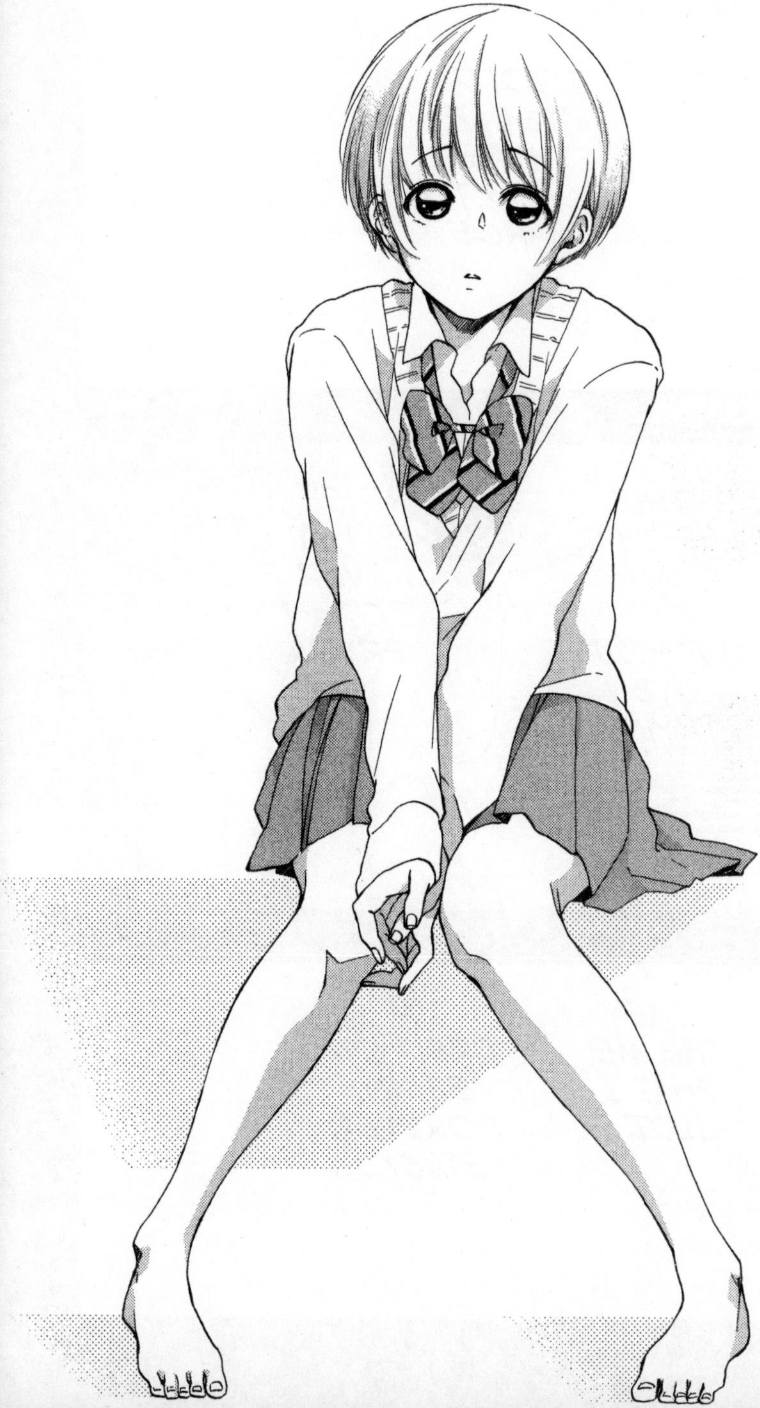

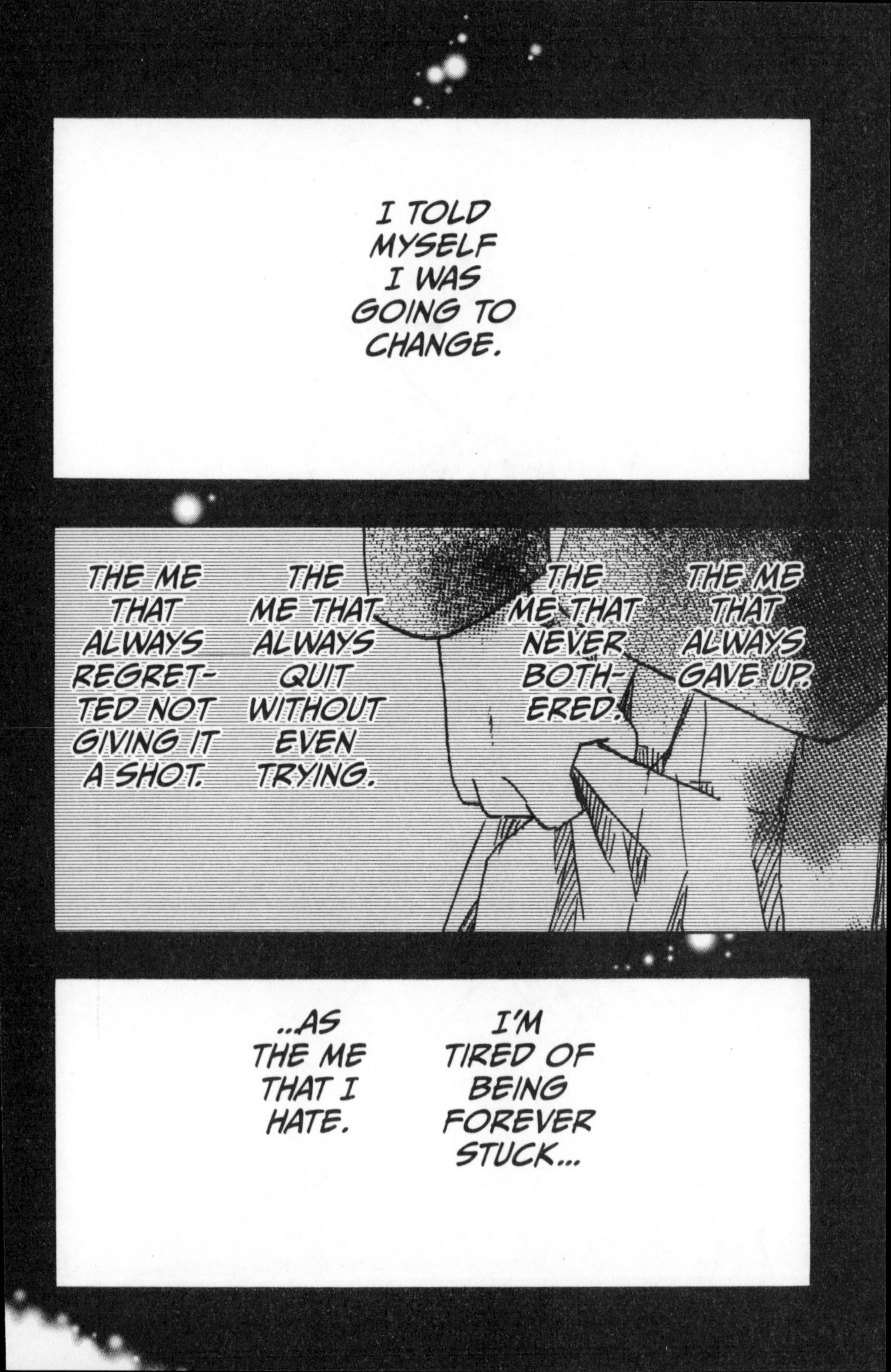
I TOLD MYSELF I WAS GOING TO CHANGE.
THE ME THAT ALWAYS GAVE UP.
THE ME THAT NEVER BOTHERED.
THE ME THAT ALWAYS QUIT WITHOUT EVEN TRYING.
THE ME THAT ALWAYS REGRETTED NOT GIVING IT A SHOT.
I'M TIRED OF BEING FOREVER STUCK...
...AS THE ME THAT I HATE.

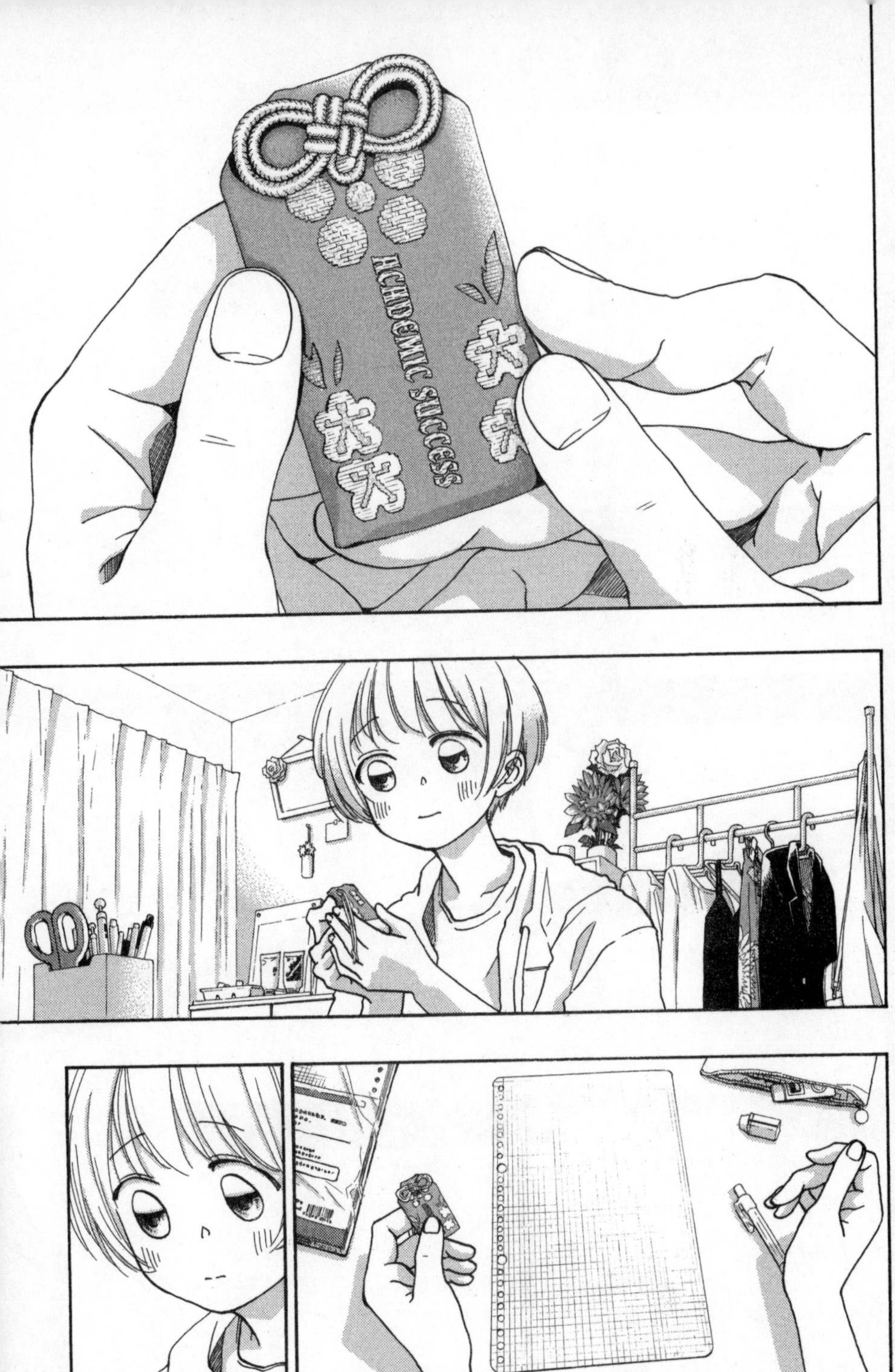
ACADEMIC SUCCESS

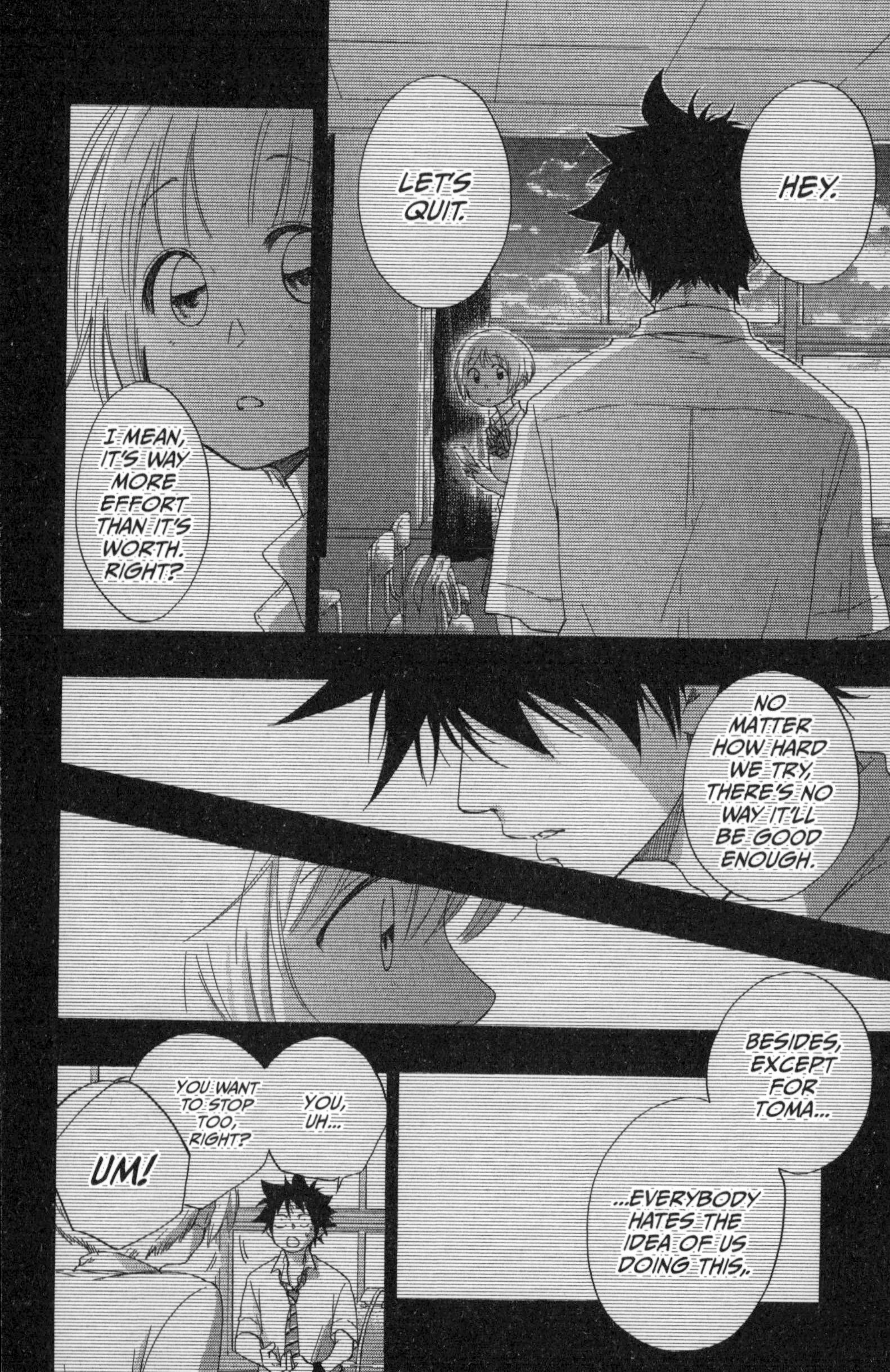
HEY.
LET'S QUIT.
I MEAN, IT'S WAY MORE EFFORT THAN IT'S WORTH. RIGHT?
NO MATTER HOW HARD WE TRY, THERE'S NO WAY IT'LL BE GOOD ENOUGH.
BESIDES, EXCEPT FOR TOMA...
...EVERYBODY HATES THE IDEA OF US DOING THIS.
YOU, UH...
YOU WANT TO STOP TOO, RIGHT?
UM!

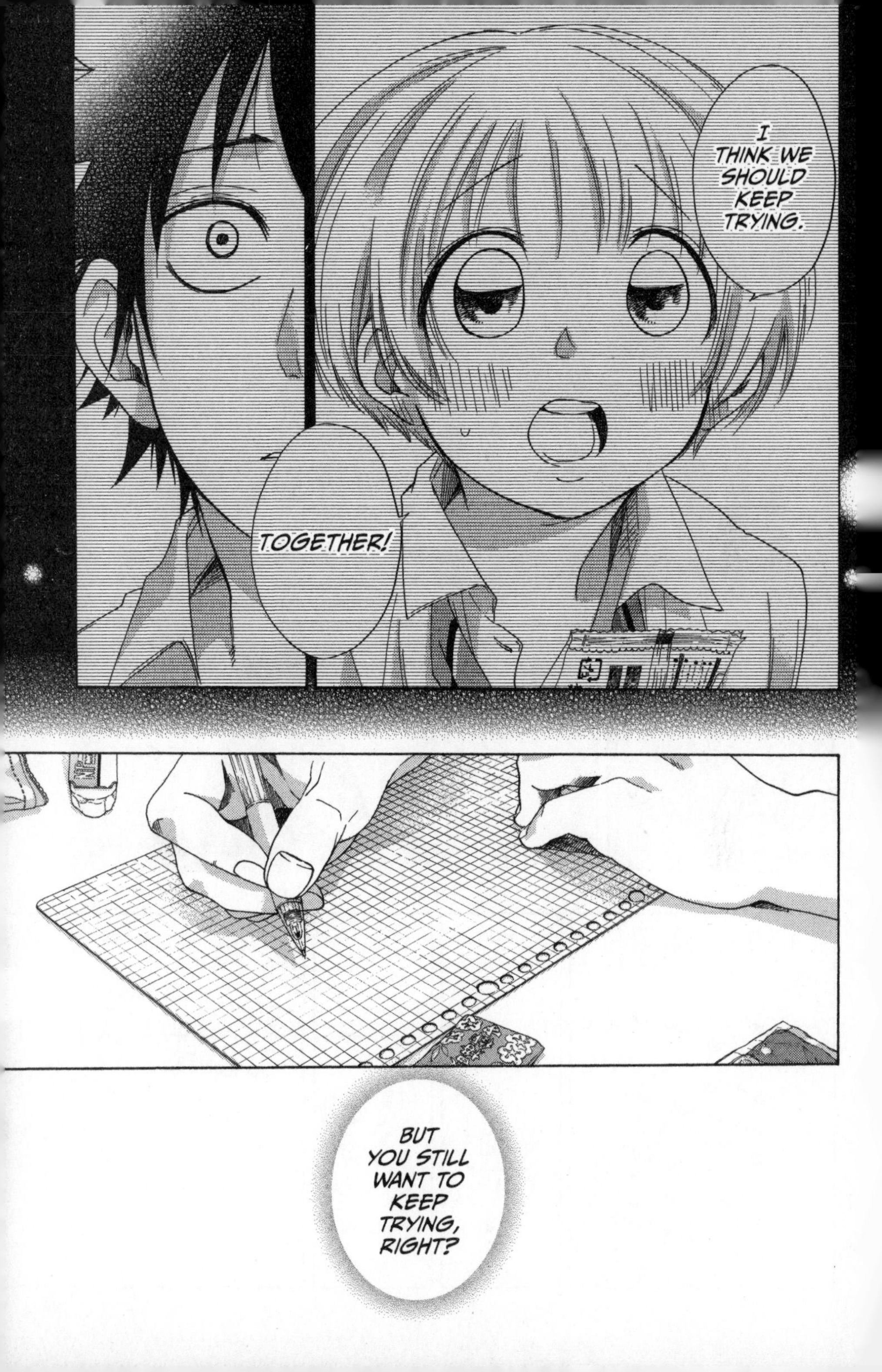
I THINK WE SHOULD KEEP TRYING.
TOGETHER!
BUT YOU STILL WANT TO KEEP TRYING, RIGHT?

...THE BIGGEST QUESTION IS, WHAT DO YOU WANT TO DO MOST?

RIGHT NOW...

LET'S START BY WRITING IT ALL OUT.

private

- Best one I can get into with my GPA
- Good rep
- Probably has more job opportunities
- Recommended by parents & teachers
- Campus looks fun

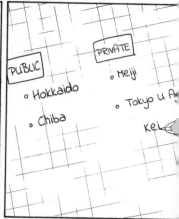

PUBLIC
- Hokkaido
- Chiba

PRIVATE
- Meiji
- Tokyo U A
- Kei

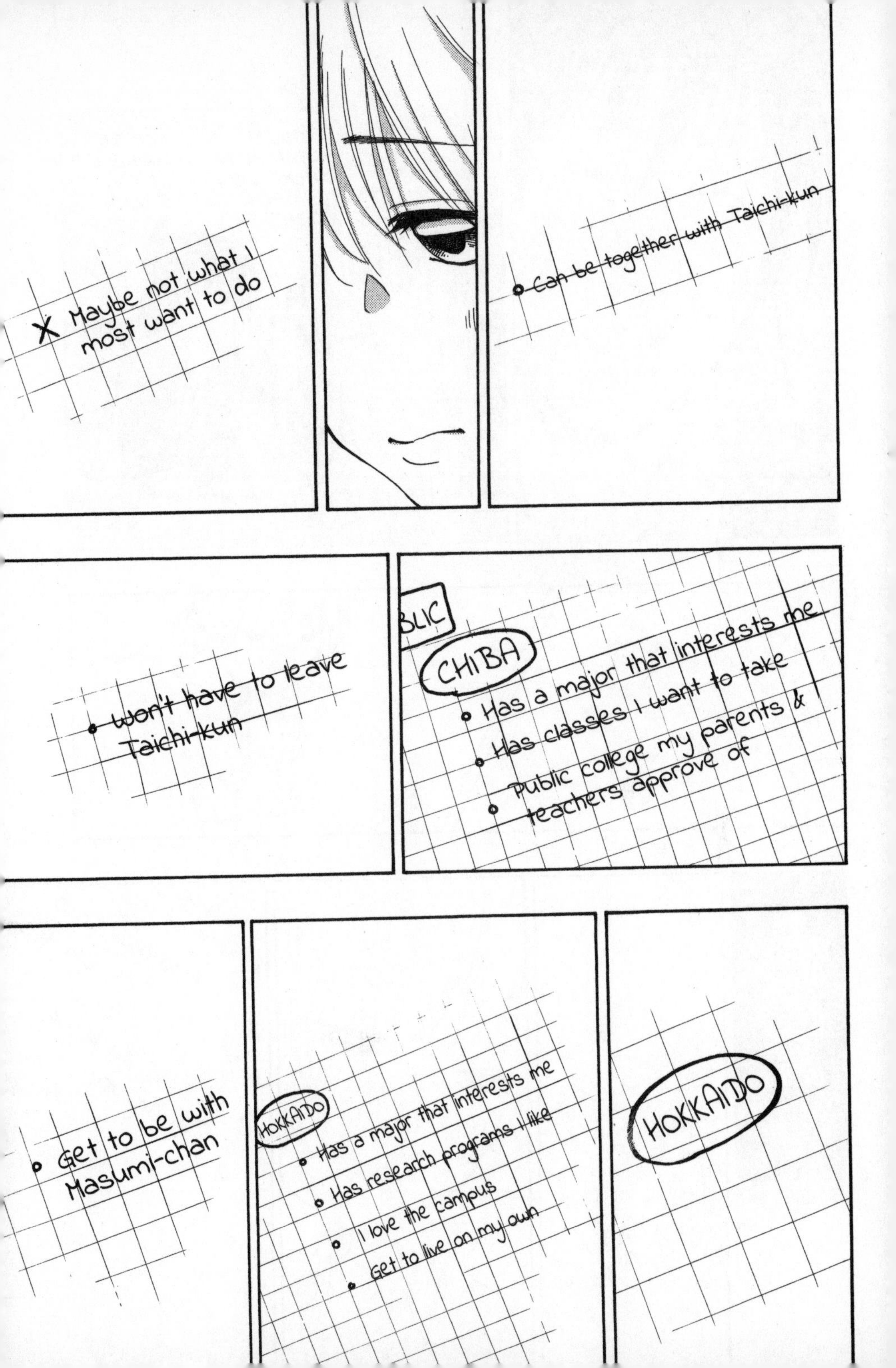

Can be together with Taichi-kun
X Maybe not what I most want to do
BLIC
CHIBA
Has a major that interests me
Has classes I want to take
Public college my parents & teachers approve of
Won't have to leave Taichi-kun
HOKKAIDO
HOKKAIDO
Has a major that interests me
Has research programs I like
I love the campus
Get to live on my own
Get to be with Masumi-chan

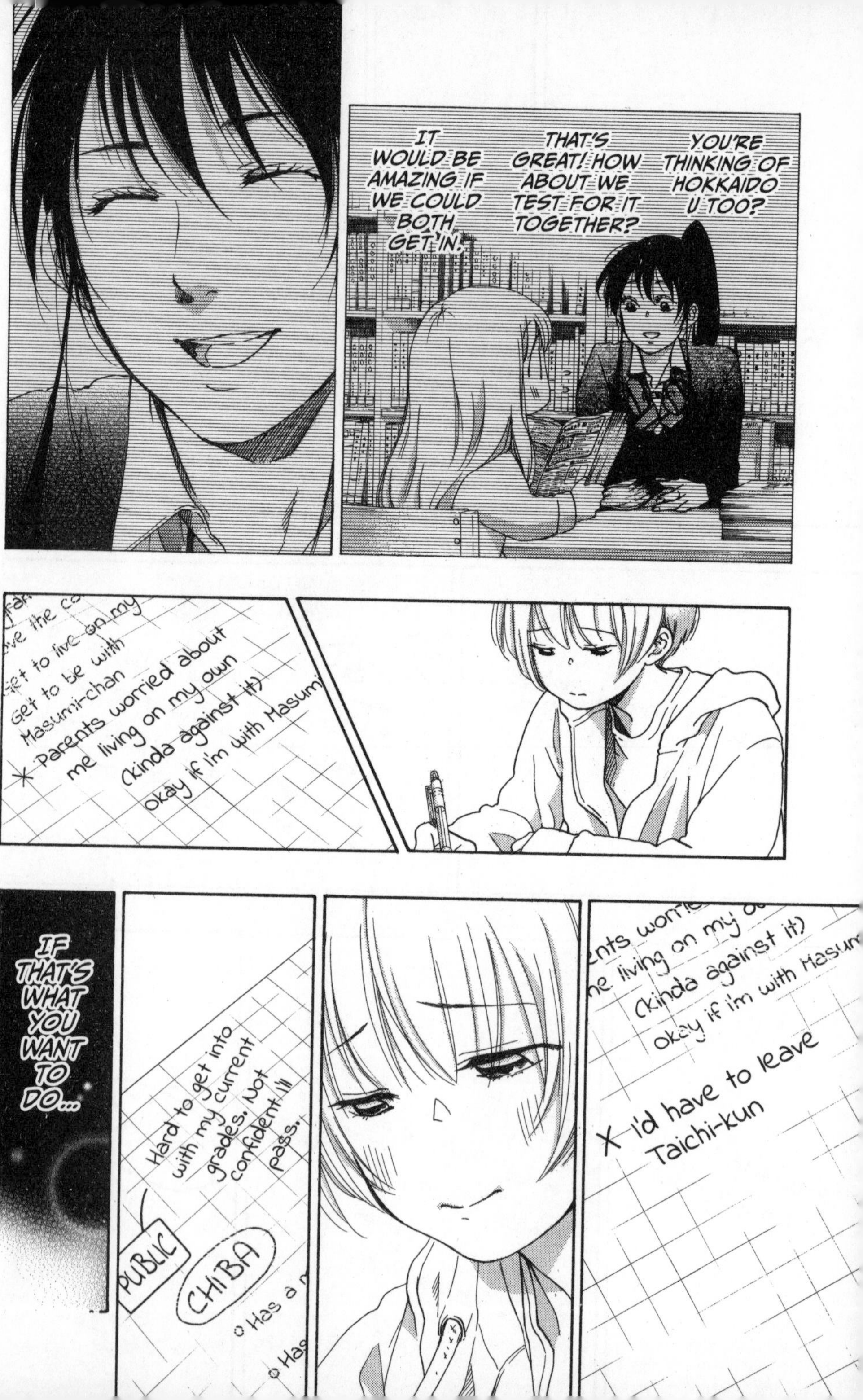
YOU'RE THINKING OF HOKKAIDO U TOO?
THAT'S GREAT! HOW ABOUT WE TEST FOR IT TOGETHER?
IT WOULD BE AMAZING IF WE COULD BOTH GET IN.
get to live on my
Get to be with Masumi-chan
✗ Parents worried about me living on my own
(kinda against it)
okay if I'm with Masumi
(kinda against it)
okay if I'm with Masum
✗ I'd have to leave Taichi-kun
Hard to get into with my current grades. Not confident I'll pass.
PUBLIC
CHIBA
IF THAT'S WHAT YOU WANT TO DO...

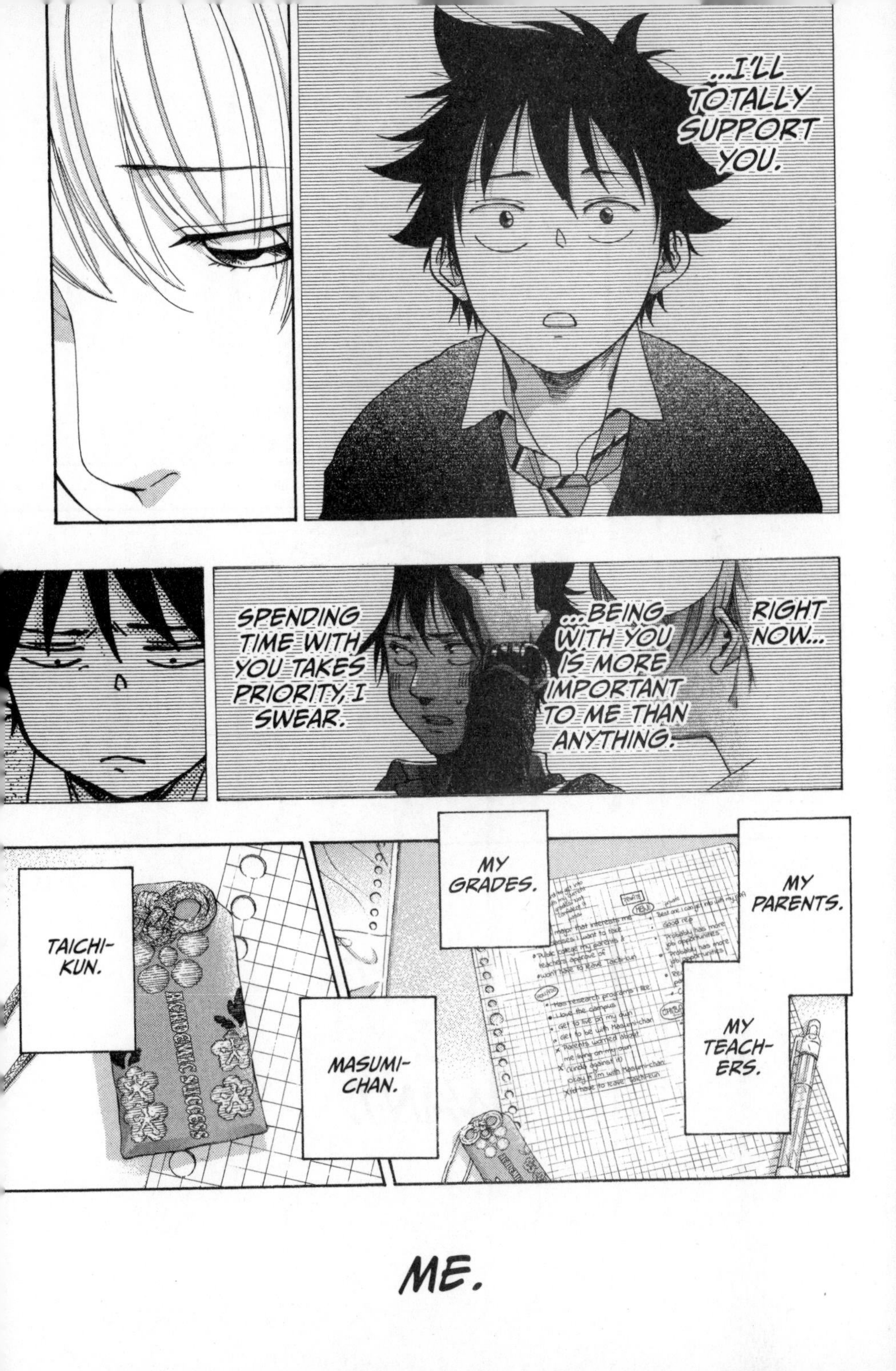
...I'LL TOTALLY SUPPORT YOU.
RIGHT NOW...
...BEING WITH YOU IS MORE IMPORTANT TO ME THAN ANYTHING.
SPENDING TIME WITH YOU TAKES PRIORITY, I SWEAR.
MY PARENTS.
MY TEACHERS.
MY GRADES.
MASUMI-CHAN.
ACADEMIC SUCCESS
TAICHI-KUN.
ME.

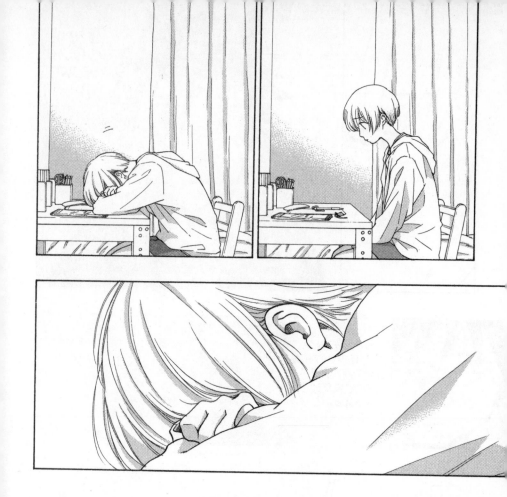

WHAT
I
WANT.

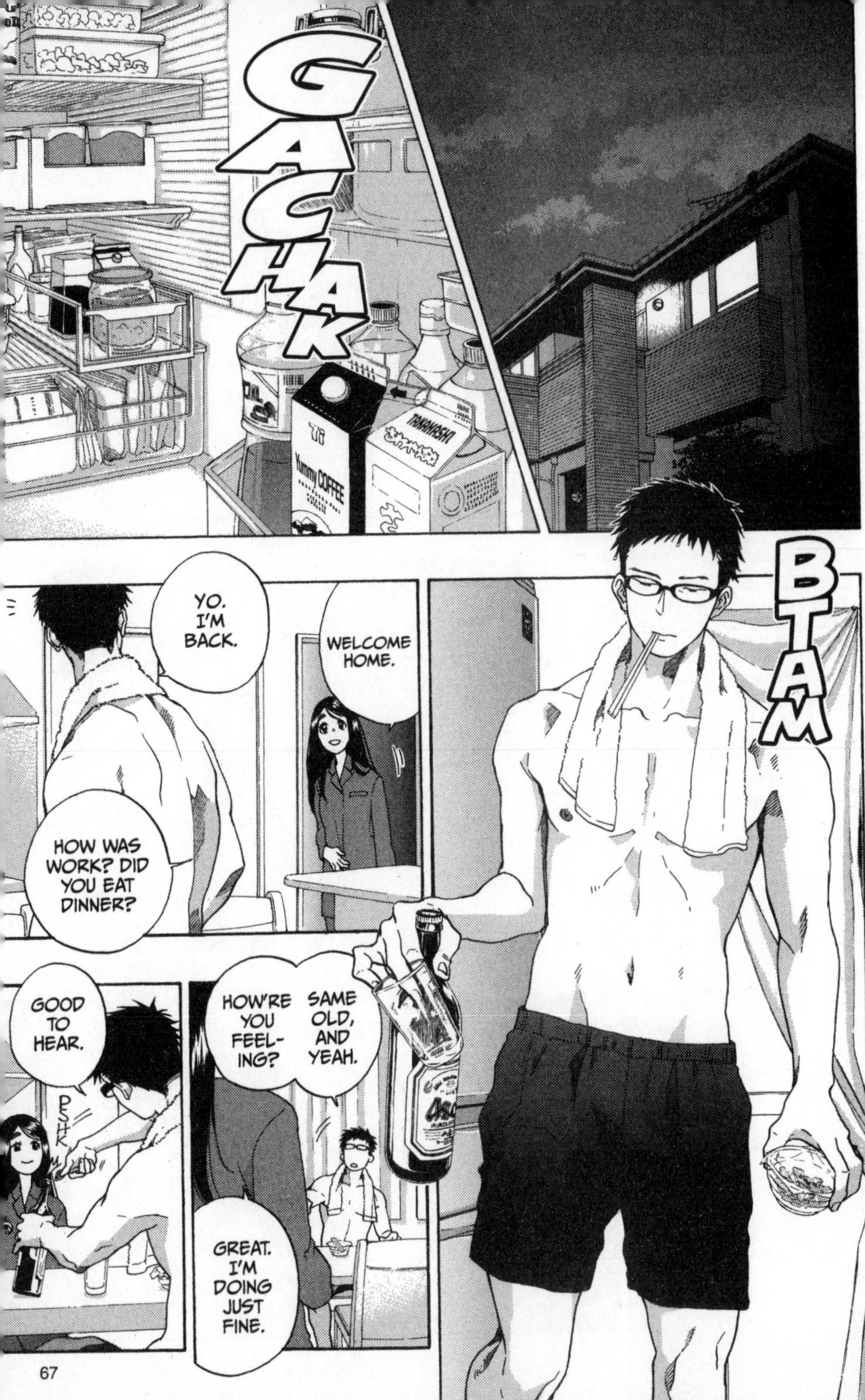

GACHAK
Yummy COFFEE
TAKAHASHI
BTAM
YO. I'M BACK.
WELCOME HOME.
HOW WAS WORK? DID YOU EAT DINNER?
SAME OLD, AND YEAH.
HOW'RE YOU FEELING?
GREAT. I'M DOING JUST FINE.
GOOD TO HEAR.
PSHK

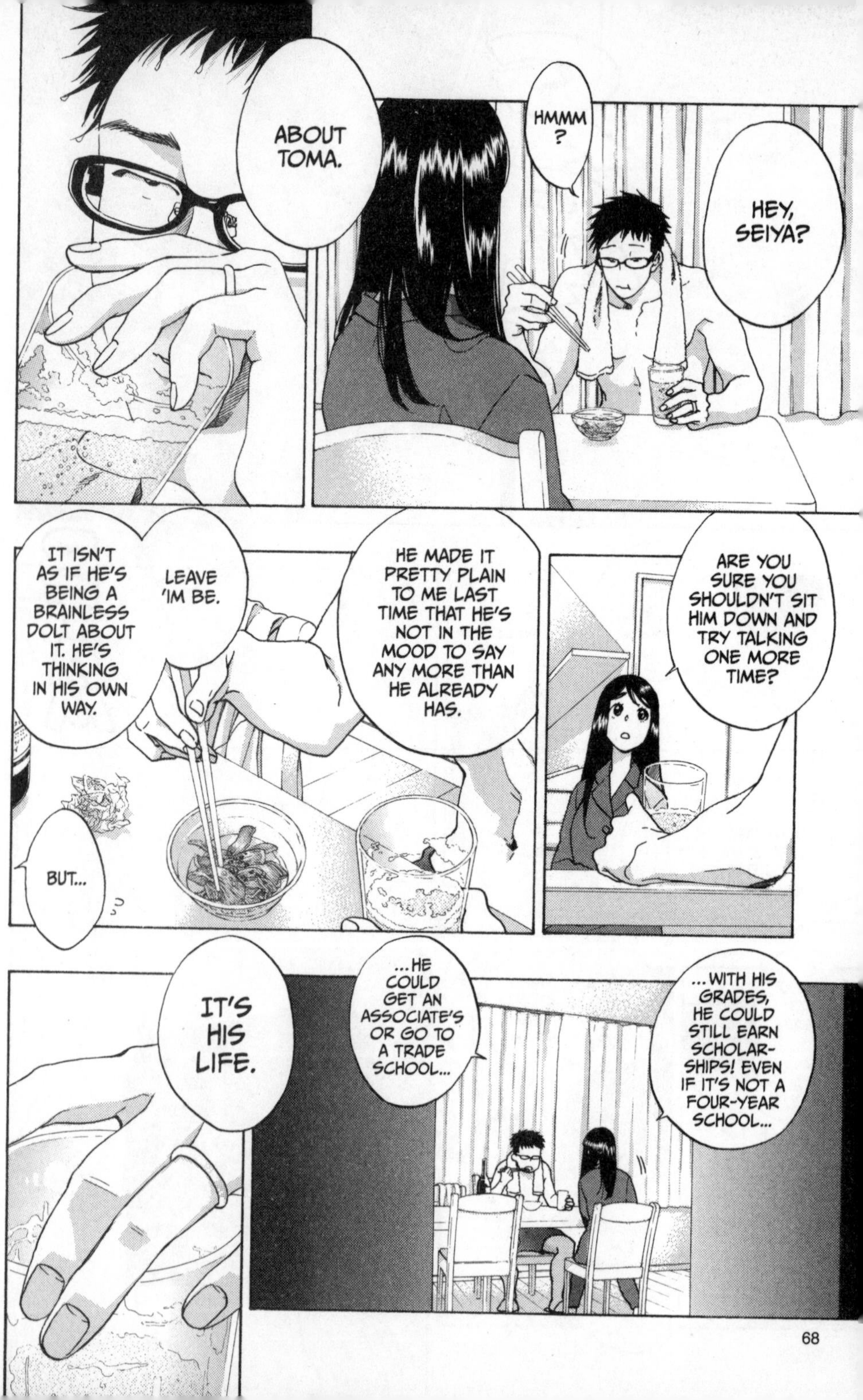
HEY, SEIYA?
HMMM?
ABOUT TOMA.
ARE YOU SURE YOU SHOULDN'T SIT HIM DOWN AND TRY TALKING ONE MORE TIME?
HE MADE IT PRETTY PLAIN TO ME LAST TIME THAT HE'S NOT IN THE MOOD TO SAY ANY MORE THAN HE ALREADY HAS.
LEAVE 'IM BE.
IT ISN'T AS IF HE'S BEING A BRAINLESS DOLT ABOUT IT. HE'S THINKING IN HIS OWN WAY.
BUT...
...WITH HIS GRADES, HE COULD STILL EARN SCHOLAR-SHIPS! EVEN IF IT'S NOT A FOUR-YEAR SCHOOL...
...HE COULD GET AN ASSOCIATE'S OR GO TO A TRADE SCHOOL...
IT'S HIS LIFE.

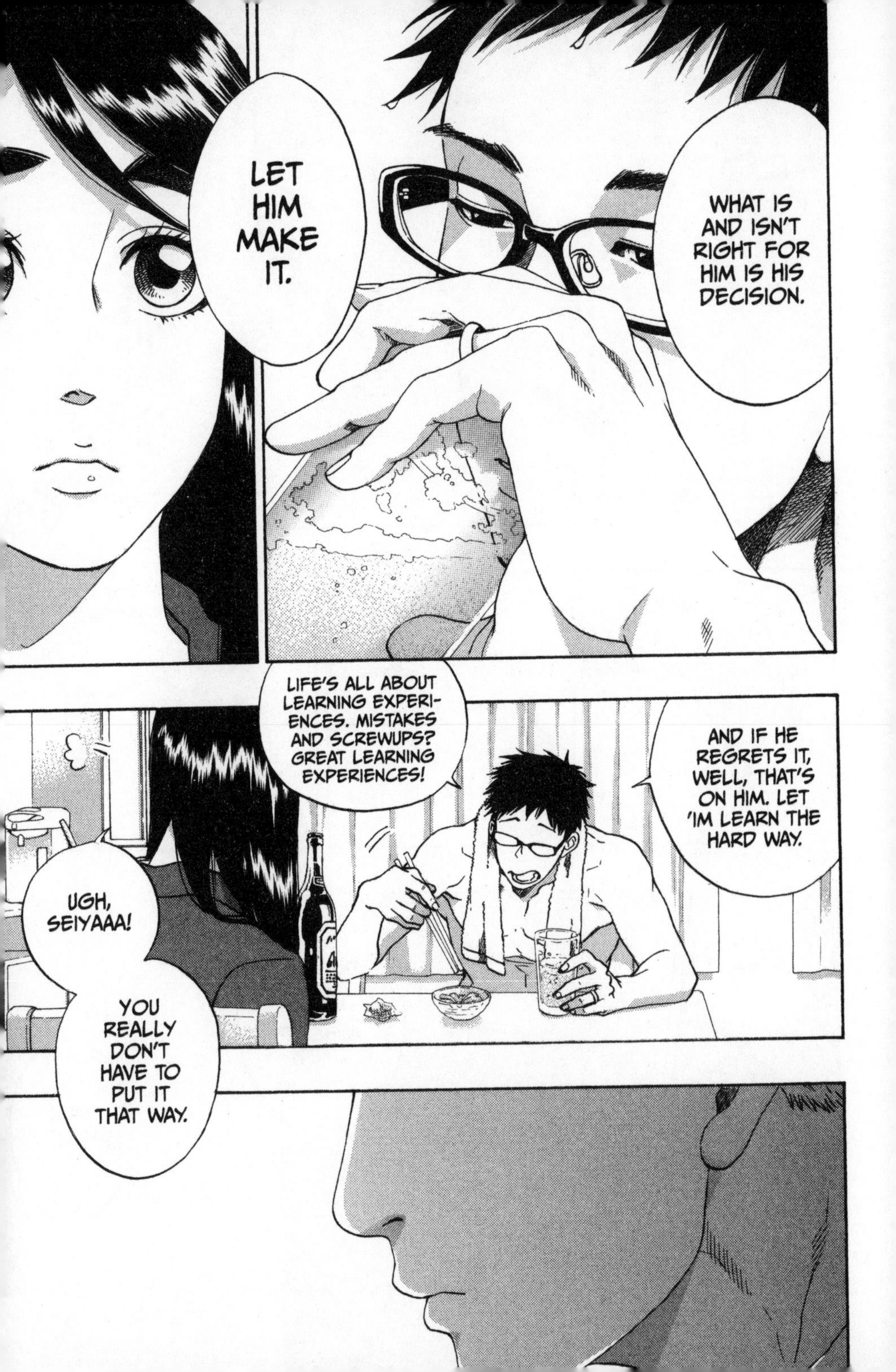
WHAT IS AND ISN'T RIGHT FOR HIM IS HIS DECISION.
LET HIM MAKE IT.
AND IF HE REGRETS IT, WELL, THAT'S ON HIM. LET 'IM LEARN THE HARD WAY.
LIFE'S ALL ABOUT LEARNING EXPERI-ENCES. MISTAKES AND SCREWUPS? GREAT LEARNING EXPERIENCES!
UGH, SEIYAAA!
YOU REALLY DON'T HAVE TO PUT IT THAT WAY.

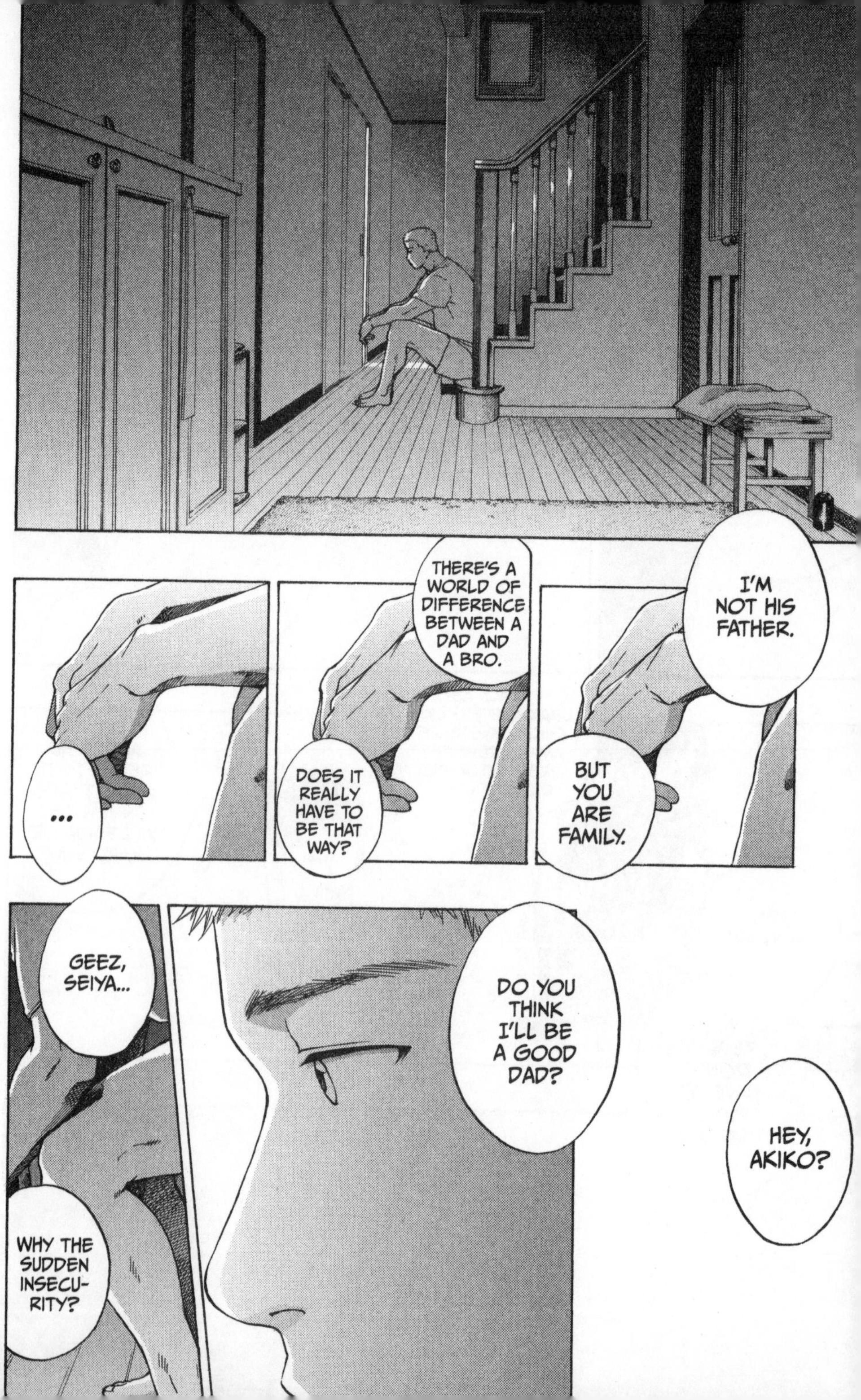
I'M NOT HIS FATHER.
BUT YOU ARE FAMILY.
THERE'S A WORLD OF DIFFERENCE BETWEEN A DAD AND A BRO.
DOES IT REALLY HAVE TO BE THAT WAY?
...
HEY, AKIKO?
DO YOU THINK I'LL BE A GOOD DAD?
GEEZ, SEIYA...
WHY THE SUDDEN INSECU-RITY?

OF COURSE YOU WILL BE.

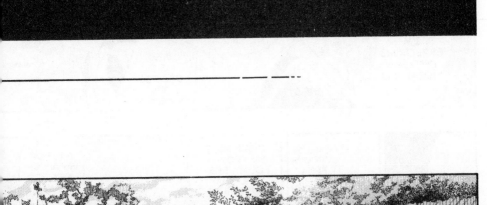

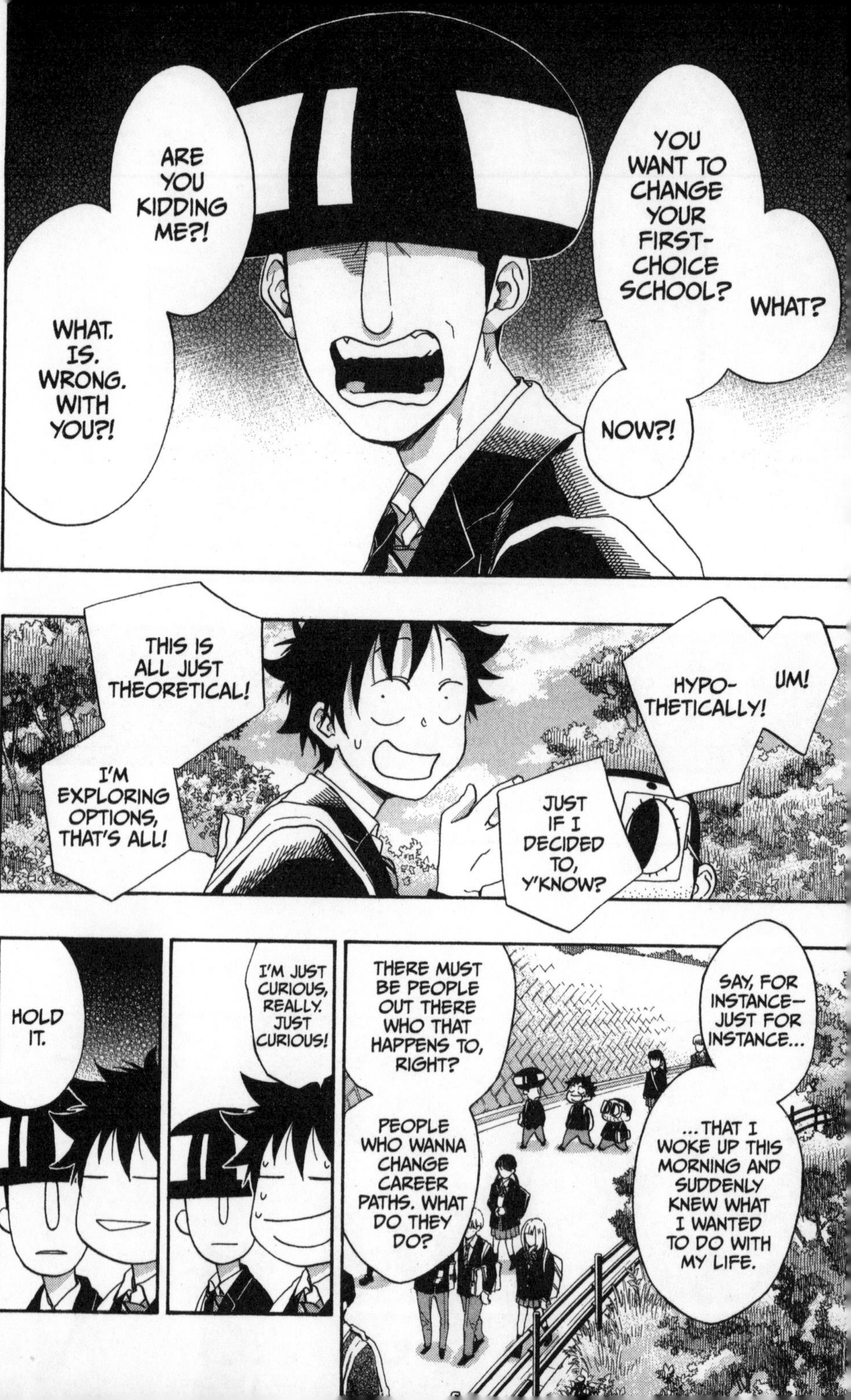
YOU WANT TO CHANGE YOUR FIRST-CHOICE SCHOOL?
WHAT?
NOW?!
ARE YOU KIDDING ME?!
WHAT. IS. WRONG. WITH YOU?!
UM!
HYPO-THETICALLY!
THIS IS ALL JUST THEORETICAL!
JUST IF I DECIDED TO, Y'KNOW?
I'M EXPLORING OPTIONS, THAT'S ALL!
SAY, FOR INSTANCE— JUST FOR INSTANCE...
...THAT I WOKE UP THIS MORNING AND SUDDENLY KNEW WHAT I WANTED TO DO WITH MY LIFE.
THERE MUST BE PEOPLE OUT THERE WHO THAT HAPPENS TO, RIGHT?
PEOPLE WHO WANNA CHANGE CAREER PATHS. WHAT DO THEY DO?
I'M JUST CURIOUS, REALLY. JUST CURIOUS!
HOLD IT.

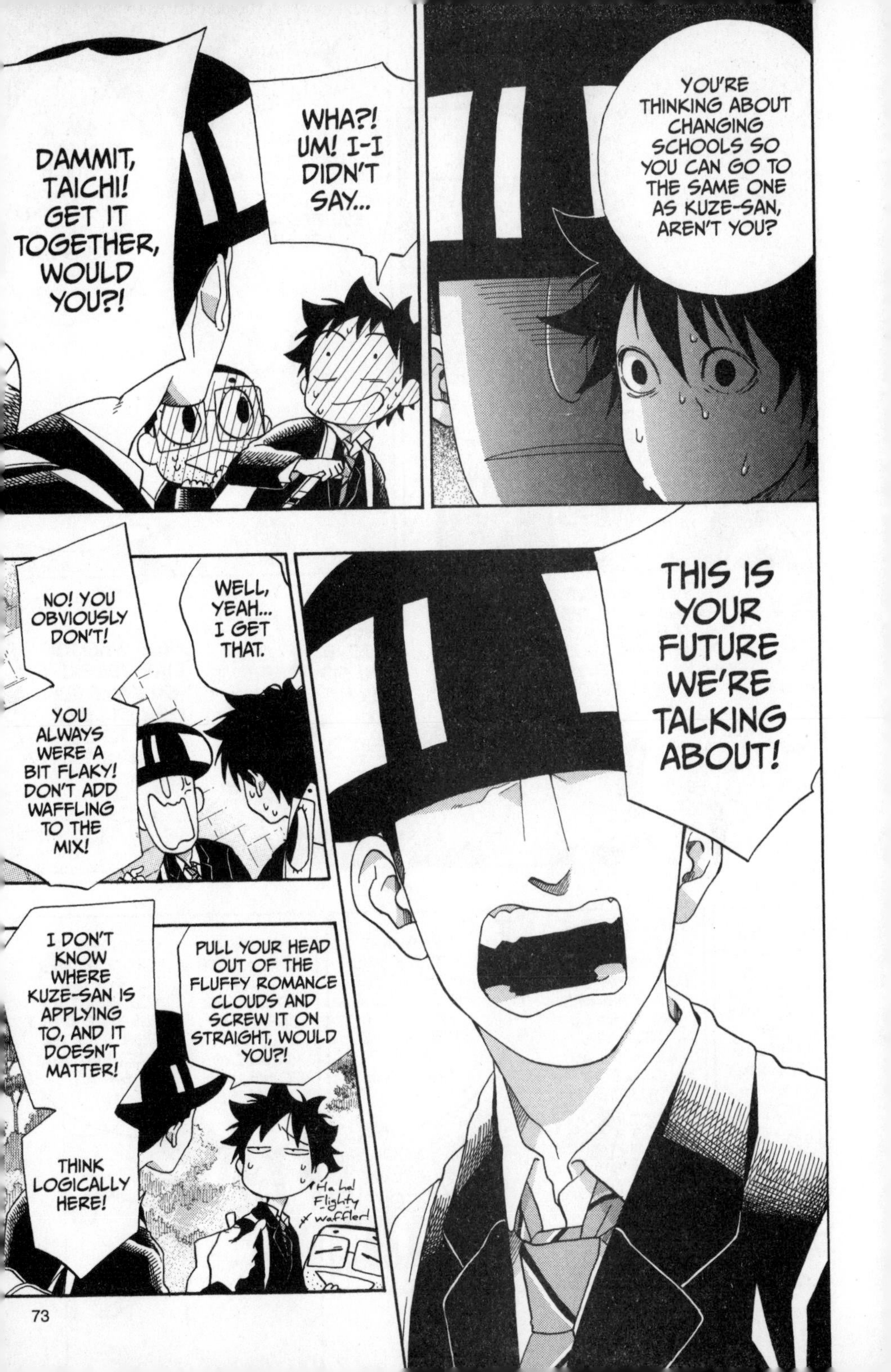
YOU'RE THINKING ABOUT CHANGING SCHOOLS SO YOU CAN GO TO THE SAME ONE AS KUZE-SAN, AREN'T YOU?
WHA?! UM! I-I DIDN'T SAY...
DAMMIT, TAICHI! GET IT TOGETHER, WOULD YOU?!
THIS IS YOUR FUTURE WE'RE TALKING ABOUT!
WELL, YEAH... I GET THAT.
NO! YOU OBVIOUSLY DON'T!
YOU ALWAYS WERE A BIT FLAKY! DON'T ADD WAFFLING TO THE MIX!
PULL YOUR HEAD OUT OF THE FLUFFY ROMANCE CLOUDS AND SCREW IT ON STRAIGHT, WOULD YOU?!
I DON'T KNOW WHERE KUZE-SAN IS APPLYING TO, AND IT DOESN'T MATTER!
THINK LOGICALLY HERE!
Ha ha! Flighty waffler!

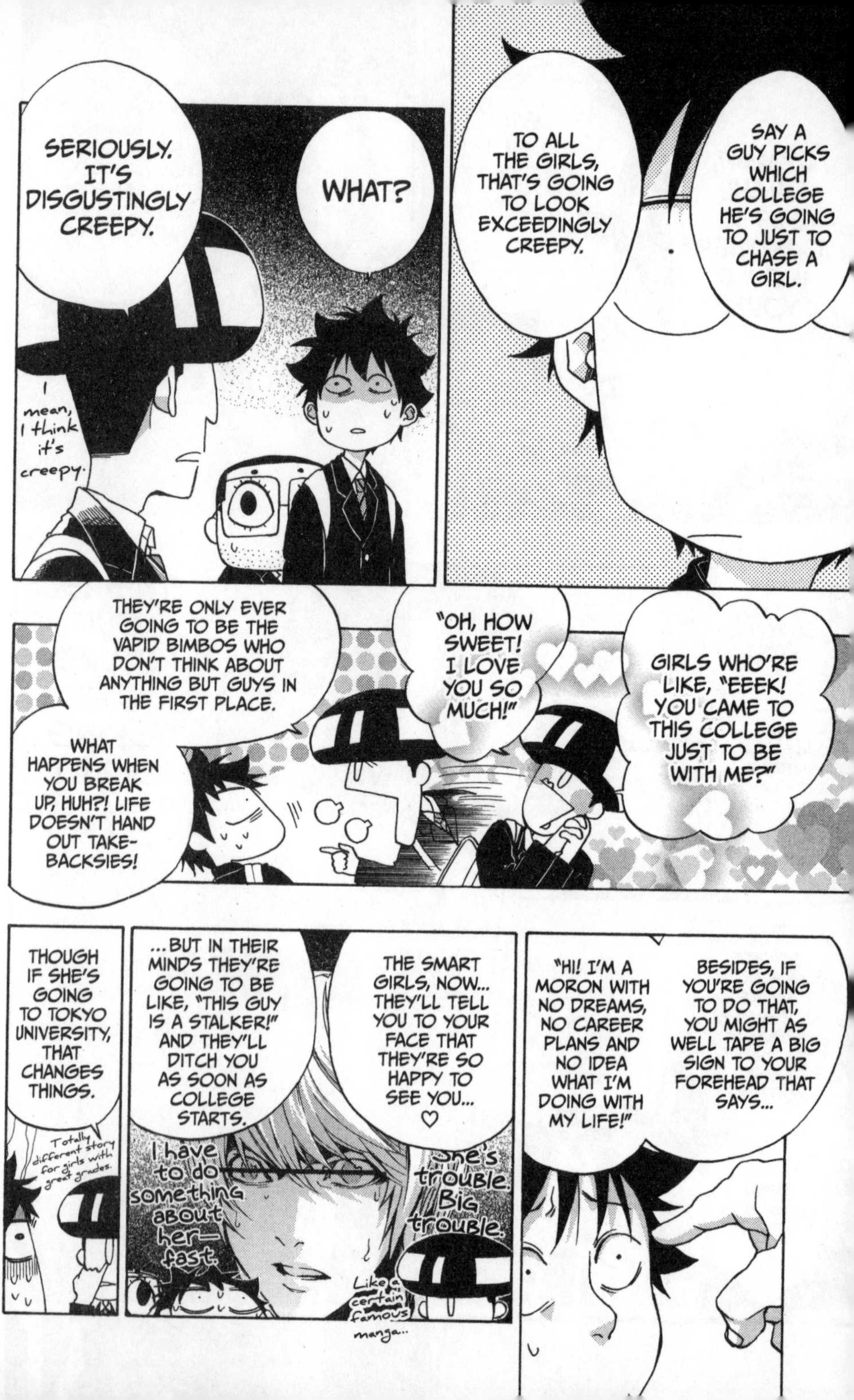
SAY A GUY PICKS WHICH COLLEGE HE'S GOING TO JUST TO CHASE A GIRL.
TO ALL THE GIRLS, THAT'S GOING TO LOOK EXCEEDINGLY CREEPY.
WHAT?
SERIOUSLY. IT'S DISGUSTINGLY CREEPY.
I mean, I think it's creepy.
GIRLS WHO'RE LIKE, "EEEK! YOU CAME TO THIS COLLEGE JUST TO BE WITH ME?"
"OH, HOW SWEET! I LOVE YOU SO MUCH!"
THEY'RE ONLY EVER GOING TO BE THE VAPID BIMBOS WHO DON'T THINK ABOUT ANYTHING BUT GUYS IN THE FIRST PLACE.
WHAT HAPPENS WHEN YOU BREAK UP, HUH?! LIFE DOESN'T HAND OUT TAKE-BACKSIES!
BESIDES, IF YOU'RE GOING TO DO THAT, YOU MIGHT AS WELL TAPE A BIG SIGN TO YOUR FOREHEAD THAT SAYS...
"HI! I'M A MORON WITH NO DREAMS, NO CAREER PLANS AND NO IDEA WHAT I'M DOING WITH MY LIFE!"
THE SMART GIRLS, NOW... THEY'LL TELL YOU TO YOUR FACE THAT THEY'RE SO HAPPY TO SEE YOU... ♡
...BUT IN THEIR MINDS THEY'RE GOING TO BE LIKE, "THIS GUY IS A STALKER!" AND THEY'LL DITCH YOU AS SOON AS COLLEGE STARTS.
She's trouble. Big trouble.
I have to do something about her—fast.
Like a certain famous manga...
THOUGH IF SHE'S GOING TO TOKYO UNIVERSITY, THAT CHANGES THINGS.
Totally different story for girls with great grades.

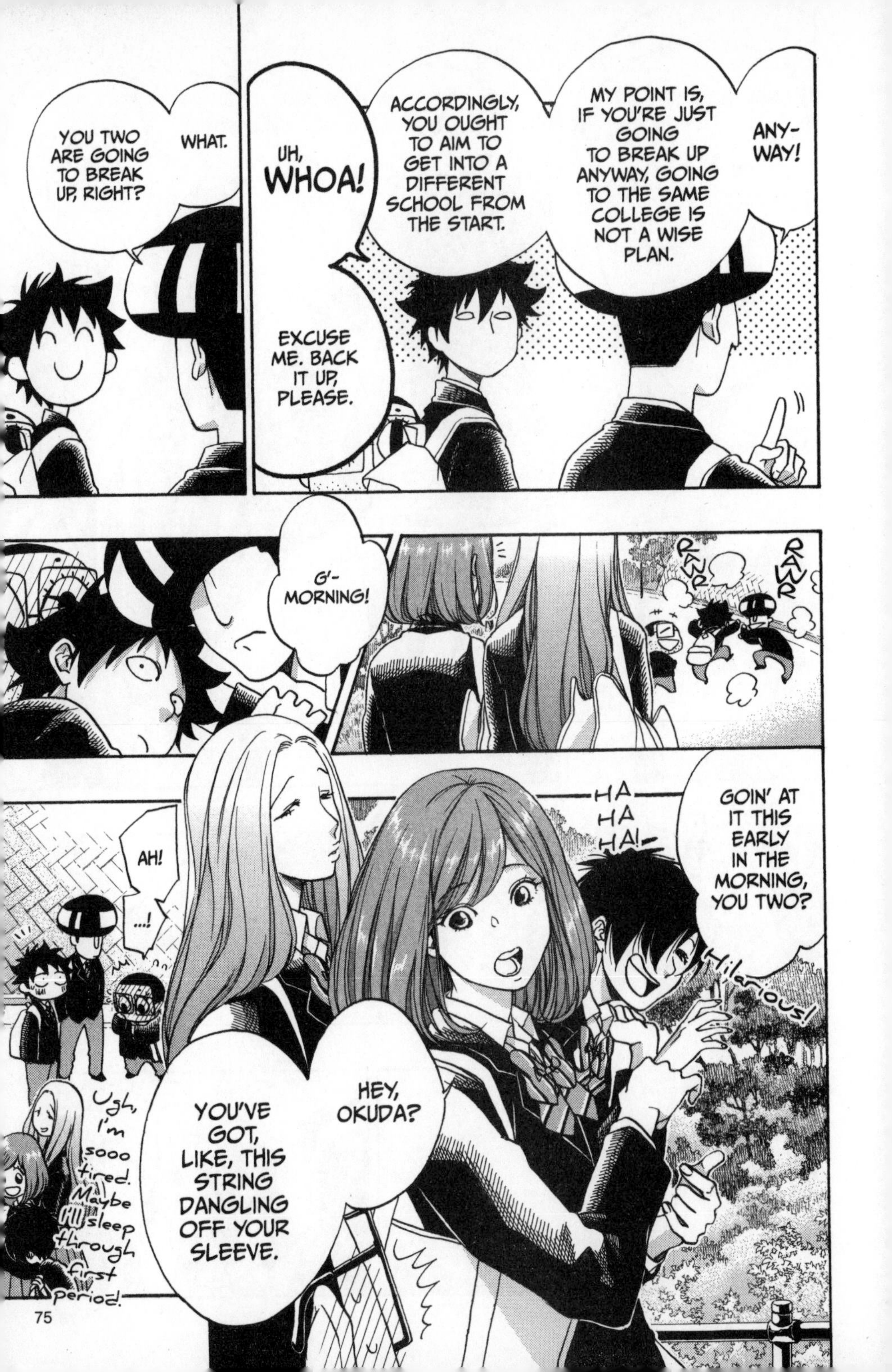
ANY-WAY!
MY POINT IS, IF YOU'RE JUST GOING TO BREAK UP ANYWAY, GOING TO THE SAME COLLEGE IS NOT A WISE PLAN.
ACCORDINGLY, YOU OUGHT TO AIM TO GET INTO A DIFFERENT SCHOOL FROM THE START.
UH, WHOA!
EXCUSE ME. BACK IT UP, PLEASE.
WHAT.
YOU TWO ARE GOING TO BREAK UP, RIGHT?
RAWR
RAWR
G'-MORNING!
GOIN' AT IT THIS EARLY IN THE MORNING, YOU TWO?
HA HA HA!
Hilarious!
AH!
...!
HEY, OKUDA?
YOU'VE GOT, LIKE, THIS STRING DANGLING OFF YOUR SLEEVE.
Ugh, I'm sooo tired. Maybe I'll sleep through first period.

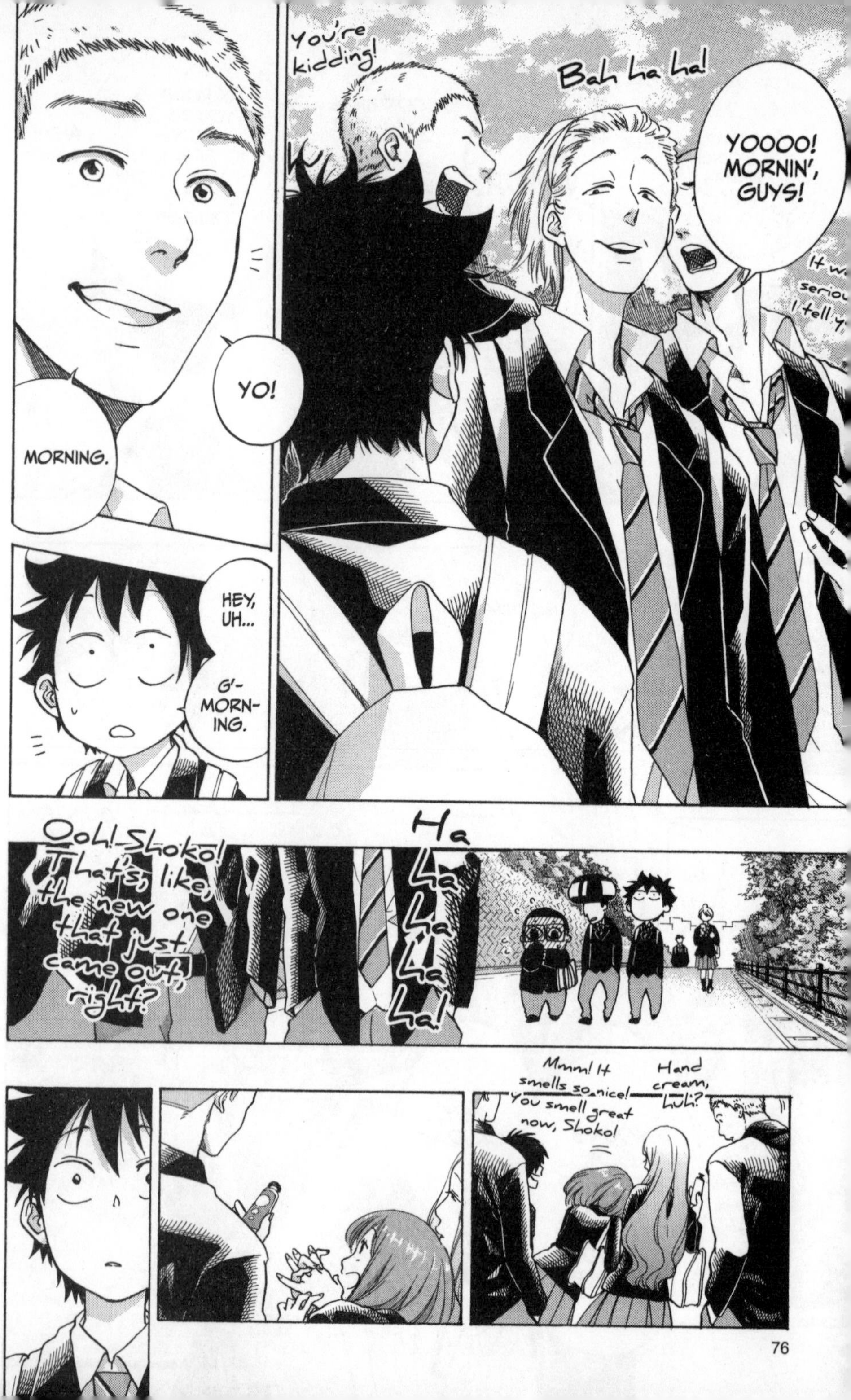

Bah ha ha!
YOOOO! MORNIN', GUYS!
You're kidding!
YO!
MORNING.
HEY, UH...
G'-MORNING.
Ha ha ha ha ha!
Ooh! Shoko! That's, like, the new one that just came out, right?
Hand cream, huh?
Mmm! It smells so nice! You smell great now, Shoko!

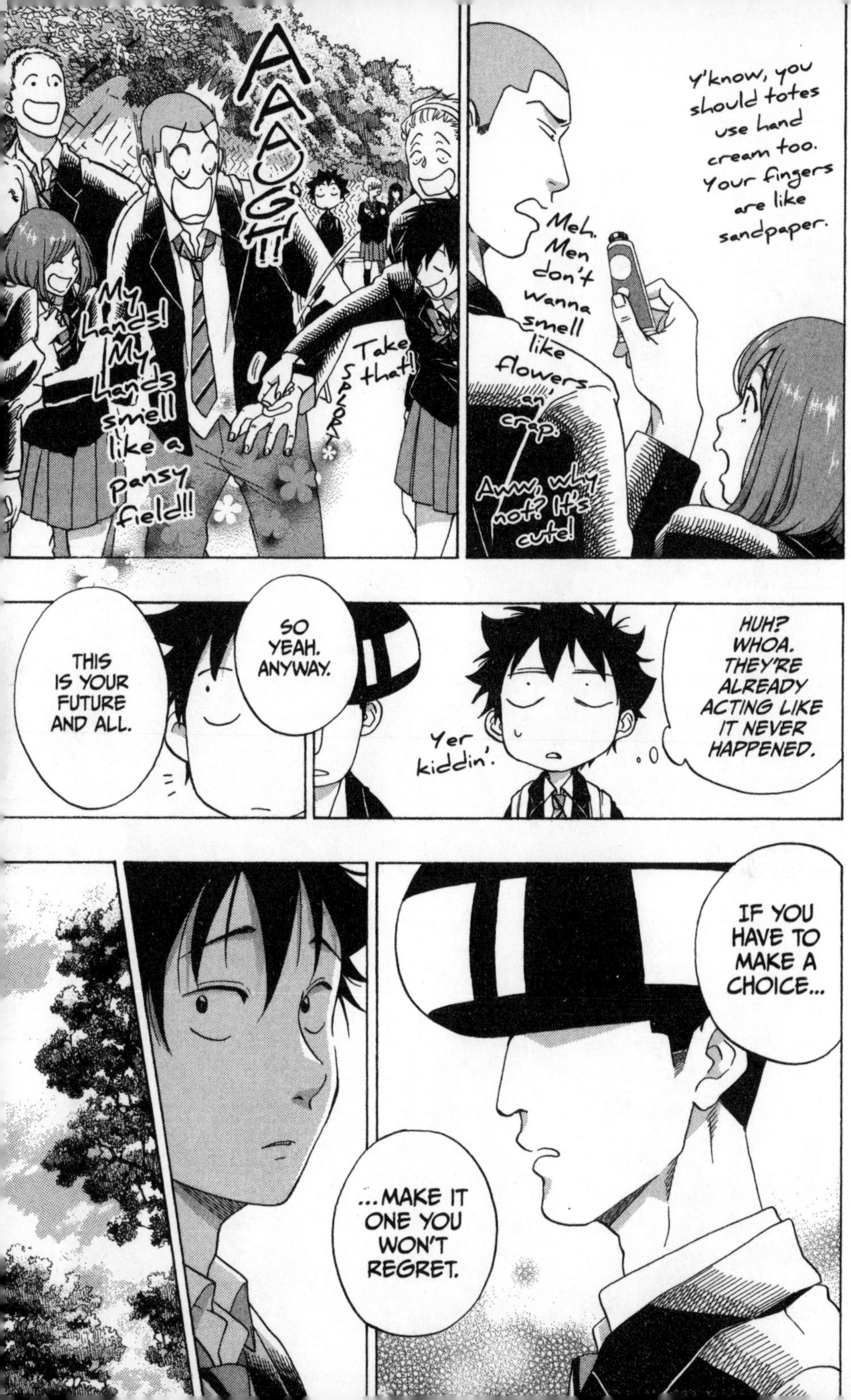
Y'know, you should totes use hand cream too. Your fingers are like sandpaper.
Meh. Men don't wanna smell like flowers an' crap.
Aww, why not? It's cute!
AAAUGH!!
My hands! My hands smell like a pansy field!!
Take that!
SPLORT
HUH? WHOA. THEY'RE ALREADY ACTING LIKE IT NEVER HAPPENED.
Yer kiddin'.
SO YEAH. ANYWAY.
THIS IS YOUR FUTURE AND ALL.
IF YOU HAVE TO MAKE A CHOICE...
...MAKE IT ONE YOU WON'T REGRET.

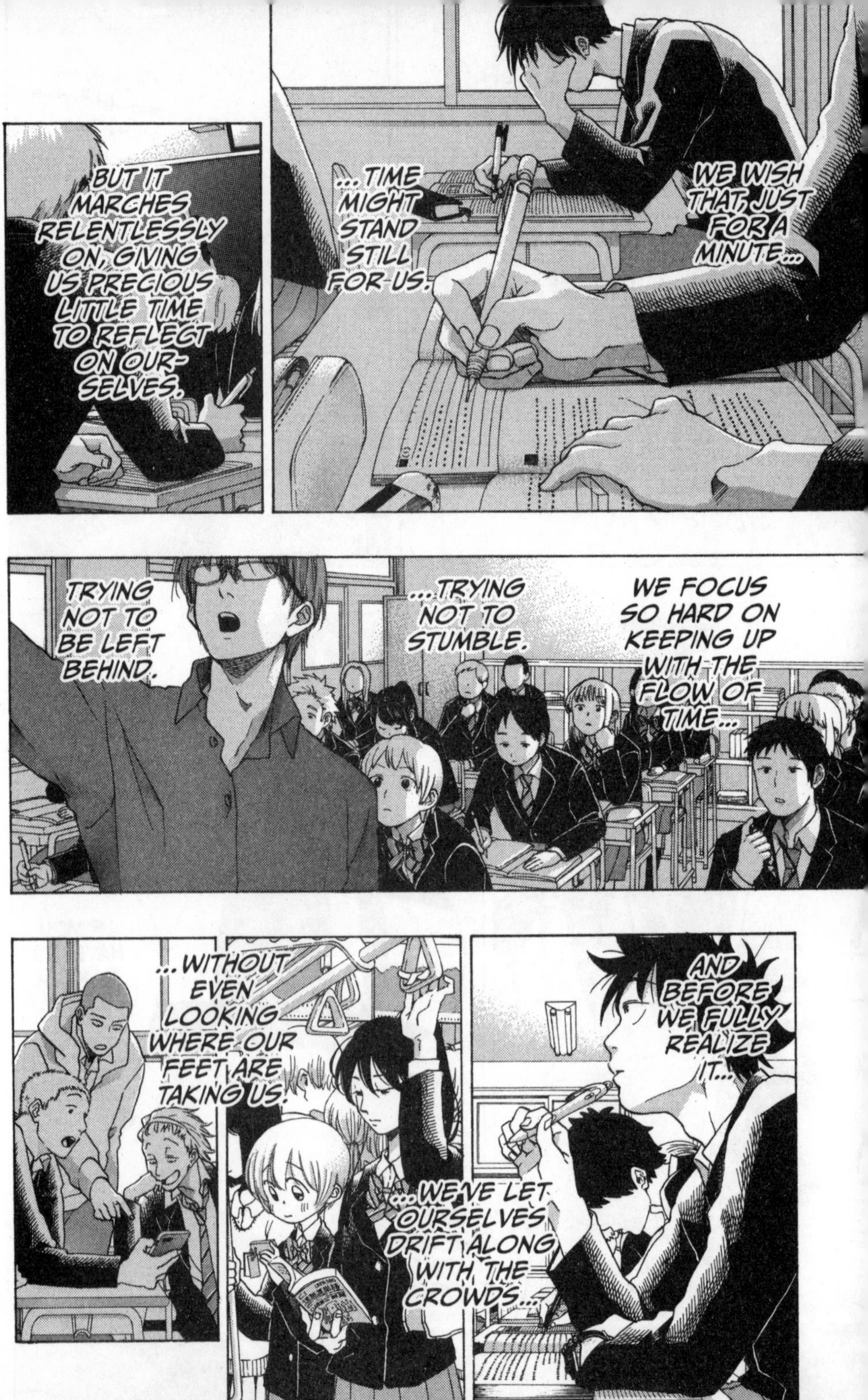
WE WISH THAT, JUST FOR A MINUTE...
...TIME MIGHT STAND STILL FOR US.
BUT IT MARCHES RELENTLESSLY ON, GIVING US PRECIOUS LITTLE TIME TO REFLECT ON OURSELVES.
WE FOCUS SO HARD ON KEEPING UP WITH THE FLOW OF TIME...
...TRYING NOT TO STUMBLE.
TRYING NOT TO BE LEFT BEHIND.
AND BEFORE WE FULLY REALIZE IT...
...WE'VE LET OURSELVES DRIFT ALONG WITH THE CROWDS...
...WITHOUT EVEN LOOKING WHERE OUR FEET ARE TAKING US.

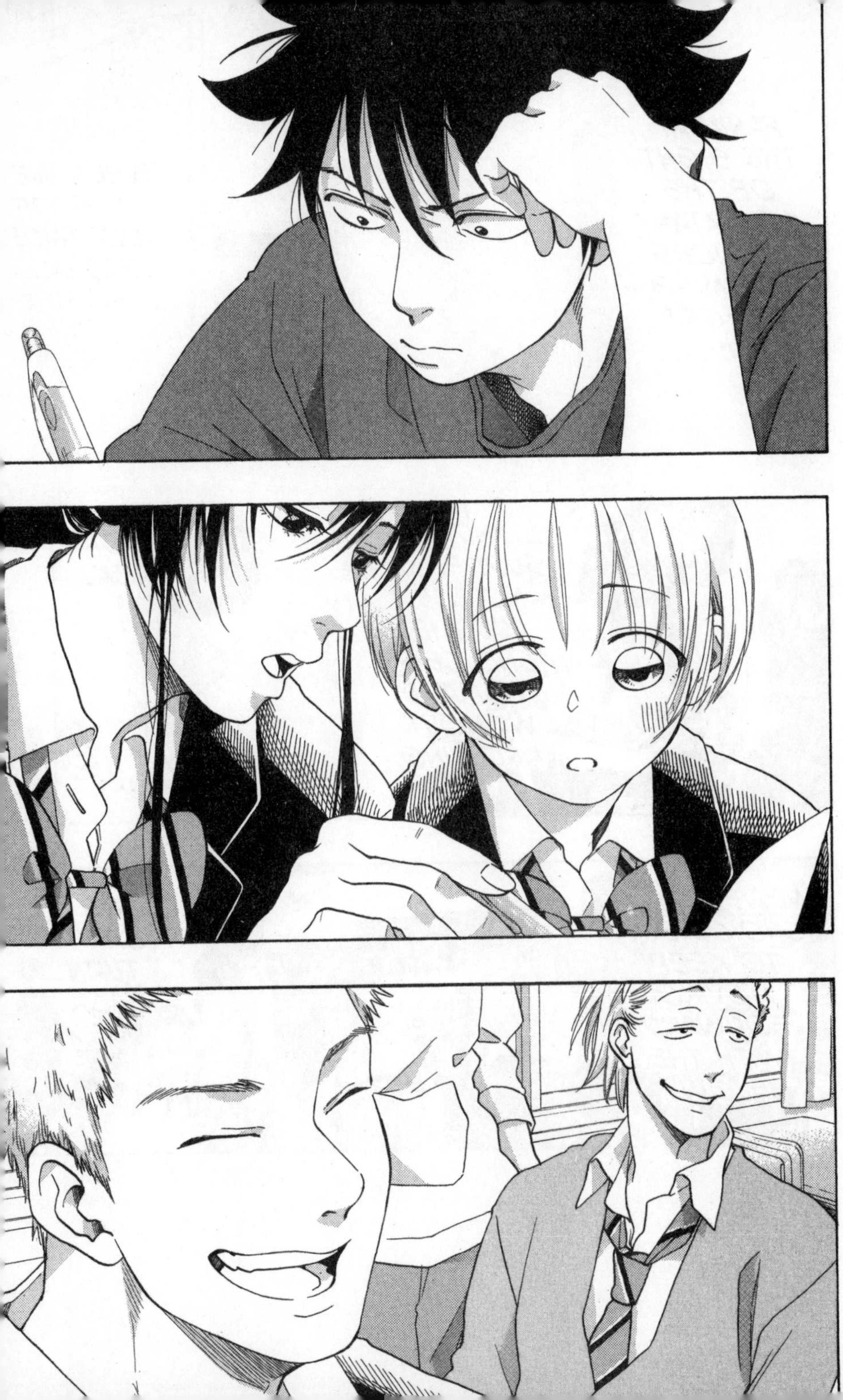

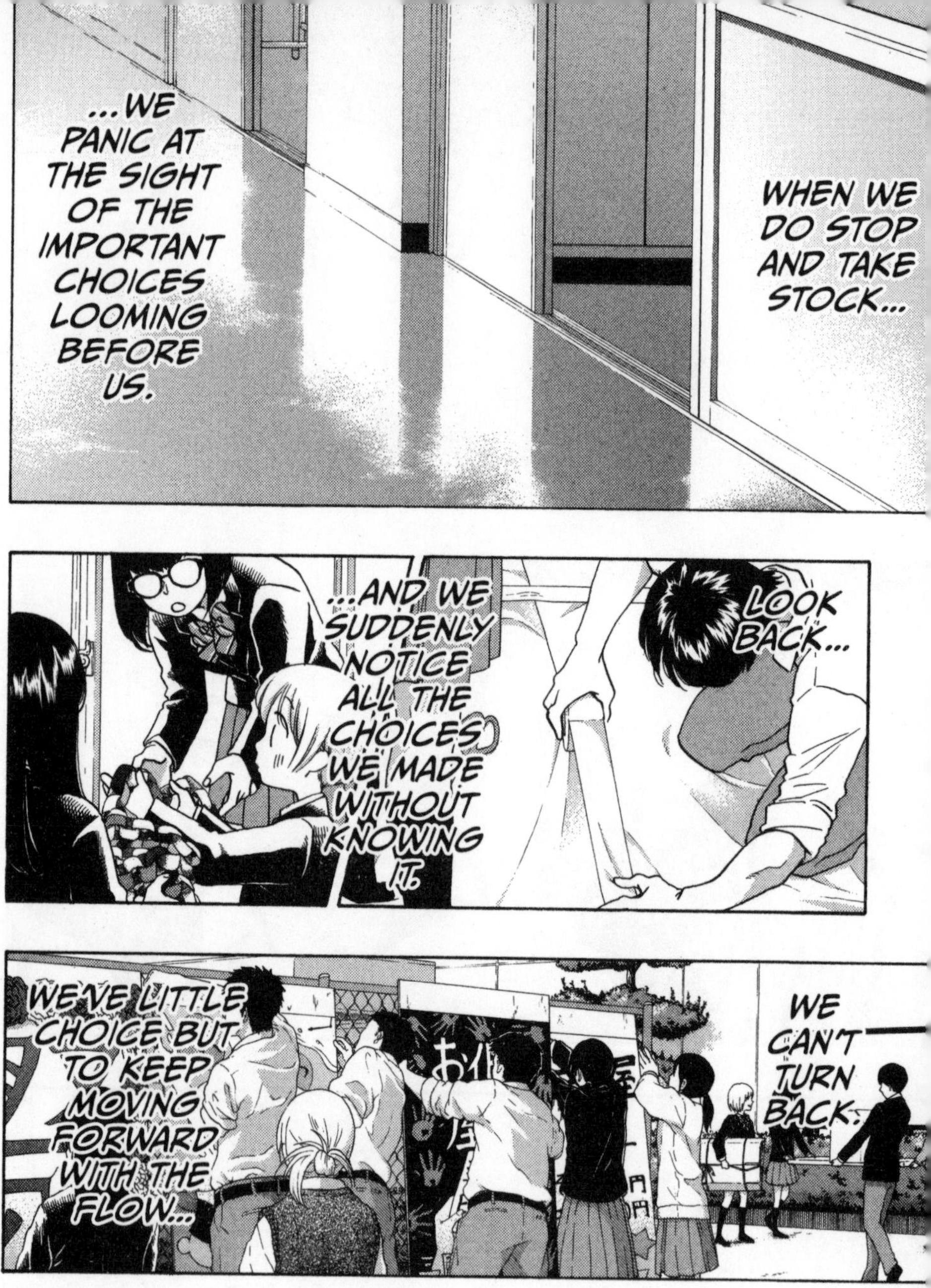
WHEN WE DO STOP AND TAKE STOCK...
...WE PANIC AT THE SIGHT OF THE IMPORTANT CHOICES LOOMING BEFORE US.
LOOK BACK...
...AND WE SUDDENLY NOTICE ALL THE CHOICES WE MADE WITHOUT KNOWING IT.
WE CAN'T TURN BACK.
WE'VE LITTLE CHOICE BUT TO KEEP MOVING FORWARD WITH THE FLOW...

UNTIL ONCE AGAIN CHOICE LOOMS BEFORE US.

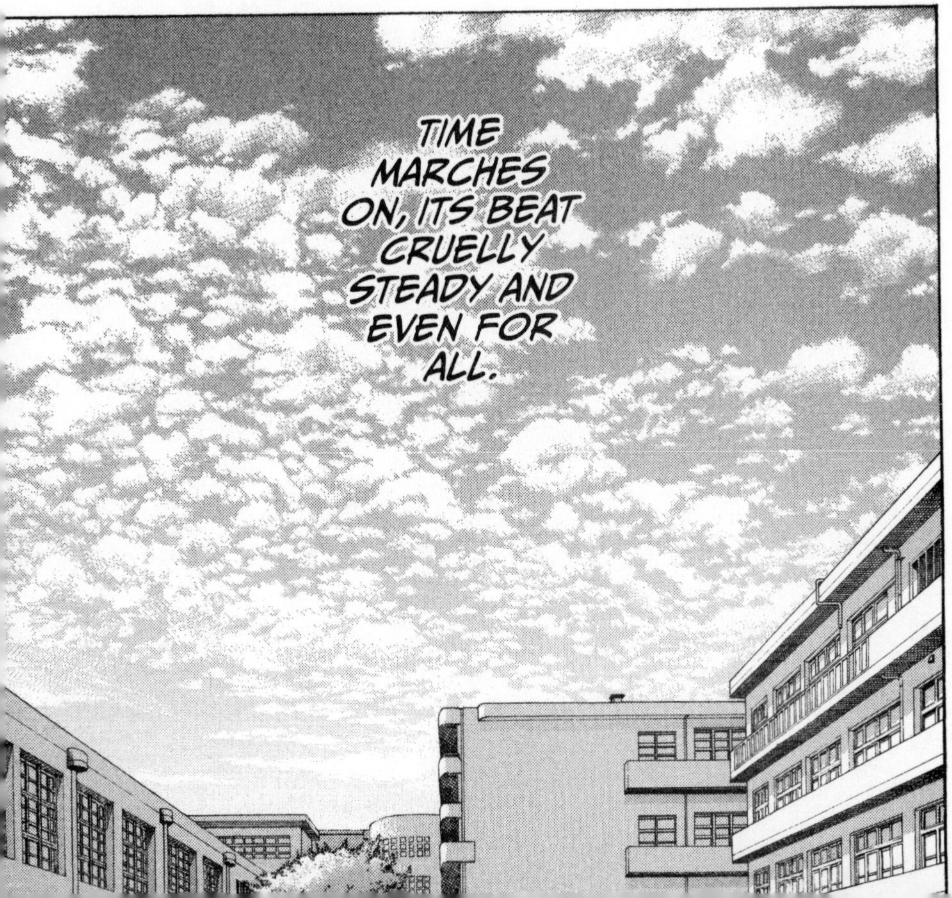
TIME MARCHES ON, ITS BEAT CRUELLY STEADY AND EVEN FOR ALL.

Big brother Seiya's
evening snack

Menma
bamboo
shoots

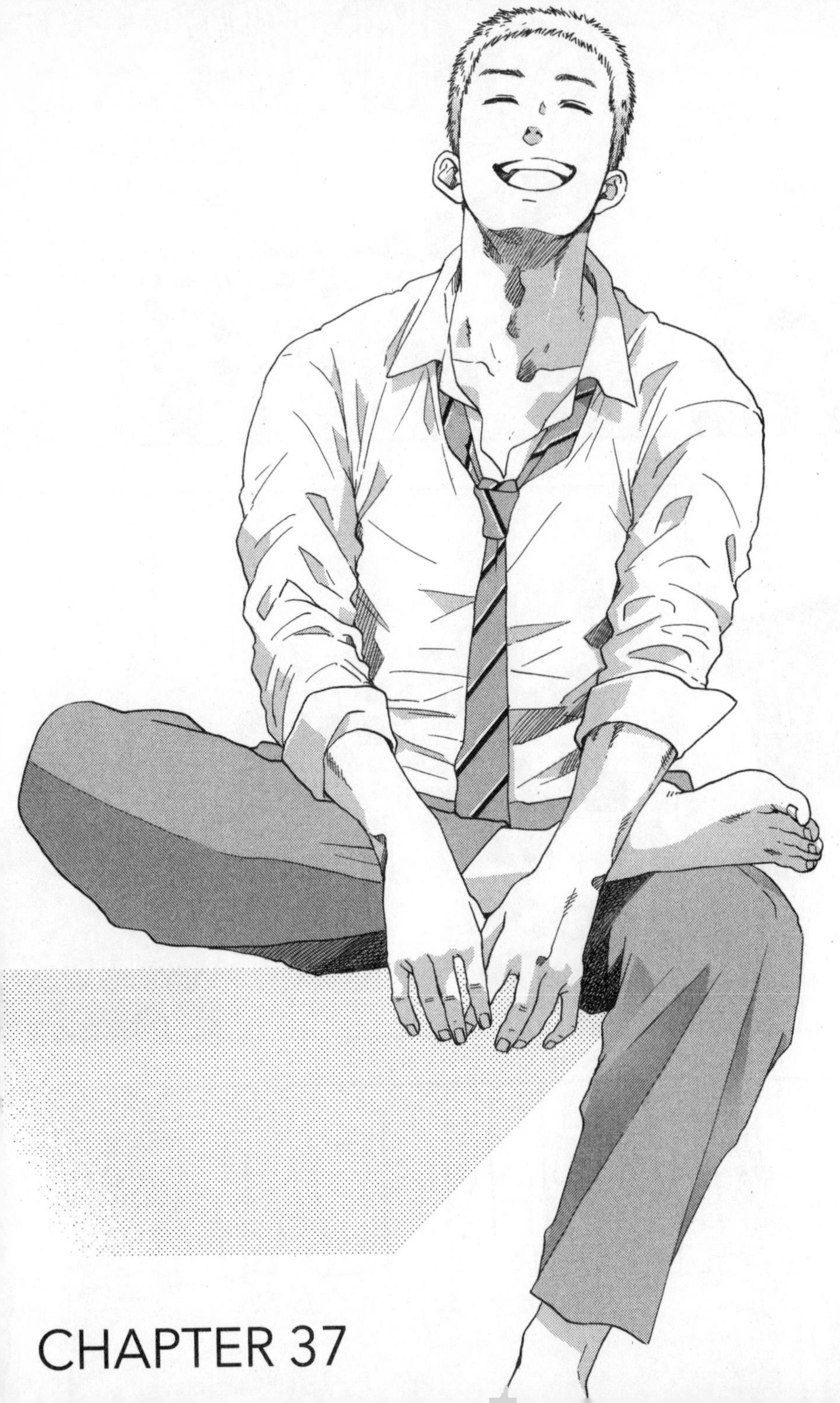

CHAPTER 37

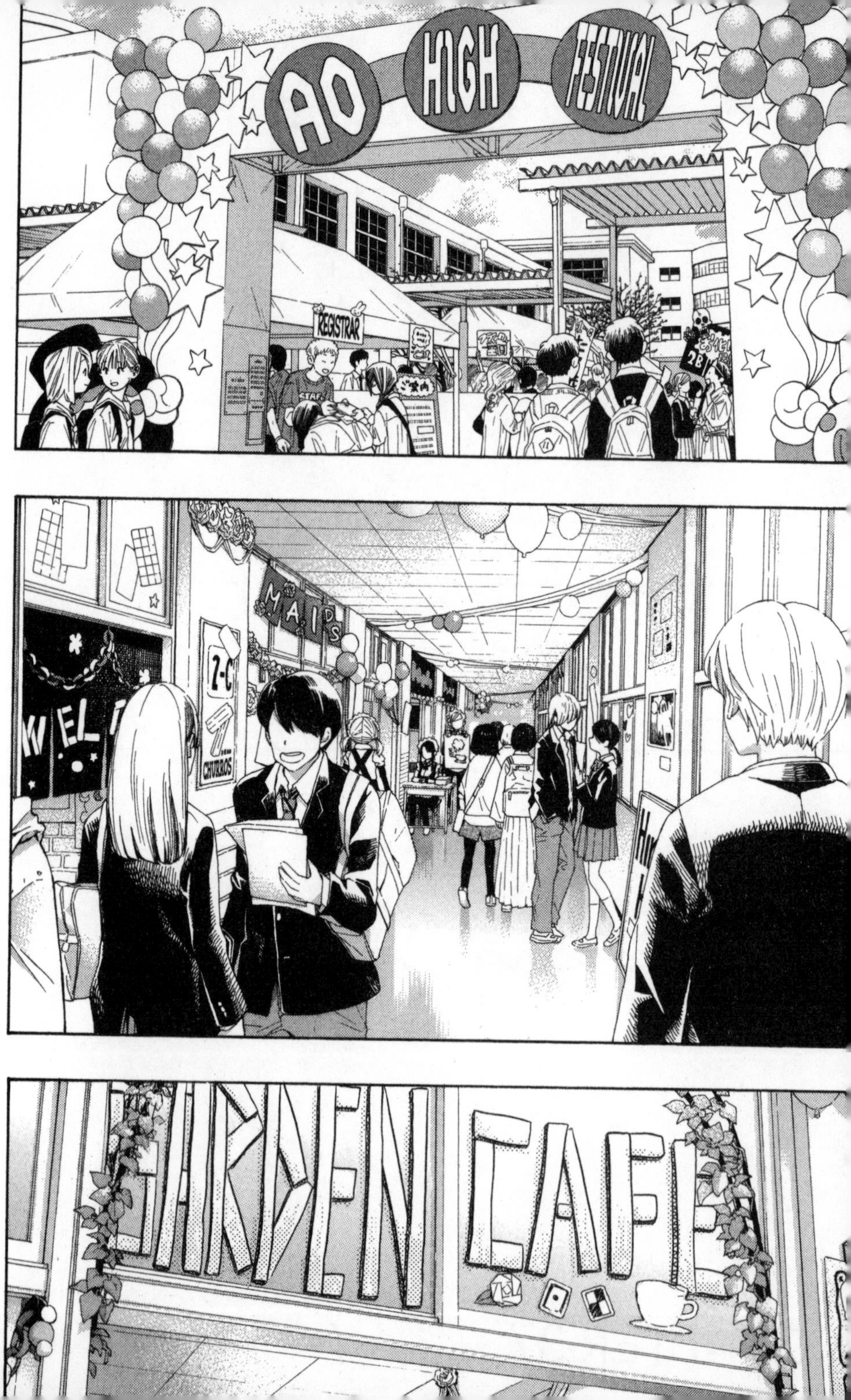
AO HIGH FESTIVAL
REGISTRAR
ご案内
2B
MAIDS
2-C
CHURROS
CAFE

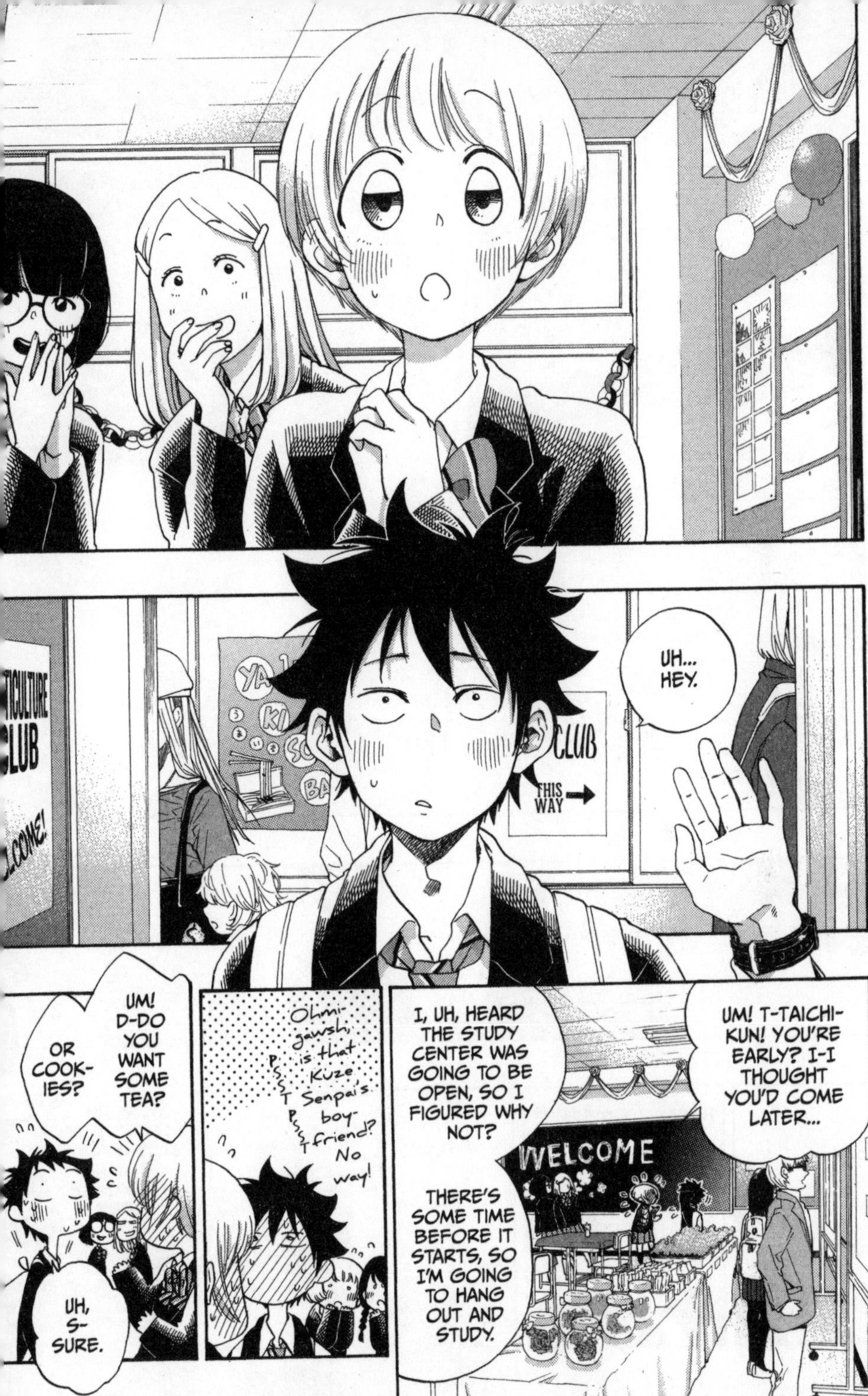
UH... HEY.
CLUB
CLUB
THIS WAY
UM! T-TAICHI-KUN! YOU'RE EARLY? I-I THOUGHT YOU'D COME LATER...
I, UH, HEARD THE STUDY CENTER WAS GOING TO BE OPEN, SO I FIGURED WHY NOT?
THERE'S SOME TIME BEFORE IT STARTS, SO I'M GOING TO HANG OUT AND STUDY.
WELCOME
Ohmi-gawsh, is that Kuze Senpai's boy-friend? No way!
PSST PSST
UM! D-DO YOU WANT SOME TEA?
OR COOK-IES?
UH, S-SURE.

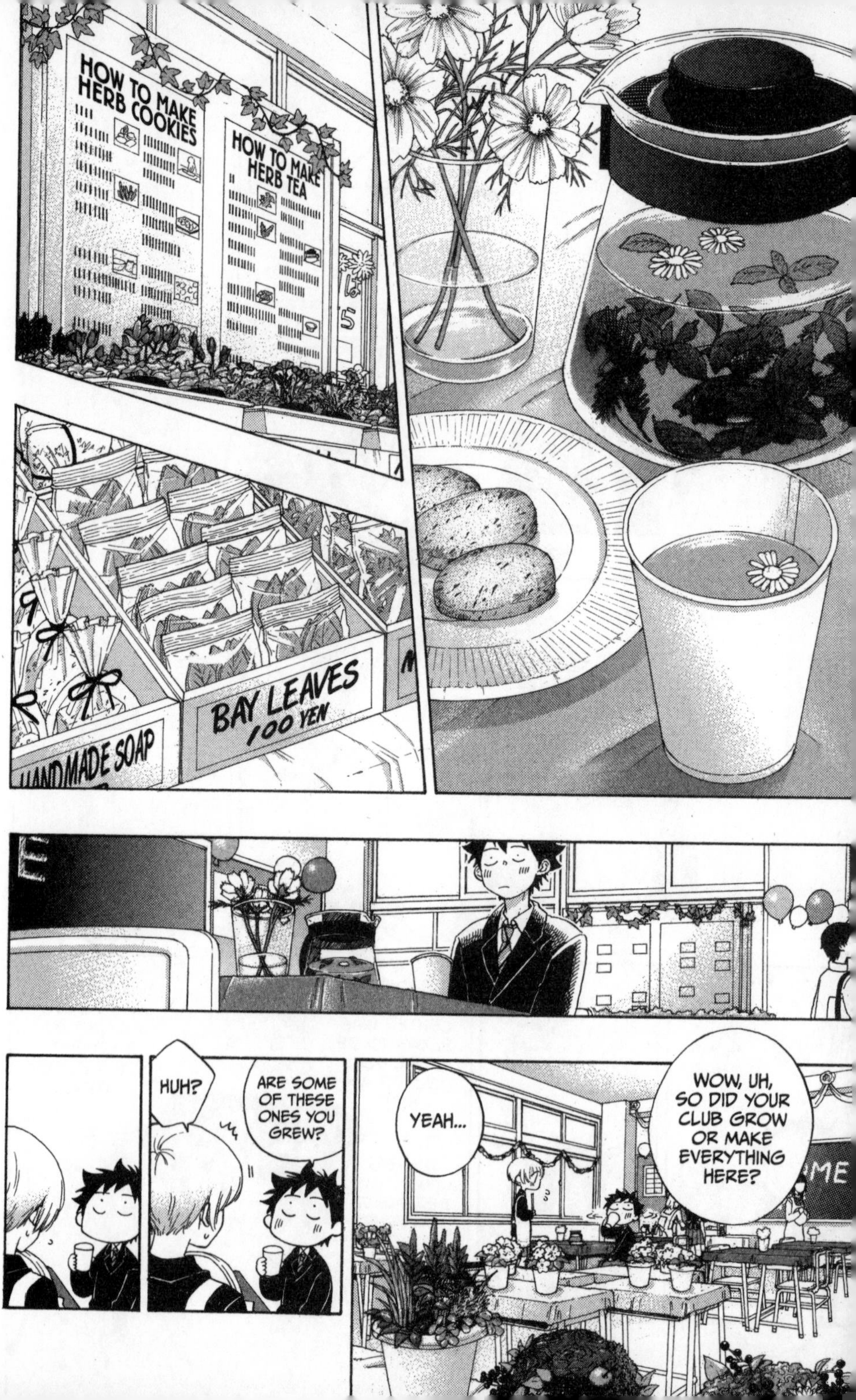
HOW TO MAKE HERB COOKIES
HOW TO MAKE HERB TEA
BAY LEAVES 100 YEN
HANDMADE SOAP
WOW, UH, SO DID YOUR CLUB GROW OR MAKE EVERYTHING HERE?
YEAH...
ARE SOME OF THESE ONES YOU GREW?
HUH?

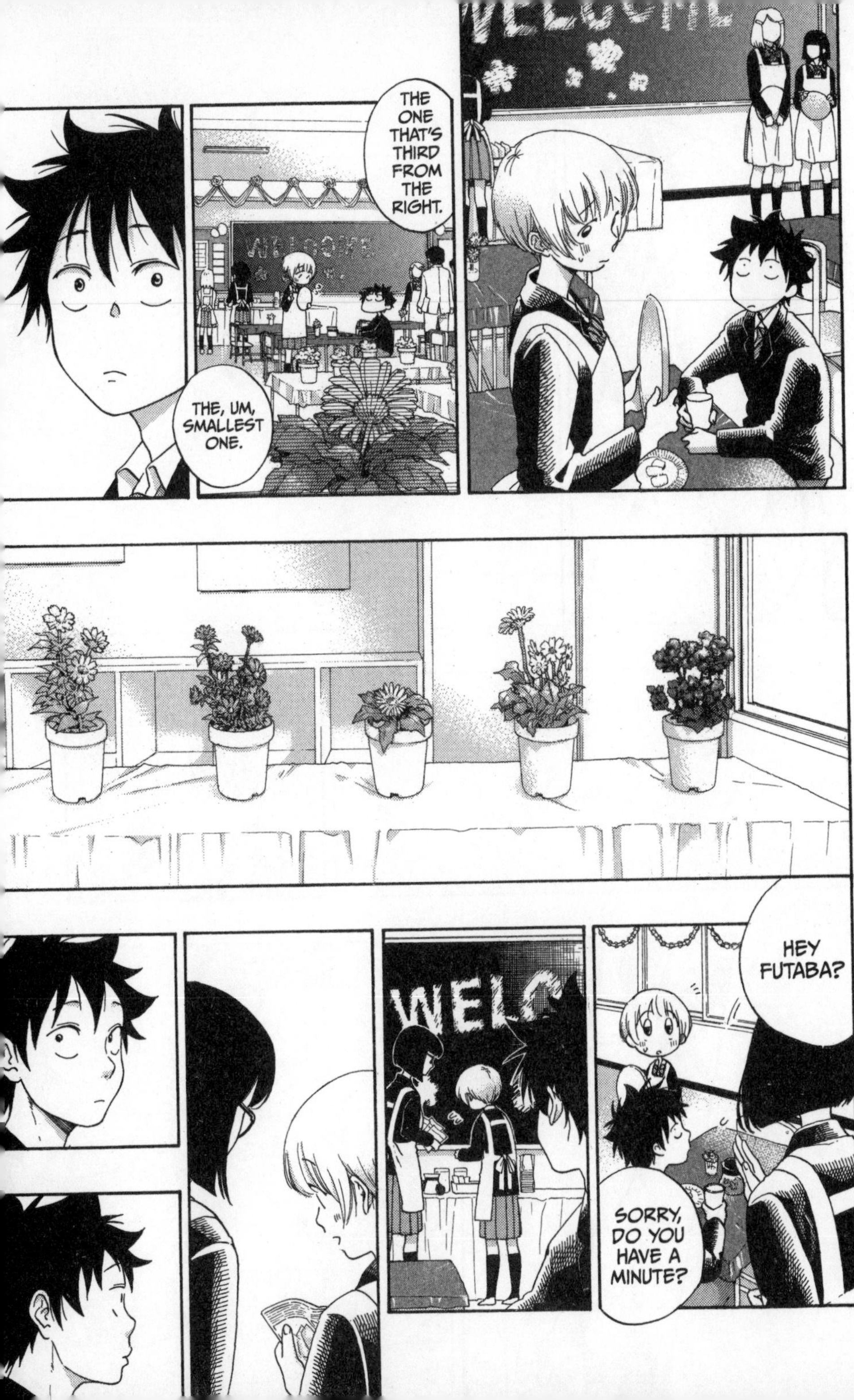
THE ONE THAT'S THIRD FROM THE RIGHT.
THE, UM, SMALLEST ONE.
HEY FUTABA?
SORRY, DO YOU HAVE A MINUTE?

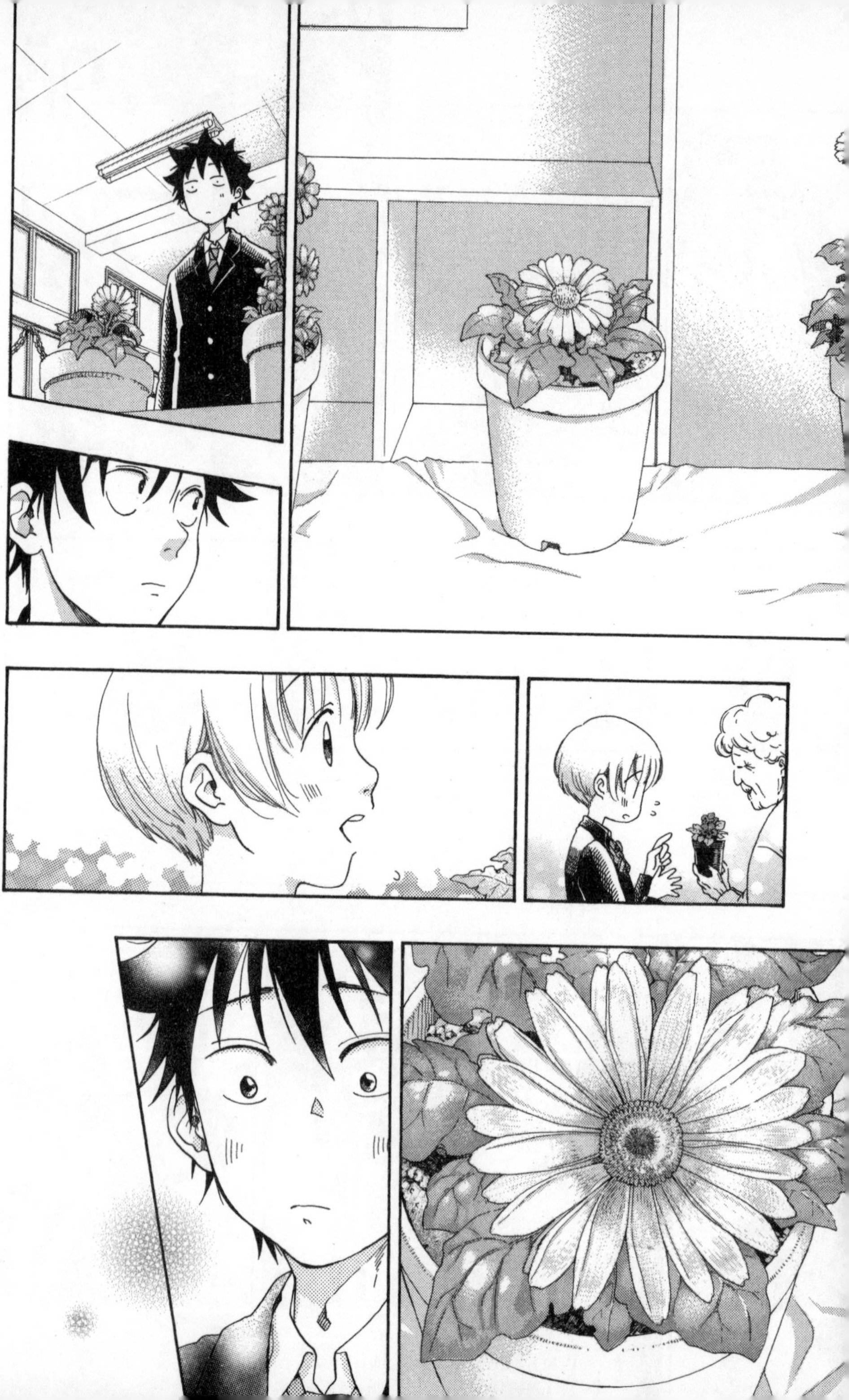

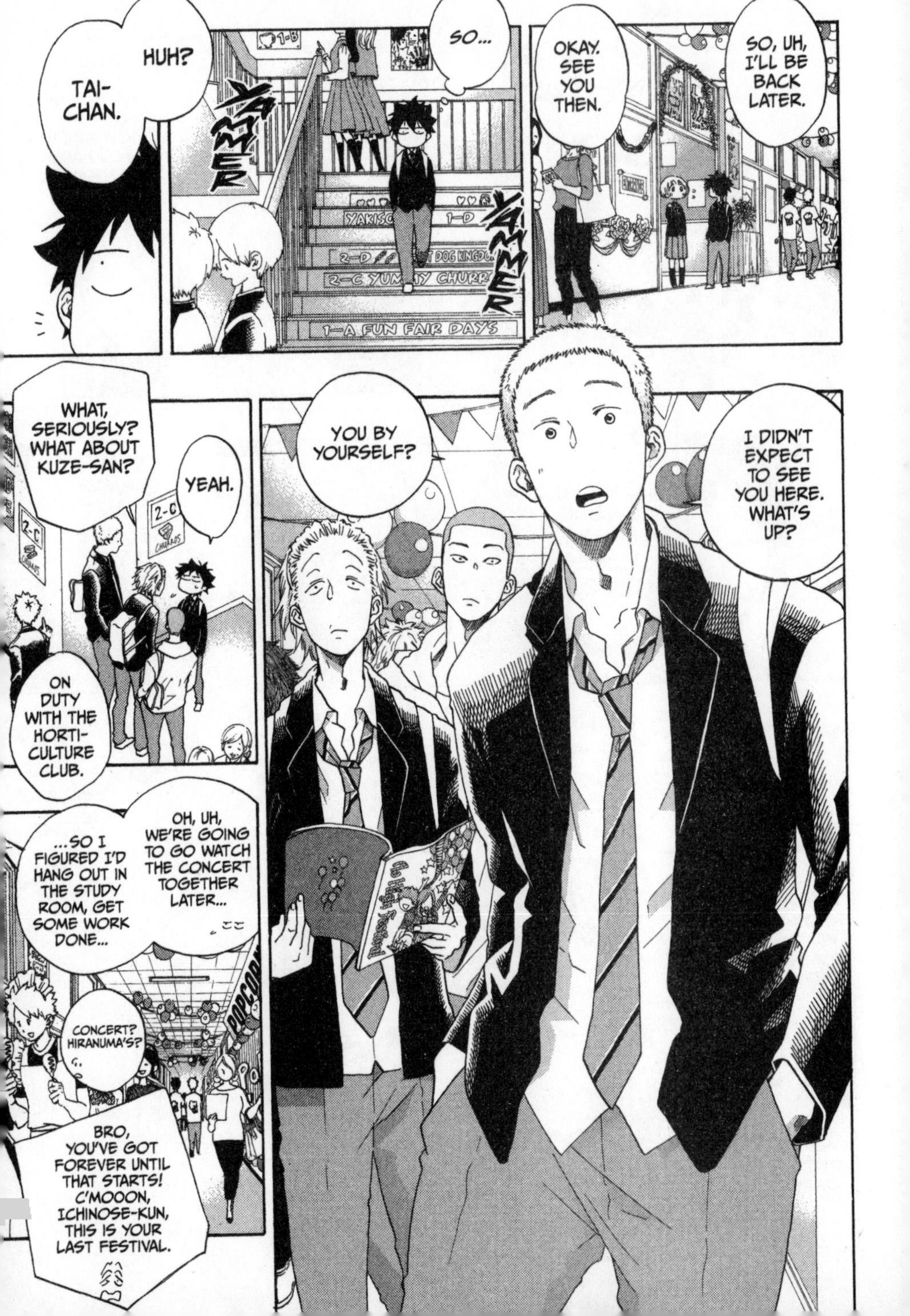
SO, UH, I'LL BE BACK LATER.
OKAY. SEE YOU THEN.
SO...
YAMMER
YAMMER
1-B
1-D
2-C YUMMY CHURR
1-A FUN FAIR DAYS
HUH?
TAI-CHAN.
I DIDN'T EXPECT TO SEE YOU HERE. WHAT'S UP?
YOU BY YOURSELF?
YEAH.
WHAT, SERIOUSLY? WHAT ABOUT KUZE-SAN?
2-C
ON DUTY WITH THE HORTI-CULTURE CLUB.
OH, UH, WE'RE GOING TO GO WATCH THE CONCERT TOGETHER LATER...
...SO I FIGURED I'D HANG OUT IN THE STUDY ROOM, GET SOME WORK DONE...
POPCORN
CONCERT? HIRANUMA'S?
BRO, YOU'VE GOT FOREVER UNTIL THAT STARTS! C'MOOON, ICHINOSE-KUN, THIS IS YOUR LAST FESTIVAL.

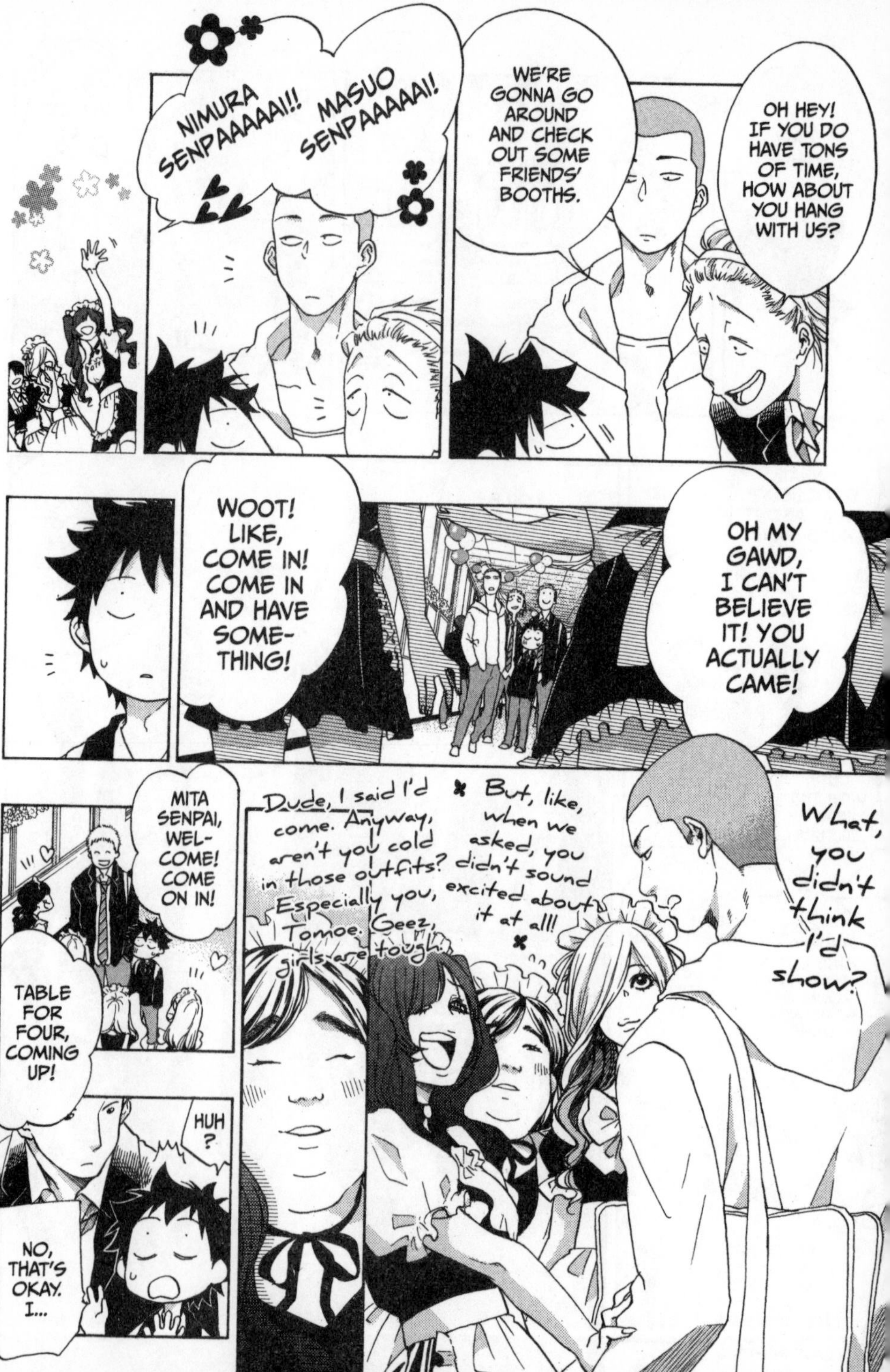
WE'RE GONNA GO AROUND AND CHECK OUT SOME FRIENDS' BOOTHS.
OH HEY! IF YOU DO HAVE TONS OF TIME, HOW ABOUT YOU HANG WITH US?
NIMURA SENPAAAAAI!! MASUO SENPAAAAAI!
OH MY GAWD, I CAN'T BELIEVE IT! YOU ACTUALLY CAME!
WOOT! LIKE, COME IN! COME IN AND HAVE SOME-THING!
What, you didn't think I'd show?
But, like, when we asked, you didn't sound excited about it at all!
Dude, I said I'd come. Anyway, aren't you cold in those outfits? Especially you, Tomoe. Geez, girls are tough.
MITA SENPAI, WEL-COME! COME ON IN!
TABLE FOR FOUR, COMING UP!
HUH?
NO, THAT'S OKAY. I...

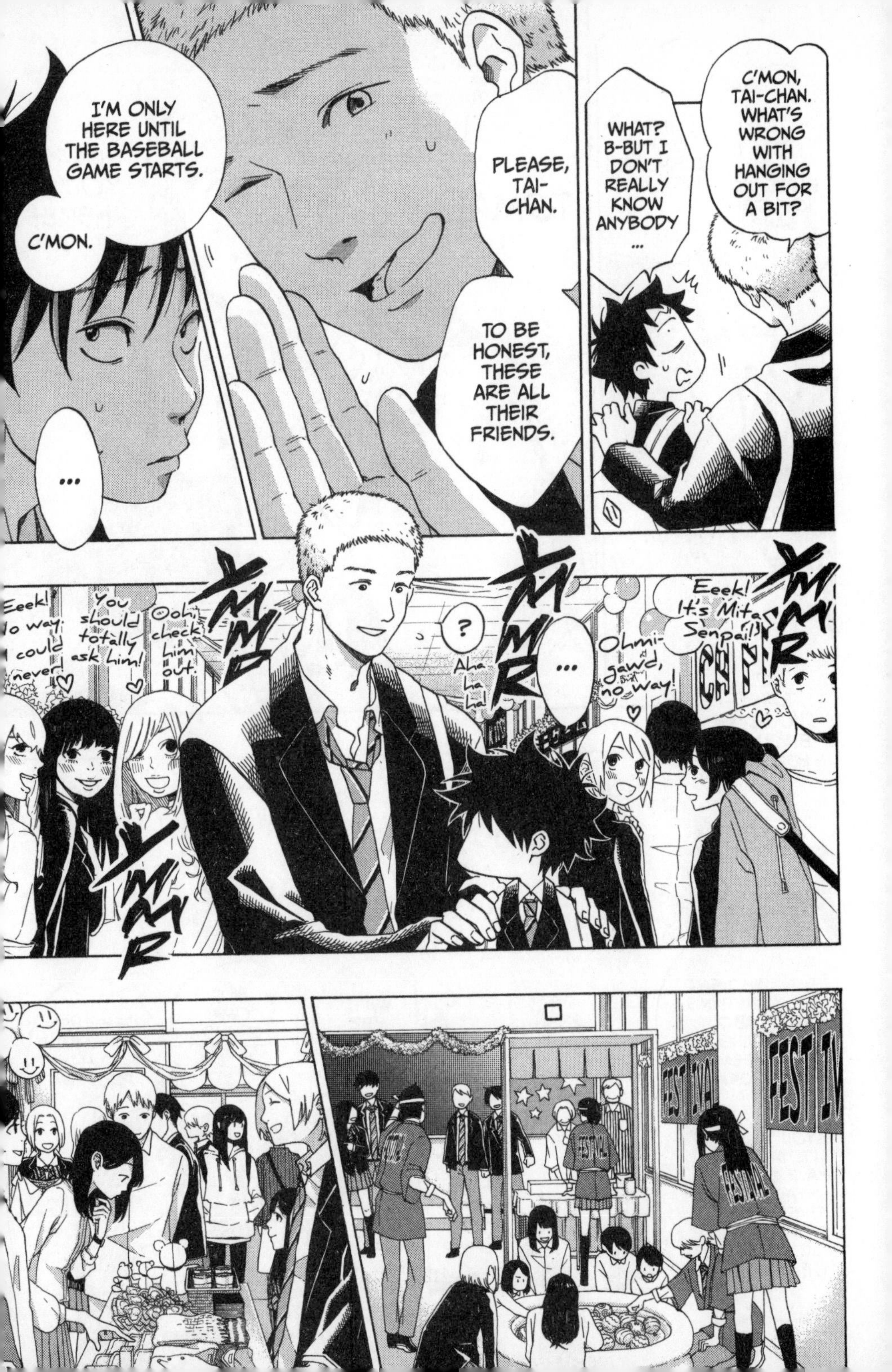

C'MON, TAI-CHAN. WHAT'S WRONG WITH HANGING OUT FOR A BIT?
WHAT? B-BUT I DON'T REALLY KNOW ANYBODY...
PLEASE, TAI-CHAN.
TO BE HONEST, THESE ARE ALL THEIR FRIENDS.
I'M ONLY HERE UNTIL THE BASEBALL GAME STARTS.
C'MON.
...
MMMR
Eeek! It's Mita Senpai!
Ohmigawd, no way!
MMMR
...
?
Aha ha ha!
Oohh, check him out.
You should totally ask him!
Eeek! o way. could never!
MMMR
MMMR
FESTIVAL
FEST IVAL
FEST IV

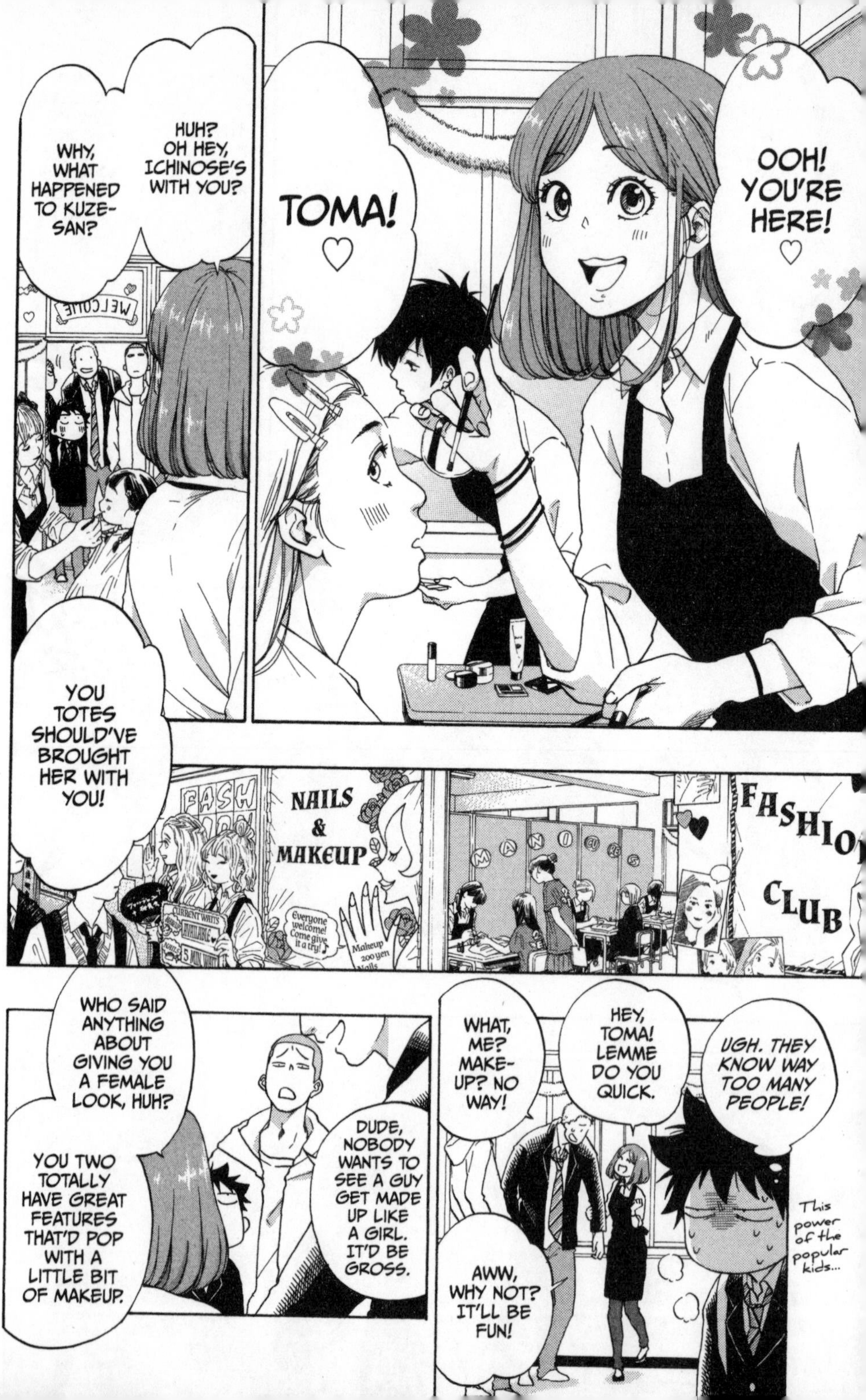
OOH! YOU'RE HERE! ♡
TOMA! ♡
HUH? OH HEY, ICHINOSE'S WITH YOU?
WHY, WHAT HAPPENED TO KUZE-SAN?
YOU TOTES SHOULD'VE BROUGHT HER WITH YOU!
FASHIO
CLUB
NAILS & MAKEUP
Everyone welcome! Come give it a try!
Makeup 200 yen
CURRENT WAITS
UGH. THEY KNOW WAY TOO MANY PEOPLE!
This power of the popular kids...
HEY, TOMA! LEMME DO YOU QUICK.
WHAT, ME? MAKE-UP? NO WAY!
AWW, WHY NOT? IT'LL BE FUN!
DUDE, NOBODY WANTS TO SEE A GUY GET MADE UP LIKE A GIRL. IT'D BE GROSS.
WHO SAID ANYTHING ABOUT GIVING YOU A FEMALE LOOK, HUH?
YOU TWO TOTALLY HAVE GREAT FEATURES THAT'D POP WITH A LITTLE BIT OF MAKEUP.

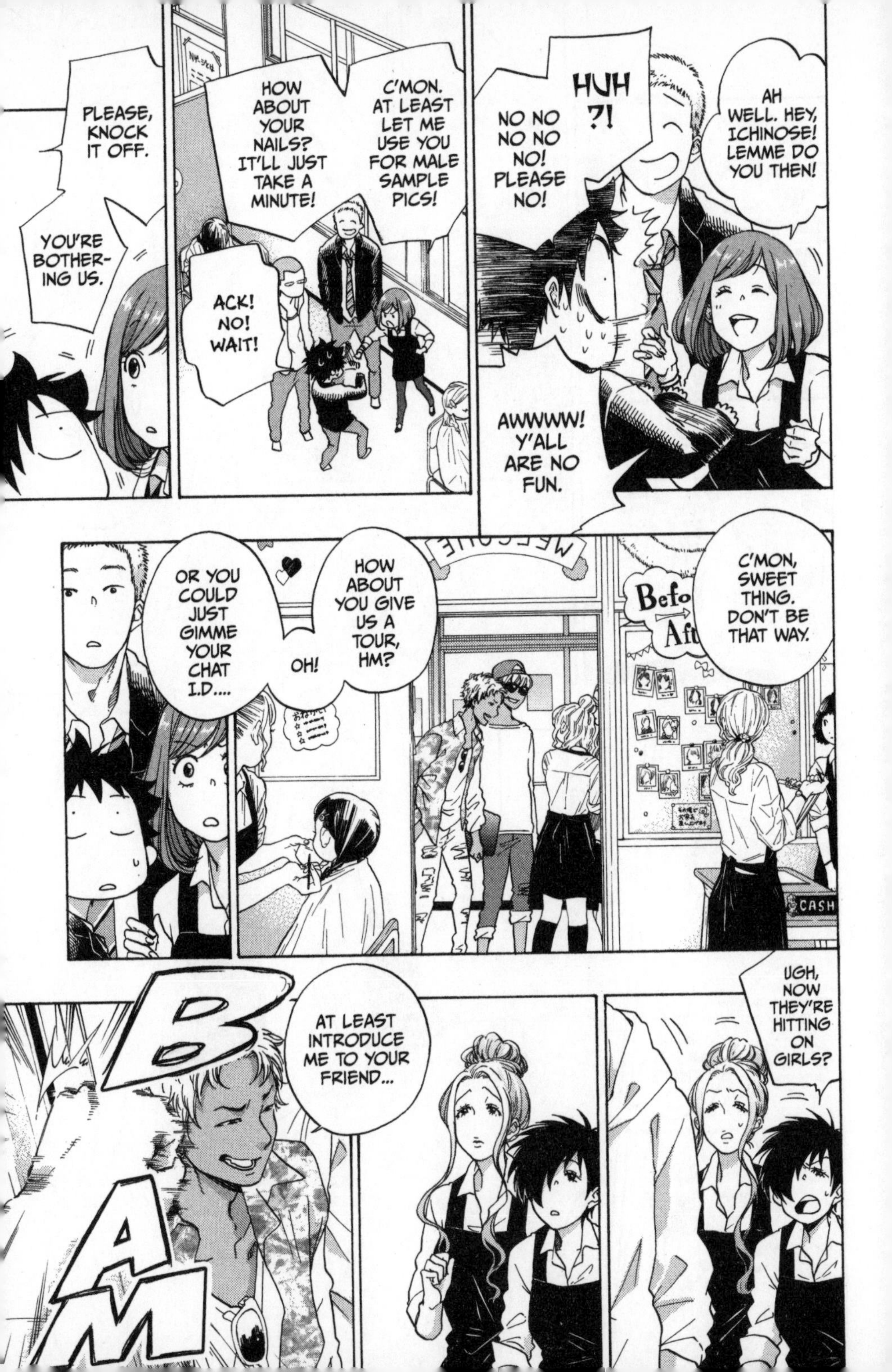
AH WELL. HEY, ICHINOSE! LEMME DO YOU THEN!
HUH ?!
NO NO NO NO NO! PLEASE NO!
AWWWW! Y'ALL ARE NO FUN.
C'MON. AT LEAST LET ME USE YOU FOR MALE SAMPLE PICS!
HOW ABOUT YOUR NAILS? IT'LL JUST TAKE A MINUTE!
ACK! NO! WAIT!
PLEASE, KNOCK IT OFF.
YOU'RE BOTHERING US.
C'MON, SWEET THING. DON'T BE THAT WAY.
CASH
HOW ABOUT YOU GIVE US A TOUR, HM?
OH!
OR YOU COULD JUST GIMME YOUR CHAT I.D....
UGH, NOW THEY'RE HITTING ON GIRLS?
AT LEAST INTRODUCE ME TO YOUR FRIEND...
BAM

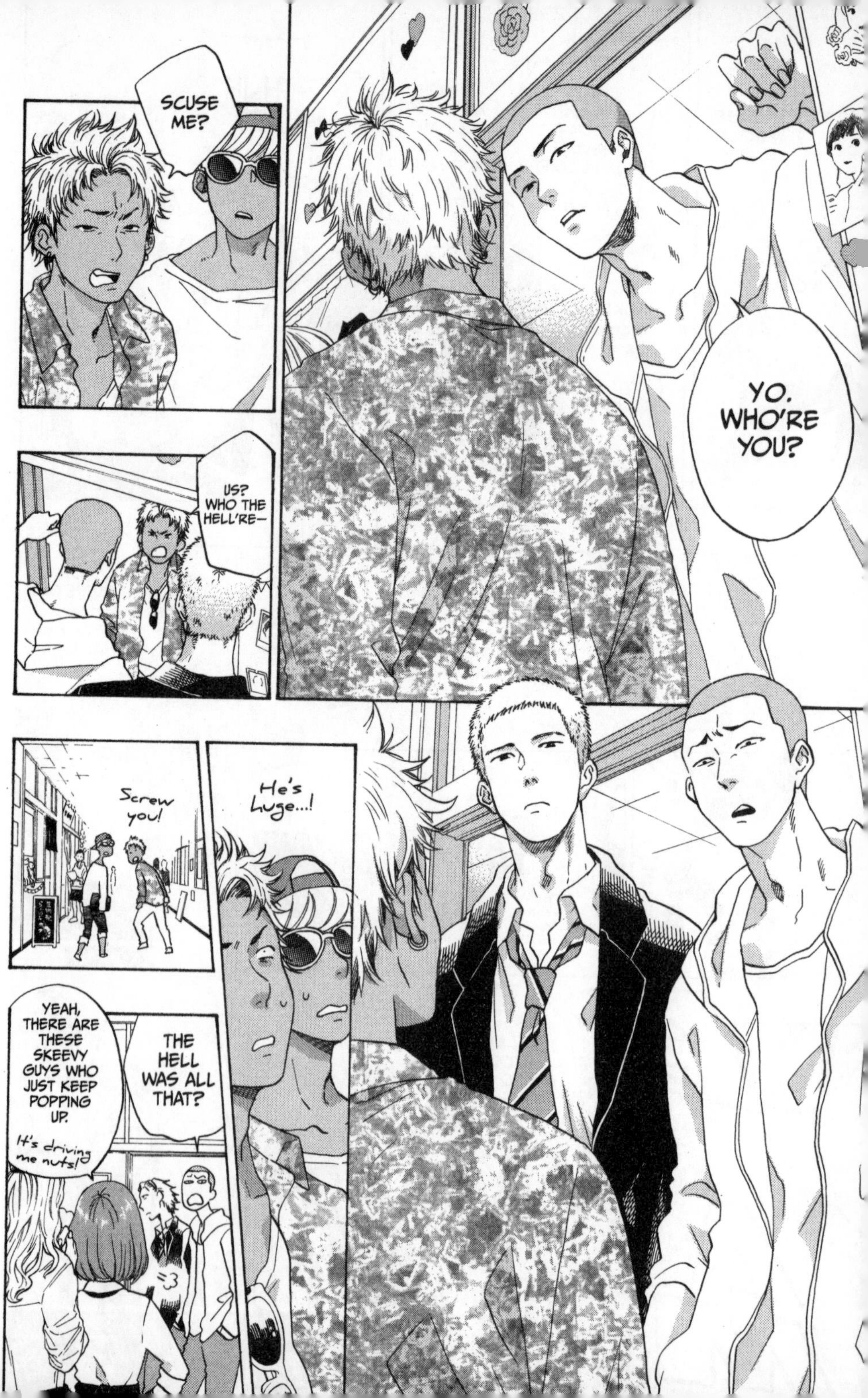
YO. WHO'RE YOU?
SCUSE ME?
US? WHO THE HELL'RE—
He's huge...!
Screw you!
THE HELL WAS ALL THAT?
YEAH, THERE ARE THESE SKEEVY GUYS WHO JUST KEEP POPPING UP.
It's driving me nuts!

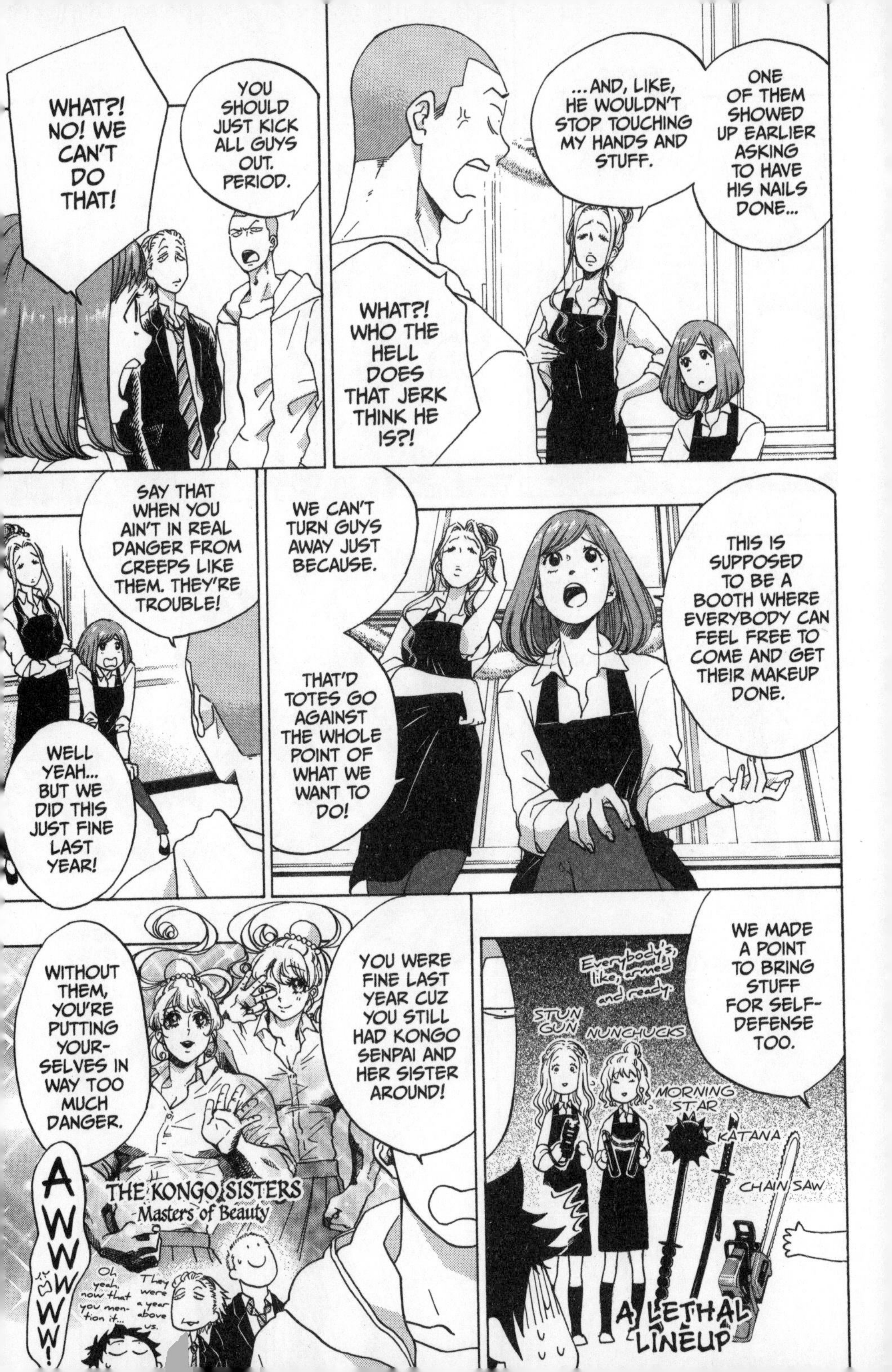
ONE OF THEM SHOWED UP EARLIER ASKING TO HAVE HIS NAILS DONE...
...AND, LIKE, HE WOULDN'T STOP TOUCHING MY HANDS AND STUFF.
WHAT?! WHO THE HELL DOES THAT JERK THINK HE IS?!
YOU SHOULD JUST KICK ALL GUYS OUT. PERIOD.
WHAT?! NO! WE CAN'T DO THAT!
THIS IS SUPPOSED TO BE A BOOTH WHERE EVERYBODY CAN FEEL FREE TO COME AND GET THEIR MAKEUP DONE.
WE CAN'T TURN GUYS AWAY JUST BECAUSE.
THAT'D TOTES GO AGAINST THE WHOLE POINT OF WHAT WE WANT TO DO!
SAY THAT WHEN YOU AIN'T IN REAL DANGER FROM CREEPS LIKE THEM. THEY'RE TROUBLE!
WELL YEAH... BUT WE DID THIS JUST FINE LAST YEAR!
WE MADE A POINT TO BRING STUFF FOR SELF-DEFENSE TOO.
Everybody's, like, armed and ready.
STUN GUN
NUNCHUCKS
MORNING STAR
KATANA
CHAIN SAW
A LETHAL LINEUP
YOU WERE FINE LAST YEAR CUZ YOU STILL HAD KONGO SENPAI AND HER SISTER AROUND!
WITHOUT THEM, YOU'RE PUTTING YOURSELVES IN WAY TOO MUCH DANGER.
THE KONGO SISTERS
Masters of Beauty
AWWWWWW!
Oh yeah, now that you mention it...
They were a year above us.

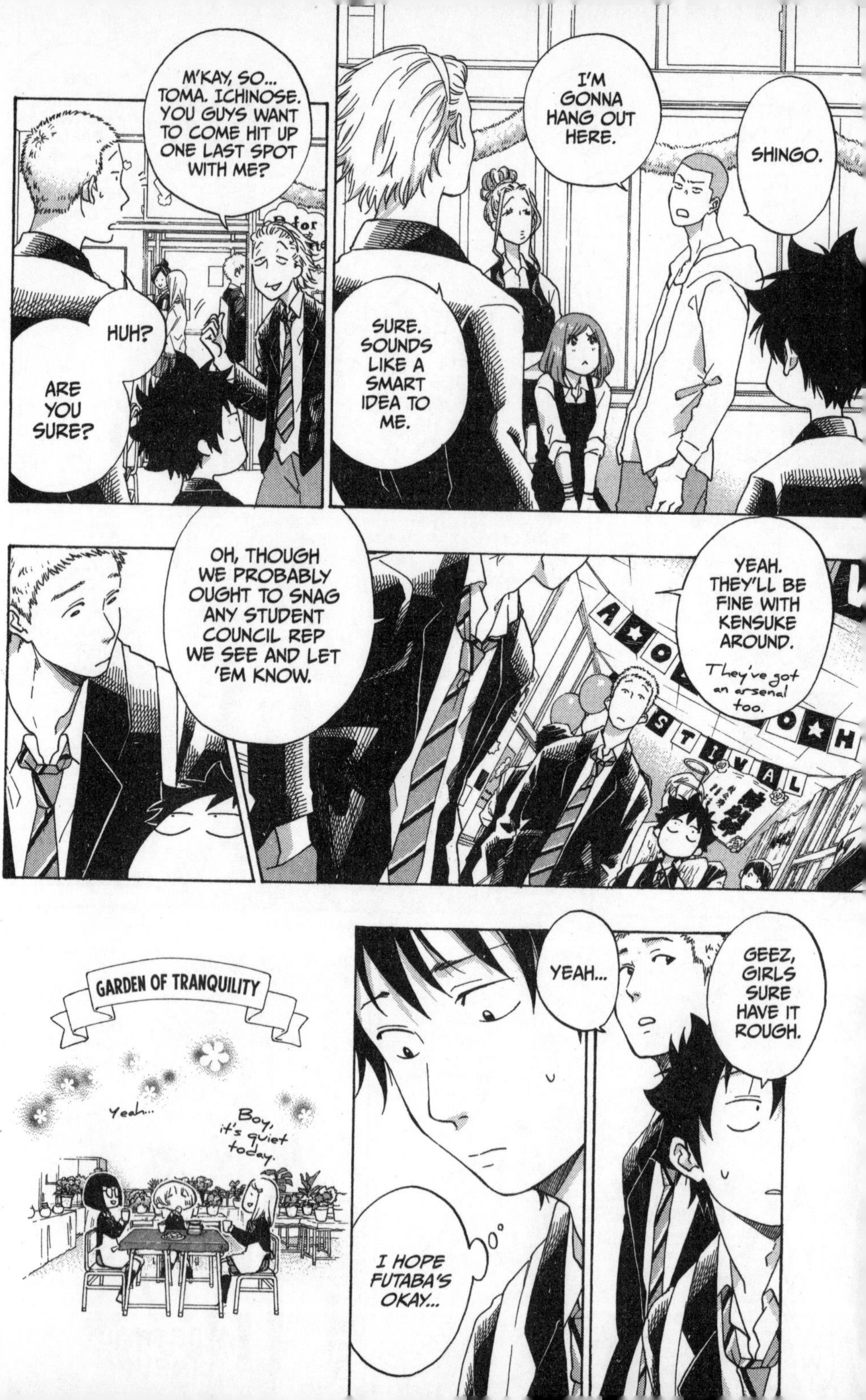
SHINGO.
I'M GONNA HANG OUT HERE.
SURE. SOUNDS LIKE A SMART IDEA TO ME.
M'KAY, SO... TOMA. ICHINOSE. YOU GUYS WANT TO COME HIT UP ONE LAST SPOT WITH ME?
HUH?
ARE YOU SURE?
YEAH. THEY'LL BE FINE WITH KENSUKE AROUND.
They've got an arsenal too.
OH, THOUGH WE PROBABLY OUGHT TO SNAG ANY STUDENT COUNCIL REP WE SEE AND LET 'EM KNOW.
GEEZ, GIRLS SURE HAVE IT ROUGH.
YEAH...
I HOPE FUTABA'S OKAY...
GARDEN OF TRANQUILITY
Boy, it's quiet today.
Yeah...

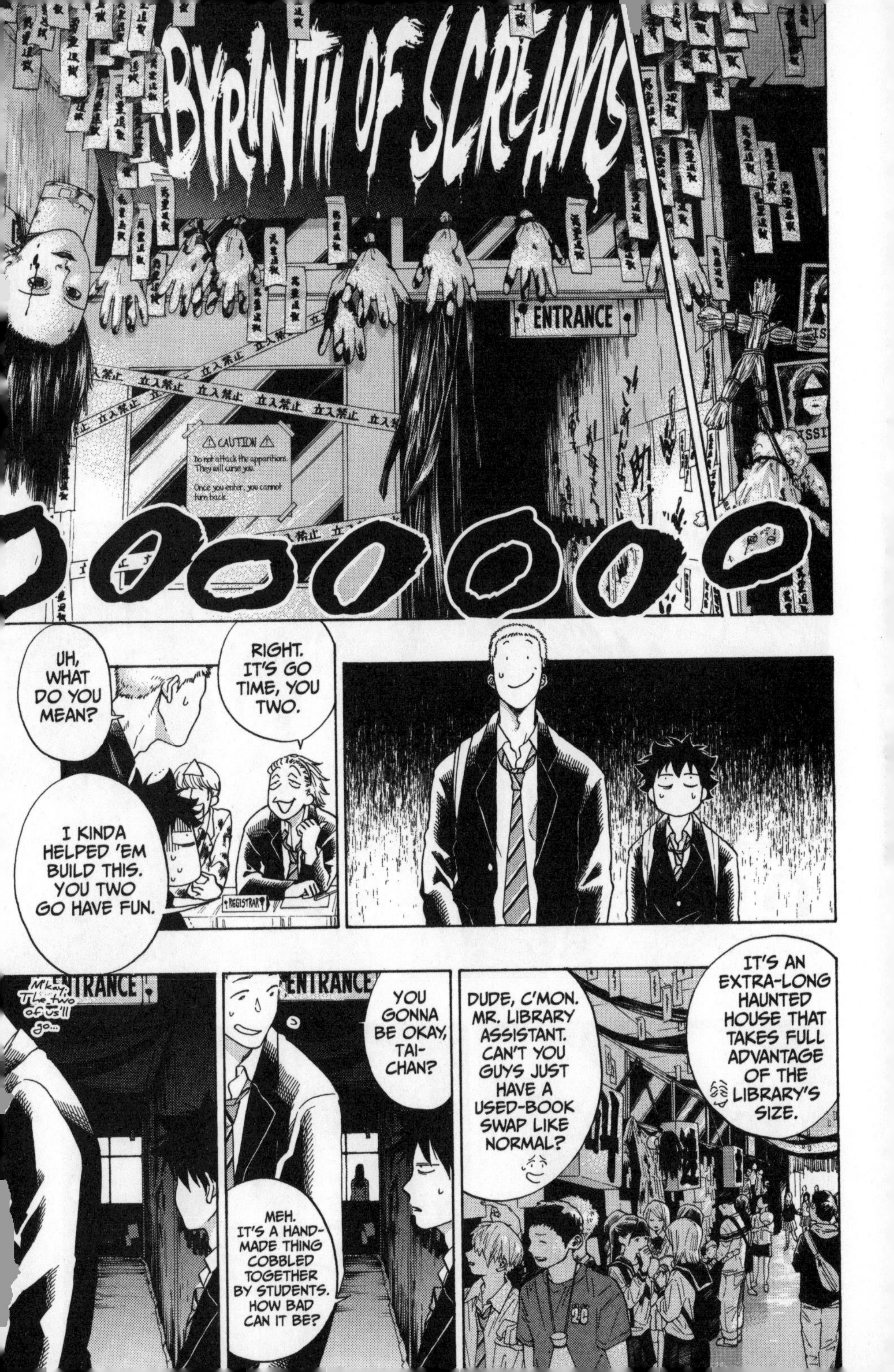
BYRINTH OF SCREAMS
ENTRANCE
CAUTION
Do not attack the apparitions. They will curse you.
Once you enter, you cannot turn back.
OOOOOOO
RIGHT. IT'S GO TIME, YOU TWO.
UH, WHAT DO YOU MEAN?
I KINDA HELPED 'EM BUILD THIS. YOU TWO GO HAVE FUN.
REGISTRAR
IT'S AN EXTRA-LONG HAUNTED HOUSE THAT TAKES FULL ADVANTAGE OF THE LIBRARY'S SIZE.
DUDE, C'MON. MR. LIBRARY ASSISTANT. CAN'T YOU GUYS JUST HAVE A USED-BOOK SWAP LIKE NORMAL?
ENTRANCE
YOU GONNA BE OKAY, TAI-CHAN?
MEH. IT'S A HAND-MADE THING COBBLED TOGETHER BY STUDENTS. HOW BAD CAN IT BE?
ENTRANCE
M'kay. The two of us'll go...

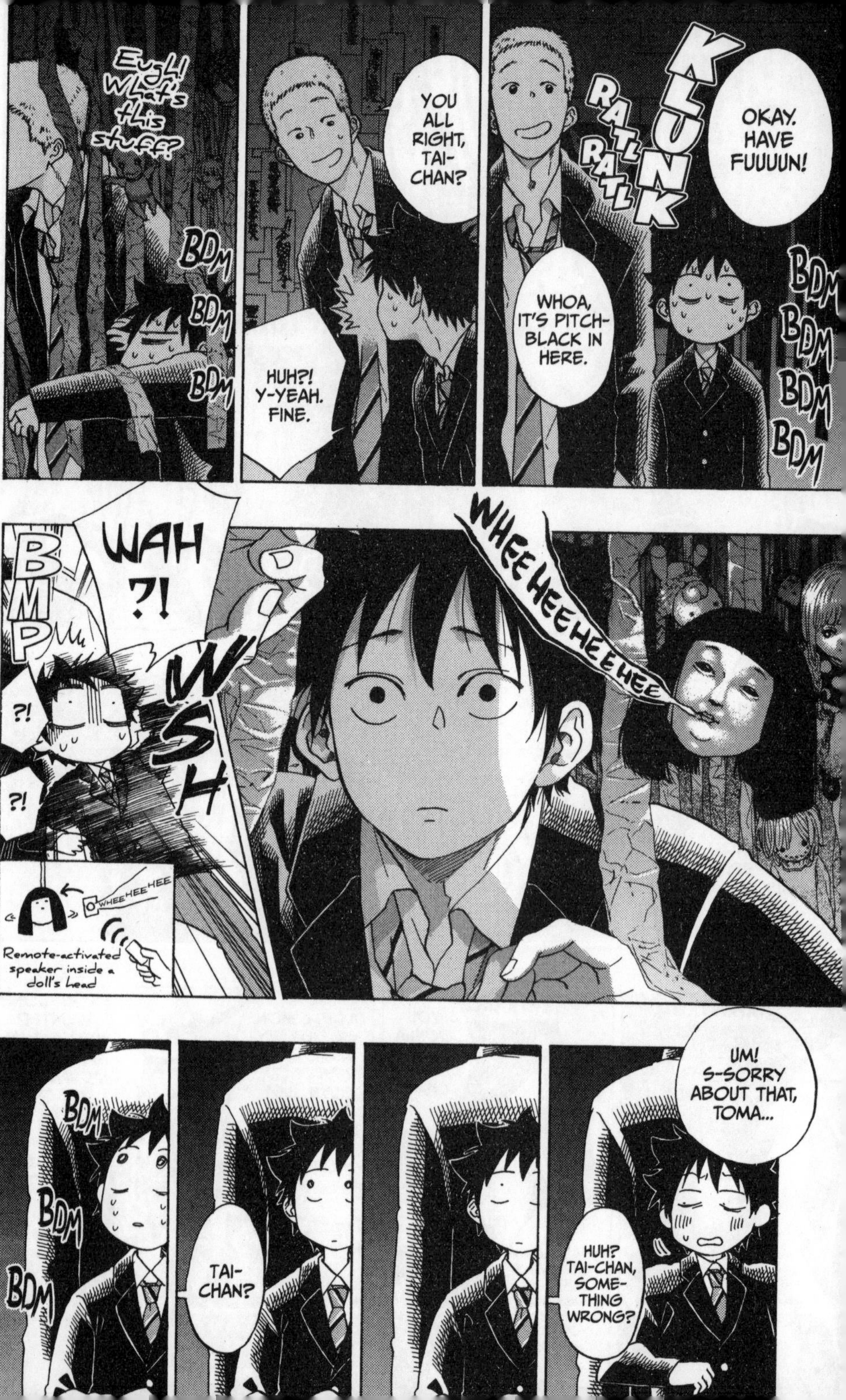
KLUNK
RATTL RATTL
OKAY. HAVE FUUUUN!
WHOA, IT'S PITCH-BLACK IN HERE.
BDM BDM BDM BDM
YOU ALL RIGHT, TAI-CHAN?
HUH?! Y-YEAH. FINE.
Eugh! What's this stuff?
BDM BDM BDM
WHEE HEE HEE HEE HEE
WAH?!
BMP
WSSH
?!
?!
WHEE HEE HEE
Remote-activated speaker inside a doll's head
UM! S-SORRY ABOUT THAT, TOMA...
HUH? TAI-CHAN, SOME-THING WRONG?
TAI-CHAN?
BDM BDM BDM

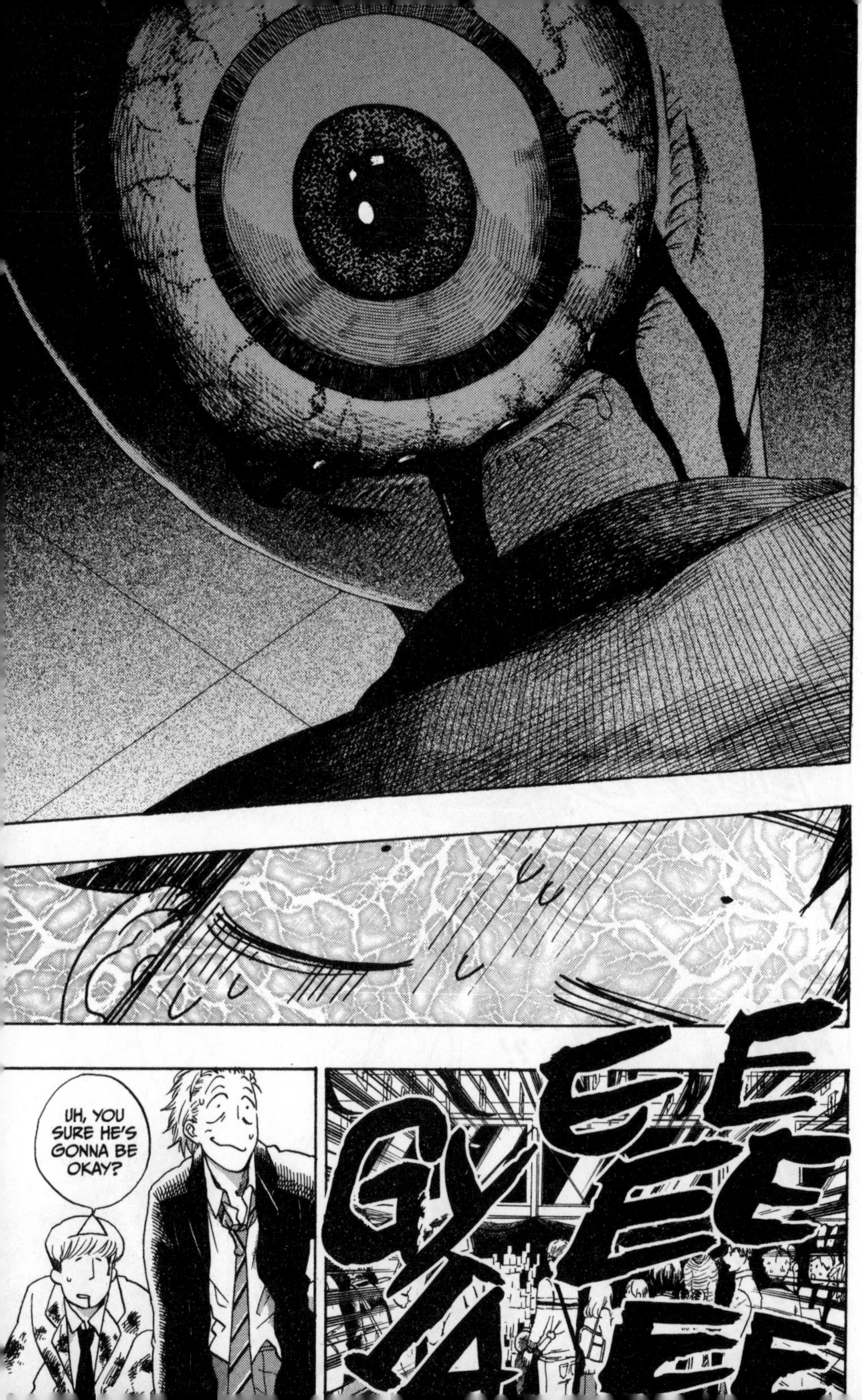
UH, YOU SURE HE'S GONNA BE OKAY?

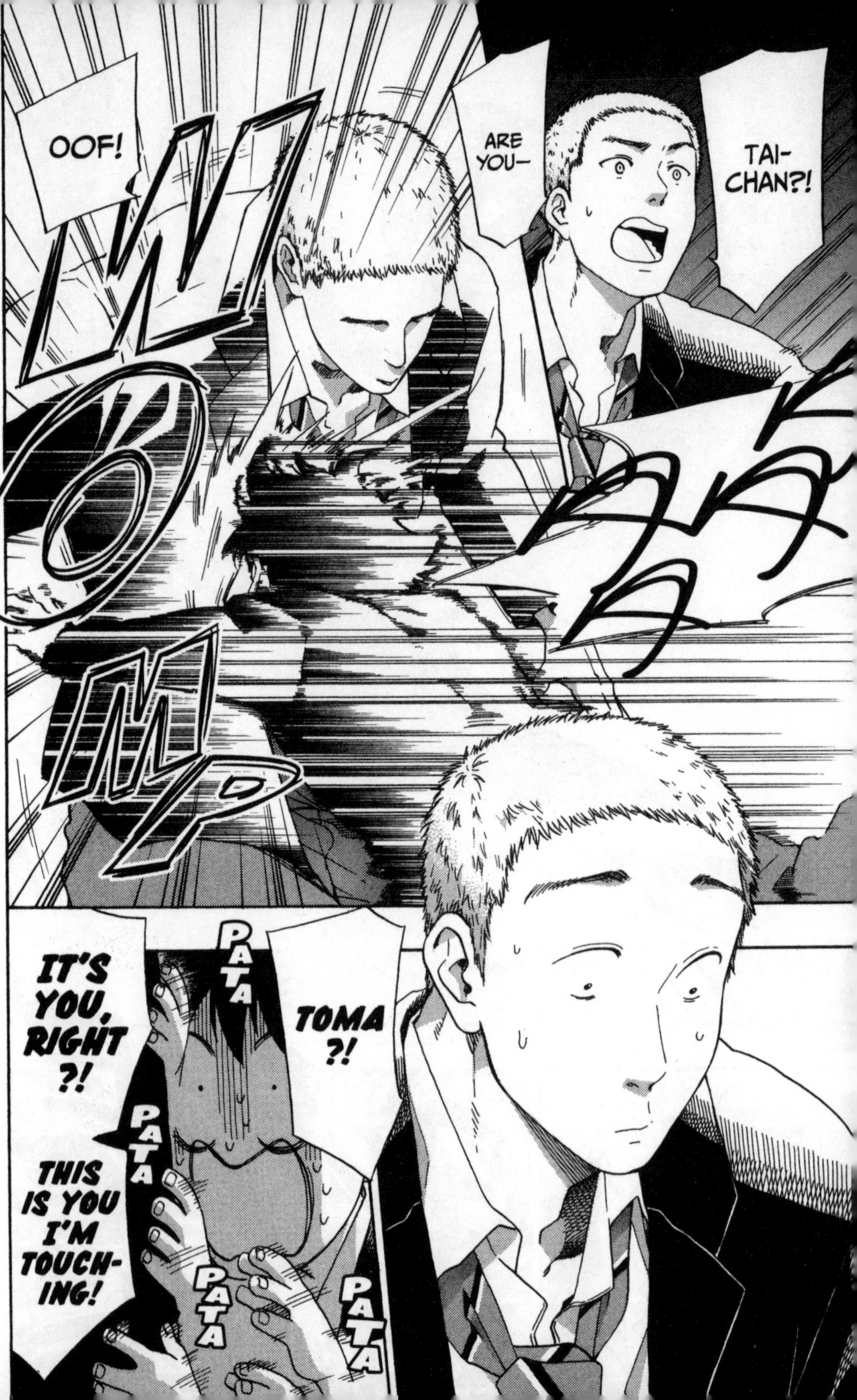
TAI-CHAN?!
ARE YOU—
OOF!
TOMA?!
IT'S YOU, RIGHT?!
PATA
PATA
THIS IS YOU I'M TOUCHING!
PATA
PATA

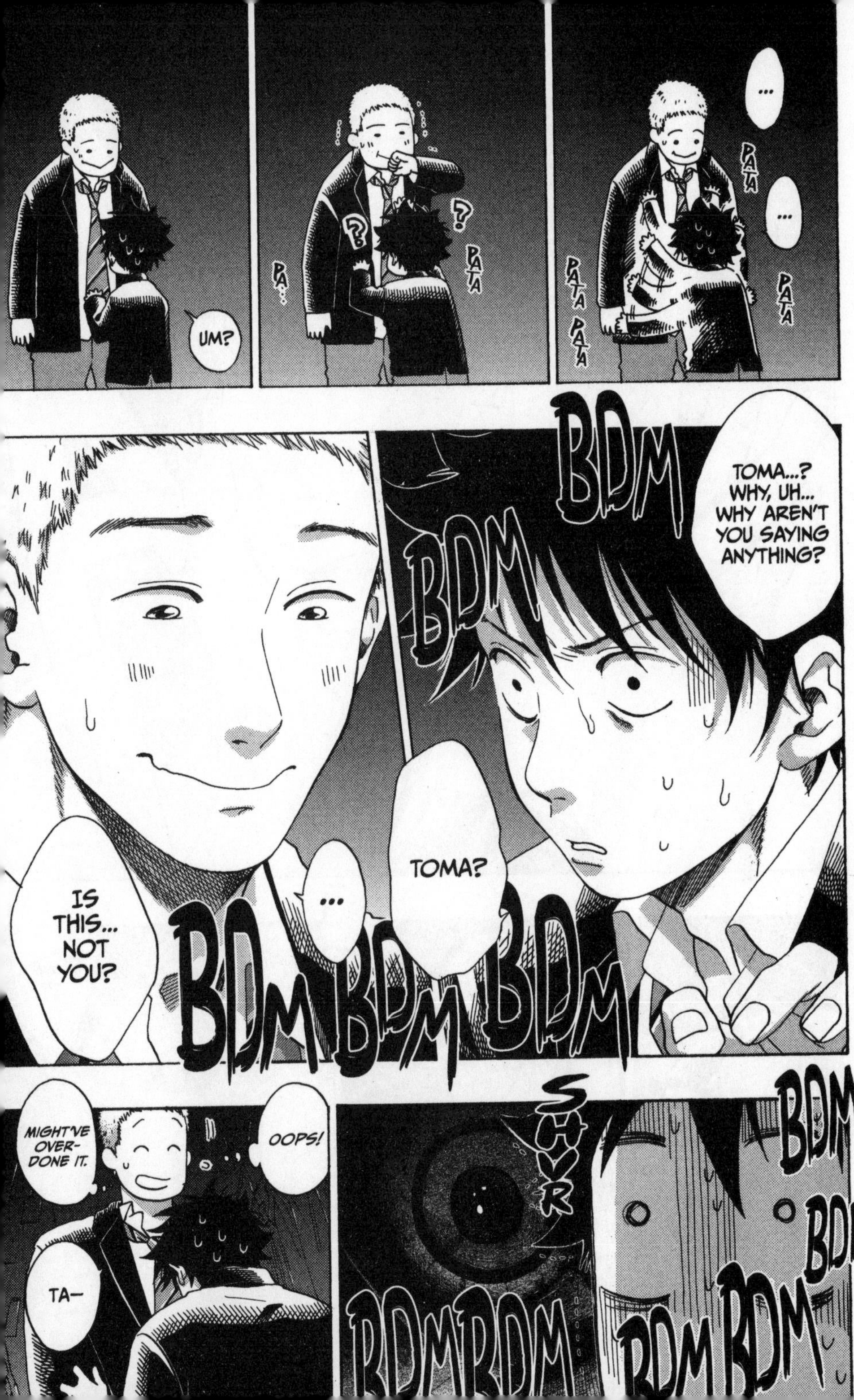
...
PATA
...
PATA
PATA PATA PATA
?
?
PATA
PA...
UM?
BDM
TOMA...? WHY, UH... WHY AREN'T YOU SAYING ANYTHING?
BDM
TOMA?
...
IS THIS... NOT YOU?
BDM BDM BDM
BDM
BDM
BDM
BDM BDM
SHVR
BDM BDM
OOPS!
MIGHT'VE OVER-DONE IT.
TA—

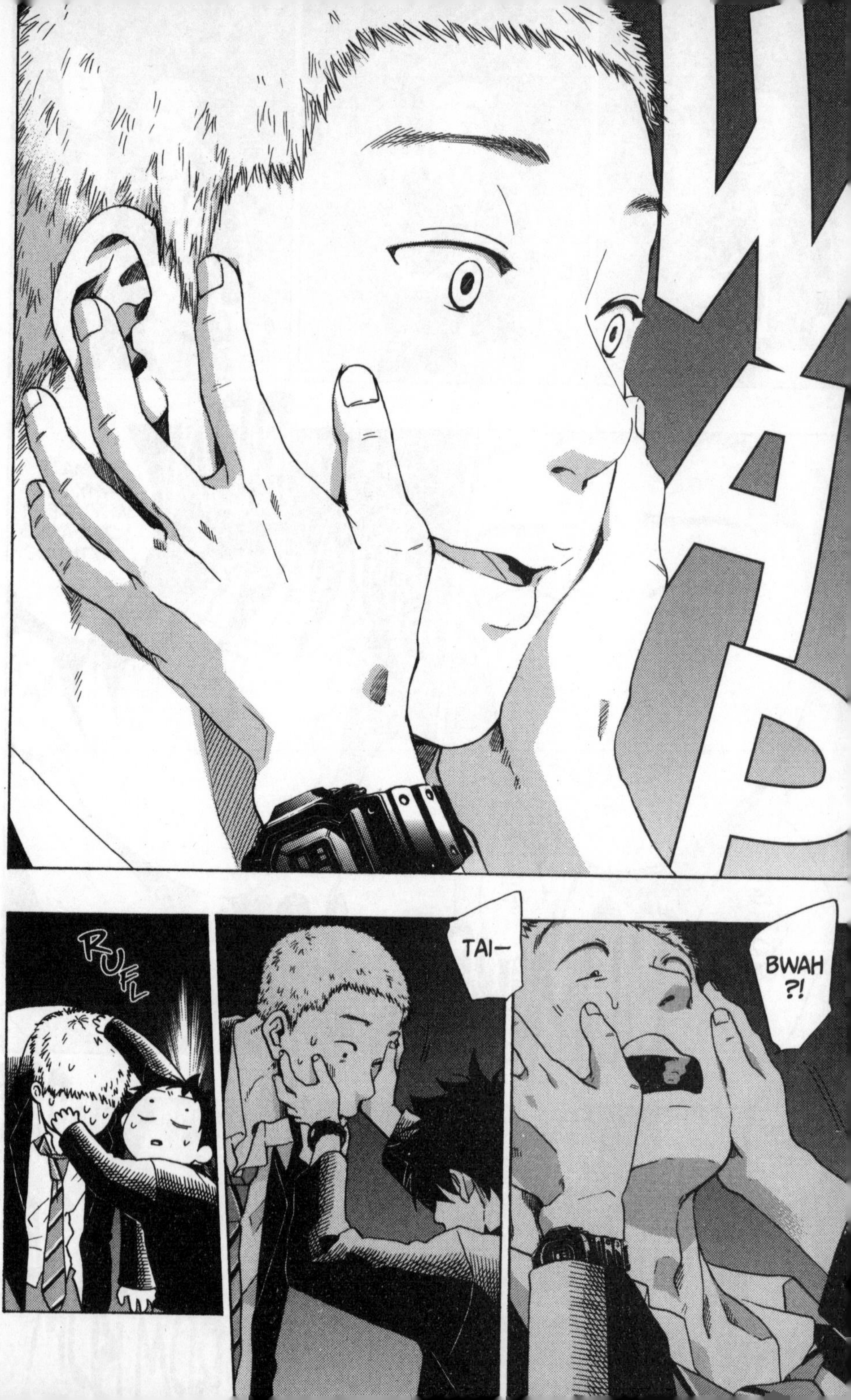
WAP
BWAH ?!
TAI—
RUFL

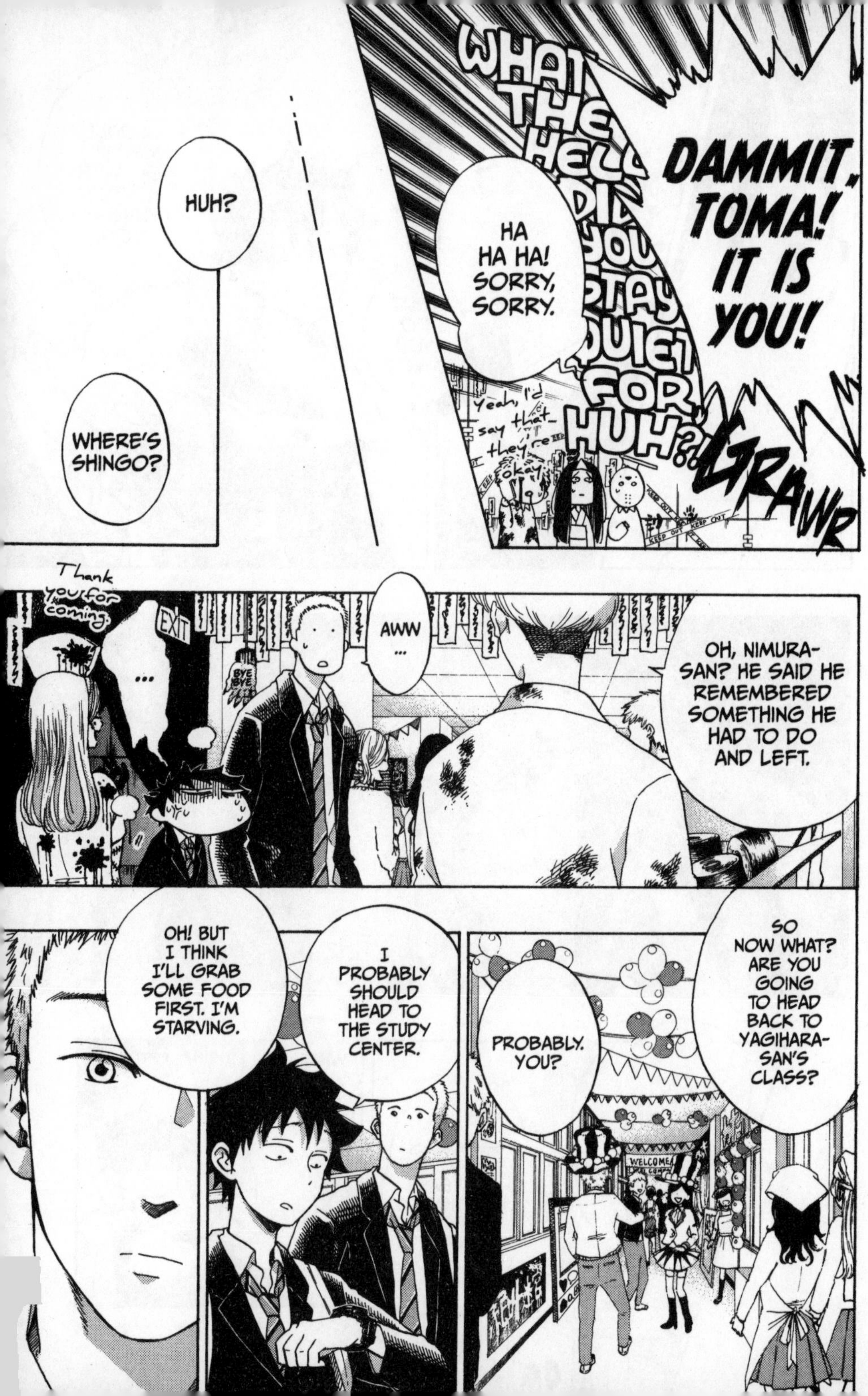
DAMMIT, TOMA! IT IS YOU!
WHAT THE HELL DID YOU STAY QUIET FOR, HUH?!
HA HA HA! SORRY, SORRY.
Yeah, I'd say that they're okay.
GRAWR
HUH?
WHERE'S SHINGO?
OH, NIMURA-SAN? HE SAID HE REMEMBERED SOMETHING HE HAD TO DO AND LEFT.
AWW ...
BYE BYE
...
EXIT
Thank you for coming.
SO NOW WHAT? ARE YOU GOING TO HEAD BACK TO YAGIHARA-SAN'S CLASS?
PROBABLY. YOU?
WELCOME
I PROBABLY SHOULD HEAD TO THE STUDY CENTER.
OH! BUT I THINK I'LL GRAB SOME FOOD FIRST. I'M STARVING.

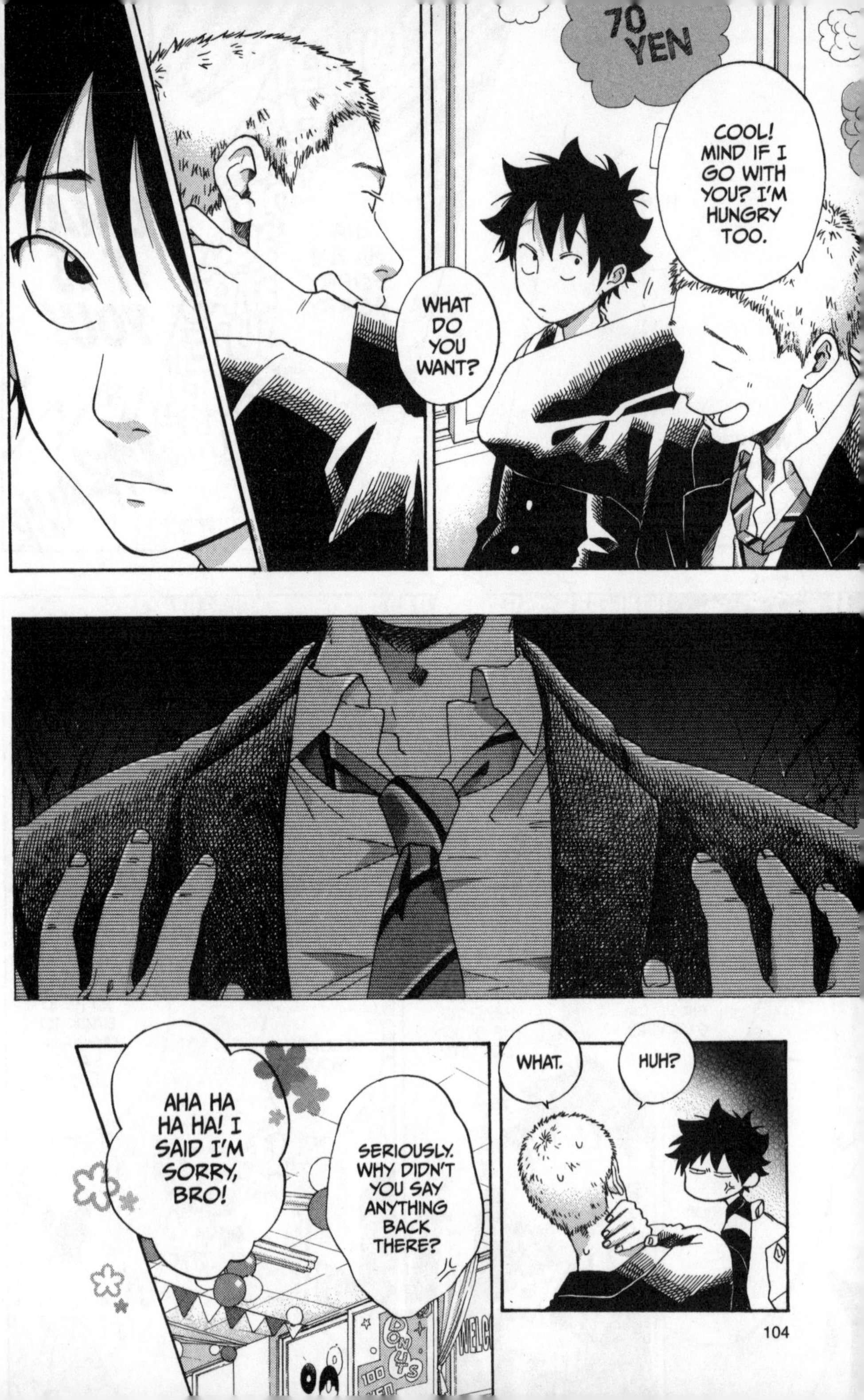
70 YEN
COOL! MIND IF I GO WITH YOU? I'M HUNGRY TOO.
WHAT DO YOU WANT?
HUH?
WHAT.
SERIOUSLY. WHY DIDN'T YOU SAY ANYTHING BACK THERE?
AHA HA HA HA! I SAID I'M SORRY, BRO!
DONUTS

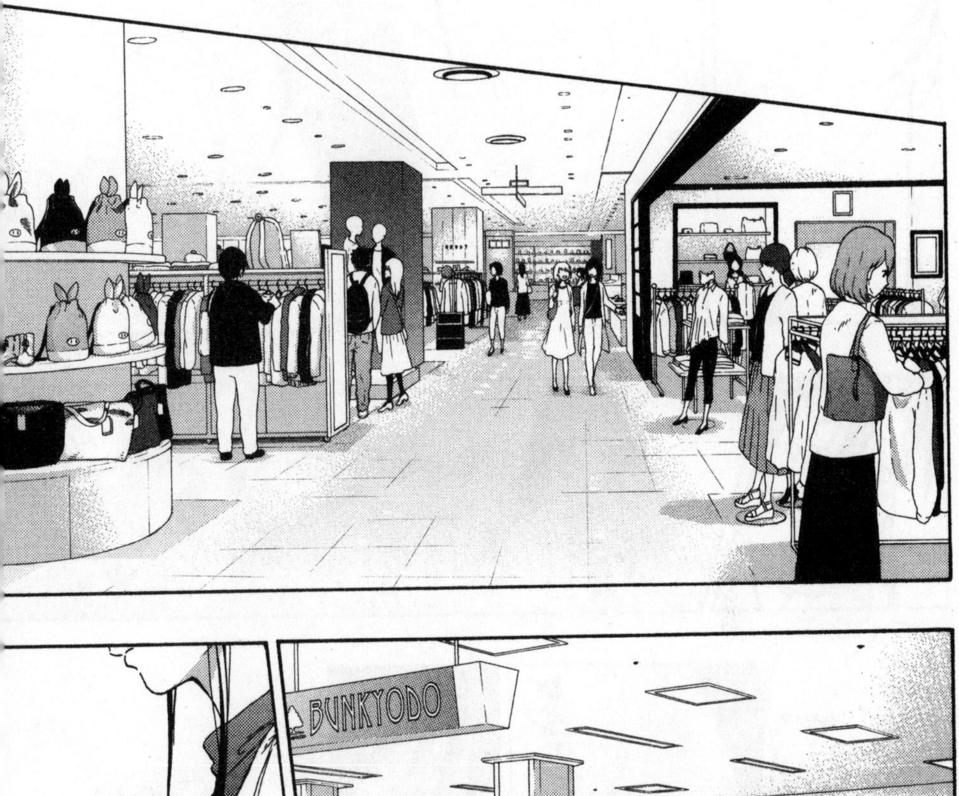

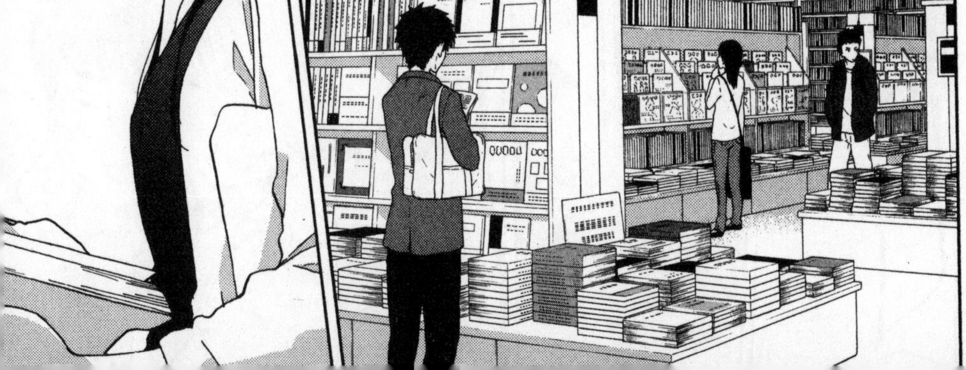
BUNKYODO

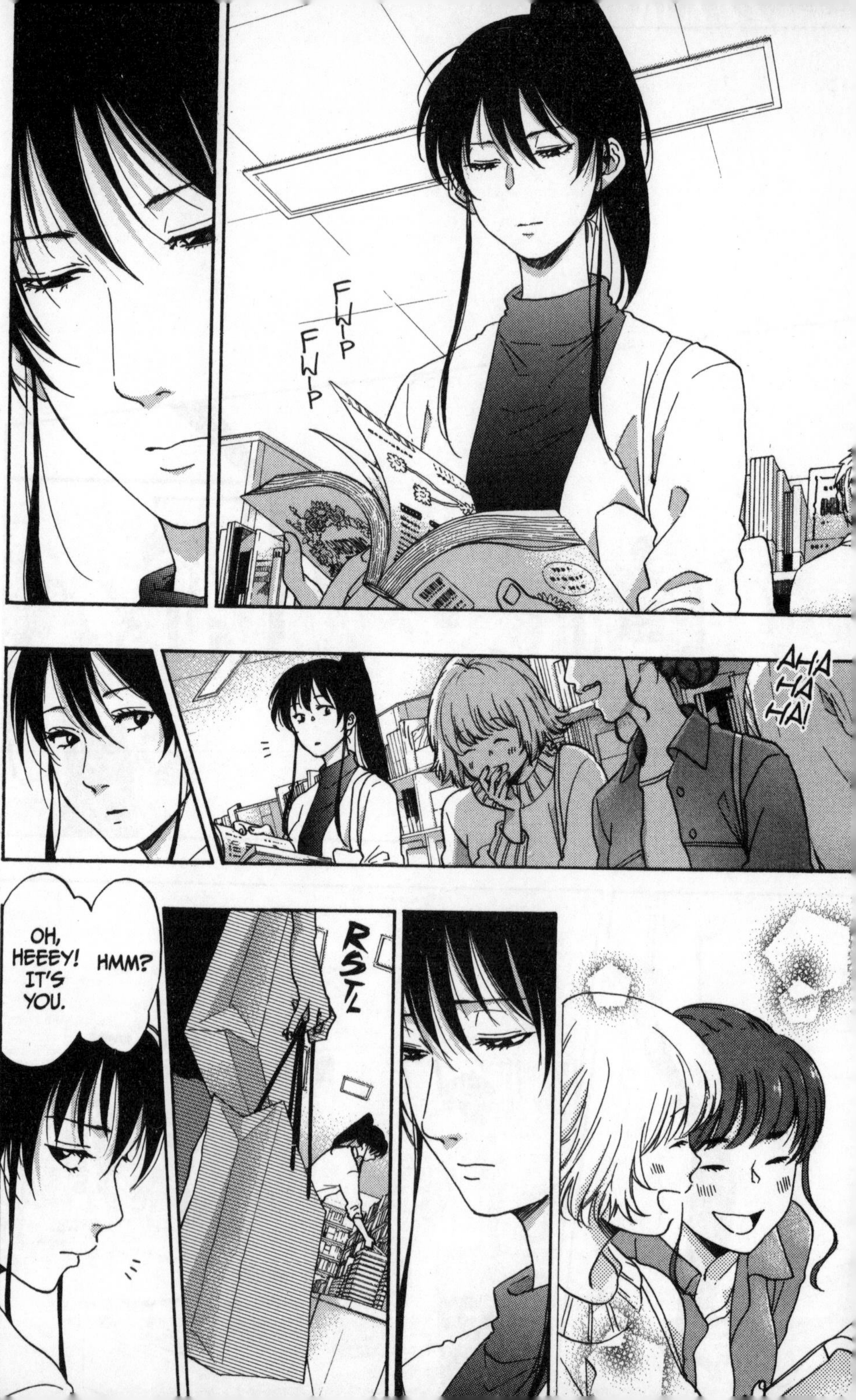
FWIP
FWIP
AHA HA HA!
RSTL
HMM?
OH, HEEEY! IT'S YOU.

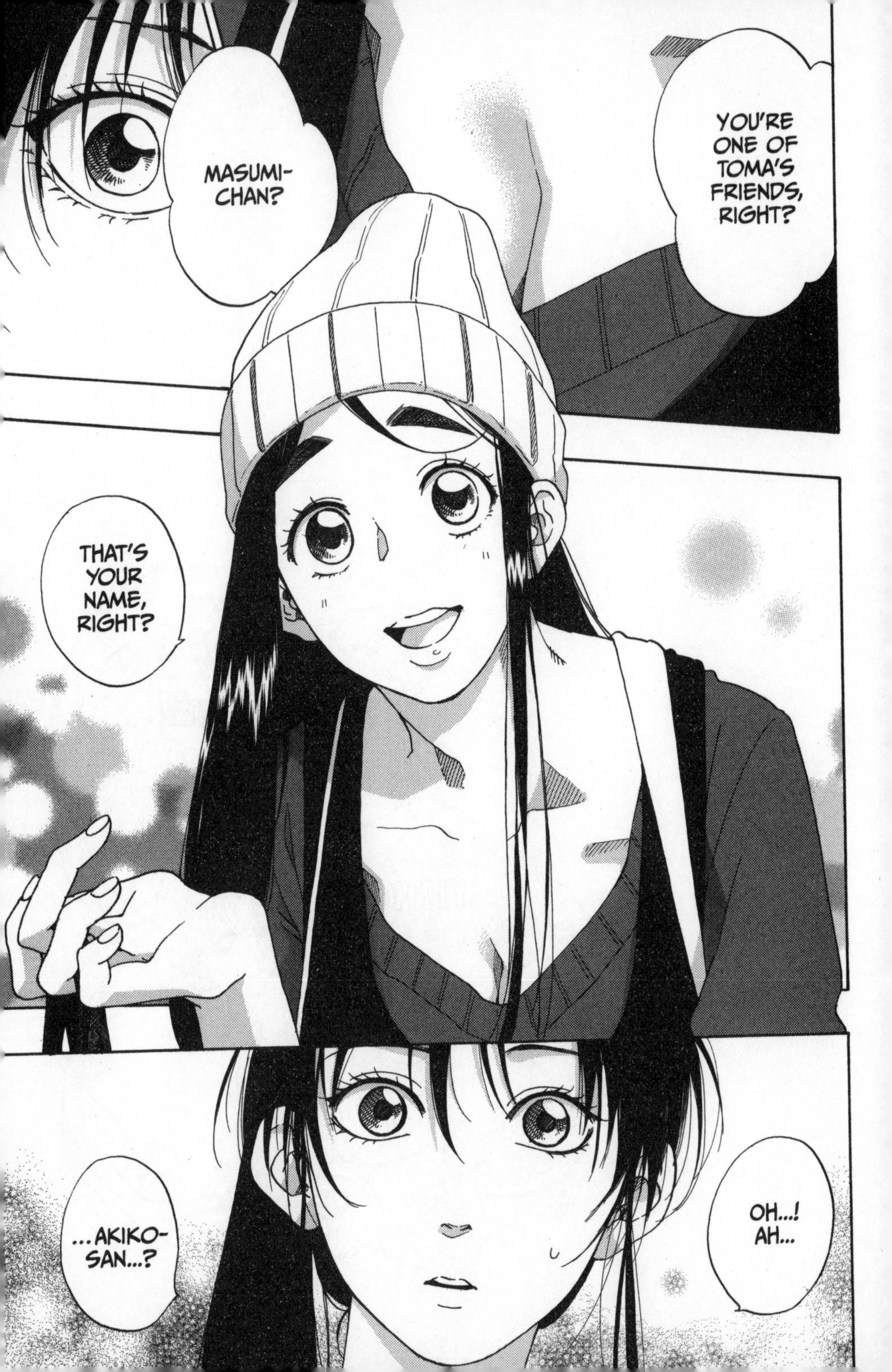
YOU'RE ONE OF TOMA'S FRIENDS, RIGHT?
MASUMI-CHAN?
THAT'S YOUR NAME, RIGHT?
OH...! AH...
...AKIKO-SAN...?

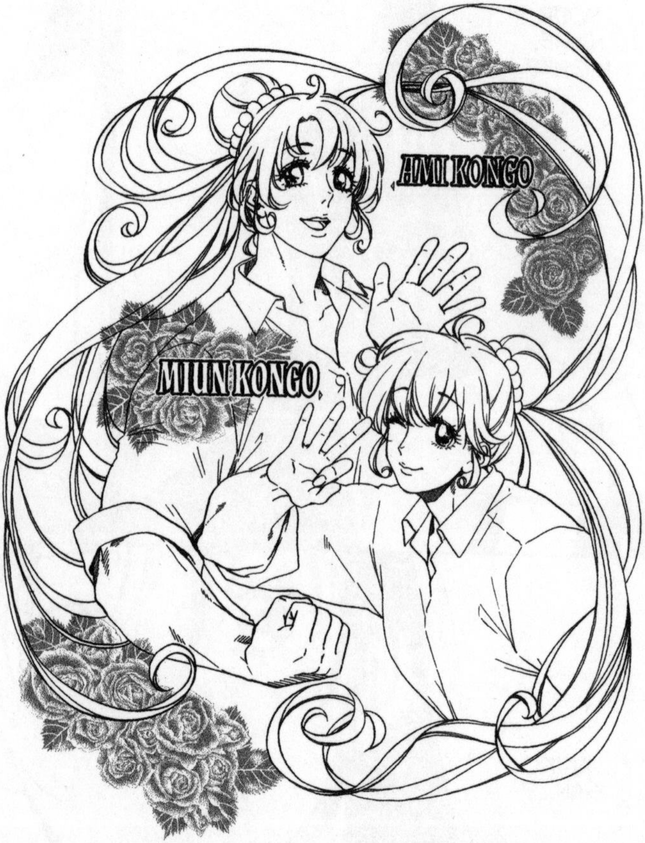
AMI KONGO
MIUN KONGO

CHAPTER 38

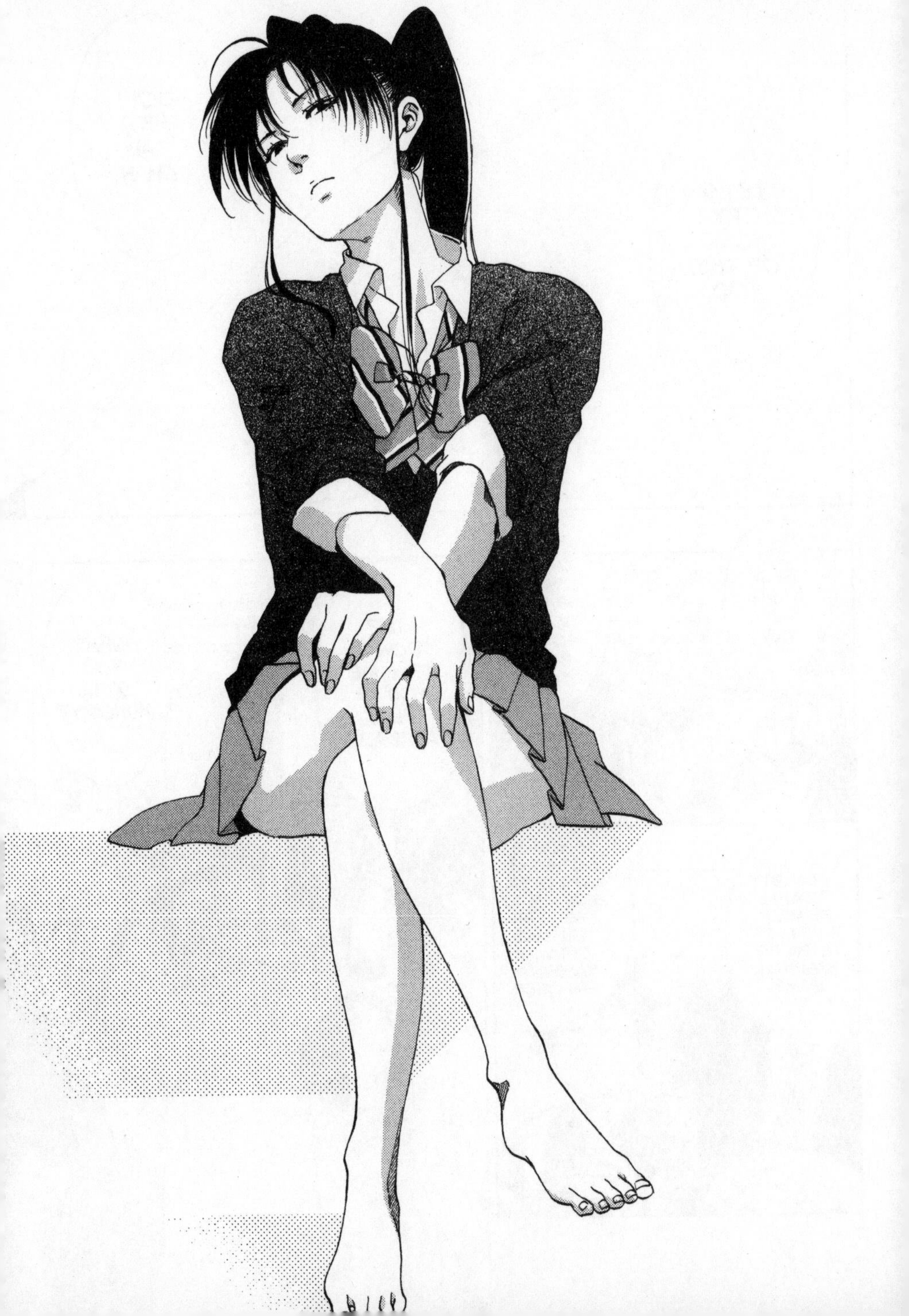

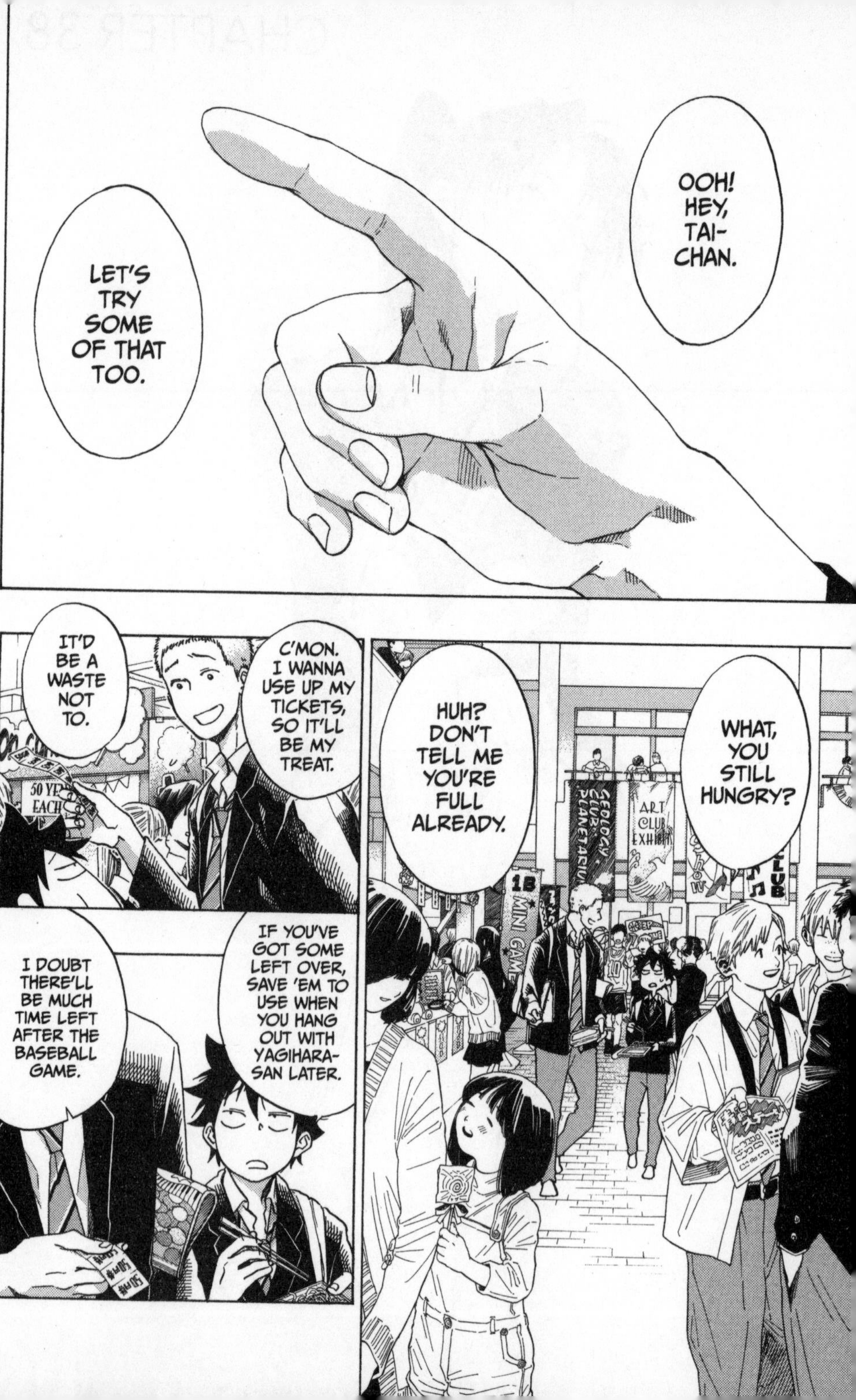
OOH! HEY, TAI-CHAN.
LET'S TRY SOME OF THAT TOO.
WHAT, YOU STILL HUNGRY?
HUH? DON'T TELL ME YOU'RE FULL ALREADY.
C'MON. I WANNA USE UP MY TICKETS, SO IT'LL BE MY TREAT.
IT'D BE A WASTE NOT TO.
IF YOU'VE GOT SOME LEFT OVER, SAVE 'EM TO USE WHEN YOU HANG OUT WITH YAGIHARA-SAN LATER.
I DOUBT THERE'LL BE MUCH TIME LEFT AFTER THE BASEBALL GAME.

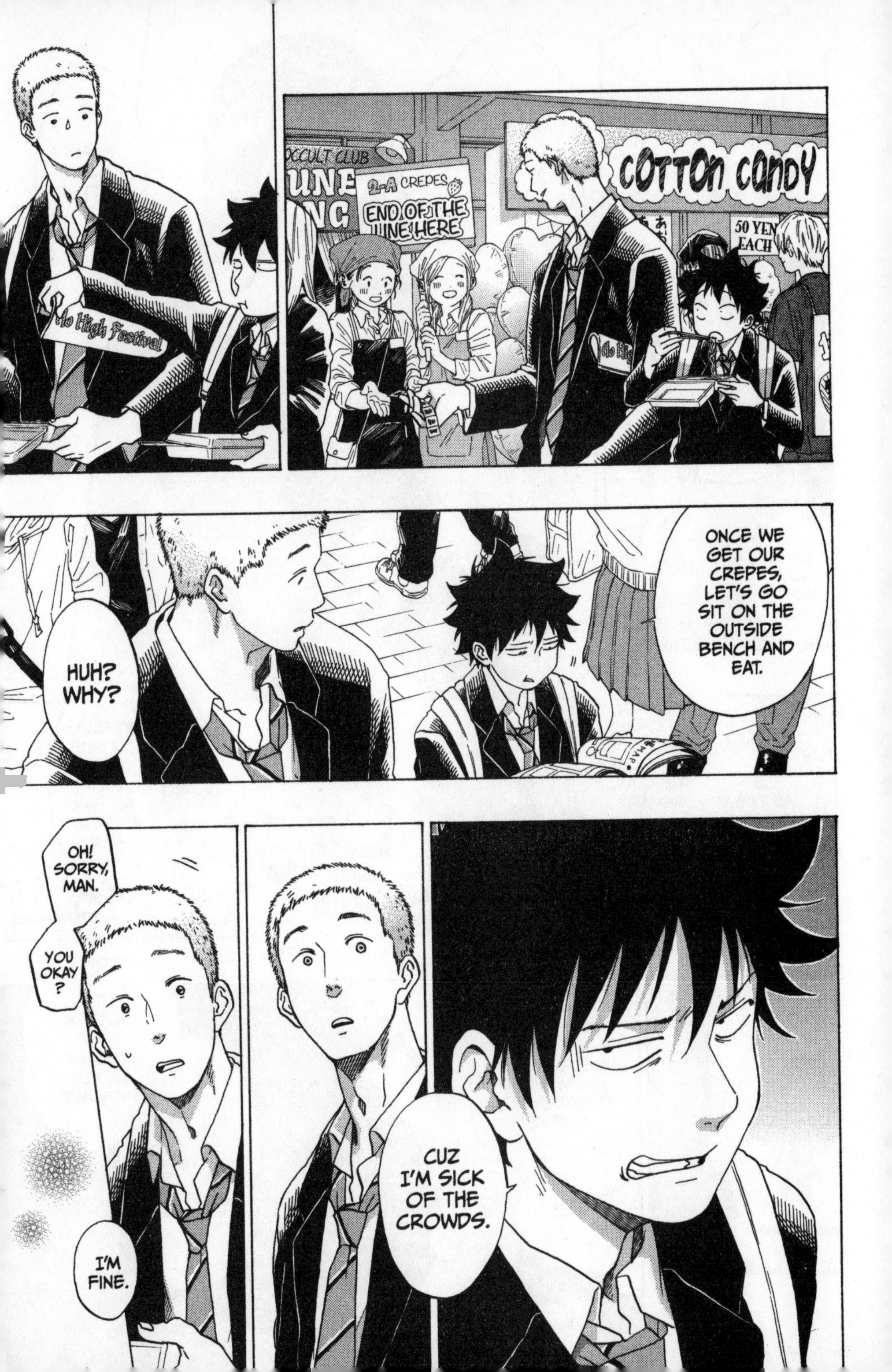
OCCULT CLUB
2-A CREPES
END OF THE LINE HERE
COTTON CANDY
50 YEN EACH
Ao High
Ao High Festival
ONCE WE GET OUR CREPES, LET'S GO SIT ON THE OUTSIDE BENCH AND EAT.
HUH? WHY?
MAP
CUZ I'M SICK OF THE CROWDS.
OH! SORRY, MAN.
YOU OKAY?
I'M FINE.

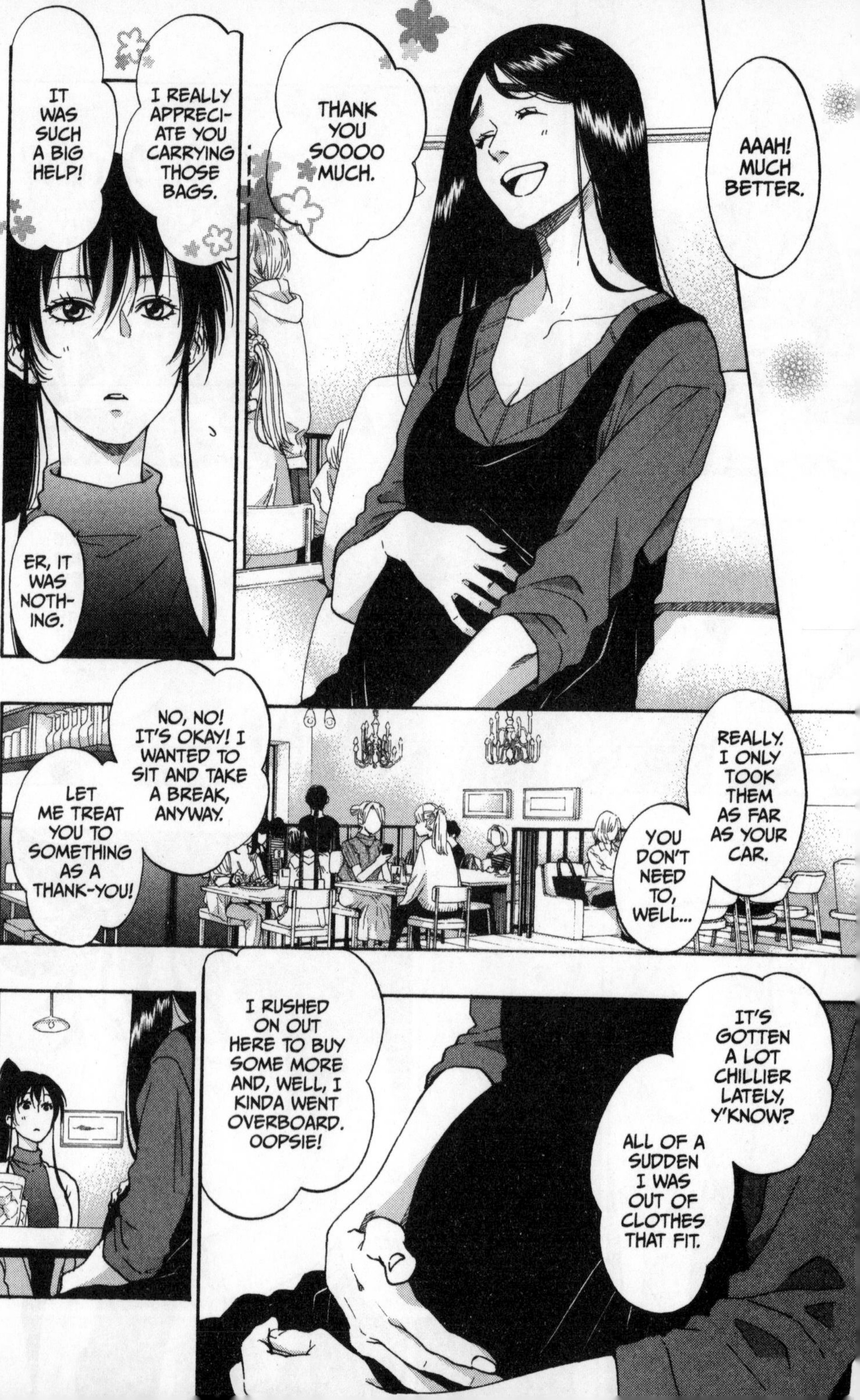
AAAH! MUCH BETTER.
THANK YOU SOOOO MUCH.
I REALLY APPRECIATE YOU CARRYING THOSE BAGS.
IT WAS SUCH A BIG HELP!
ER, IT WAS NOTHING.
REALLY. I ONLY TOOK THEM AS FAR AS YOUR CAR.
YOU DON'T NEED TO, WELL...
NO, NO! IT'S OKAY! I WANTED TO SIT AND TAKE A BREAK, ANYWAY.
LET ME TREAT YOU TO SOMETHING AS A THANK-YOU!
IT'S GOTTEN A LOT CHILLIER LATELY, Y'KNOW?
ALL OF A SUDDEN I WAS OUT OF CLOTHES THAT FIT.
I RUSHED ON OUT HERE TO BUY SOME MORE AND, WELL, I KINDA WENT OVERBOARD. OOPSIE!

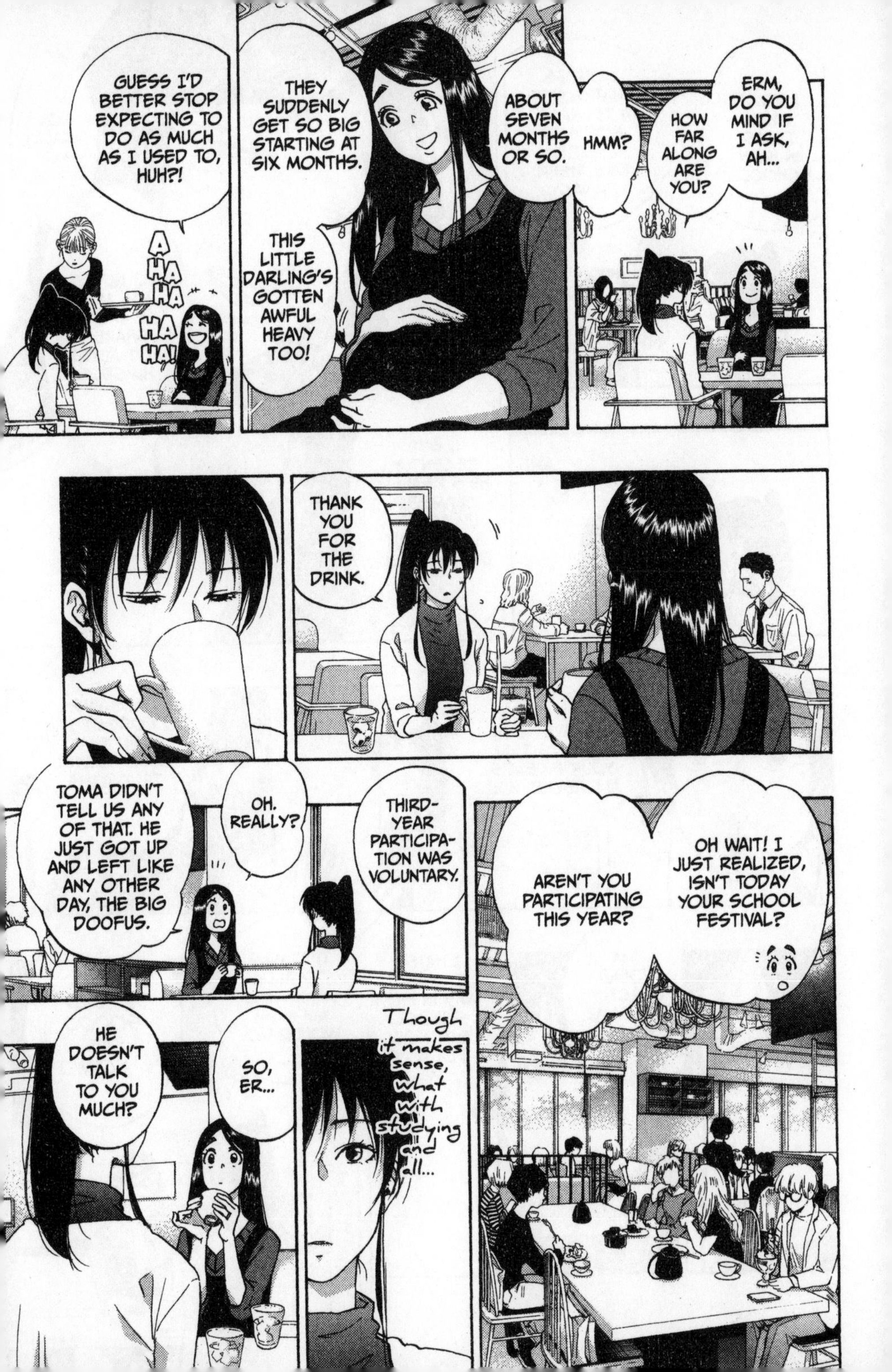

ERM, DO YOU MIND IF I ASK, AH...
HOW FAR ALONG ARE YOU?
HMM?
ABOUT SEVEN MONTHS OR SO.
THEY SUDDENLY GET SO BIG STARTING AT SIX MONTHS.
THIS LITTLE DARLING'S GOTTEN AWFUL HEAVY TOO!
GUESS I'D BETTER STOP EXPECTING TO DO AS MUCH AS I USED TO, HUH?!
A HA HA HA HA!
THANK YOU FOR THE DRINK.
OH WAIT! I JUST REALIZED, ISN'T TODAY YOUR SCHOOL FESTIVAL?
AREN'T YOU PARTICIPATING THIS YEAR?
THIRD-YEAR PARTICIPATION WAS VOLUNTARY.
OH. REALLY?
TOMA DIDN'T TELL US ANY OF THAT. HE JUST GOT UP AND LEFT LIKE ANY OTHER DAY, THE BIG DOOFUS.
Though it makes sense, what with studying and all...
SO, ER...
HE DOESN'T TALK TO YOU MUCH?

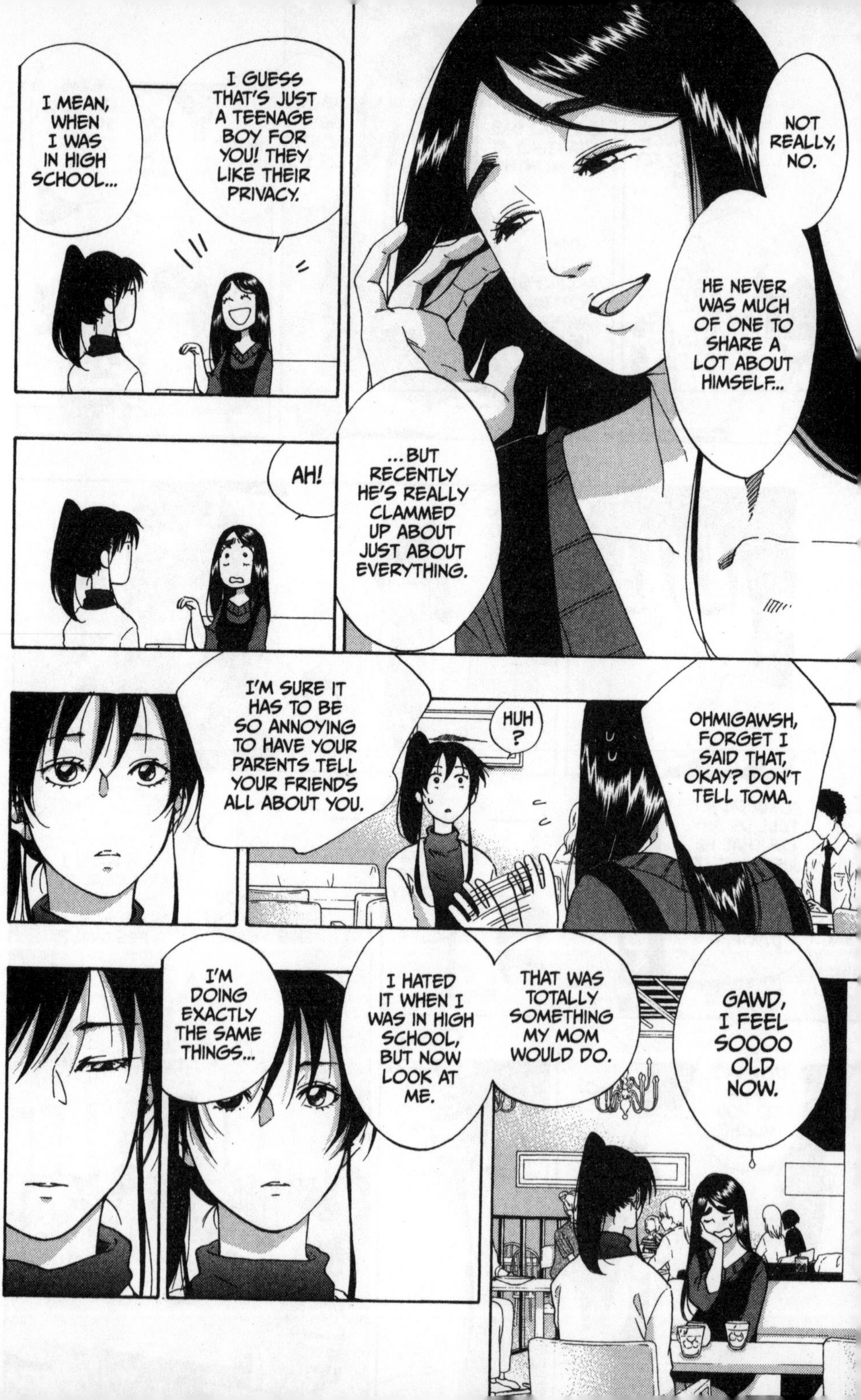
NOT REALLY, NO.
HE NEVER WAS MUCH OF ONE TO SHARE A LOT ABOUT HIMSELF...
...BUT RECENTLY HE'S REALLY CLAMMED UP ABOUT JUST ABOUT EVERYTHING.
I GUESS THAT'S JUST A TEENAGE BOY FOR YOU! THEY LIKE THEIR PRIVACY.
I MEAN, WHEN I WAS IN HIGH SCHOOL...
AH!
OHMIGAWSH, FORGET I SAID THAT, OKAY? DON'T TELL TOMA.
HUH?
I'M SURE IT HAS TO BE SO ANNOYING TO HAVE YOUR PARENTS TELL YOUR FRIENDS ALL ABOUT YOU.
GAWD, I FEEL SOOOO OLD NOW.
THAT WAS TOTALLY SOMETHING MY MOM WOULD DO.
I HATED IT WHEN I WAS IN HIGH SCHOOL, BUT NOW LOOK AT ME.
I'M DOING EXACTLY THE SAME THINGS...

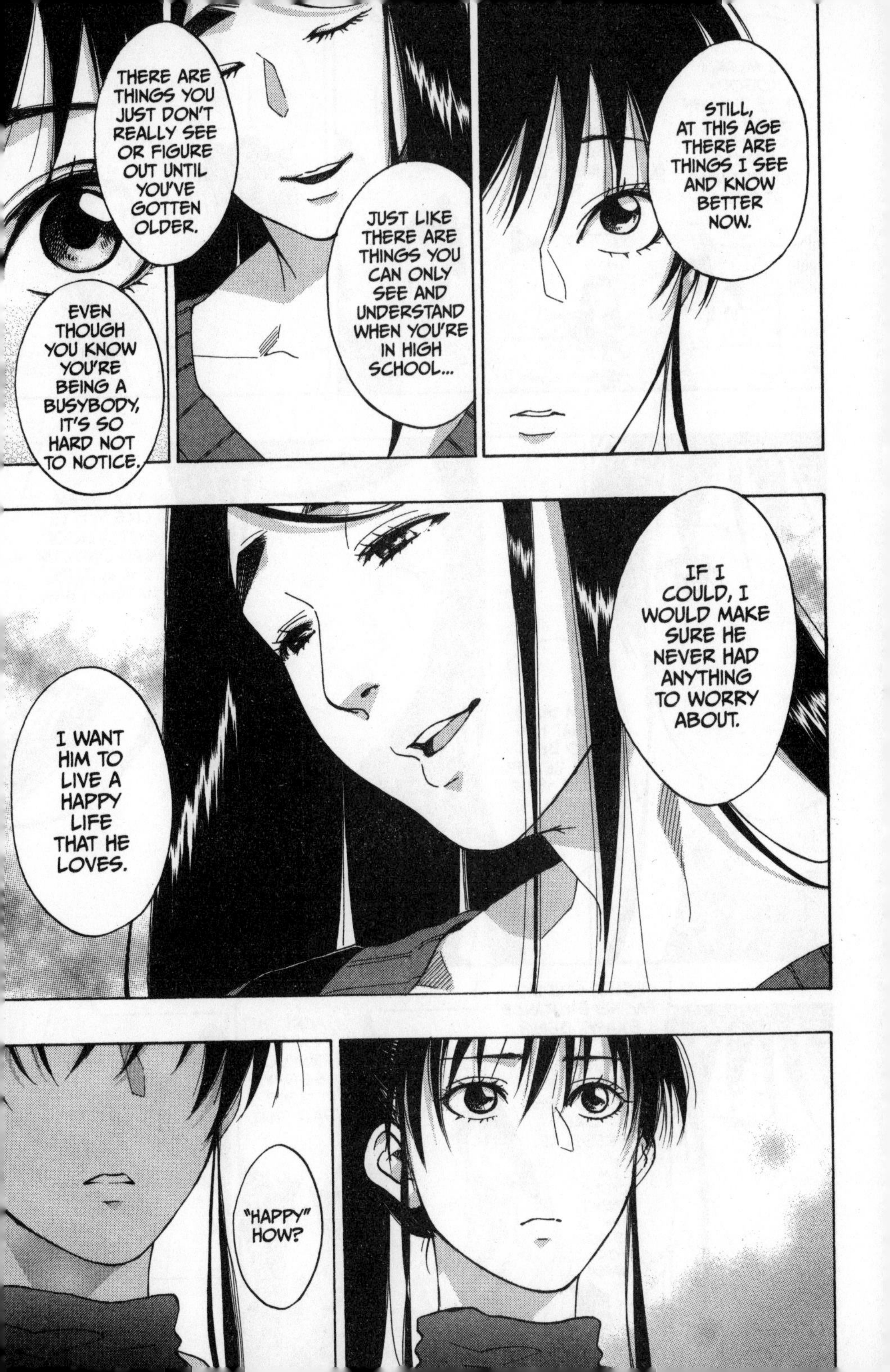
STILL, AT THIS AGE THERE ARE THINGS I SEE AND KNOW BETTER NOW.
JUST LIKE THERE ARE THINGS YOU CAN ONLY SEE AND UNDERSTAND WHEN YOU'RE IN HIGH SCHOOL...
THERE ARE THINGS YOU JUST DON'T REALLY SEE OR FIGURE OUT UNTIL YOU'VE GOTTEN OLDER.
EVEN THOUGH YOU KNOW YOU'RE BEING A BUSYBODY, IT'S SO HARD NOT TO NOTICE.
IF I COULD, I WOULD MAKE SURE HE NEVER HAD ANYTHING TO WORRY ABOUT.
I WANT HIM TO LIVE A HAPPY LIFE THAT HE LOVES.
"HAPPY" HOW?

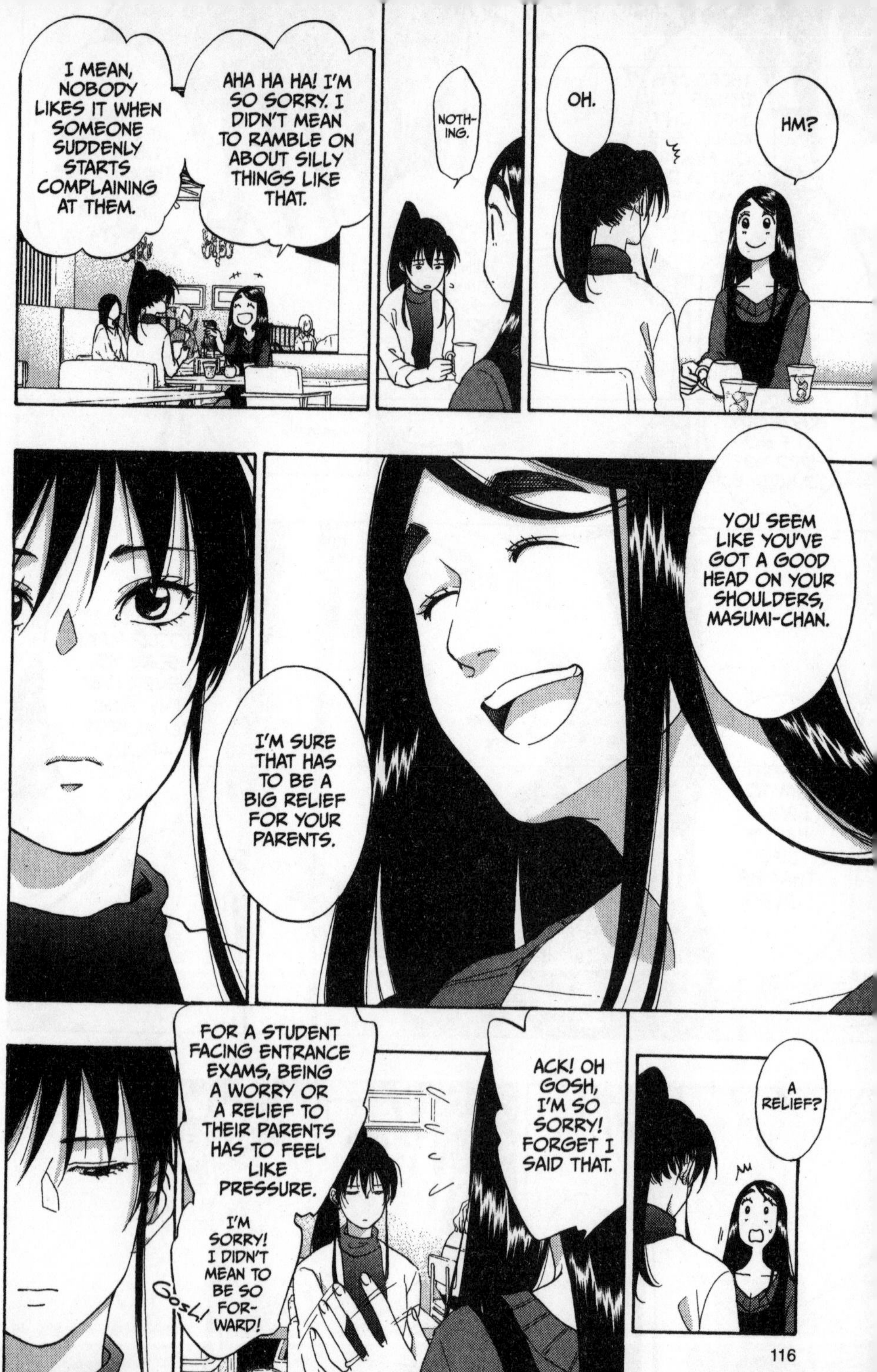
OH.
HM?
NOTH-ING.
AHA HA HA! I'M SO SORRY. I DIDN'T MEAN TO RAMBLE ON ABOUT SILLY THINGS LIKE THAT.
I MEAN, NOBODY LIKES IT WHEN SOMEONE SUDDENLY STARTS COMPLAINING AT THEM.
YOU SEEM LIKE YOU'VE GOT A GOOD HEAD ON YOUR SHOULDERS, MASUMI-CHAN.
I'M SURE THAT HAS TO BE A BIG RELIEF FOR YOUR PARENTS.
A RELIEF?
FOR A STUDENT FACING ENTRANCE EXAMS, BEING A WORRY OR A RELIEF TO THEIR PARENTS HAS TO FEEL LIKE PRESSURE.
ACK! OH GOSH, I'M SO SORRY! FORGET I SAID THAT.
I'M SORRY! I DIDN'T MEAN TO BE SO FOR-WARD!
GOSH!

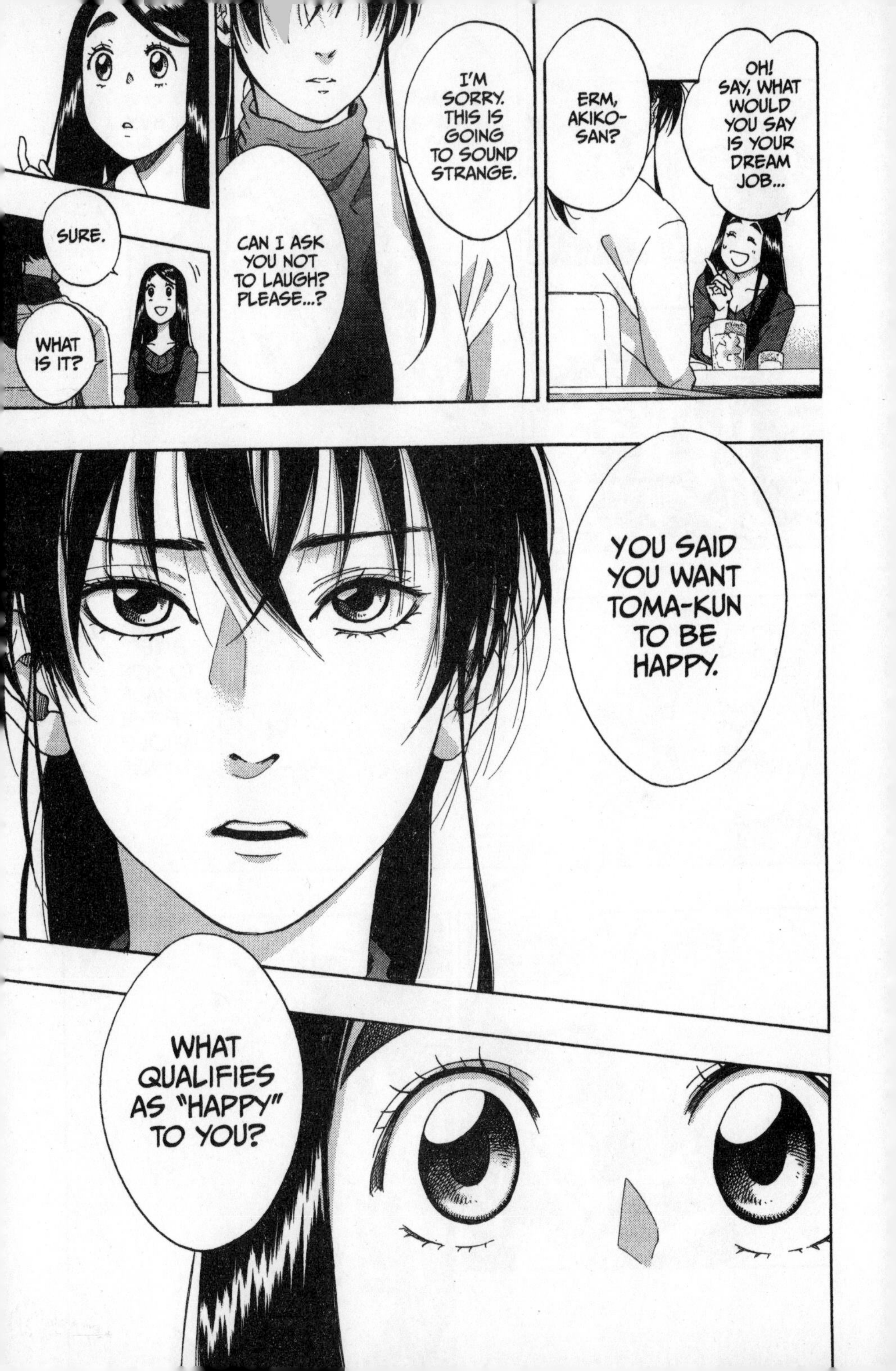
OH! SAY, WHAT WOULD YOU SAY IS YOUR DREAM JOB...
ERM, AKIKO-SAN?
I'M SORRY. THIS IS GOING TO SOUND STRANGE.
CAN I ASK YOU NOT TO LAUGH? PLEASE...?
SURE.
WHAT IS IT?
YOU SAID YOU WANT TOMA-KUN TO BE HAPPY.
WHAT QUALIFIES AS "HAPPY" TO YOU?

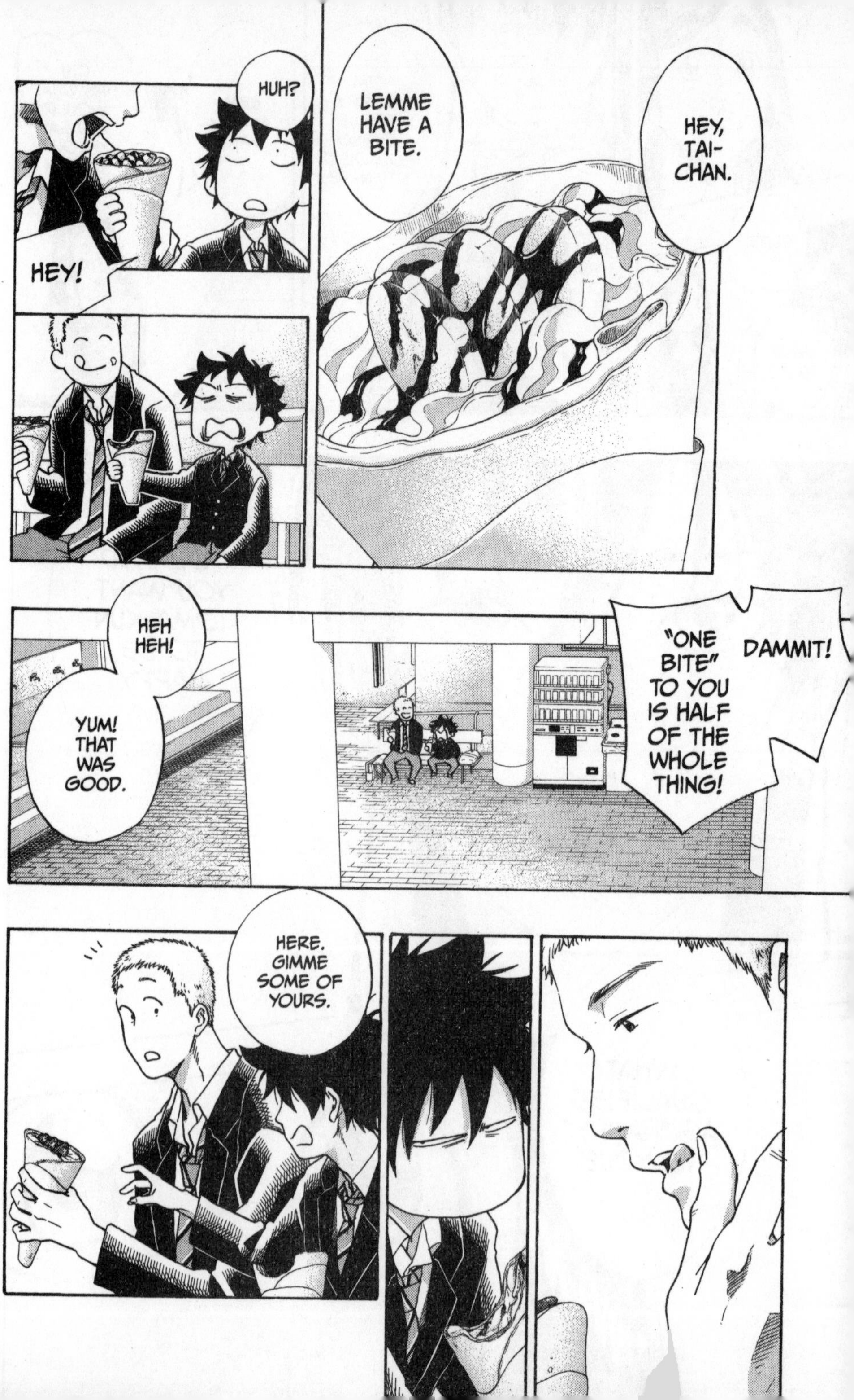
HEY, TAI-CHAN.
LEMME HAVE A BITE.
HUH?
HEY!
DAMMIT!
"ONE BITE" TO YOU IS HALF OF THE WHOLE THING!
HEH HEH!
YUM! THAT WAS GOOD.
HERE. GIMME SOME OF YOURS.

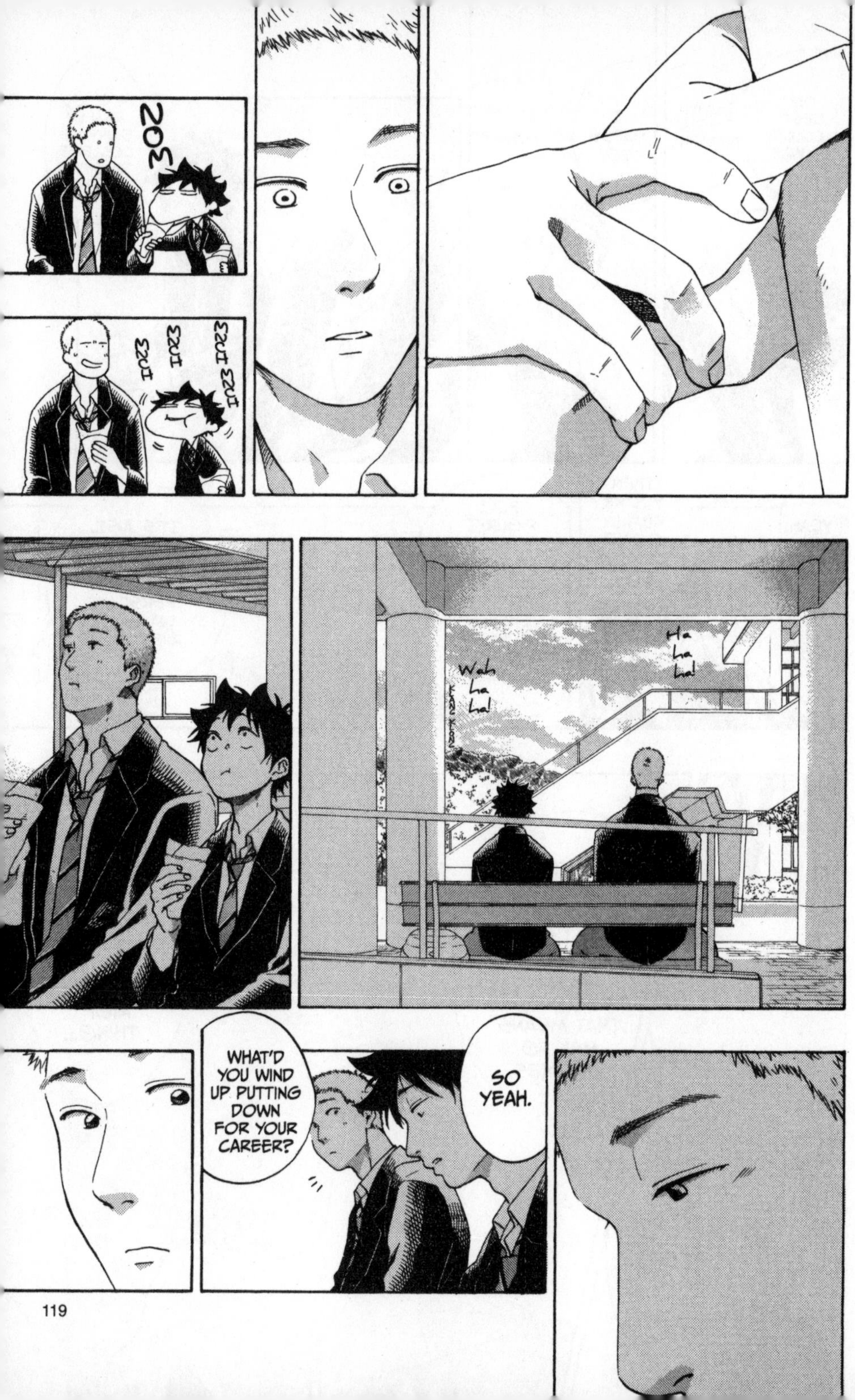
NOM
MNCH MNCH
MNCH
MNCH
Ha ha ha!
Wah ha ha!
KLANG KLONG
SO YEAH.
WHAT'D YOU WIND UP PUTTING DOWN FOR YOUR CAREER?

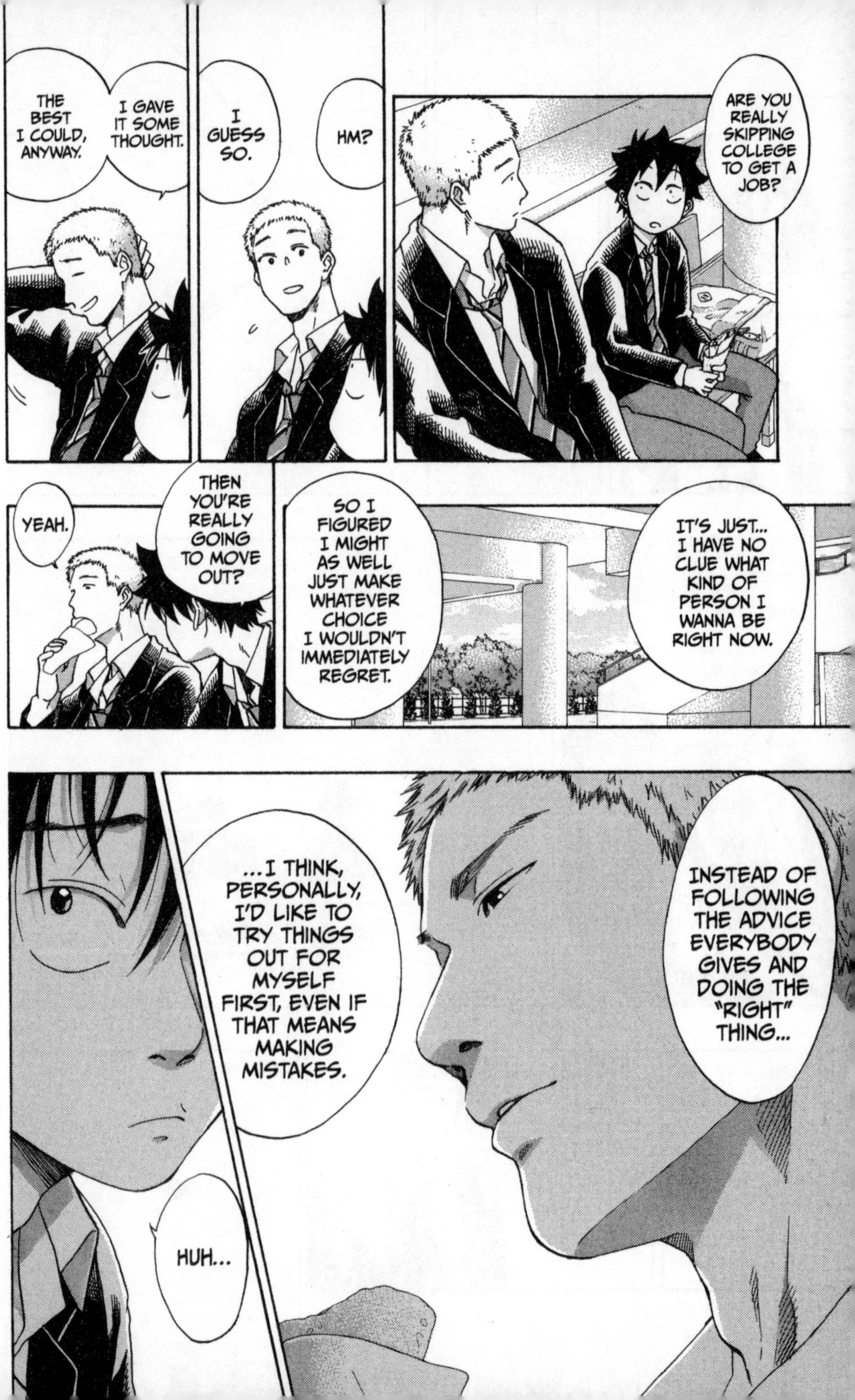
ARE YOU REALLY SKIPPING COLLEGE TO GET A JOB?
HM?
I GUESS SO.
I GAVE IT SOME THOUGHT.
THE BEST I COULD, ANYWAY.
IT'S JUST... I HAVE NO CLUE WHAT KIND OF PERSON I WANNA BE RIGHT NOW.
SO I FIGURED I MIGHT AS WELL JUST MAKE WHATEVER CHOICE I WOULDN'T IMMEDIATELY REGRET.
THEN YOU'RE REALLY GOING TO MOVE OUT?
YEAH.
INSTEAD OF FOLLOWING THE ADVICE EVERYBODY GIVES AND DOING THE "RIGHT" THING...
...I THINK, PERSONALLY, I'D LIKE TO TRY THINGS OUT FOR MYSELF FIRST, EVEN IF THAT MEANS MAKING MISTAKES.
HUH...

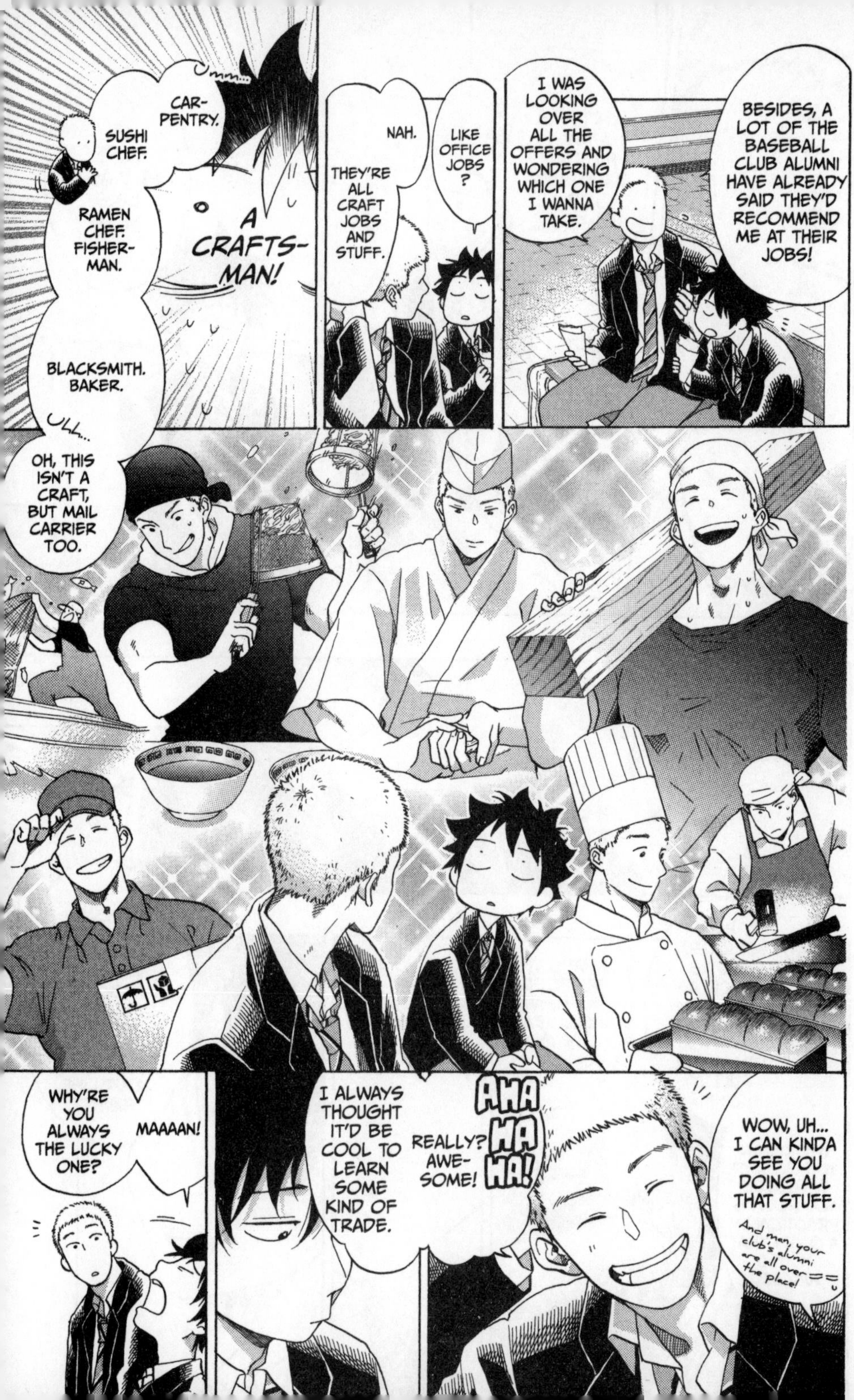
I WAS LOOKING OVER ALL THE OFFERS AND WONDERING WHICH ONE I WANNA TAKE.
BESIDES, A LOT OF THE BASEBALL CLUB ALUMNI HAVE ALREADY SAID THEY'D RECOMMEND ME AT THEIR JOBS!
LIKE OFFICE JOBS?
NAH.
THEY'RE ALL CRAFT JOBS AND STUFF.
Umm...
CAR-PENTRY.
SUSHI CHEF.
A CRAFTS-MAN!
RAMEN CHEF. FISHER-MAN.
BLACKSMITH. BAKER.
Ull...
OH, THIS ISN'T A CRAFT, BUT MAIL CARRIER TOO.
WOW, UH... I CAN KINDA SEE YOU DOING ALL THAT STUFF.
And man, your club's alumni are all over the place!
AHA HA HA!
REALLY? AWE-SOME!
I ALWAYS THOUGHT IT'D BE COOL TO LEARN SOME KIND OF TRADE.
MAAAAN!
WHY'RE YOU ALWAYS THE LUCKY ONE?

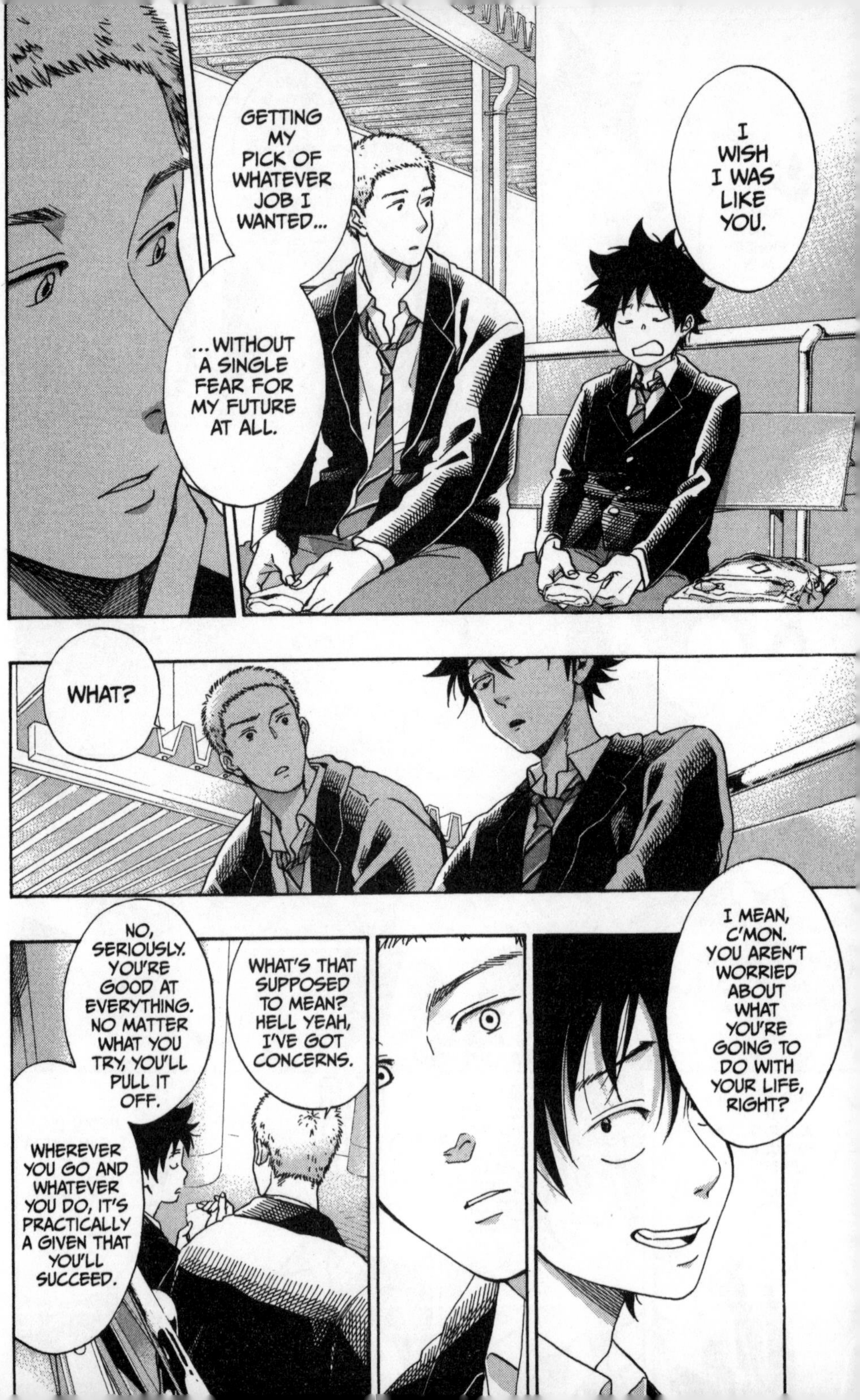
I WISH I WAS LIKE YOU.
GETTING MY PICK OF WHATEVER JOB I WANTED...
...WITHOUT A SINGLE FEAR FOR MY FUTURE AT ALL.
WHAT?
I MEAN, C'MON. YOU AREN'T WORRIED ABOUT WHAT YOU'RE GOING TO DO WITH YOUR LIFE, RIGHT?
WHAT'S THAT SUPPOSED TO MEAN? HELL YEAH, I'VE GOT CONCERNS.
NO, SERIOUSLY. YOU'RE GOOD AT EVERYTHING. NO MATTER WHAT YOU TRY, YOU'LL PULL IT OFF.
WHEREVER YOU GO AND WHATEVER YOU DO, IT'S PRACTICALLY A GIVEN THAT YOU'LL SUCCEED.

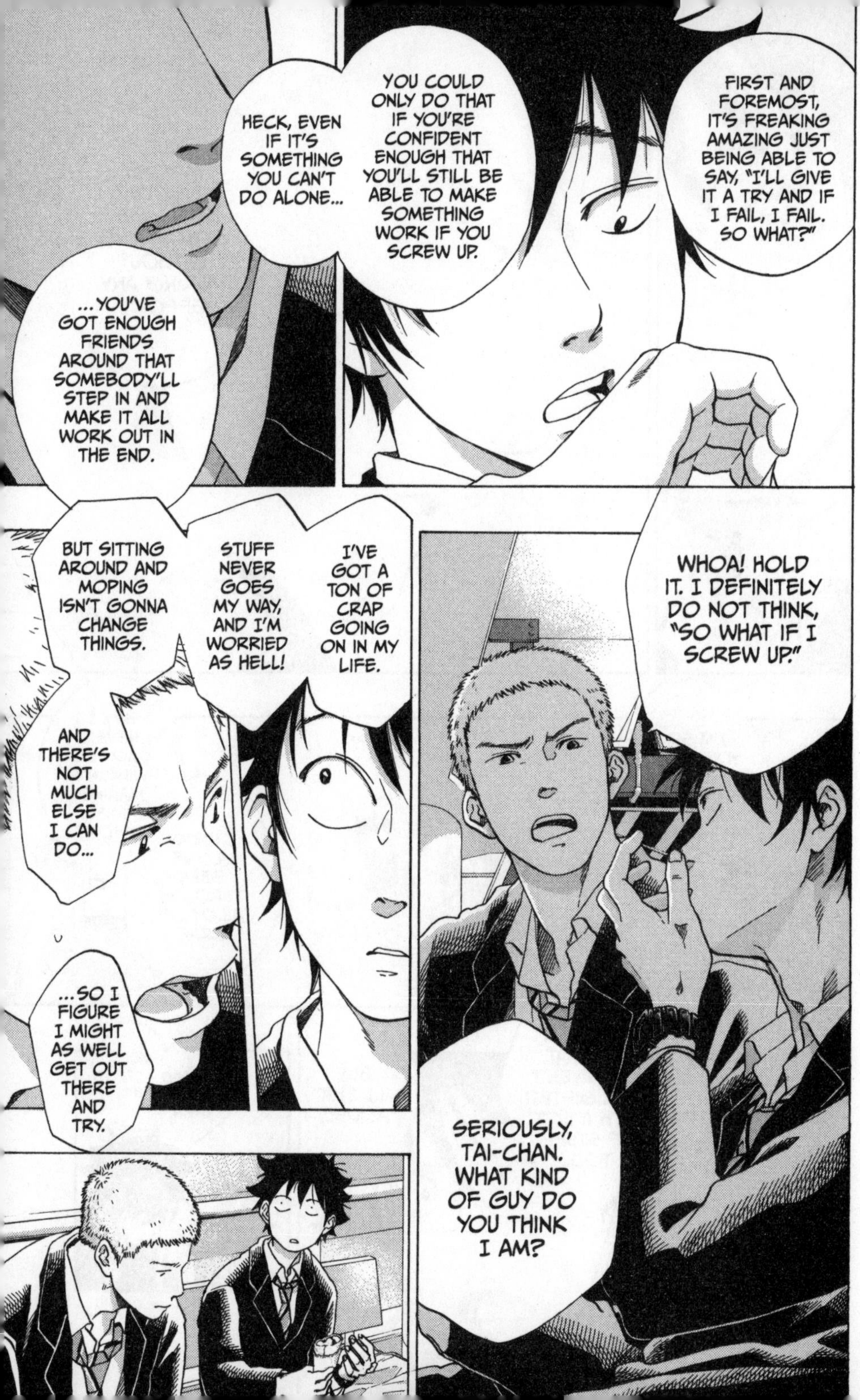
FIRST AND FOREMOST, IT'S FREAKING AMAZING JUST BEING ABLE TO SAY, "I'LL GIVE IT A TRY AND IF I FAIL, I FAIL. SO WHAT?"
YOU COULD ONLY DO THAT IF YOU'RE CONFIDENT ENOUGH THAT YOU'LL STILL BE ABLE TO MAKE SOMETHING WORK IF YOU SCREW UP.
HECK, EVEN IF IT'S SOMETHING YOU CAN'T DO ALONE...
...YOU'VE GOT ENOUGH FRIENDS AROUND THAT SOMEBODY'LL STEP IN AND MAKE IT ALL WORK OUT IN THE END.
WHOA! HOLD IT. I DEFINITELY DO NOT THINK, "SO WHAT IF I SCREW UP."
SERIOUSLY, TAI-CHAN. WHAT KIND OF GUY DO YOU THINK I AM?
I'VE GOT A TON OF CRAP GOING ON IN MY LIFE.
STUFF NEVER GOES MY WAY, AND I'M WORRIED AS HELL!
BUT SITTING AROUND AND MOPING ISN'T GONNA CHANGE THINGS.
AND THERE'S NOT MUCH ELSE I CAN DO...
...SO I FIGURE I MIGHT AS WELL GET OUT THERE AND TRY.

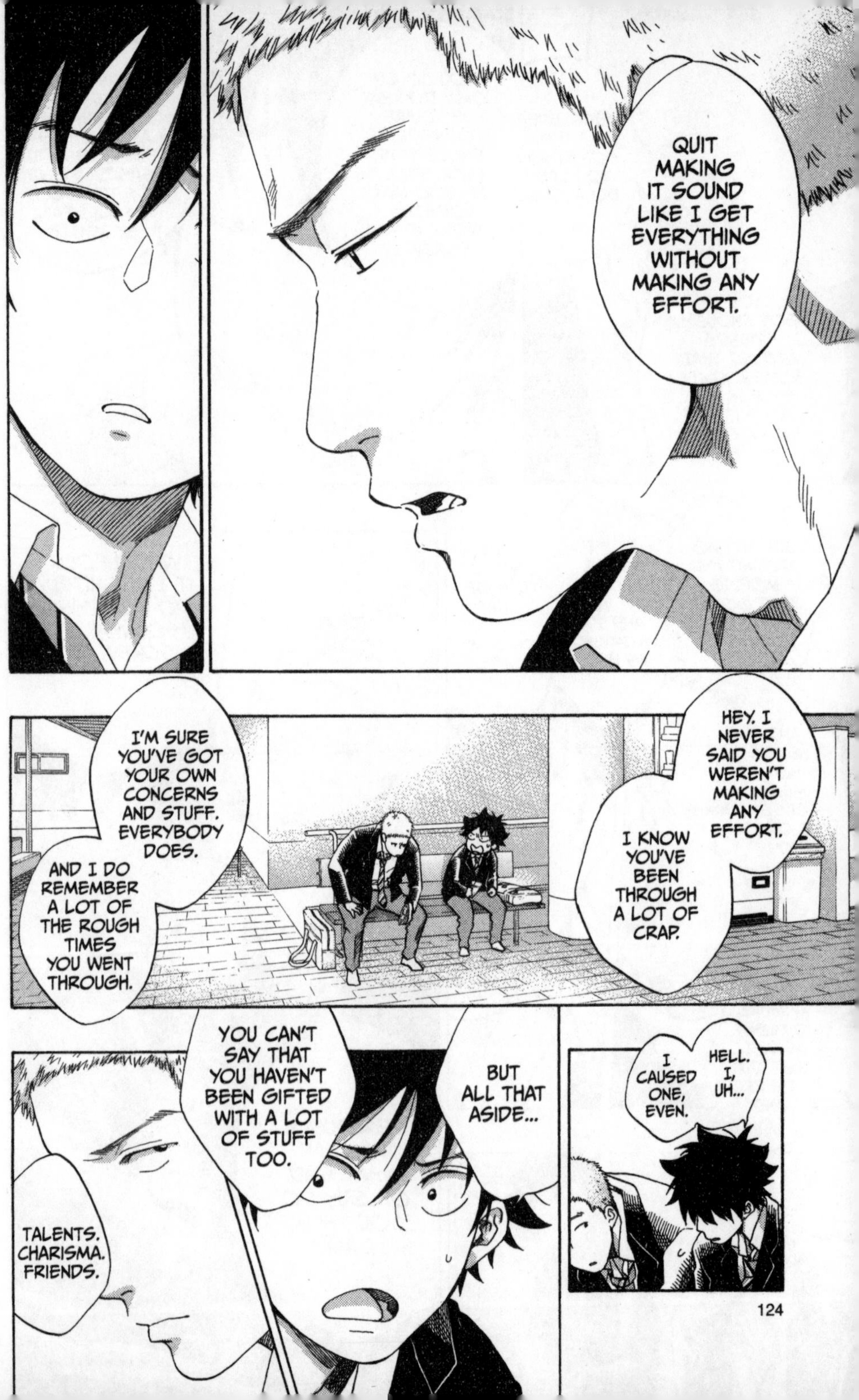
QUIT MAKING IT SOUND LIKE I GET EVERYTHING WITHOUT MAKING ANY EFFORT.
HEY. I NEVER SAID YOU WEREN'T MAKING ANY EFFORT.
I KNOW YOU'VE BEEN THROUGH A LOT OF CRAP.
I'M SURE YOU'VE GOT YOUR OWN CONCERNS AND STUFF. EVERYBODY DOES.
AND I DO REMEMBER A LOT OF THE ROUGH TIMES YOU WENT THROUGH.
HELL. I, UH...
I CAUSED ONE, EVEN.
BUT ALL THAT ASIDE...
YOU CAN'T SAY THAT YOU HAVEN'T BEEN GIFTED WITH A LOT OF STUFF TOO.
TALENTS. CHARISMA. FRIENDS.

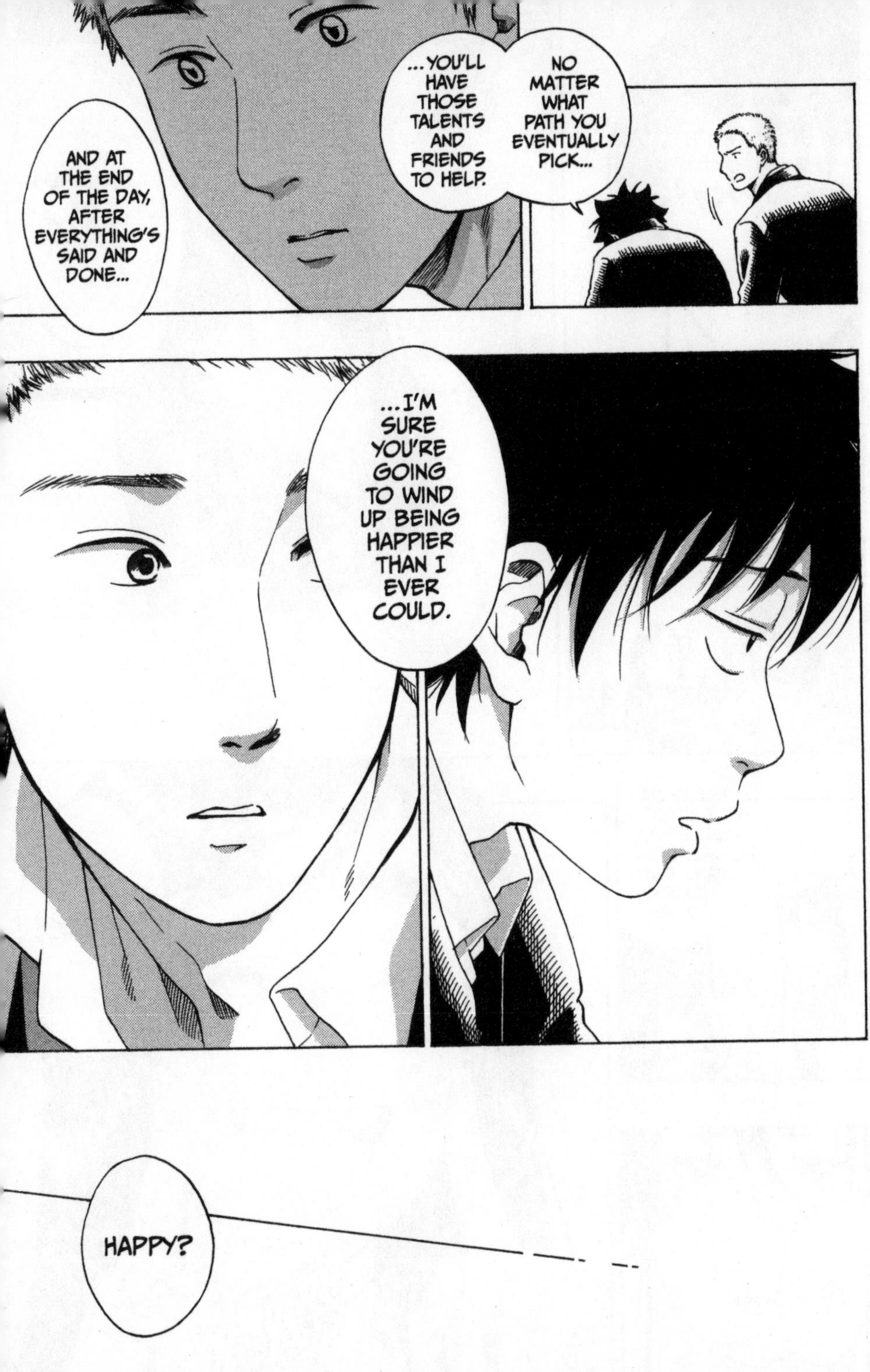
NO MATTER WHAT PATH YOU EVENTUALLY PICK...
...YOU'LL HAVE THOSE TALENTS AND FRIENDS TO HELP.
AND AT THE END OF THE DAY, AFTER EVERYTHING'S SAID AND DONE...
...I'M SURE YOU'RE GOING TO WIND UP BEING HAPPIER THAN I EVER COULD.
HAPPY?

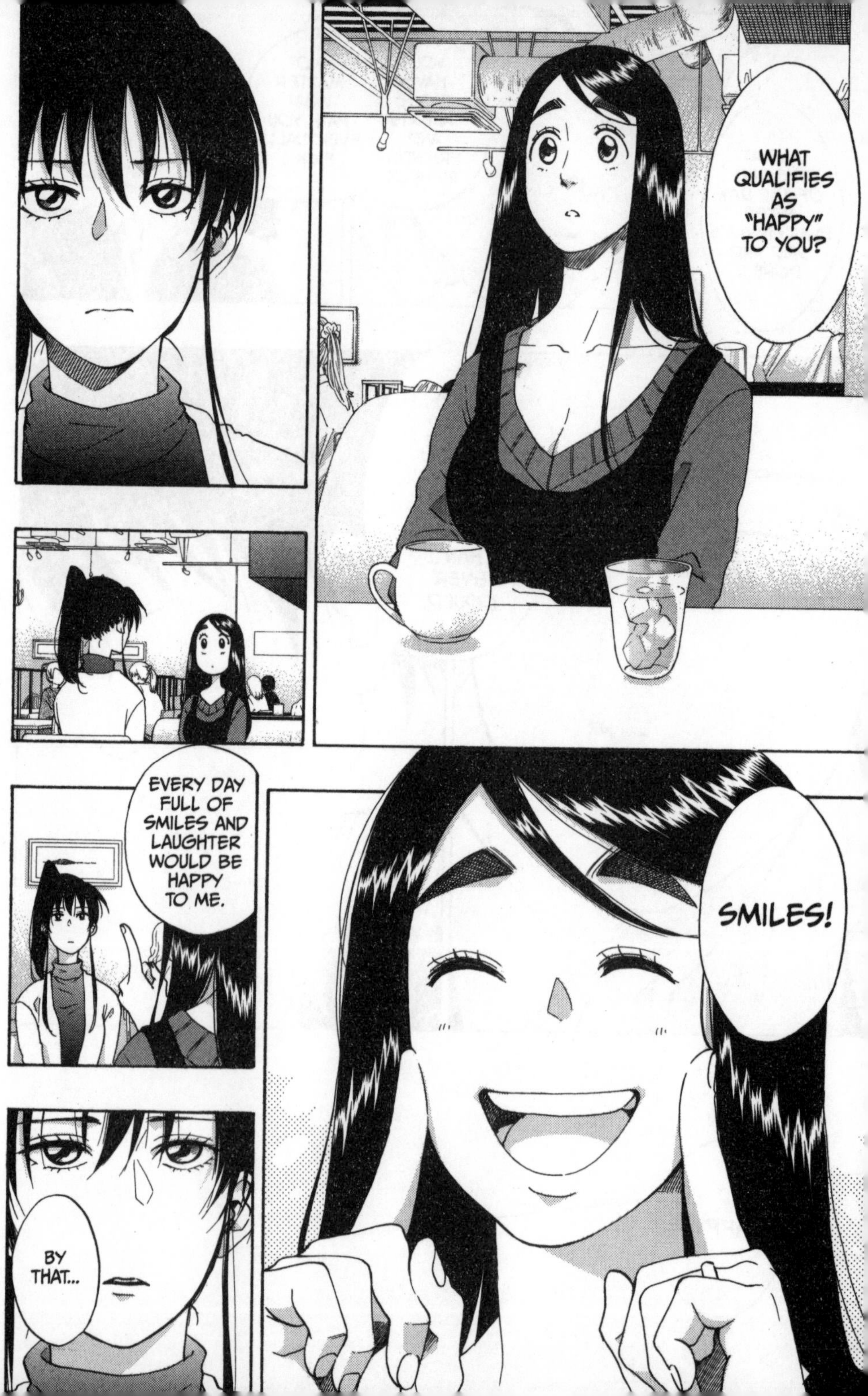
WHAT QUALIFIES AS "HAPPY" TO YOU?
SMILES!
EVERY DAY FULL OF SMILES AND LAUGHTER WOULD BE HAPPY TO ME.
BY THAT...

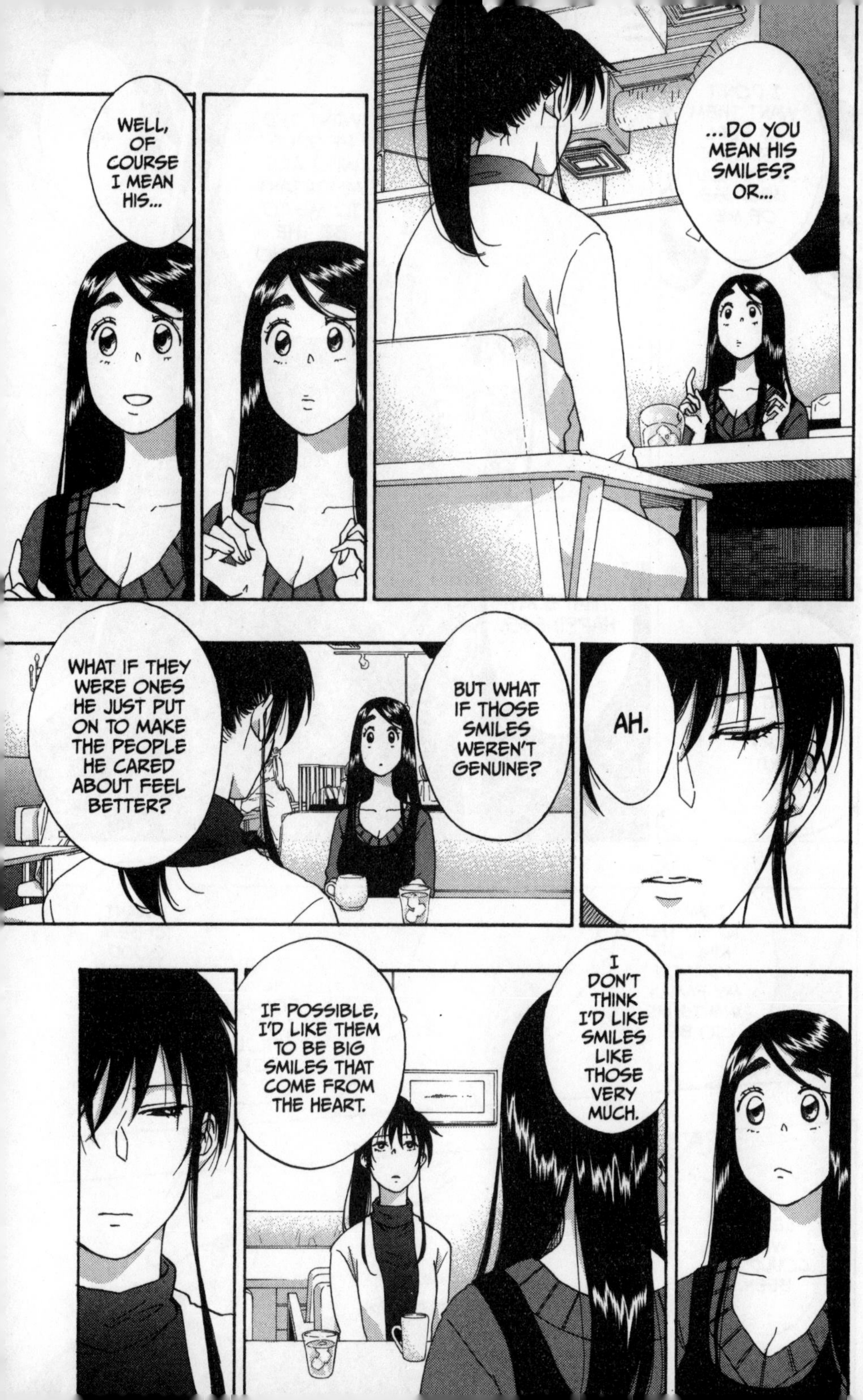
...DO YOU MEAN HIS SMILES? OR...
WELL, OF COURSE I MEAN HIS...
AH.
BUT WHAT IF THOSE SMILES WEREN'T GENUINE?
WHAT IF THEY WERE ONES HE JUST PUT ON TO MAKE THE PEOPLE HE CARED ABOUT FEEL BETTER?
I DON'T THINK I'D LIKE SMILES LIKE THOSE VERY MUCH.
IF POSSIBLE, I'D LIKE THEM TO BE BIG SMILES THAT COME FROM THE HEART.

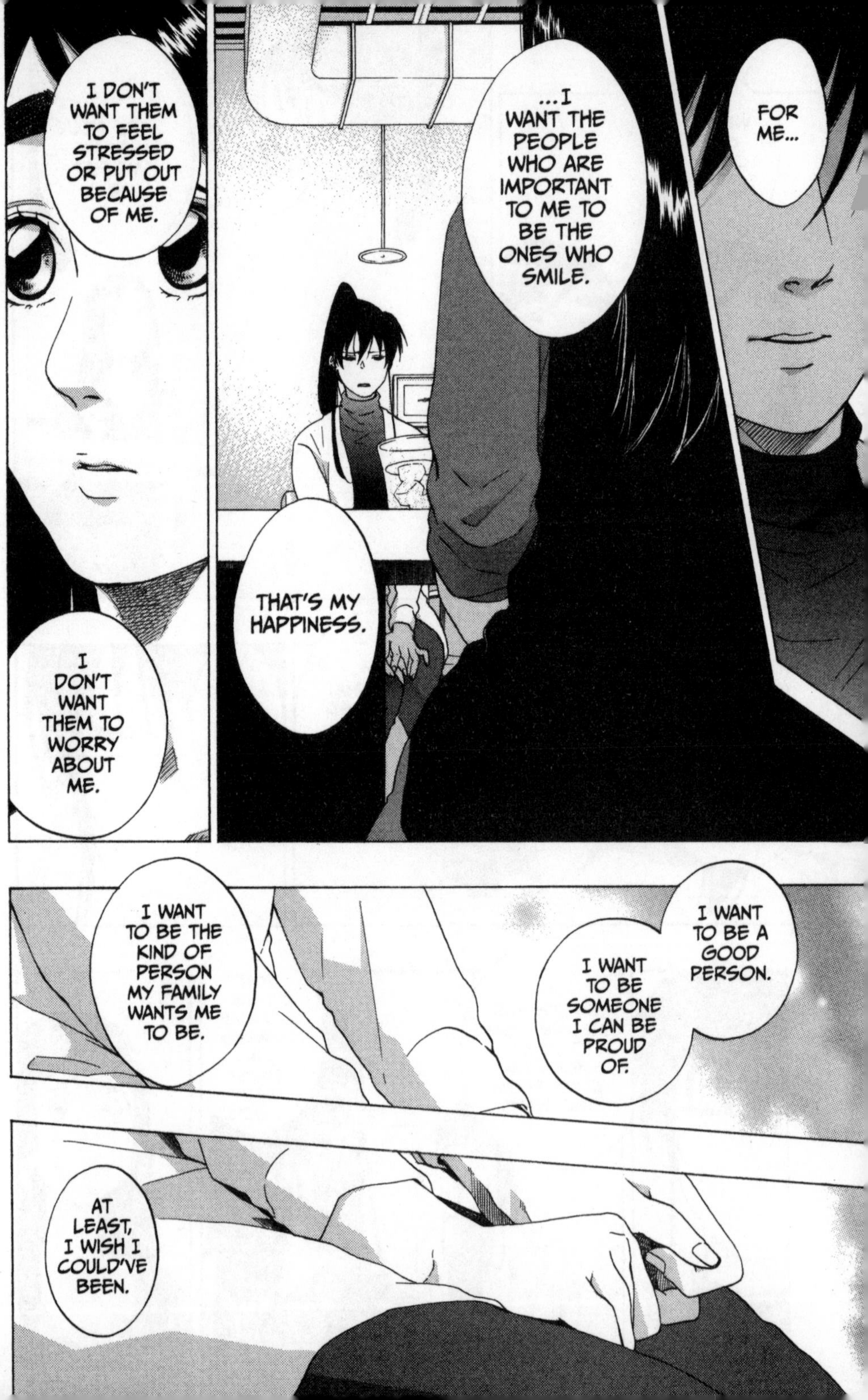
FOR ME...
...I WANT THE PEOPLE WHO ARE IMPORTANT TO ME TO BE THE ONES WHO SMILE.
THAT'S MY HAPPINESS.
I DON'T WANT THEM TO FEEL STRESSED OR PUT OUT BECAUSE OF ME.
I DON'T WANT THEM TO WORRY ABOUT ME.
I WANT TO BE A GOOD PERSON.
I WANT TO BE SOMEONE I CAN BE PROUD OF.
I WANT TO BE THE KIND OF PERSON MY FAMILY WANTS ME TO BE.
AT LEAST, I WISH I COULD'VE BEEN.

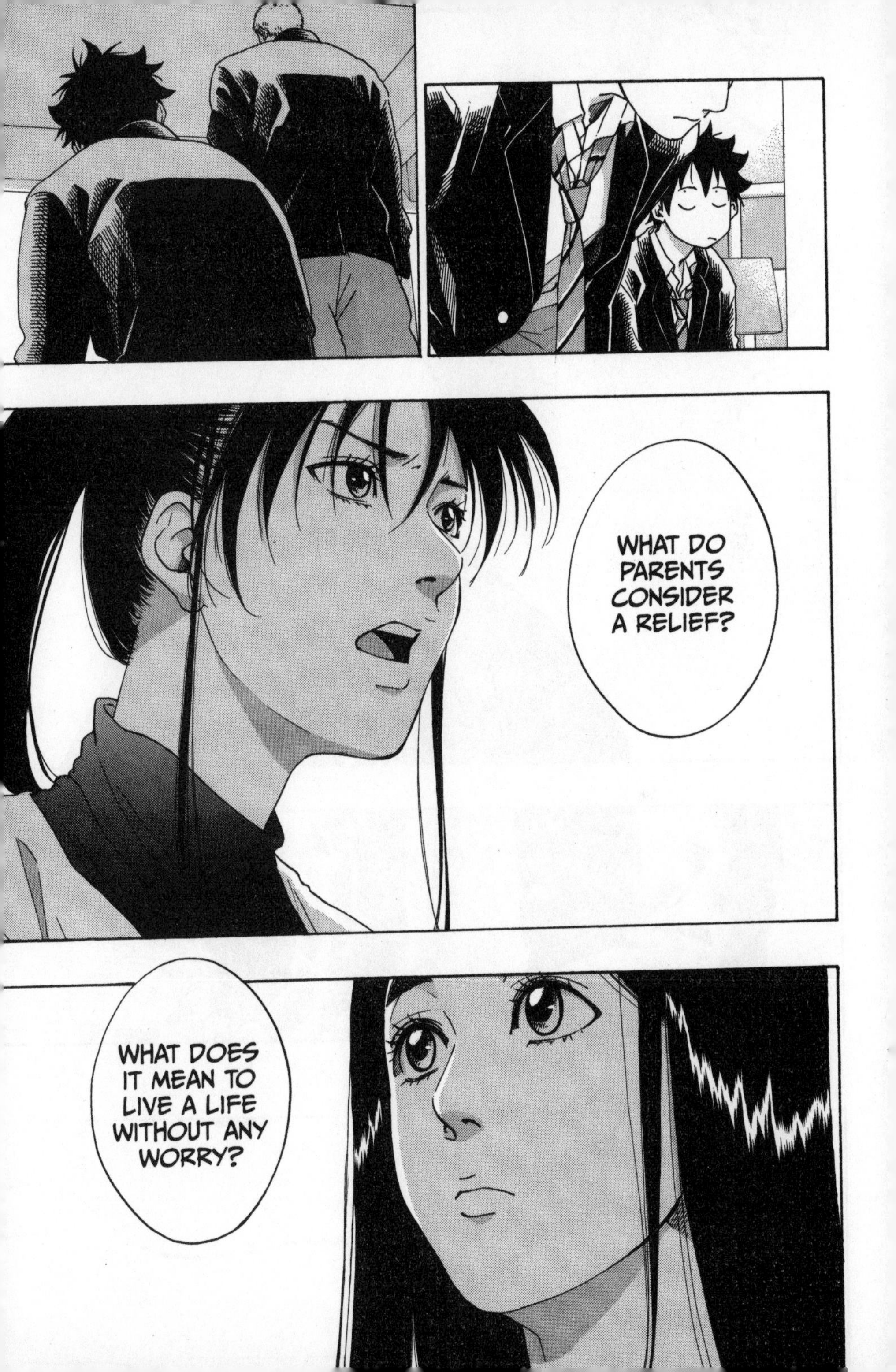
WHAT DO PARENTS CONSIDER A RELIEF?
WHAT DOES IT MEAN TO LIVE A LIFE WITHOUT ANY WORRY?

IS IT BEING NORMAL...

...AND LIVING IN THE SAME WAY AS EVERYBODY ELSE?

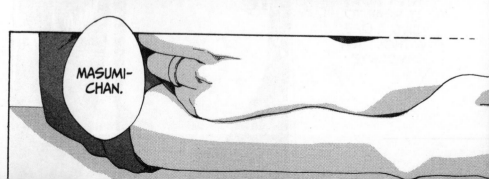

MASUMI-CHAN.

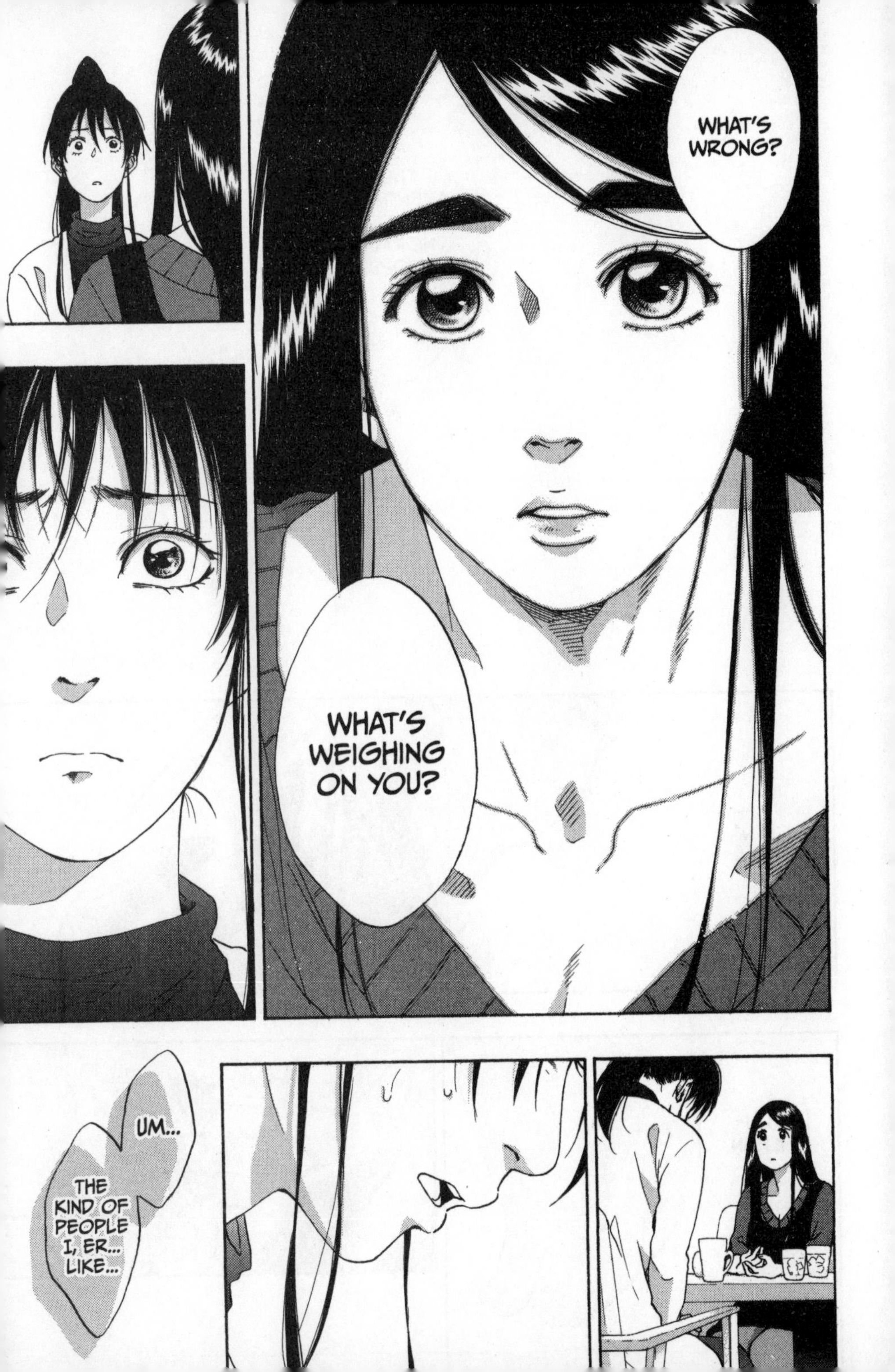
WHAT'S WRONG?
WHAT'S WEIGHING ON YOU?
UM...
THE KIND OF PEOPLE I, ER... LIKE...

THEY
AREN'T THE
SAME AS
NORMAL
PEOPLE.

TAI-
CHAN.

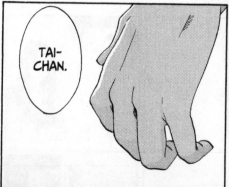

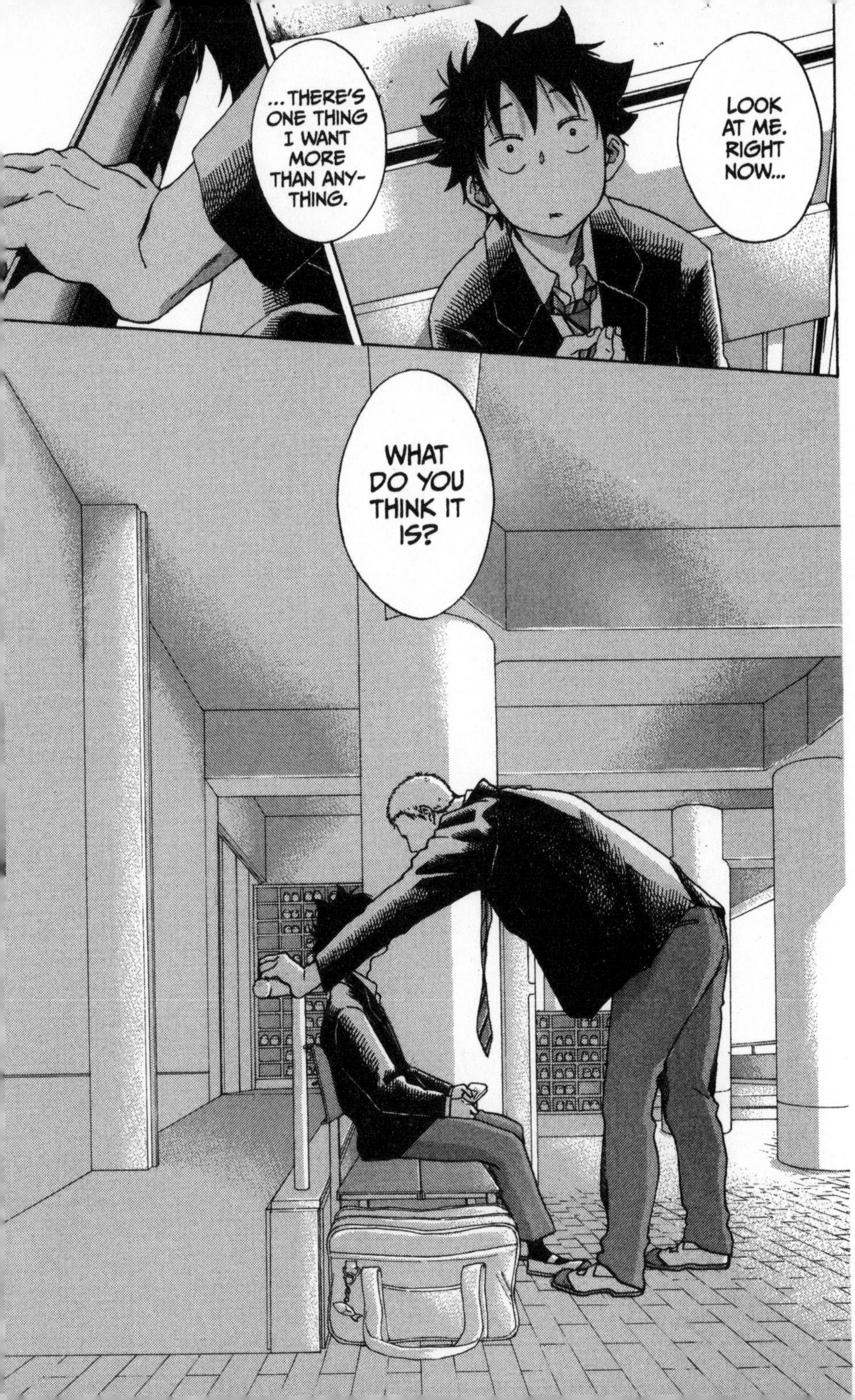
LOOK AT ME. RIGHT NOW...
...THERE'S ONE THING I WANT MORE THAN ANY-THING.
WHAT DO YOU THINK IT IS?

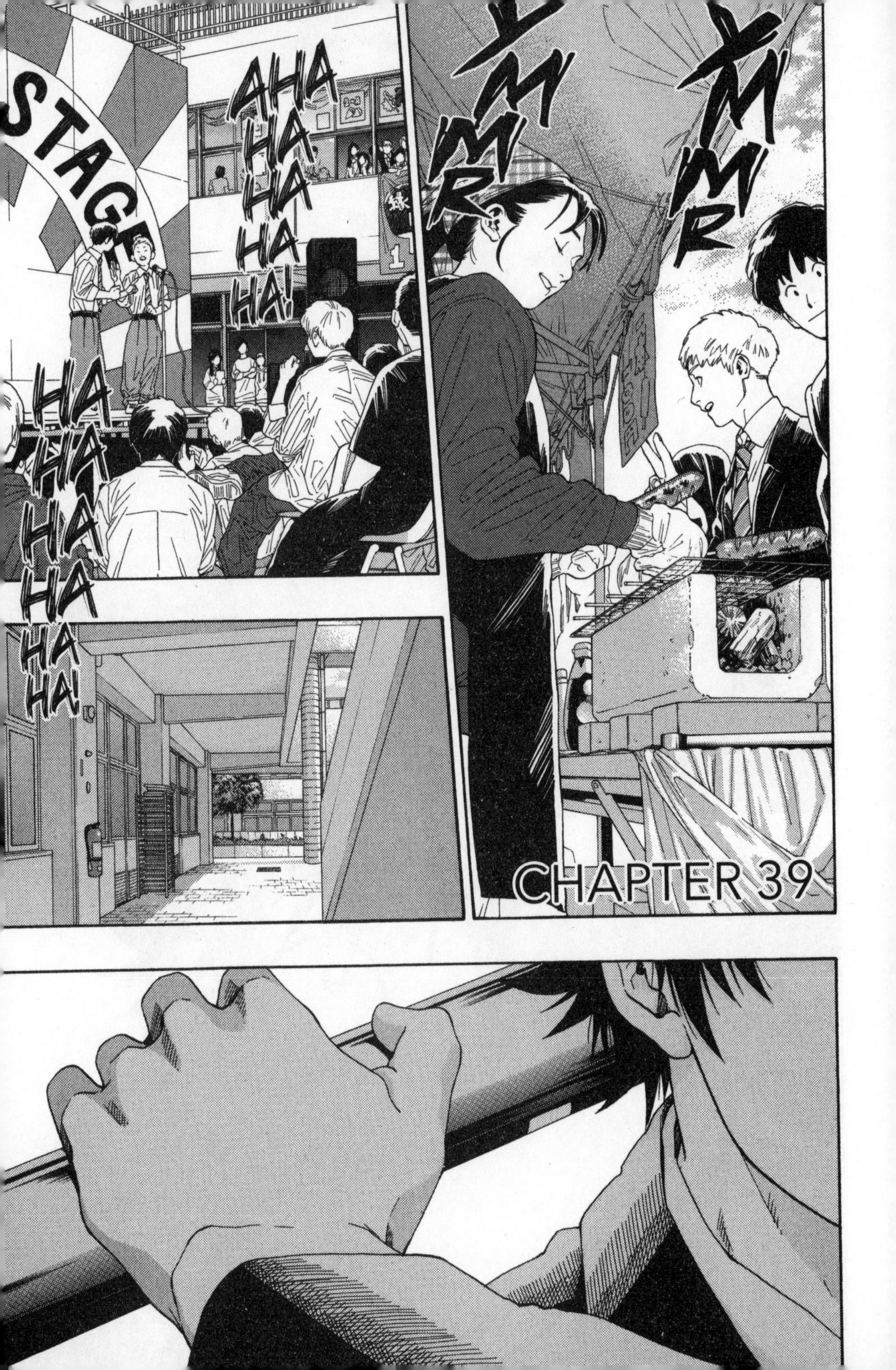
MMMR
MMMR
CHAPTER 39
STAGE
AHA HA HA HA HA HA!
HA HA HA HA HA HA HA HA!

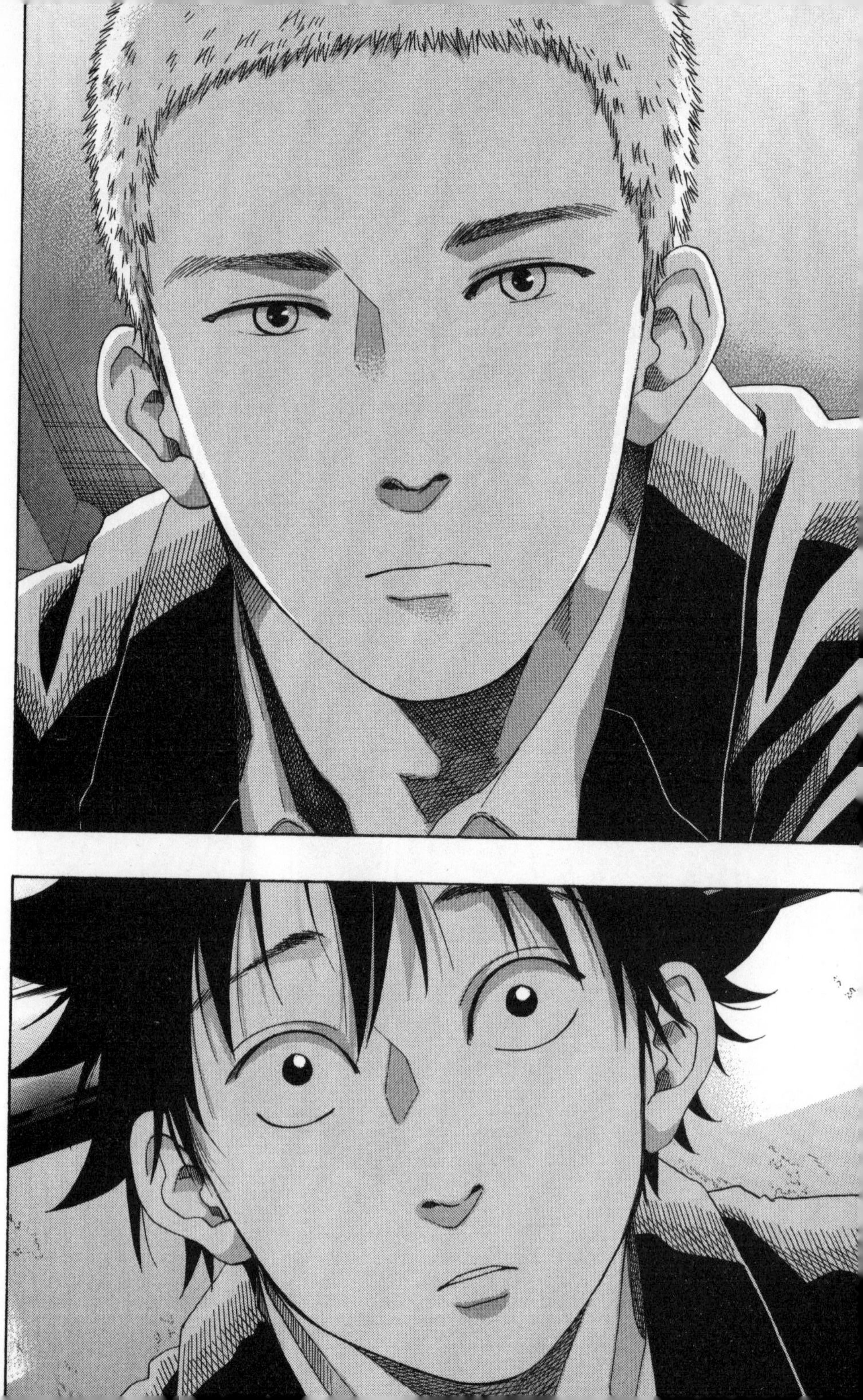

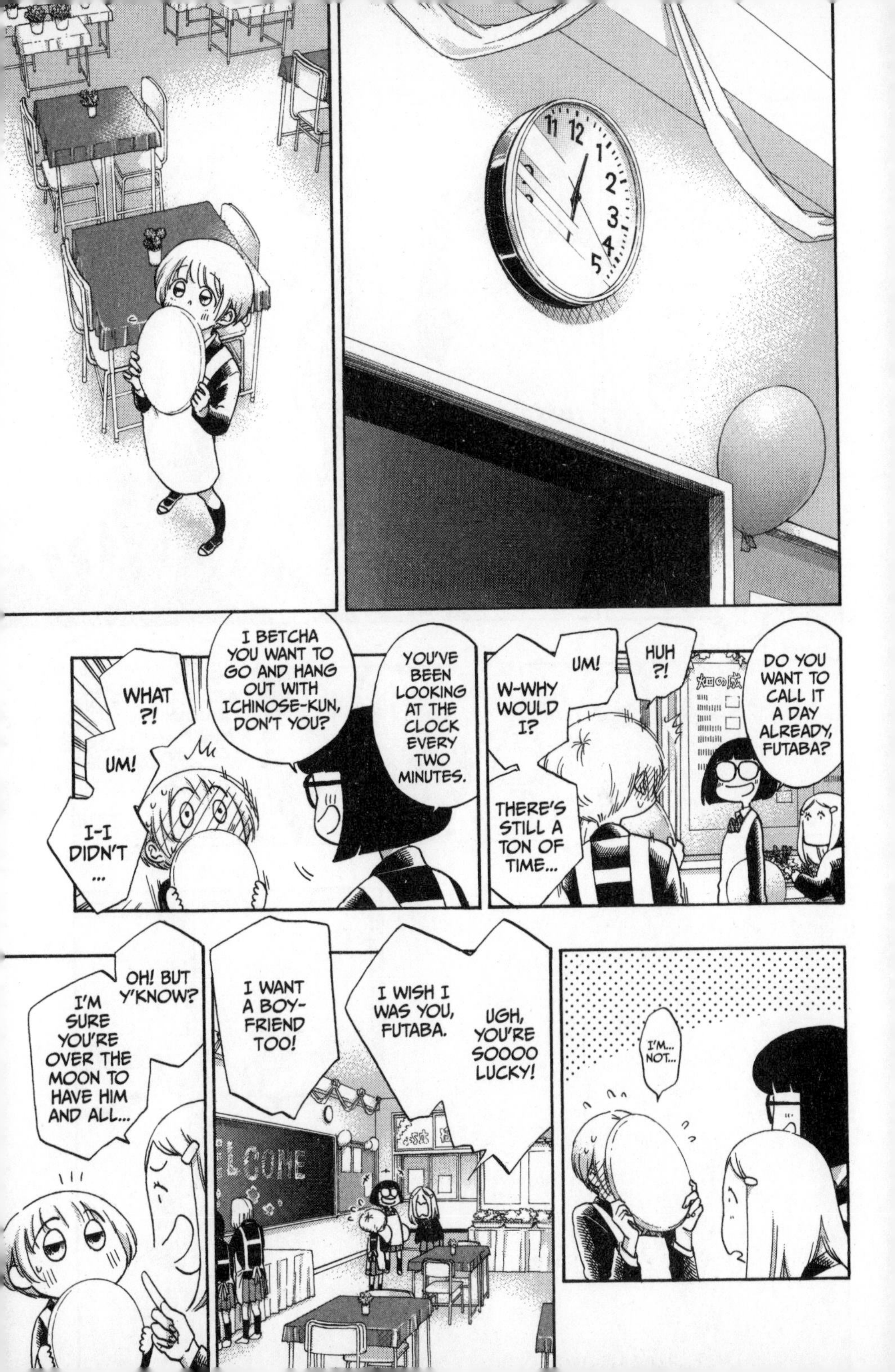
DO YOU WANT TO CALL IT A DAY ALREADY, FUTABA?
HUH?!
UM!
W-WHY WOULD I?
THERE'S STILL A TON OF TIME...
YOU'VE BEEN LOOKING AT THE CLOCK EVERY TWO MINUTES.
I BETCHA YOU WANT TO GO AND HANG OUT WITH ICHINOSE-KUN, DON'T YOU?
WHAT?!
UM!
I-I DIDN'T ...
I'M... NOT...
UGH, YOU'RE SOOOO LUCKY!
I WISH I WAS YOU, FUTABA.
I WANT A BOY-FRIEND TOO!
OH! BUT Y'KNOW?
I'M SURE YOU'RE OVER THE MOON TO HAVE HIM AND ALL...

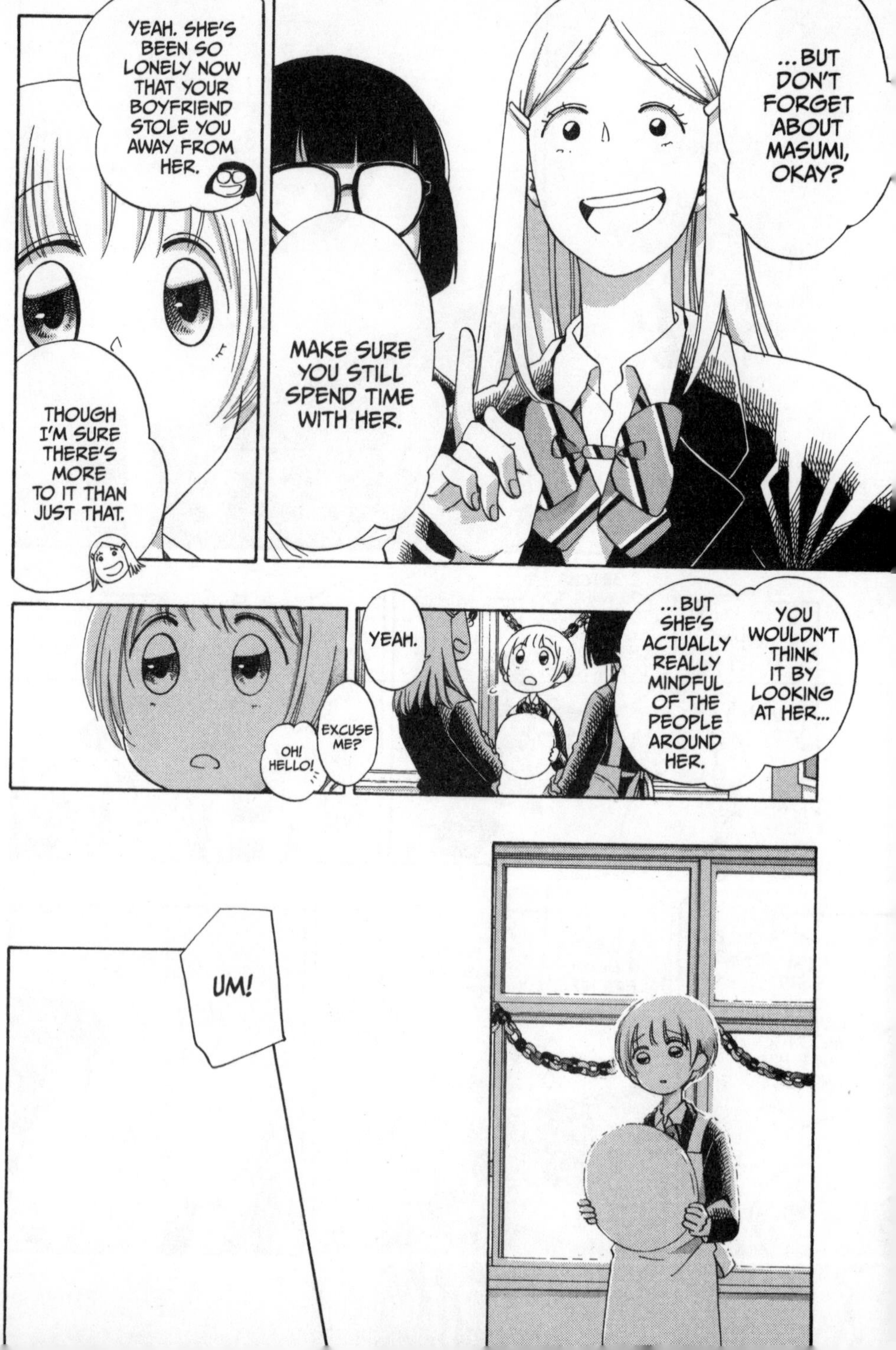
...BUT DON'T FORGET ABOUT MASUMI, OKAY?
MAKE SURE YOU STILL SPEND TIME WITH HER.
YEAH. SHE'S BEEN SO LONELY NOW THAT YOUR BOYFRIEND STOLE YOU AWAY FROM HER.
THOUGH I'M SURE THERE'S MORE TO IT THAN JUST THAT.
YOU WOULDN'T THINK IT BY LOOKING AT HER...
...BUT SHE'S ACTUALLY REALLY MINDFUL OF THE PEOPLE AROUND HER.
YEAH.
EXCUSE ME?
OH! HELLO!
UM!

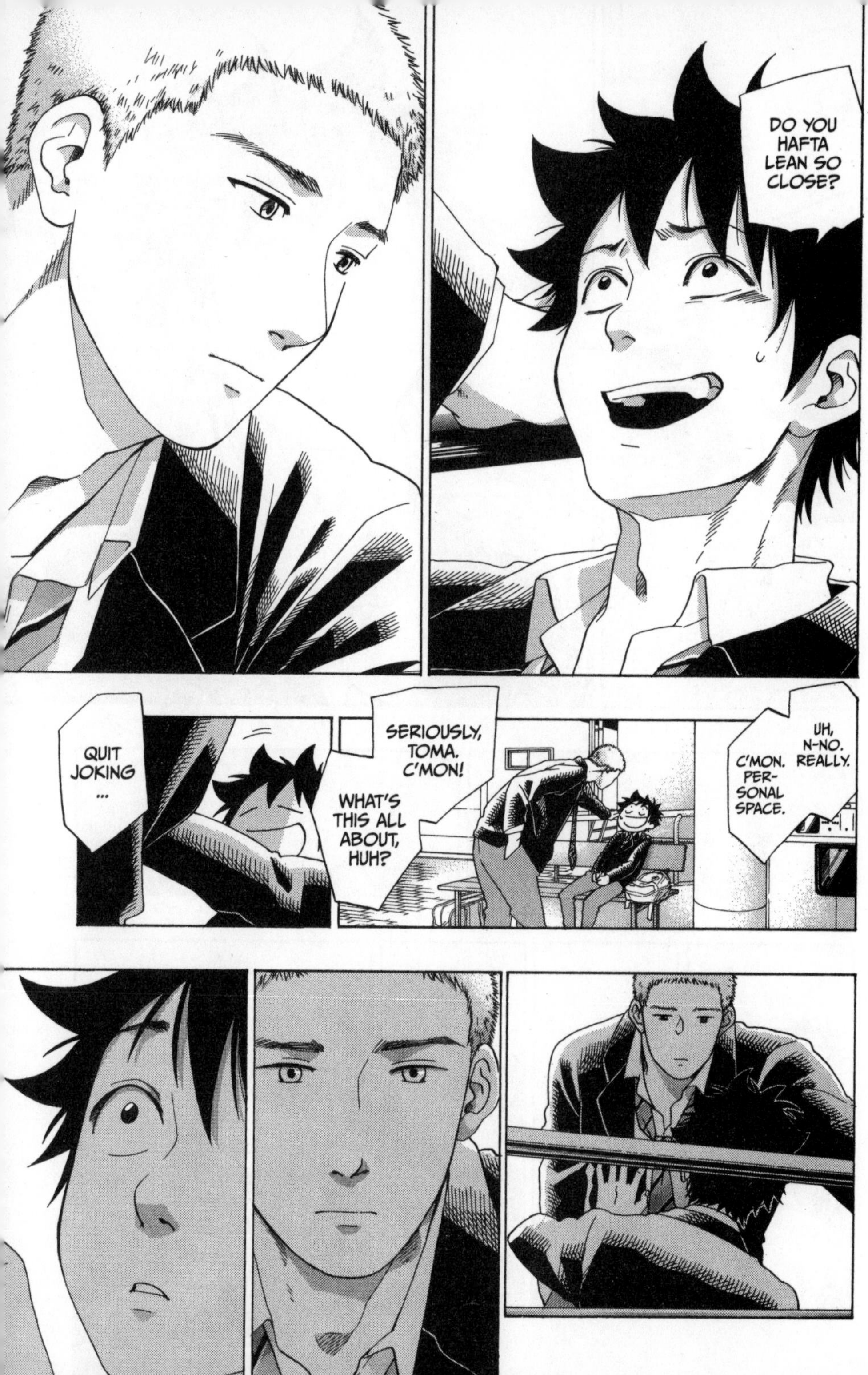
DO YOU HAFTA LEAN SO CLOSE?
UH, N-NO. REALLY.
C'MON. PERSONAL SPACE.
SERIOUSLY, TOMA. C'MON!
WHAT'S THIS ALL ABOUT, HUH?
QUIT JOKING ...

W-WHAT ...
REALLY.
I-I DON'T ...

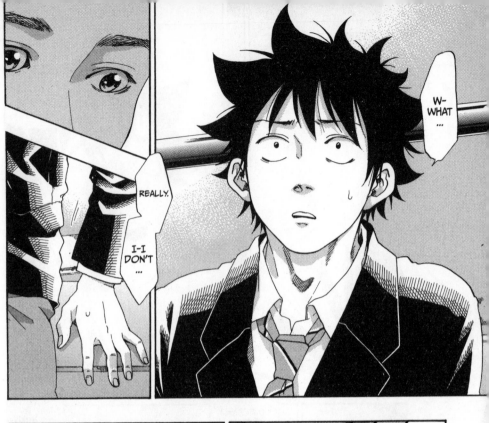

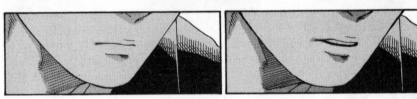

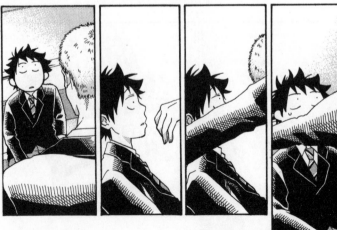

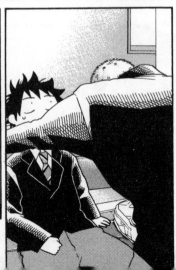

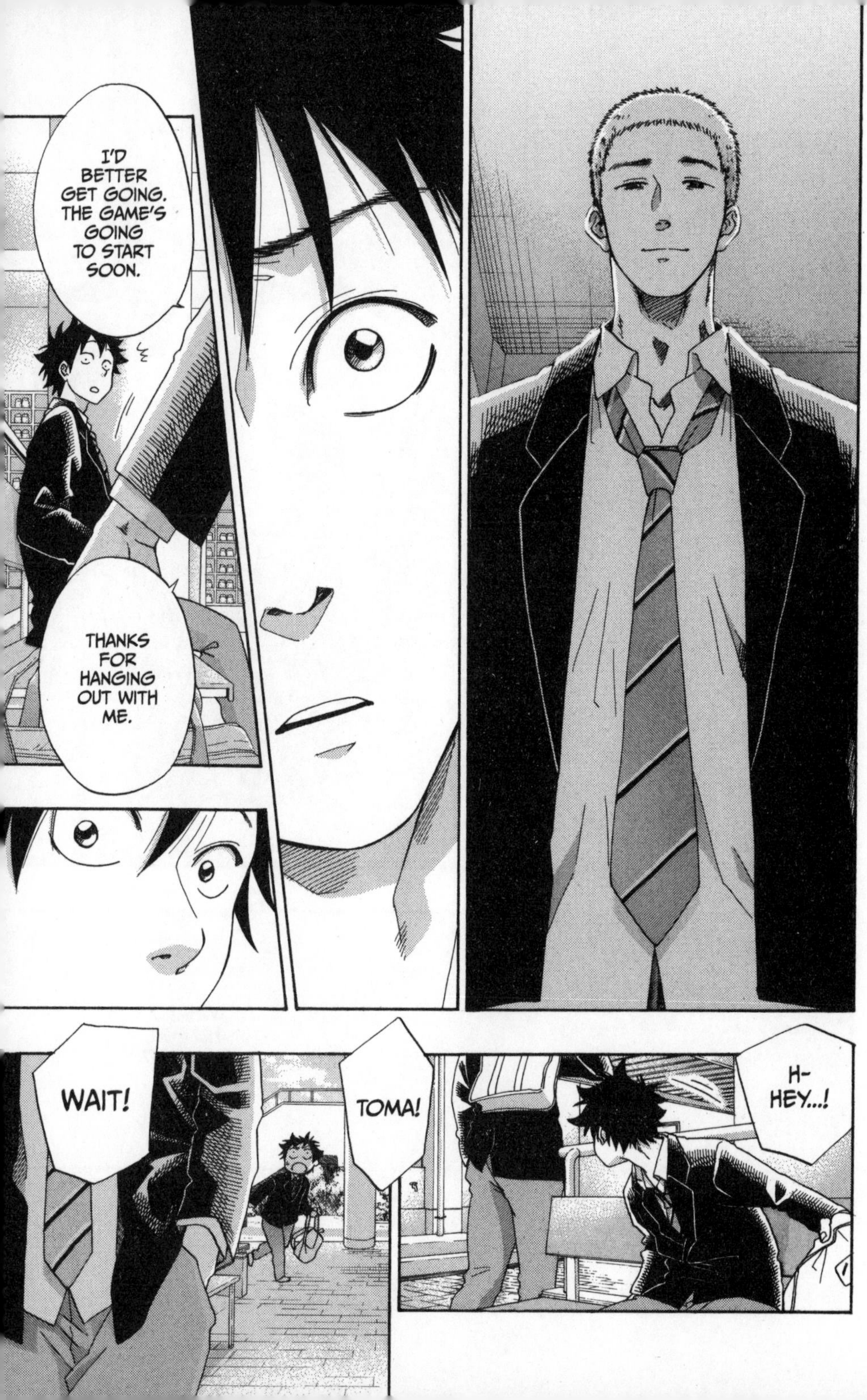
I'D BETTER GET GOING. THE GAME'S GOING TO START SOON.
THANKS FOR HANGING OUT WITH ME.
H- HEY...!
TOMA!
WAIT!

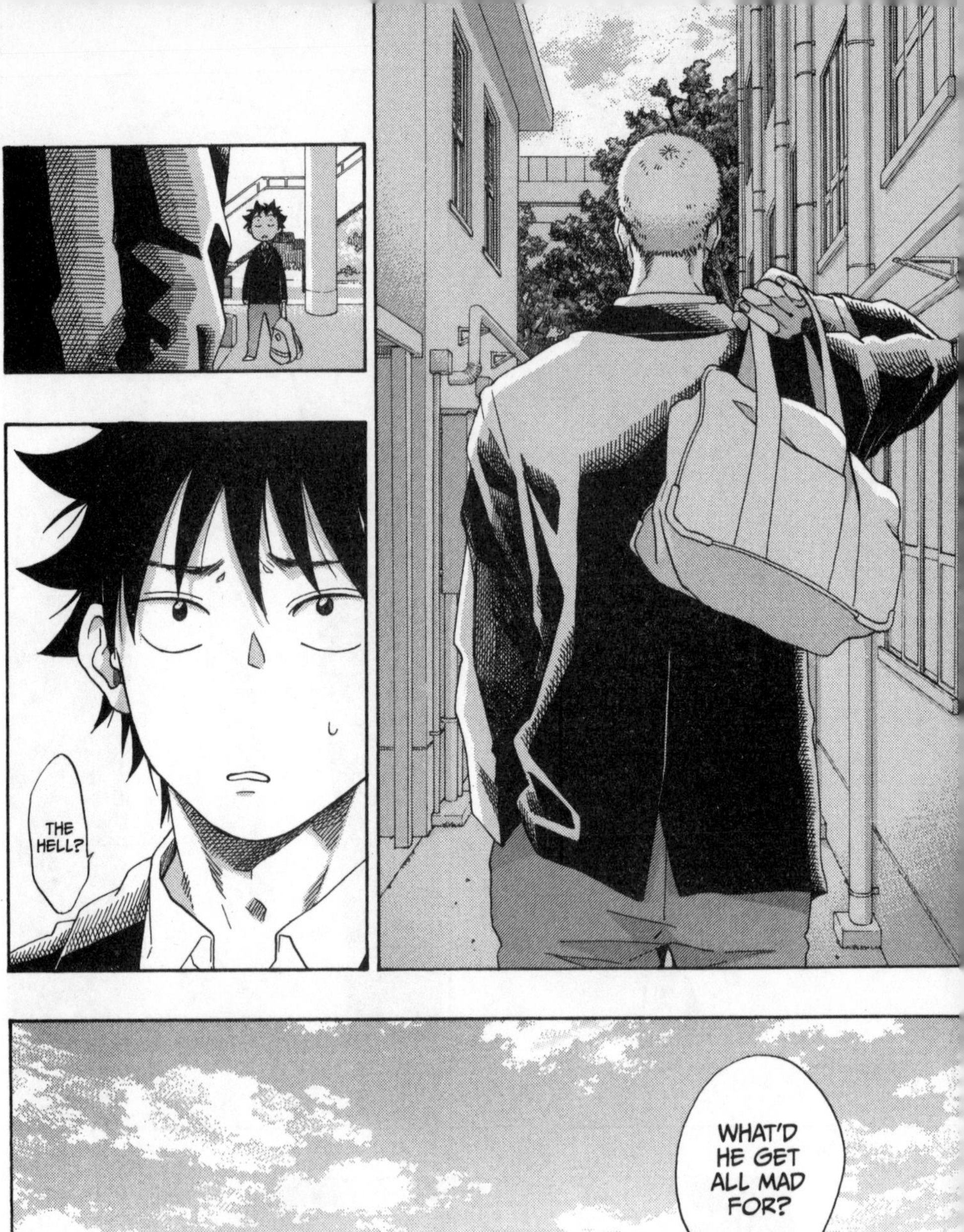
THE HELL?
WHAT'D HE GET ALL MAD FOR?

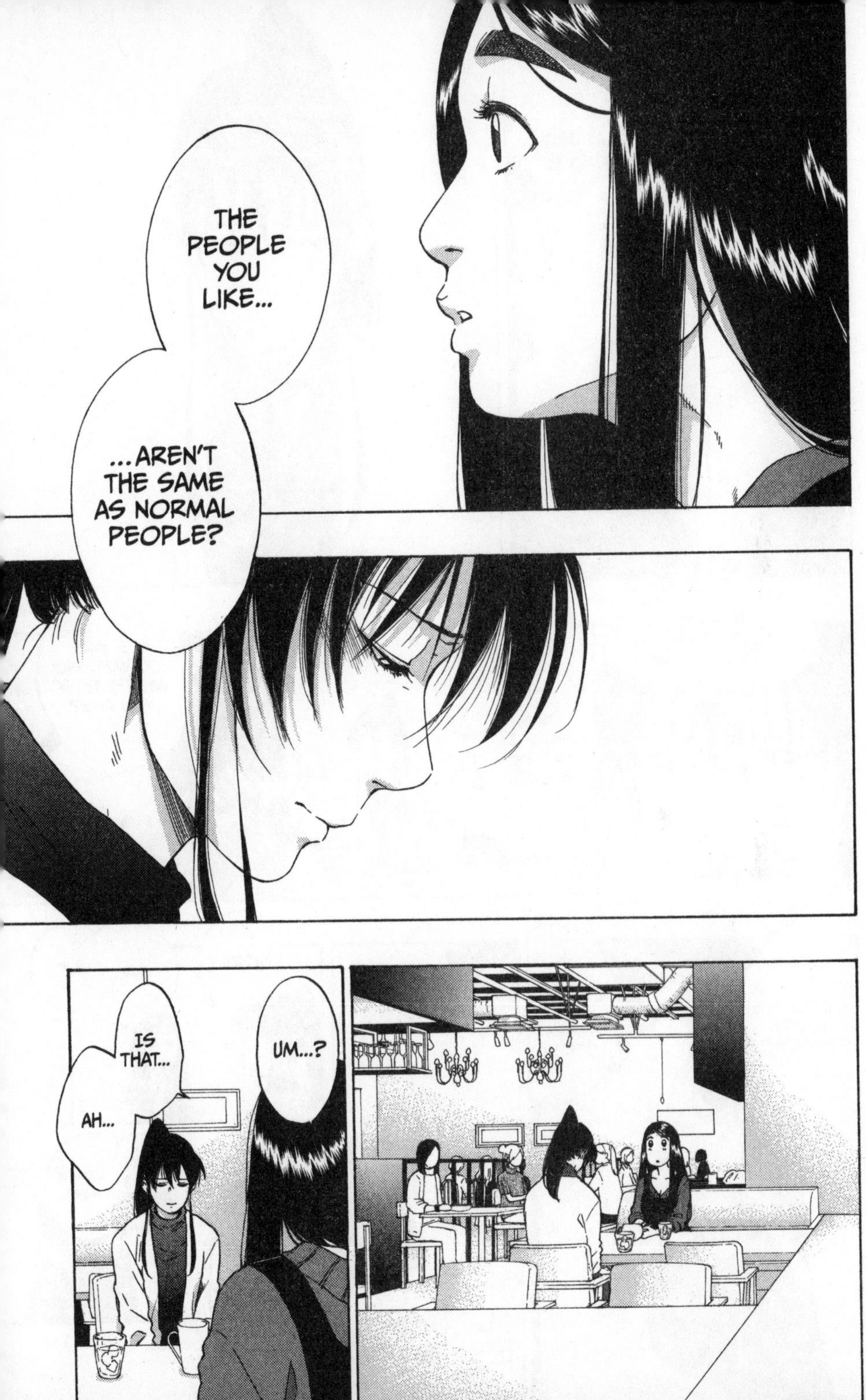
THE PEOPLE YOU LIKE...
...AREN'T THE SAME AS NORMAL PEOPLE?
UM...?
IS THAT...
AH...

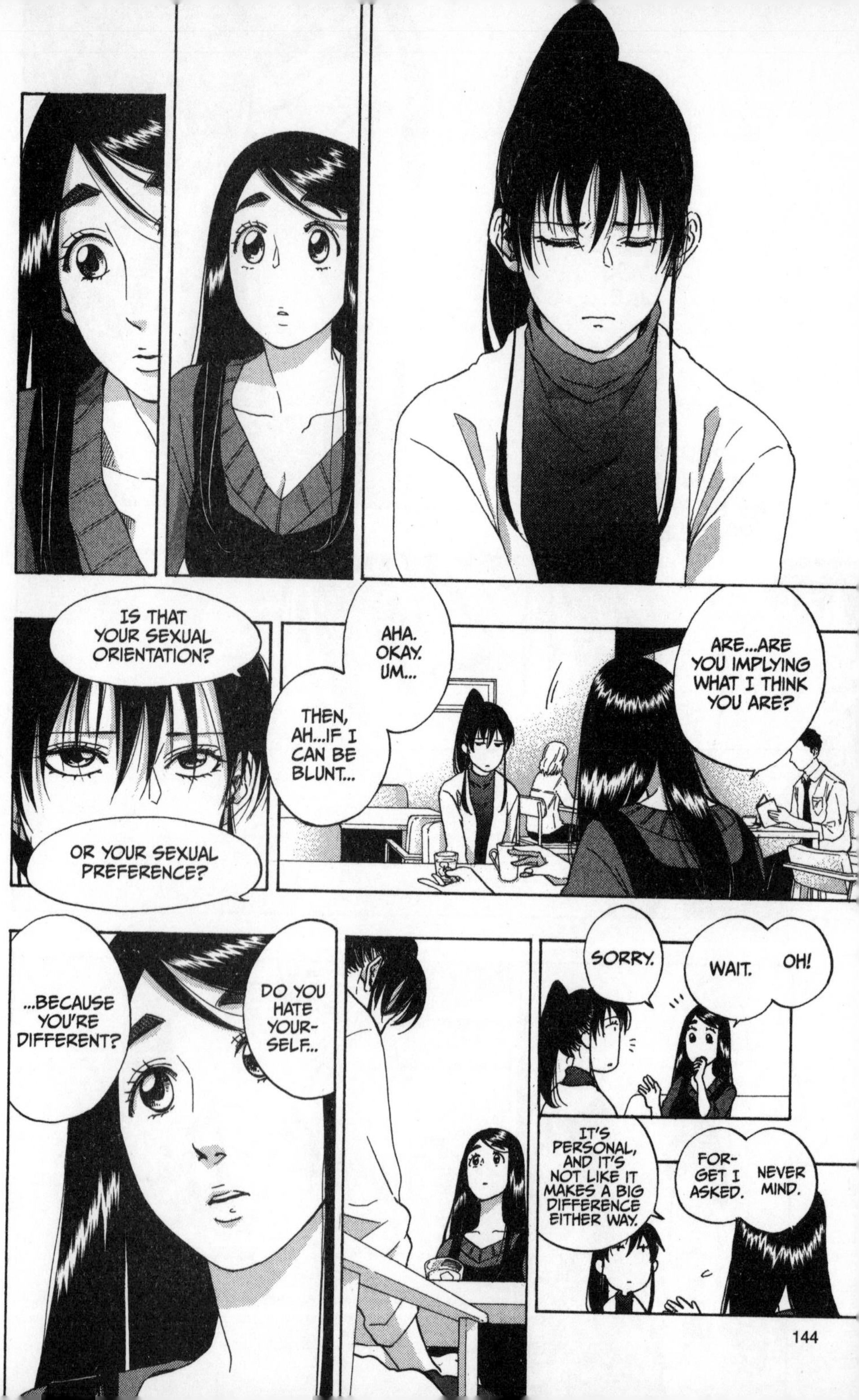
ARE...ARE YOU IMPLYING WHAT I THINK YOU ARE?
AHA. OKAY. UM...
THEN, AH...IF I CAN BE BLUNT...
IS THAT YOUR SEXUAL ORIENTATION?
OR YOUR SEXUAL PREFERENCE?
OH!
WAIT.
SORRY.
NEVER MIND.
FOR-GET I ASKED.
IT'S PERSONAL, AND IT'S NOT LIKE IT MAKES A BIG DIFFERENCE EITHER WAY.
DO YOU HATE YOUR-SELF...
...BECAUSE YOU'RE DIFFERENT?

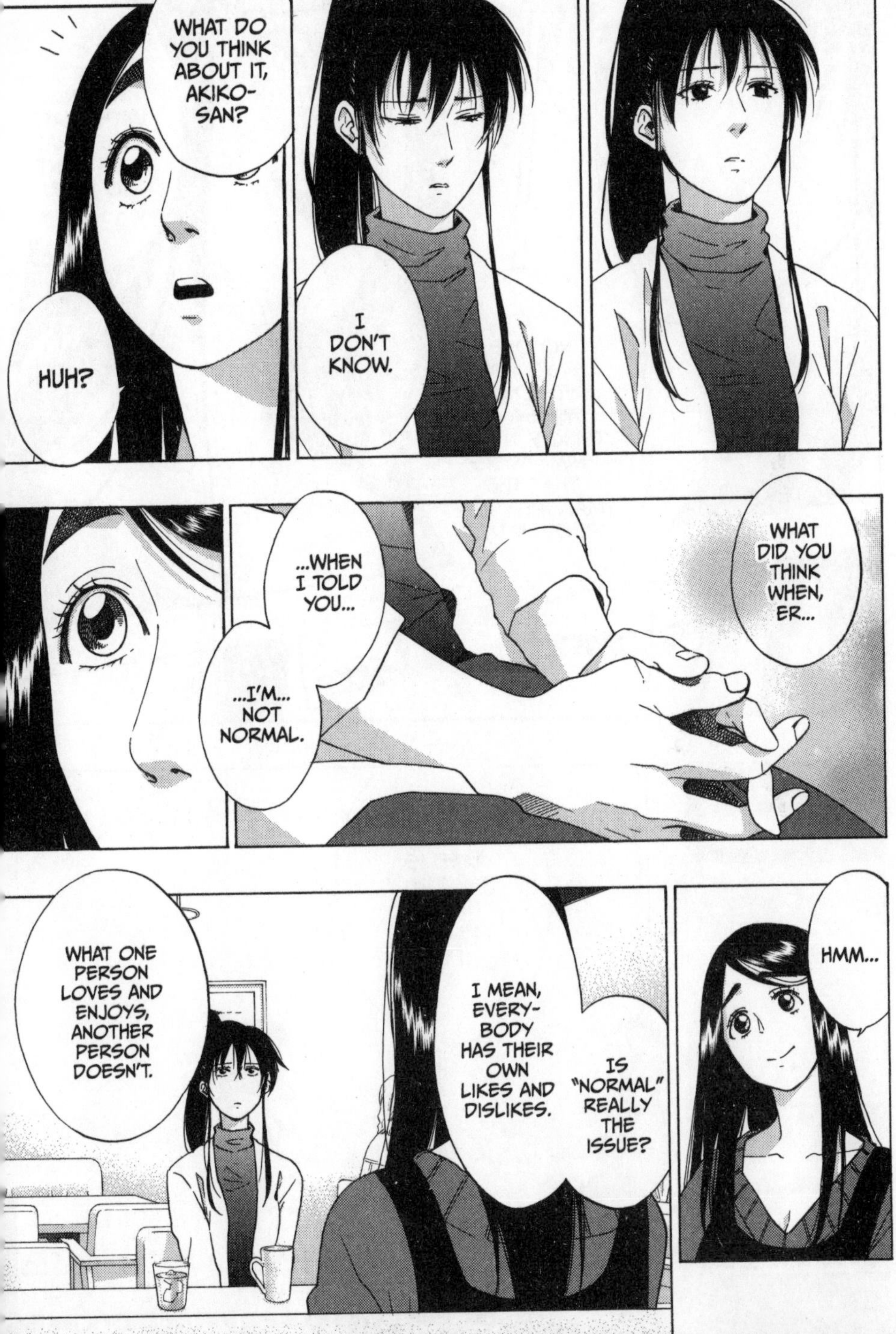
I DON'T KNOW.
WHAT DO YOU THINK ABOUT IT, AKIKO-SAN?
HUH?
WHAT DID YOU THINK WHEN, ER...
...WHEN I TOLD YOU...
...I'M... NOT NORMAL.
HMM...
IS "NORMAL" REALLY THE ISSUE?
I MEAN, EVERYBODY HAS THEIR OWN LIKES AND DISLIKES.
WHAT ONE PERSON LOVES AND ENJOYS, ANOTHER PERSON DOESN'T.

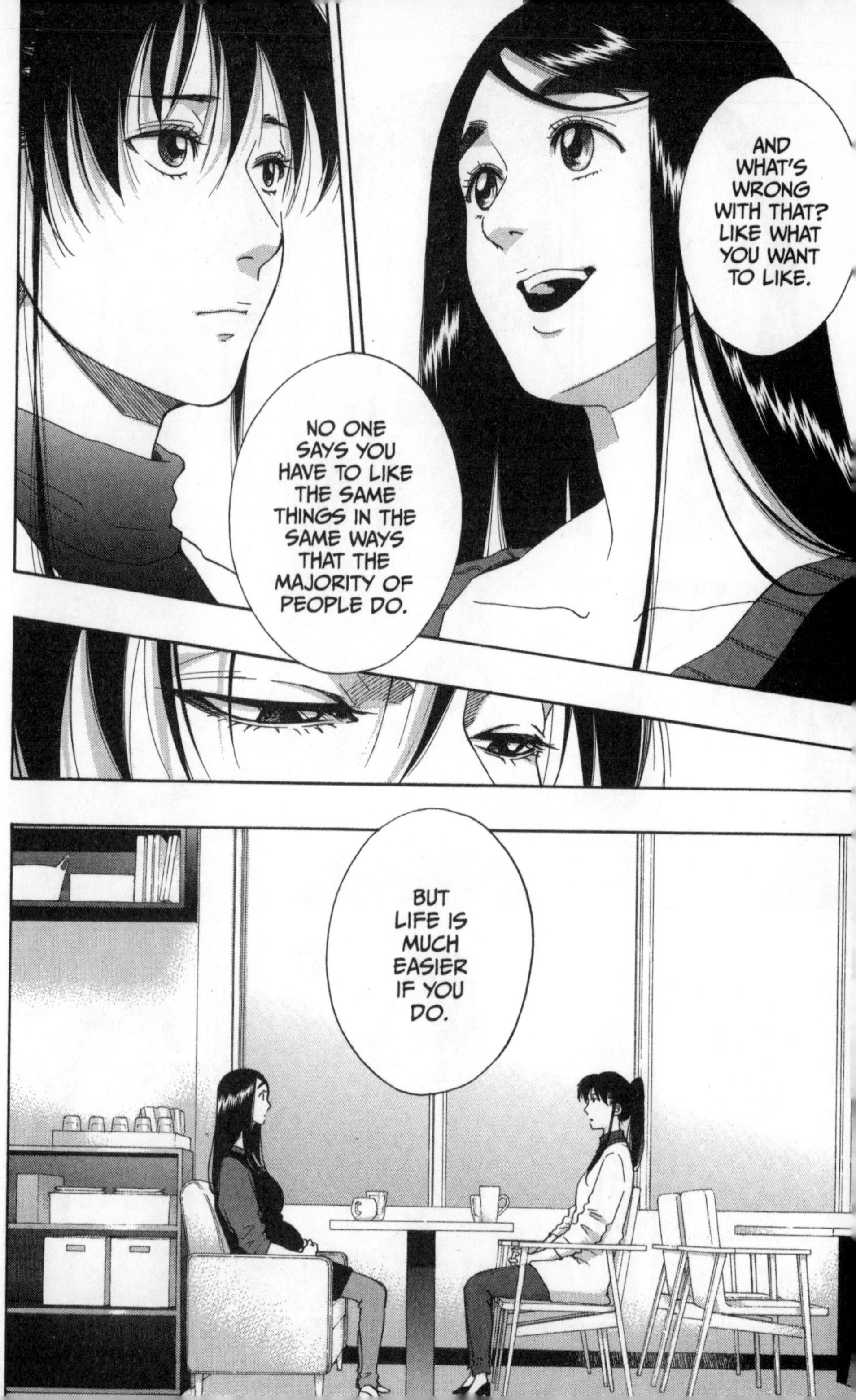
AND WHAT'S WRONG WITH THAT? LIKE WHAT YOU WANT TO LIKE.
NO ONE SAYS YOU HAVE TO LIKE THE SAME THINGS IN THE SAME WAYS THAT THE MAJORITY OF PEOPLE DO.
BUT LIFE IS MUCH EASIER IF YOU DO.

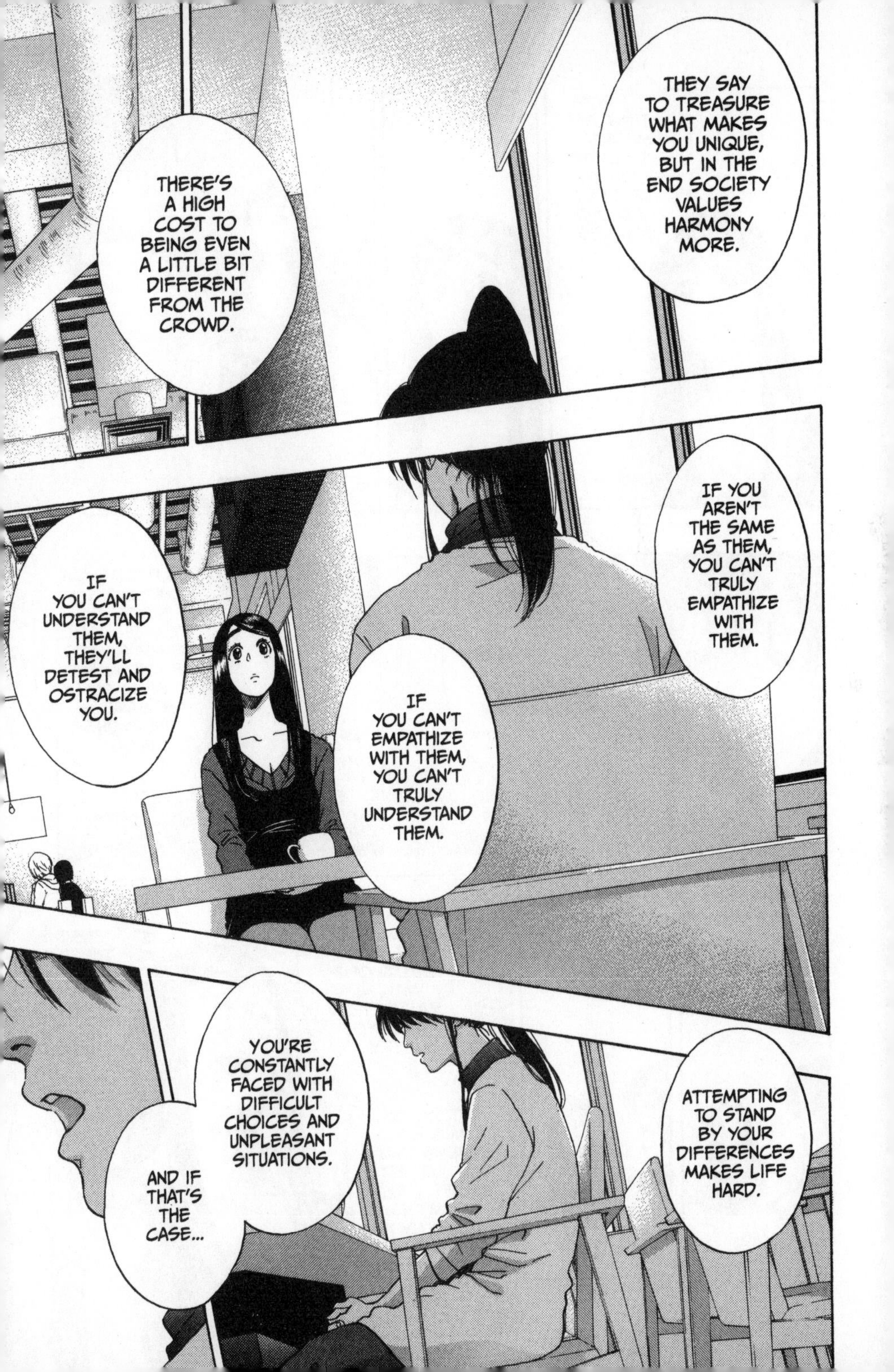
THEY SAY TO TREASURE WHAT MAKES YOU UNIQUE, BUT IN THE END SOCIETY VALUES HARMONY MORE.
THERE'S A HIGH COST TO BEING EVEN A LITTLE BIT DIFFERENT FROM THE CROWD.
IF YOU AREN'T THE SAME AS THEM, YOU CAN'T TRULY EMPATHIZE WITH THEM.
IF YOU CAN'T EMPATHIZE WITH THEM, YOU CAN'T TRULY UNDERSTAND THEM.
IF YOU CAN'T UNDERSTAND THEM, THEY'LL DETEST AND OSTRACIZE YOU.
ATTEMPTING TO STAND BY YOUR DIFFERENCES MAKES LIFE HARD.
YOU'RE CONSTANTLY FACED WITH DIFFICULT CHOICES AND UNPLEASANT SITUATIONS.
AND IF THAT'S THE CASE...

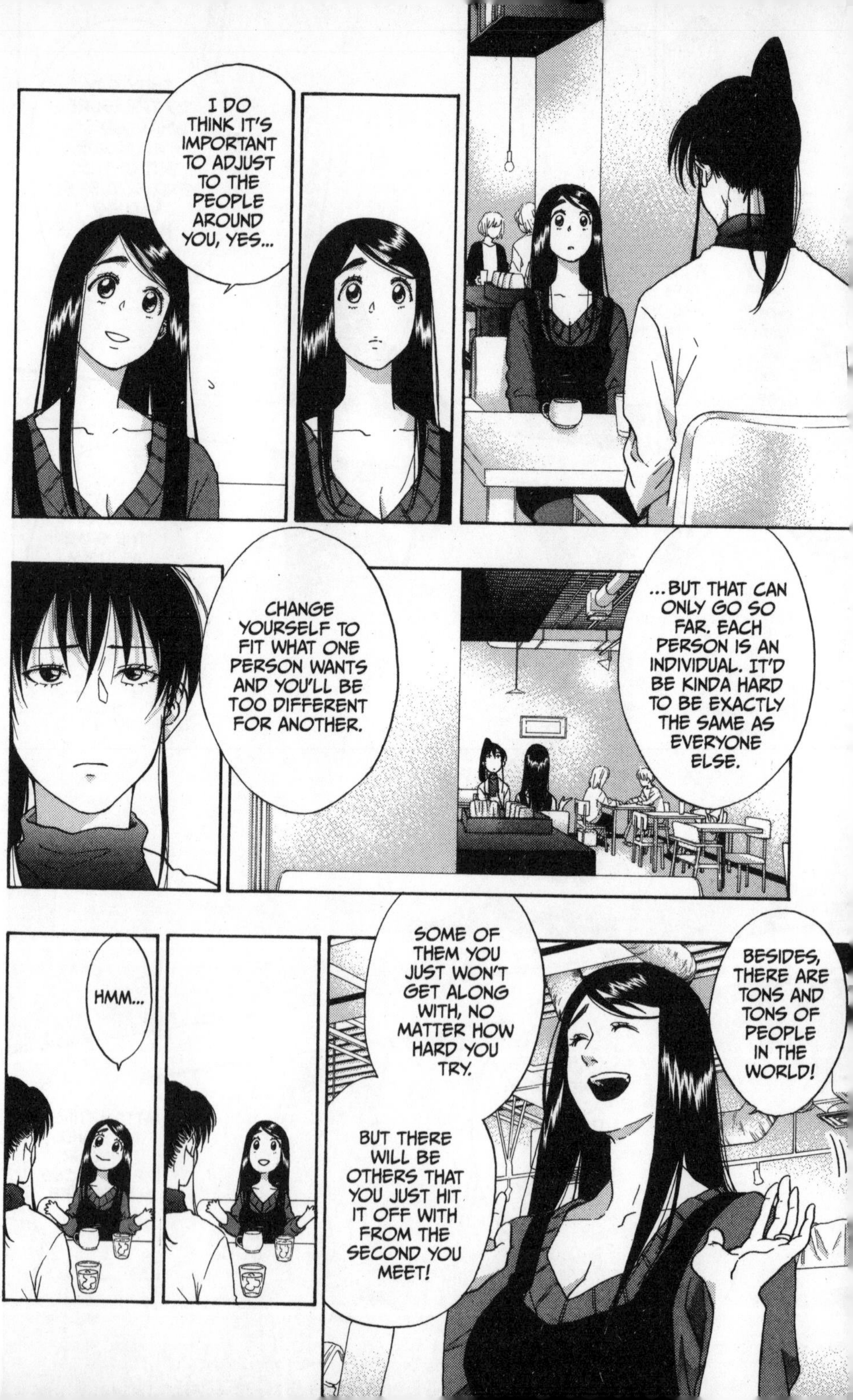
I DO THINK IT'S IMPORTANT TO ADJUST TO THE PEOPLE AROUND YOU, YES...
...BUT THAT CAN ONLY GO SO FAR. EACH PERSON IS AN INDIVIDUAL. IT'D BE KINDA HARD TO BE EXACTLY THE SAME AS EVERYONE ELSE.
CHANGE YOURSELF TO FIT WHAT ONE PERSON WANTS AND YOU'LL BE TOO DIFFERENT FOR ANOTHER.
BESIDES, THERE ARE TONS AND TONS OF PEOPLE IN THE WORLD!
SOME OF THEM YOU JUST WON'T GET ALONG WITH, NO MATTER HOW HARD YOU TRY.
BUT THERE WILL BE OTHERS THAT YOU JUST HIT IT OFF WITH FROM THE SECOND YOU MEET!
HMM...

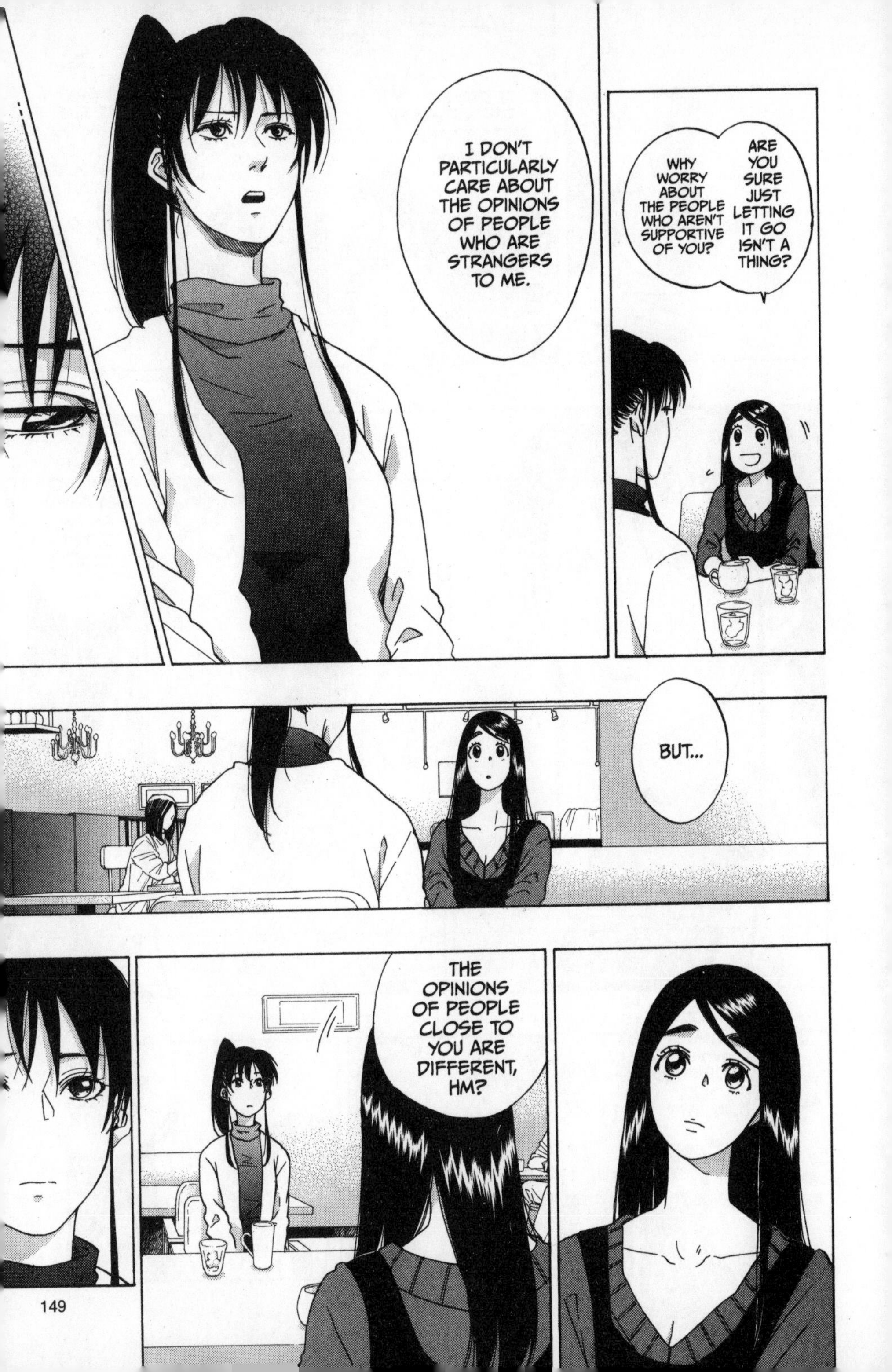
ARE YOU SURE JUST LETTING IT GO ISN'T A THING?
WHY WORRY ABOUT THE PEOPLE WHO AREN'T SUPPORTIVE OF YOU?
I DON'T PARTICULARLY CARE ABOUT THE OPINIONS OF PEOPLE WHO ARE STRANGERS TO ME.
BUT...
THE OPINIONS OF PEOPLE CLOSE TO YOU ARE DIFFERENT, HM?

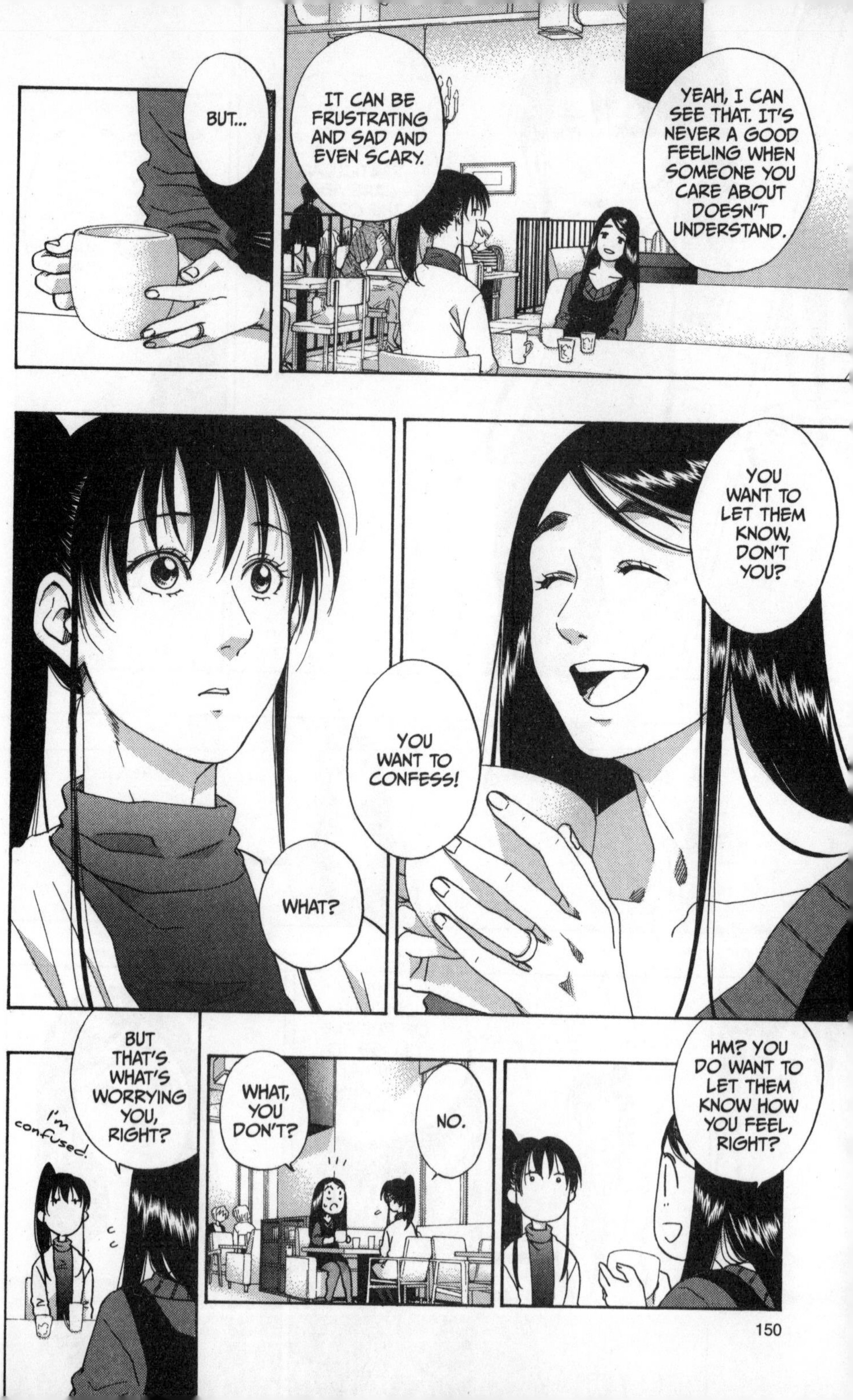
YEAH, I CAN SEE THAT. IT'S NEVER A GOOD FEELING WHEN SOMEONE YOU CARE ABOUT DOESN'T UNDERSTAND.
IT CAN BE FRUSTRATING AND SAD AND EVEN SCARY.
BUT...
YOU WANT TO LET THEM KNOW, DON'T YOU?
YOU WANT TO CONFESS!
WHAT?
HM? YOU DO WANT TO LET THEM KNOW HOW YOU FEEL, RIGHT?
NO.
WHAT, YOU DON'T?
BUT THAT'S WHAT'S WORRYING YOU, RIGHT?
I'm confused!

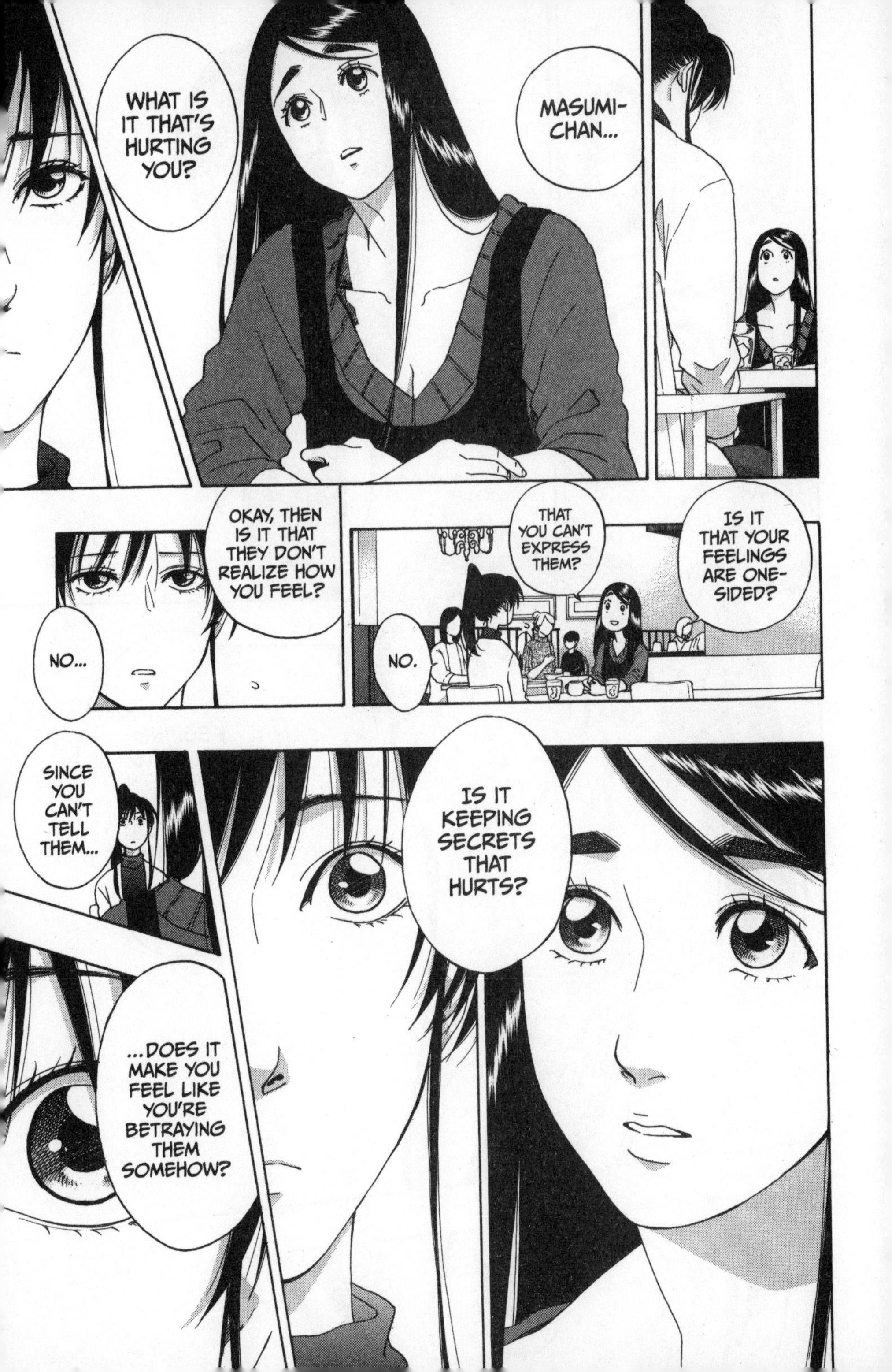
MASUMI-CHAN...
WHAT IS IT THAT'S HURTING YOU?
IS IT THAT YOUR FEELINGS ARE ONE-SIDED?
THAT YOU CAN'T EXPRESS THEM?
NO.
OKAY, THEN IS IT THAT THEY DON'T REALIZE HOW YOU FEEL?
NO...
IS IT KEEPING SECRETS THAT HURTS?
SINCE YOU CAN'T TELL THEM...
...DOES IT MAKE YOU FEEL LIKE YOU'RE BETRAYING THEM SOMEHOW?

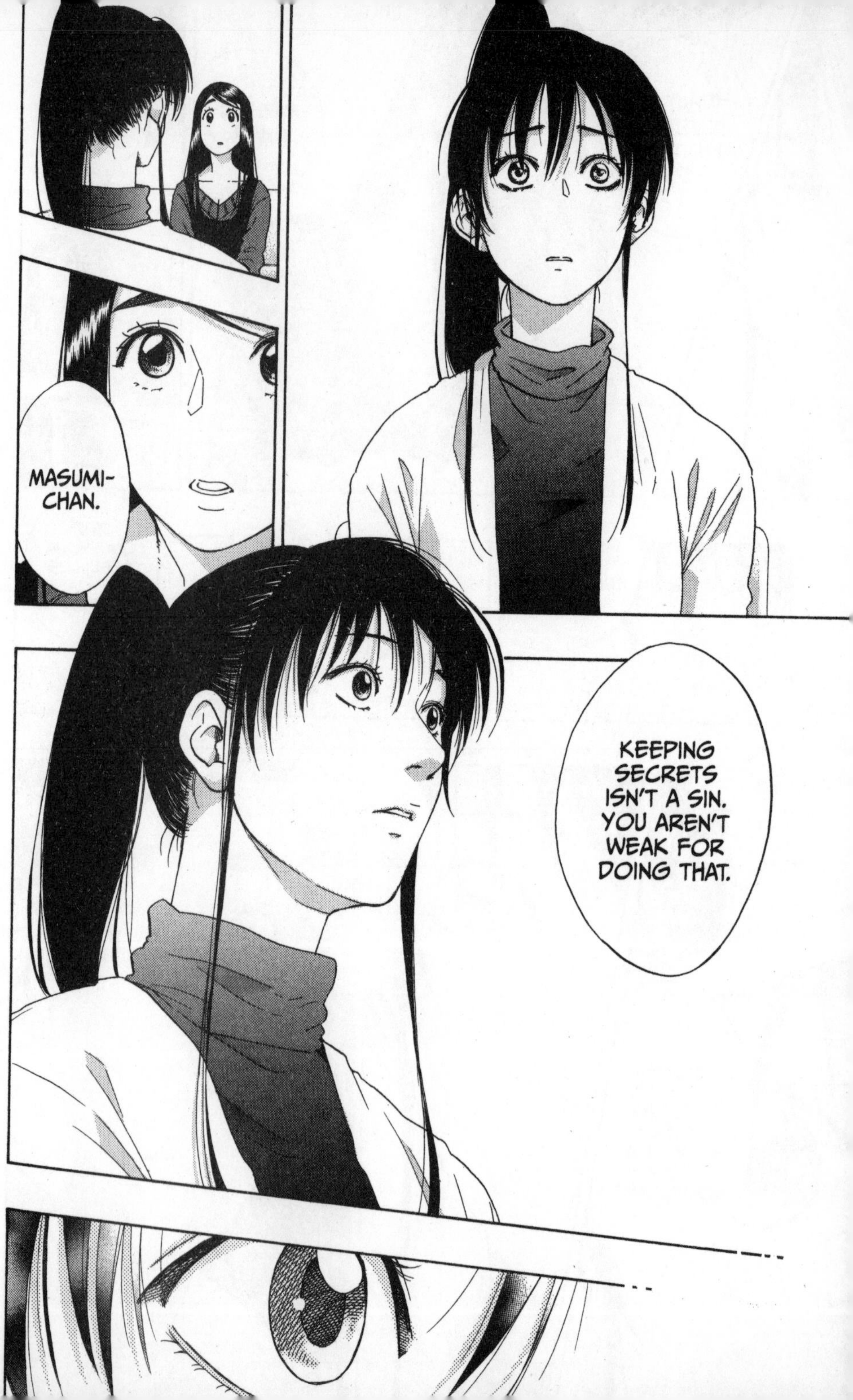
MASUMI-CHAN.
KEEPING SECRETS ISN'T A SIN. YOU AREN'T WEAK FOR DOING THAT.

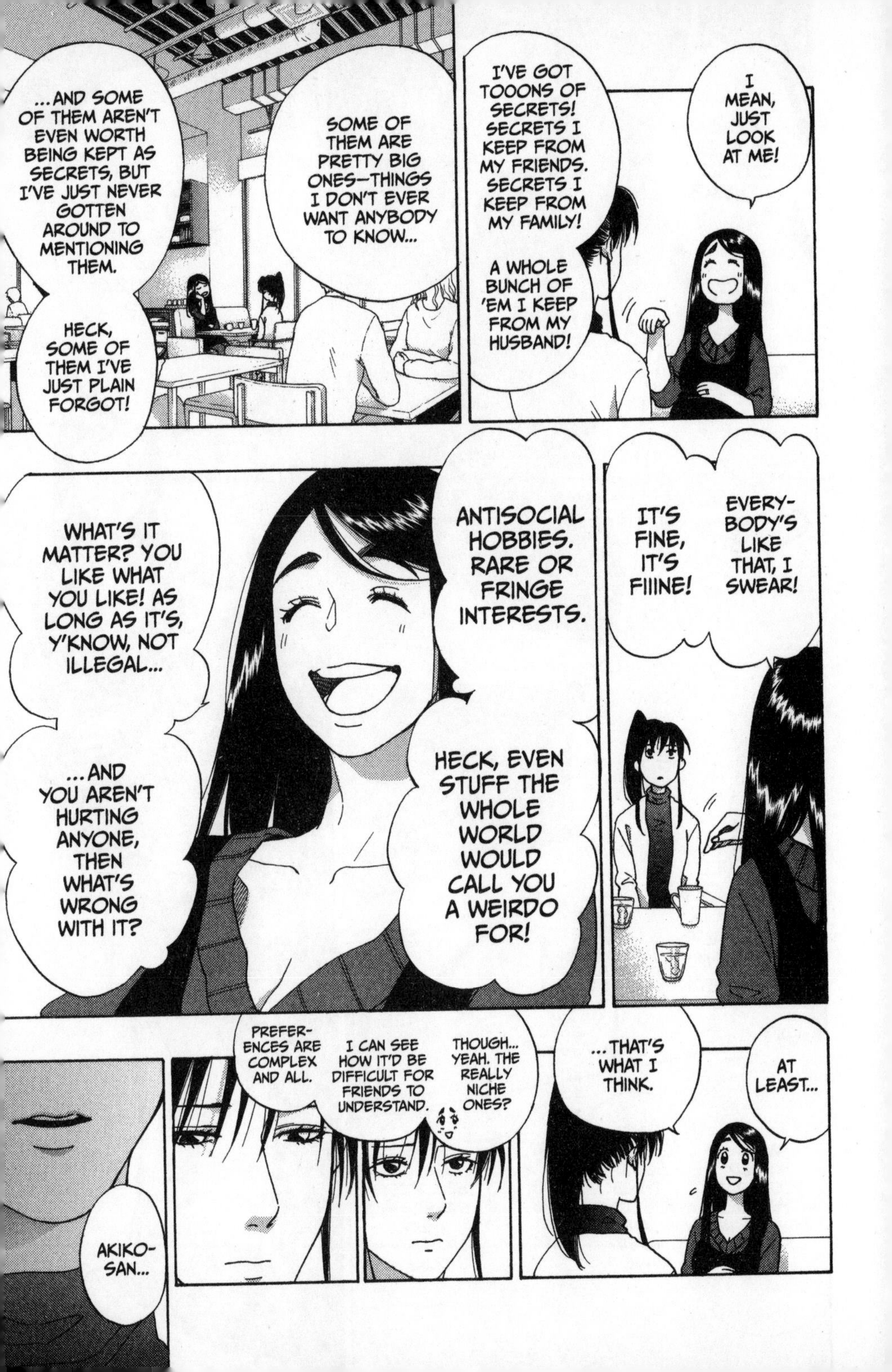
I MEAN, JUST LOOK AT ME!
I'VE GOT TOOONS OF SECRETS! SECRETS I KEEP FROM MY FRIENDS. SECRETS I KEEP FROM MY FAMILY!
A WHOLE BUNCH OF 'EM I KEEP FROM MY HUSBAND!
SOME OF THEM ARE PRETTY BIG ONES—THINGS I DON'T EVER WANT ANYBODY TO KNOW...
...AND SOME OF THEM AREN'T EVEN WORTH BEING KEPT AS SECRETS, BUT I'VE JUST NEVER GOTTEN AROUND TO MENTIONING THEM.
HECK, SOME OF THEM I'VE JUST PLAIN FORGOT!
EVERY-BODY'S LIKE THAT, I SWEAR!
IT'S FINE, IT'S FIIINE!
ANTISOCIAL HOBBIES. RARE OR FRINGE INTERESTS.
HECK, EVEN STUFF THE WHOLE WORLD WOULD CALL YOU A WEIRDO FOR!
WHAT'S IT MATTER? YOU LIKE WHAT YOU LIKE! AS LONG AS IT'S, Y'KNOW, NOT ILLEGAL...
...AND YOU AREN'T HURTING ANYONE, THEN WHAT'S WRONG WITH IT?
AT LEAST...
...THAT'S WHAT I THINK.
THOUGH... YEAH. THE REALLY NICHE ONES?
I CAN SEE HOW IT'D BE DIFFICULT FOR FRIENDS TO UNDERSTAND.
PREFER-ENCES ARE COMPLEX AND ALL.
AKIKO-SAN...

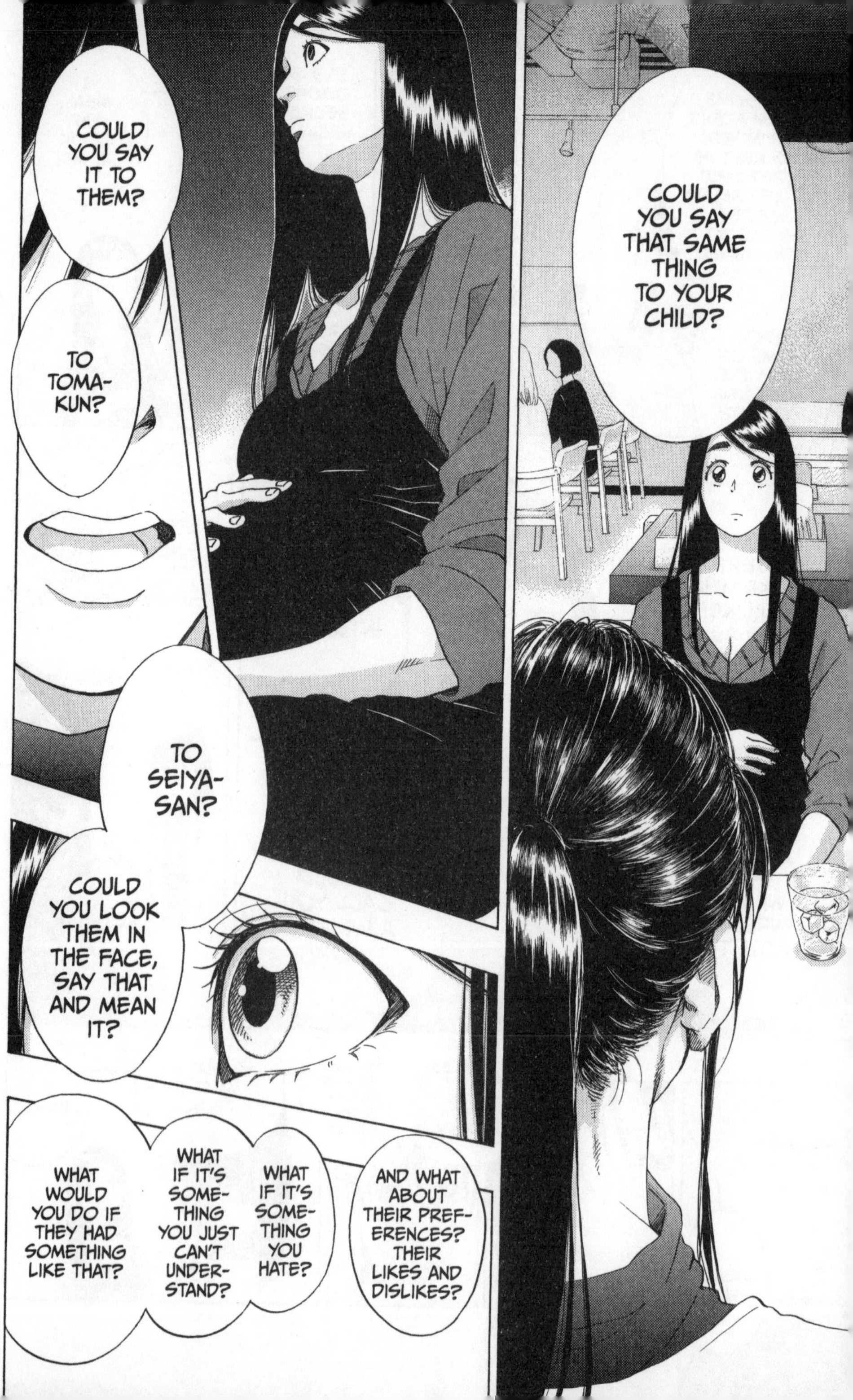
COULD YOU SAY THAT SAME THING TO YOUR CHILD?
COULD YOU SAY IT TO THEM?
TO TOMA-KUN?
TO SEIYA-SAN?
COULD YOU LOOK THEM IN THE FACE, SAY THAT AND MEAN IT?
AND WHAT ABOUT THEIR PREFERENCES? THEIR LIKES AND DISLIKES?
WHAT IF IT'S SOMETHING YOU HATE?
WHAT IF IT'S SOMETHING YOU JUST CAN'T UNDERSTAND?
WHAT WOULD YOU DO IF THEY HAD SOMETHING LIKE THAT?

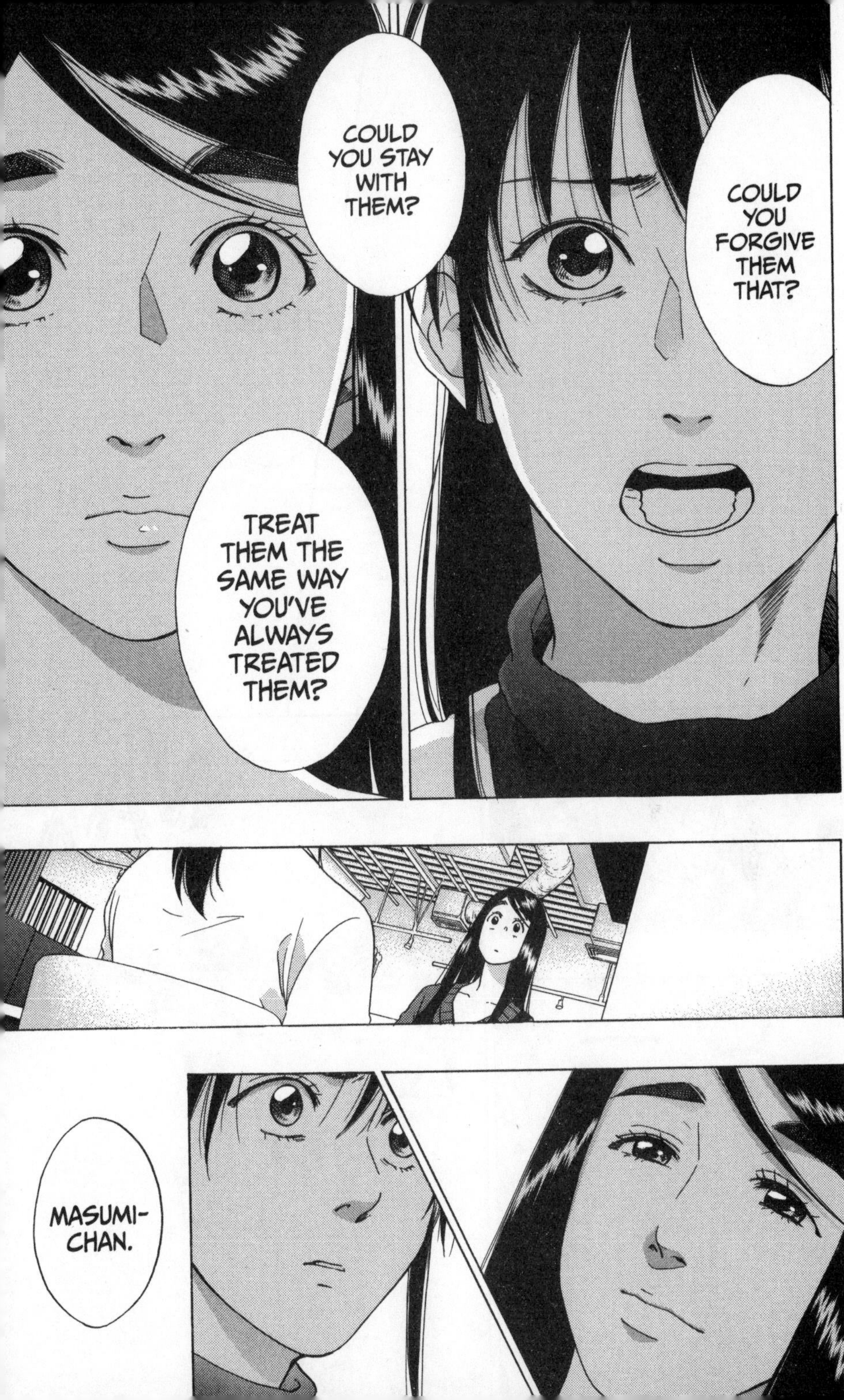
COULD YOU FORGIVE THEM THAT?
COULD YOU STAY WITH THEM?
TREAT THEM THE SAME WAY YOU'VE ALWAYS TREATED THEM?
MASUMI-CHAN.

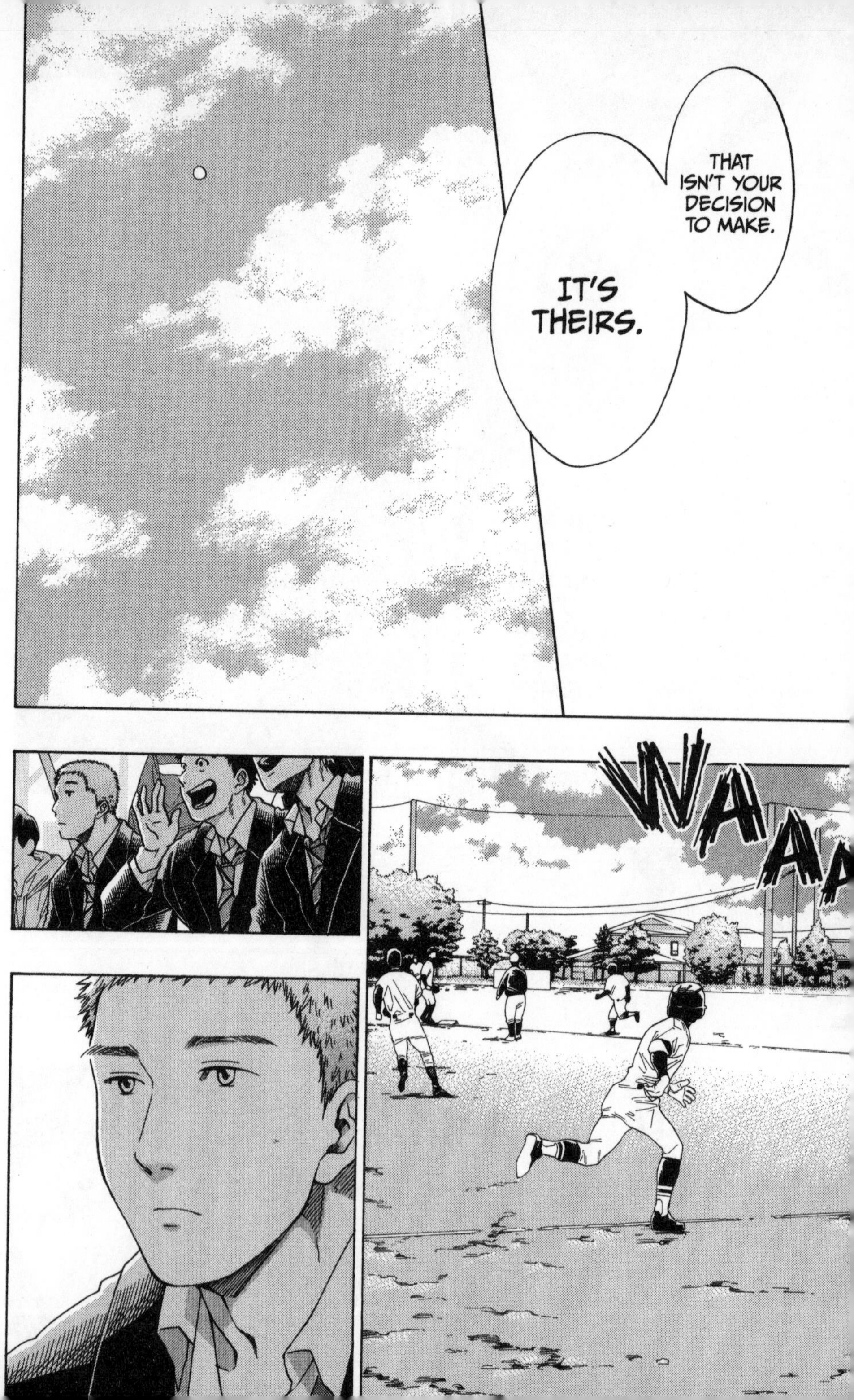
THAT ISN'T YOUR DECISION TO MAKE.
IT'S THEIRS.
WAA

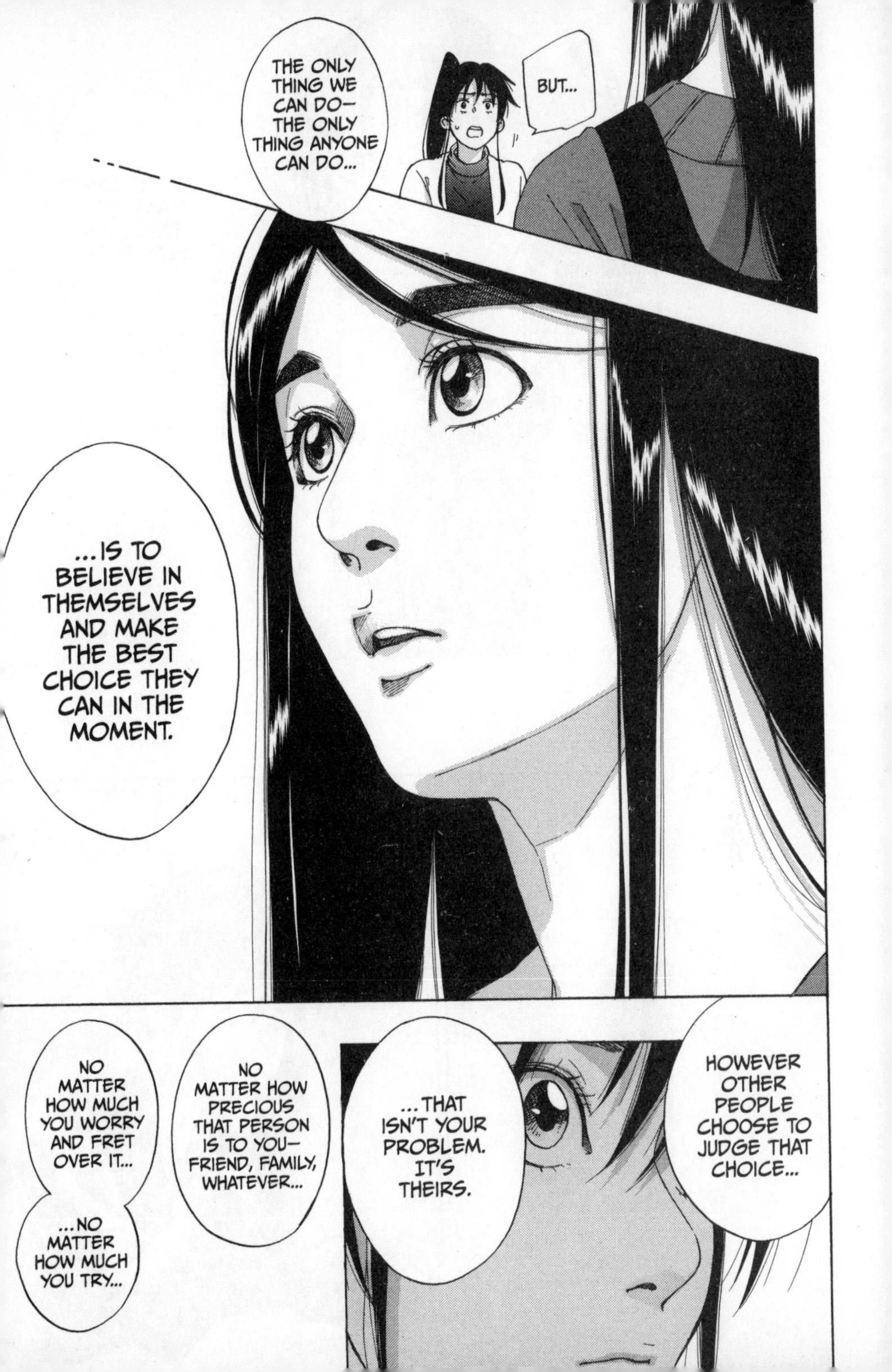
BUT...
THE ONLY THING WE CAN DO— THE ONLY THING ANYONE CAN DO...
...IS TO BELIEVE IN THEMSELVES AND MAKE THE BEST CHOICE THEY CAN IN THE MOMENT.
HOWEVER OTHER PEOPLE CHOOSE TO JUDGE THAT CHOICE...
...THAT ISN'T YOUR PROBLEM. IT'S THEIRS.
NO MATTER HOW PRECIOUS THAT PERSON IS TO YOU— FRIEND, FAMILY, WHATEVER...
NO MATTER HOW MUCH YOU WORRY AND FRET OVER IT...
...NO MATTER HOW MUCH YOU TRY...

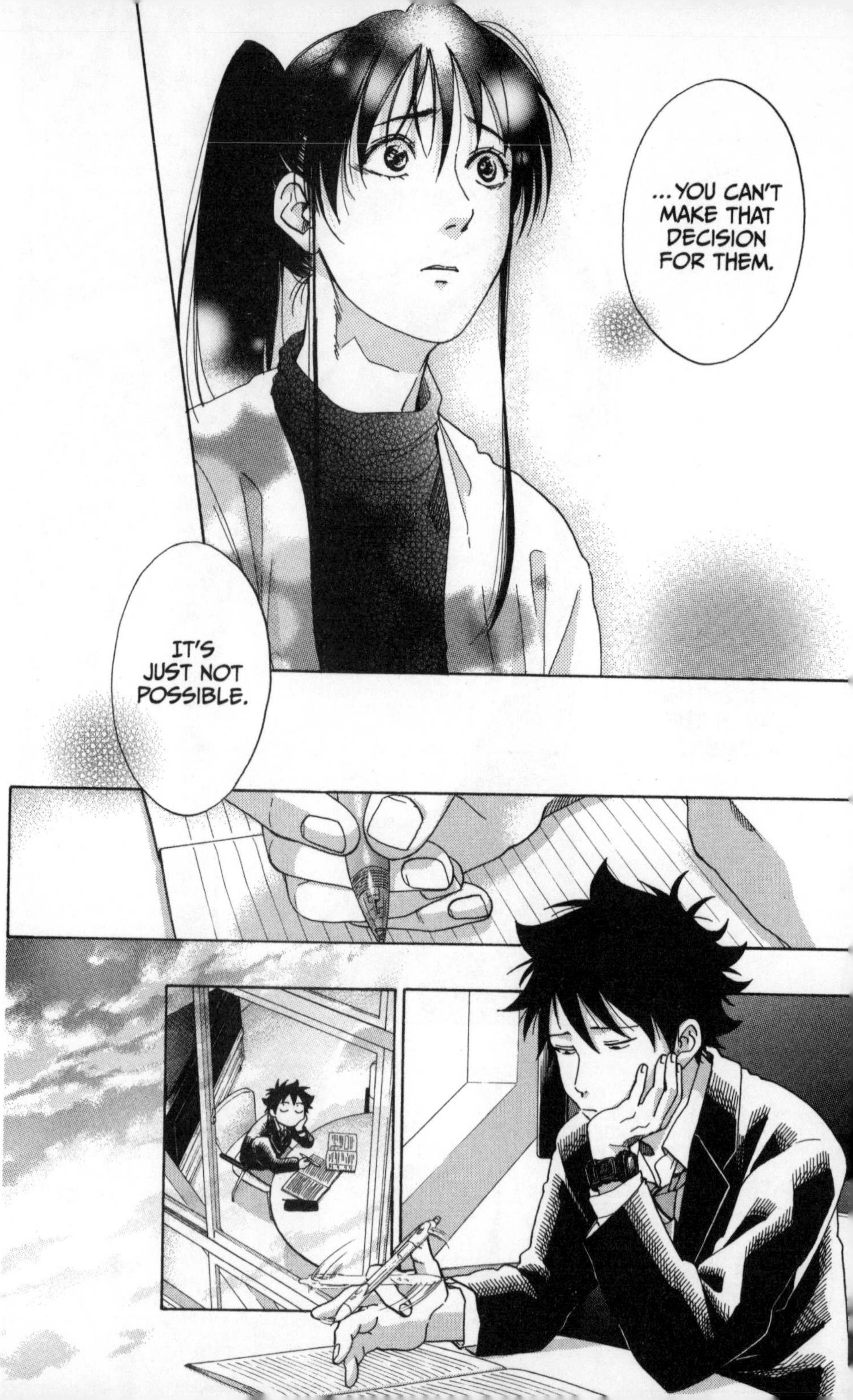
...YOU CAN'T MAKE THAT DECISION FOR THEM.
IT'S JUST NOT POSSIBLE.

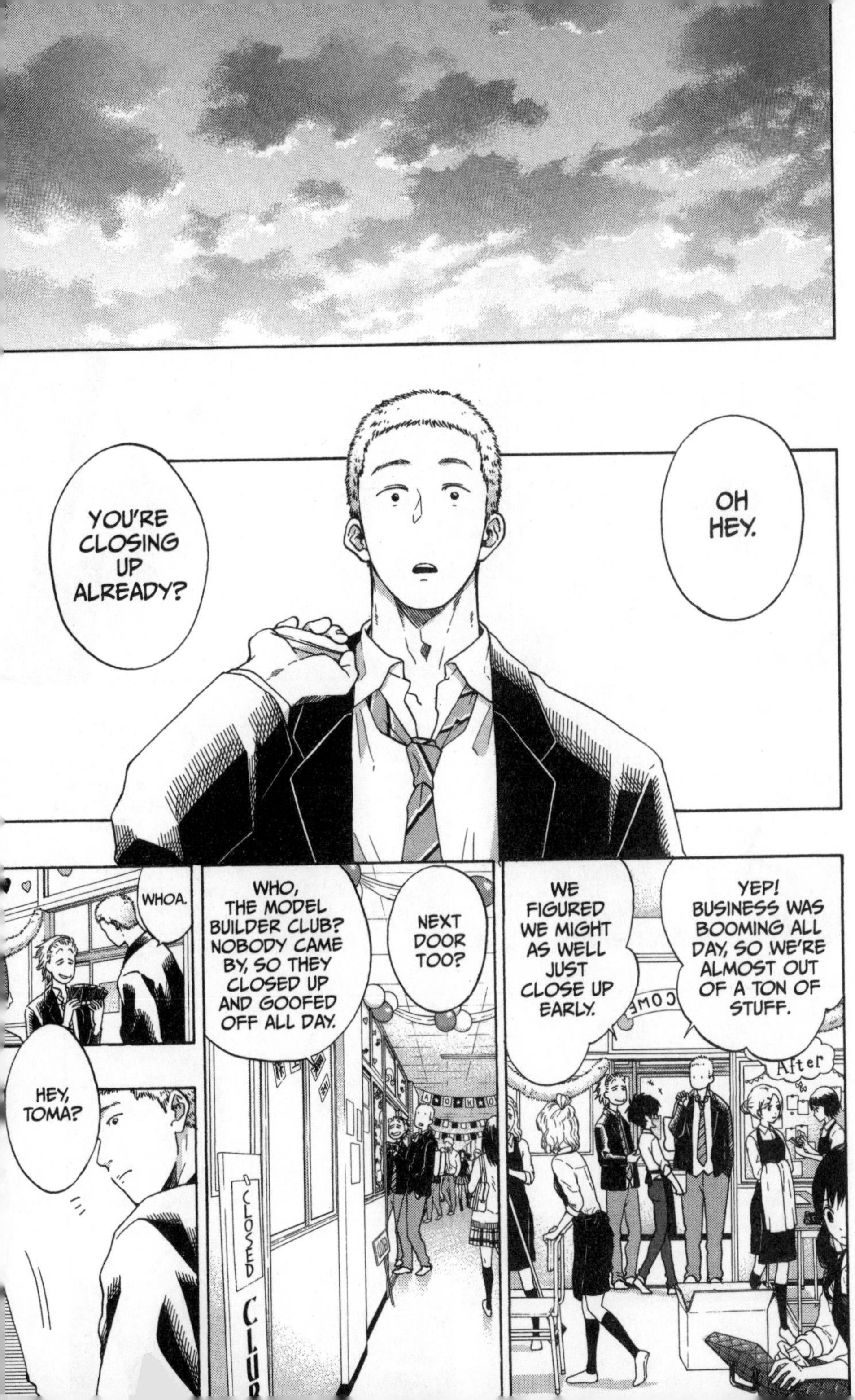
OH HEY.
YOU'RE CLOSING UP ALREADY?
YEP! BUSINESS WAS BOOMING ALL DAY, SO WE'RE ALMOST OUT OF A TON OF STUFF.
WE FIGURED WE MIGHT AS WELL JUST CLOSE UP EARLY.
After
NEXT DOOR TOO?
WHO, THE MODEL BUILDER CLUB? NOBODY CAME BY, SO THEY CLOSED UP AND GOOFED OFF ALL DAY.
CLOSED
WHOA.
HEY, TOMA?

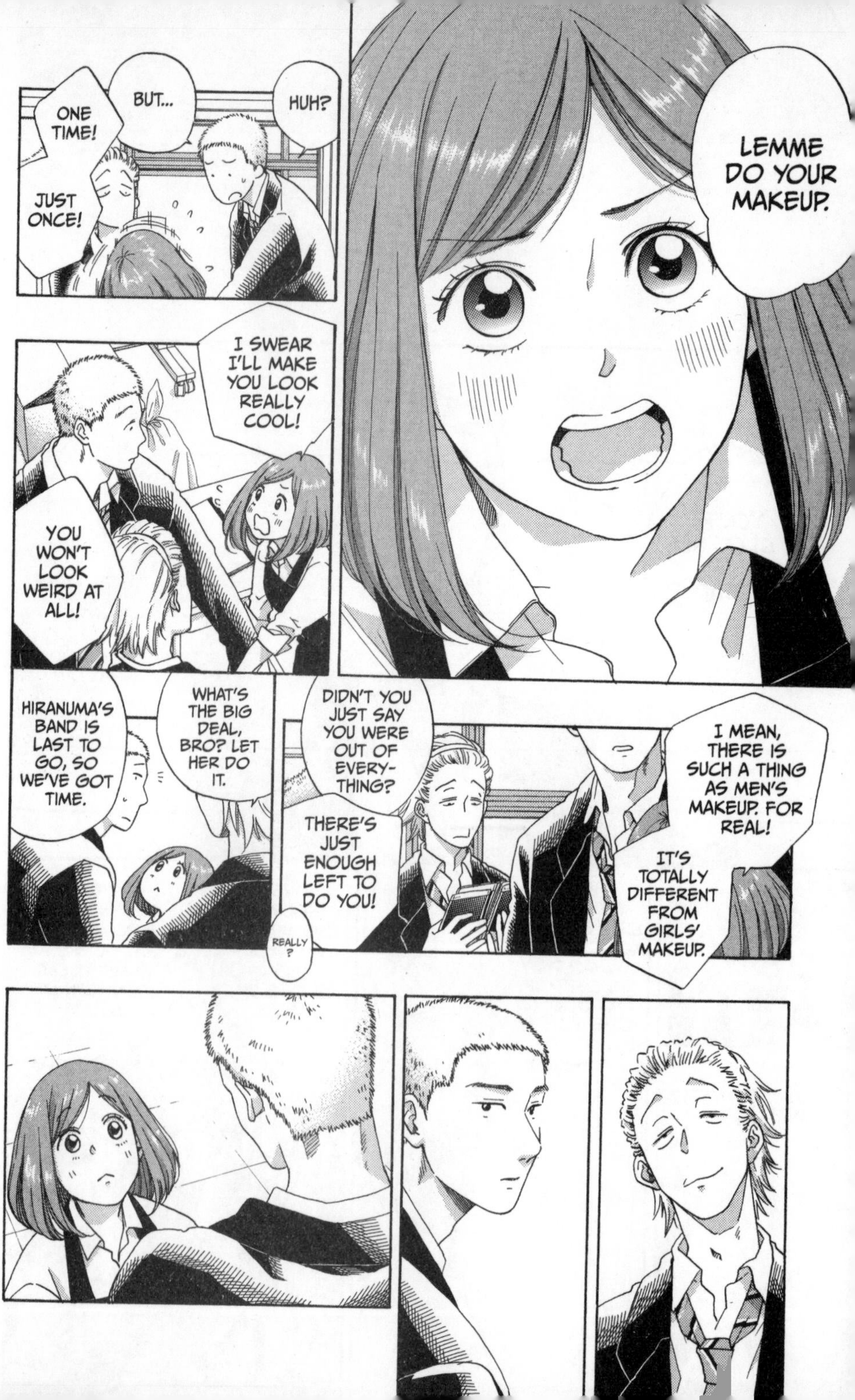
LEMME DO YOUR MAKEUP.
HUH?
BUT...
ONE TIME!
JUST ONCE!
I SWEAR I'LL MAKE YOU LOOK REALLY COOL!
YOU WON'T LOOK WEIRD AT ALL!
I MEAN, THERE IS SUCH A THING AS MEN'S MAKEUP. FOR REAL!
IT'S TOTALLY DIFFERENT FROM GIRLS' MAKEUP.
DIDN'T YOU JUST SAY YOU WERE OUT OF EVERY-THING?
THERE'S JUST ENOUGH LEFT TO DO YOU!
REALLY?
WHAT'S THE BIG DEAL, BRO? LET HER DO IT.
HIRANUMA'S BAND IS LAST TO GO, SO WE'VE GOT TIME.

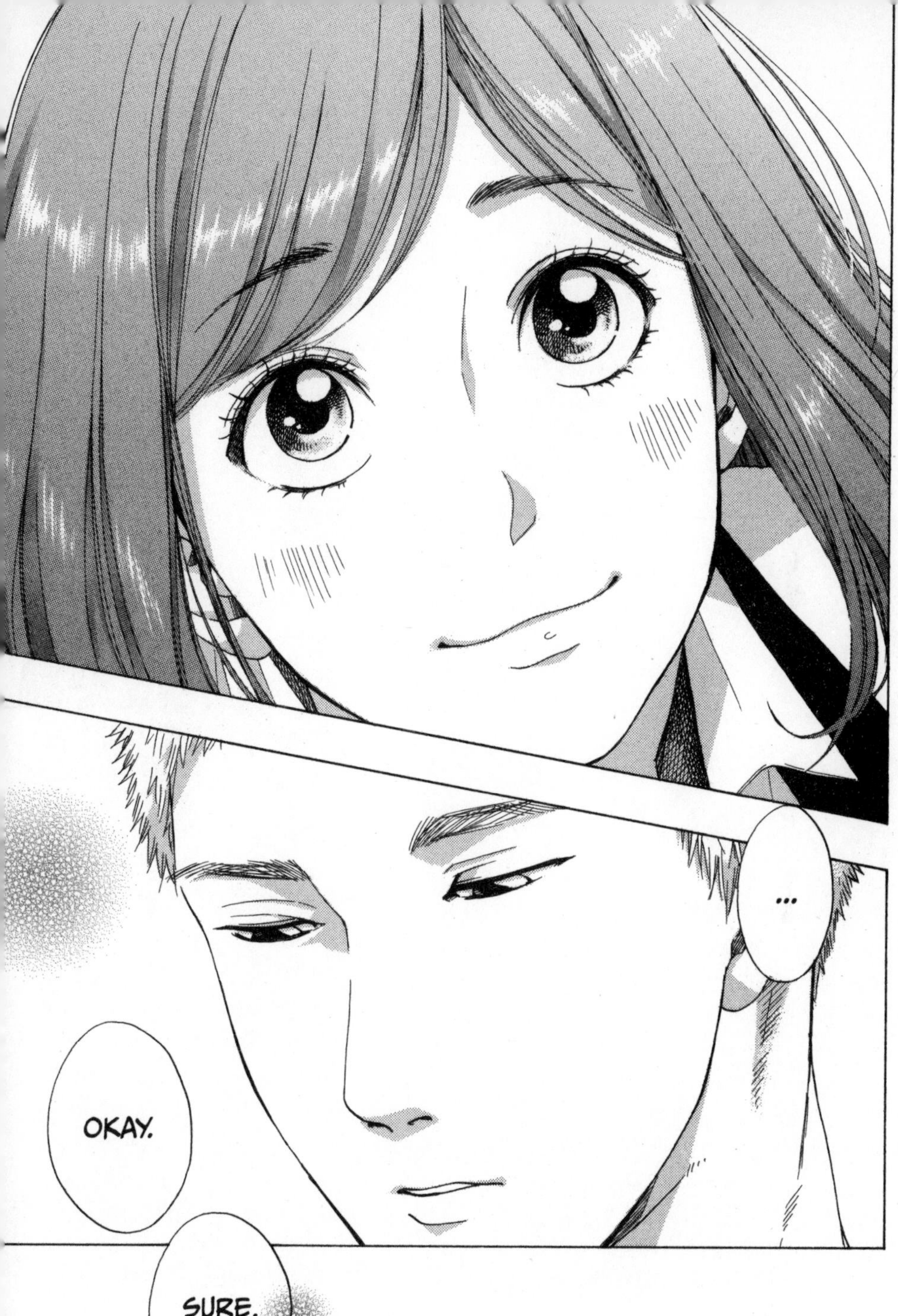
...
OKAY.
SURE.

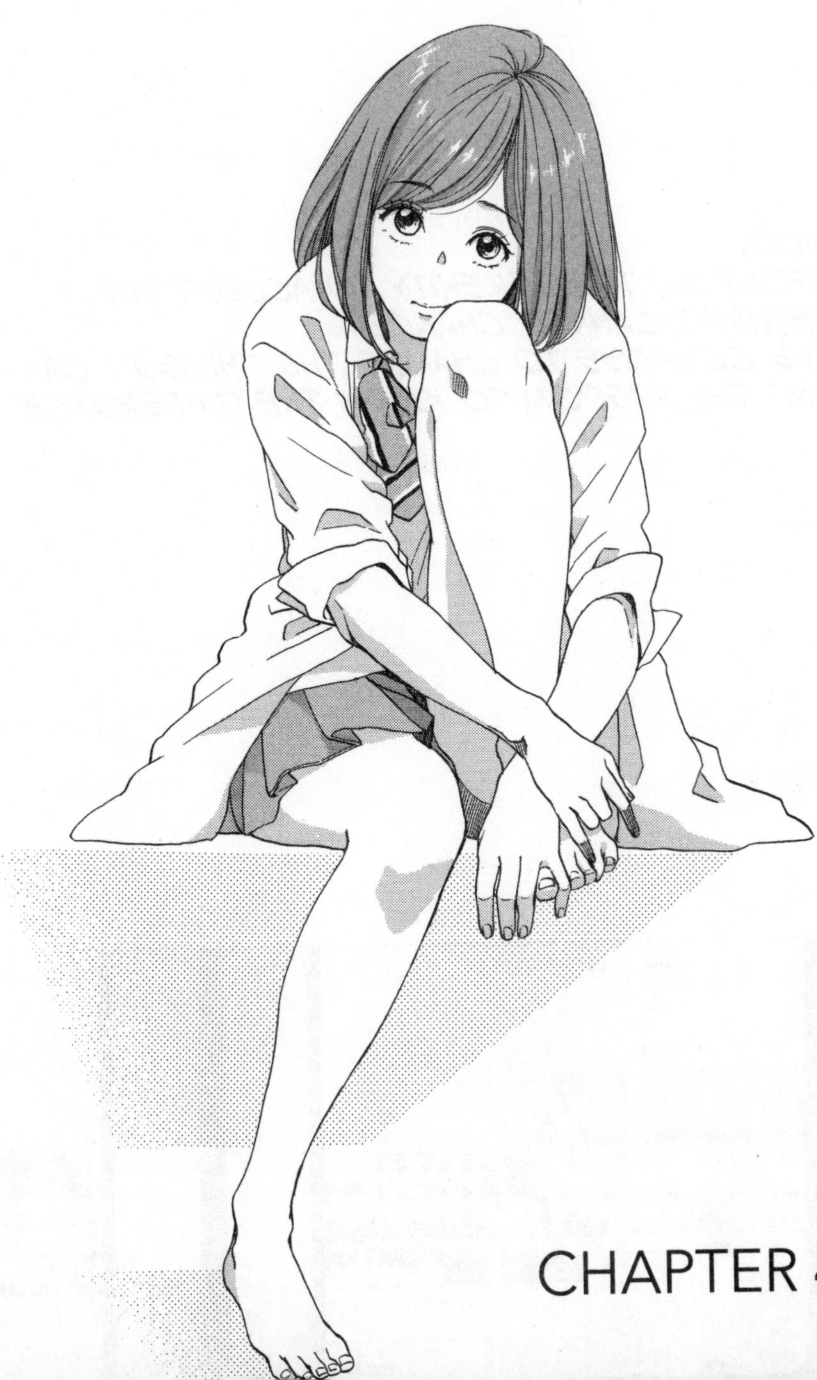

CHAPTER 40

GOD,
GRANT ME THE SERENITY TO ACCEPT THE
THINGS I CANNOT CHANGE,
THE COURAGE TO CHANGE THE THINGS I CAN
AND THE WISDOM TO KNOW THE DIFFERENCE.

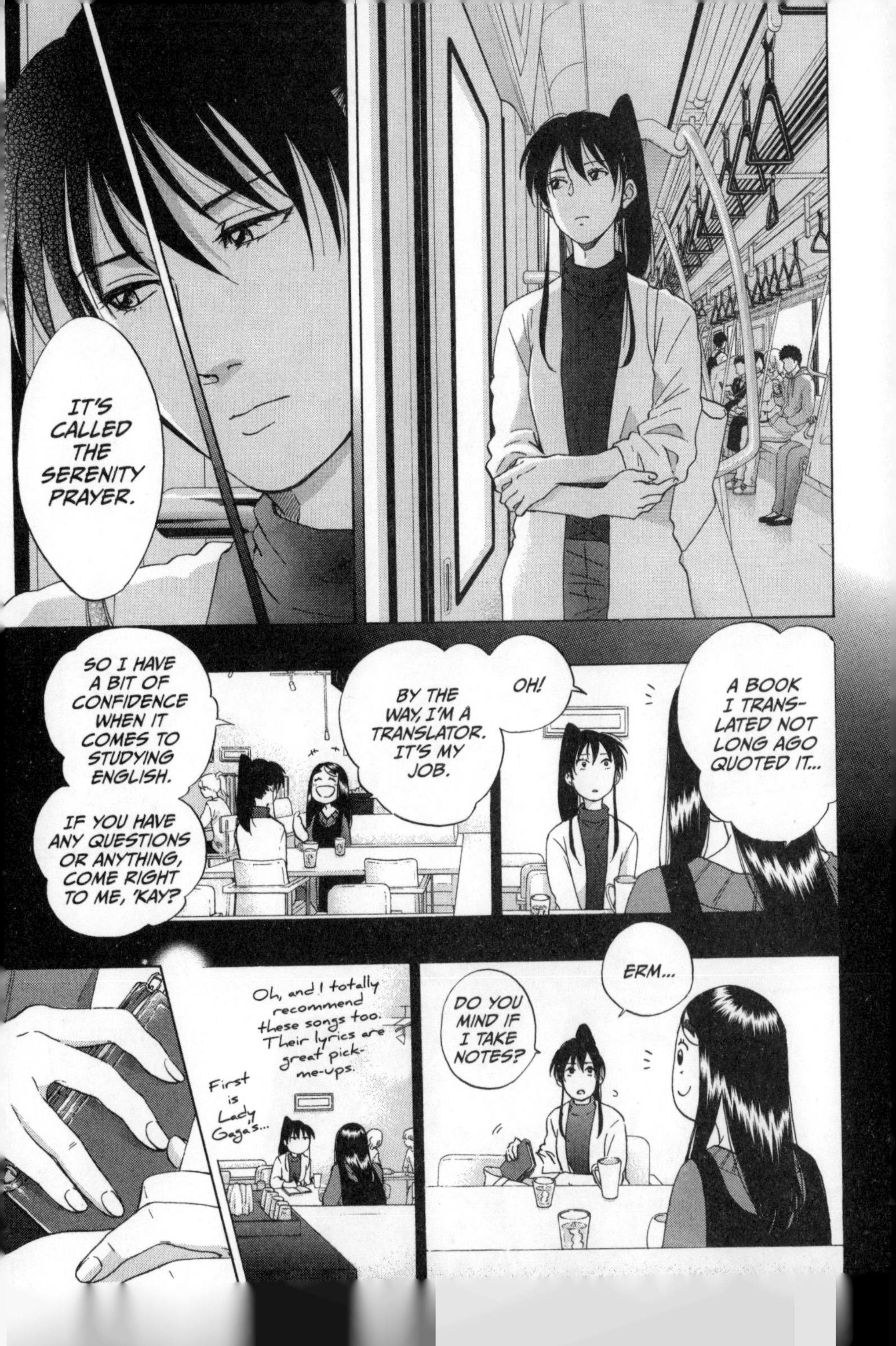
IT'S CALLED THE SERENITY PRAYER.
A BOOK I TRANSLATED NOT LONG AGO QUOTED IT...
OH!
BY THE WAY, I'M A TRANSLATOR. IT'S MY JOB.
SO I HAVE A BIT OF CONFIDENCE WHEN IT COMES TO STUDYING ENGLISH.
IF YOU HAVE ANY QUESTIONS OR ANYTHING, COME RIGHT TO ME, 'KAY?
ERM...
DO YOU MIND IF I TAKE NOTES?
Oh, and I totally recommend these songs too. Their lyrics are great pick-me-ups.
First is Lady Gaga's...

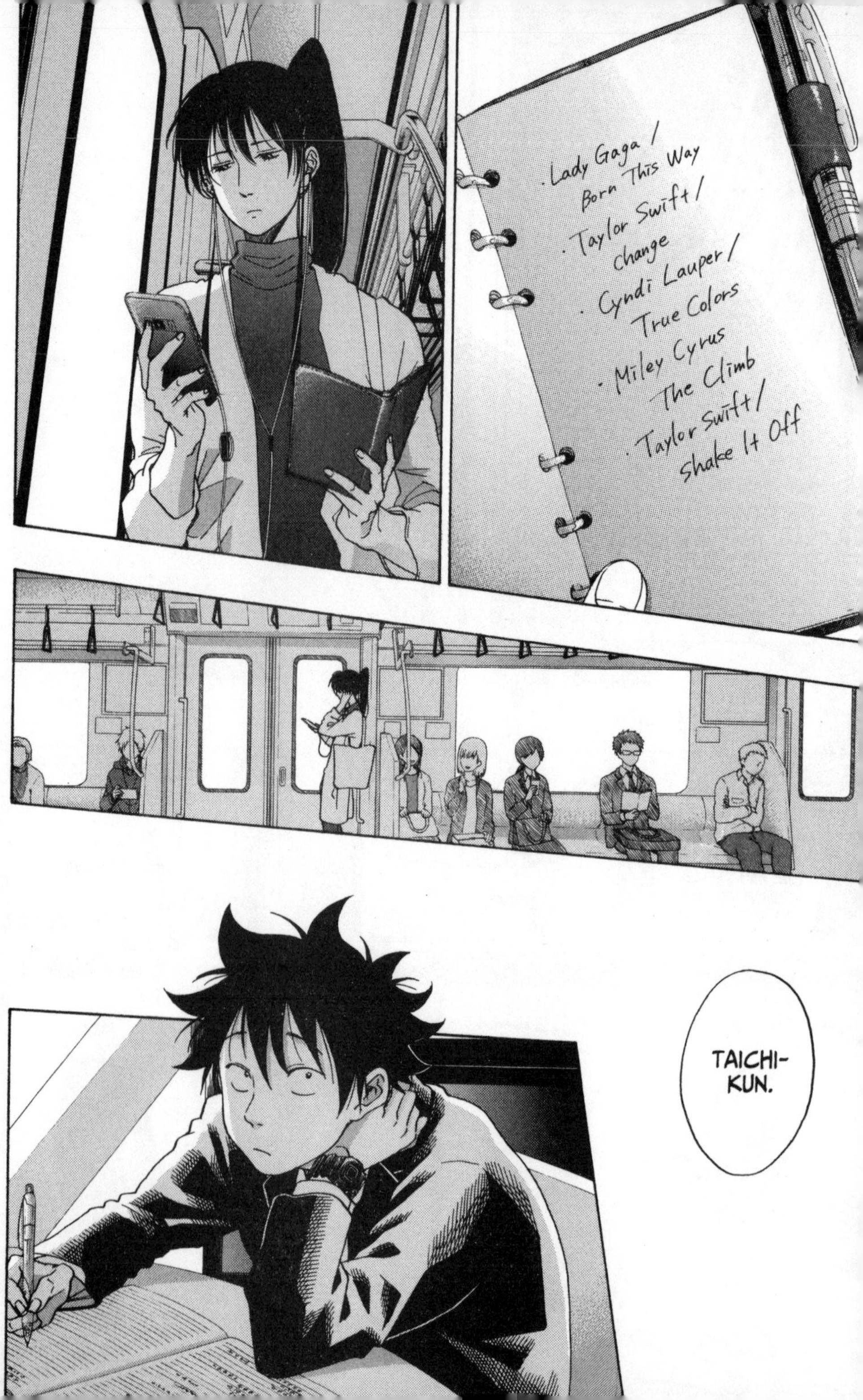
· Lady Gaga / Born This Way
· Taylor Swift / Change
· Cyndi Lauper / True Colors
· Miley Cyrus The Climb
· Taylor Swift / Shake It Off
TAICHI-KUN.

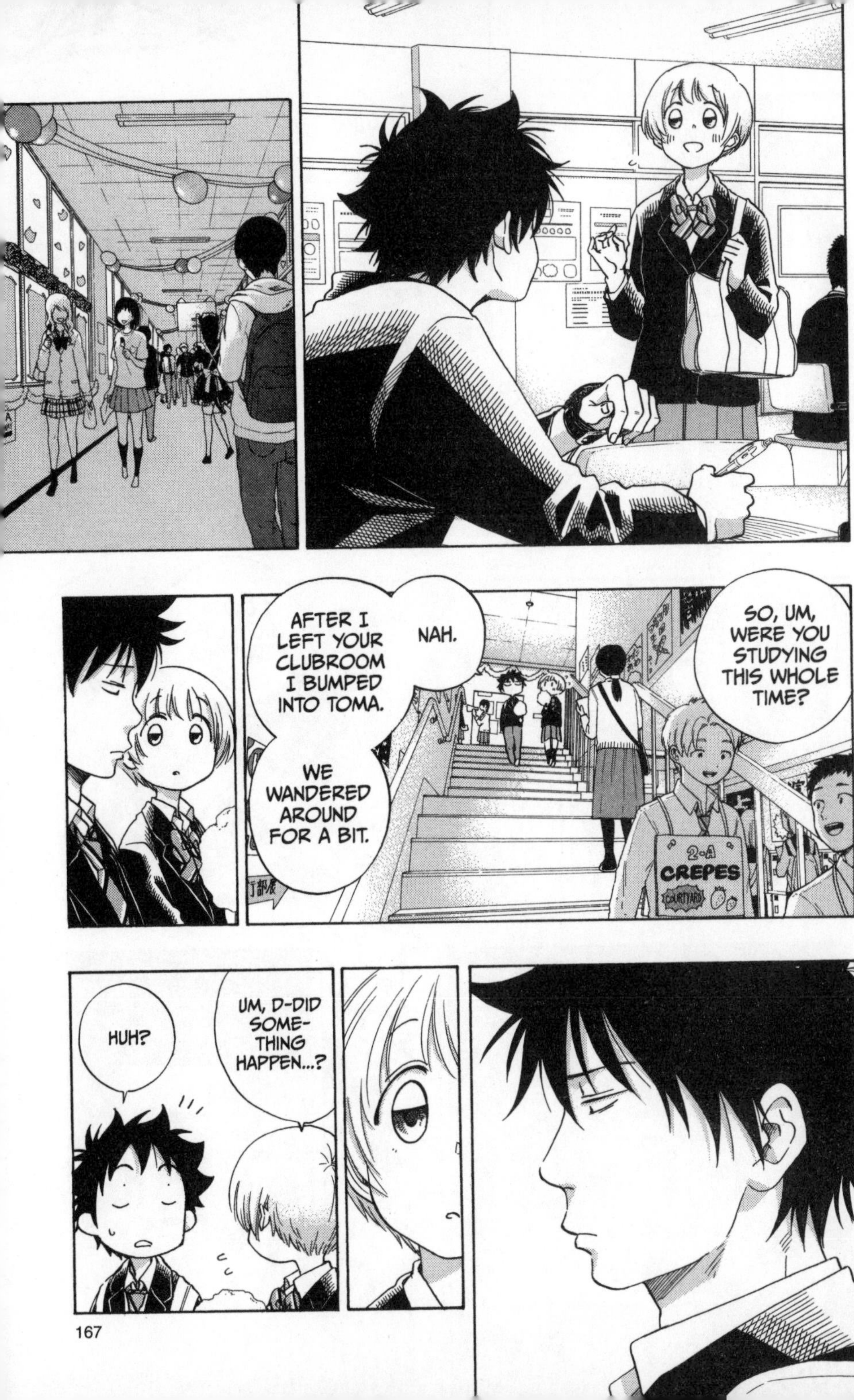
SO, UM, WERE YOU STUDYING THIS WHOLE TIME?
2-A
CREPES
COURTYARD
NAH.
AFTER I LEFT YOUR CLUBROOM I BUMPED INTO TOMA.
WE WANDERED AROUND FOR A BIT.
UM, D-DID SOME-THING HAPPEN...?
HUH?

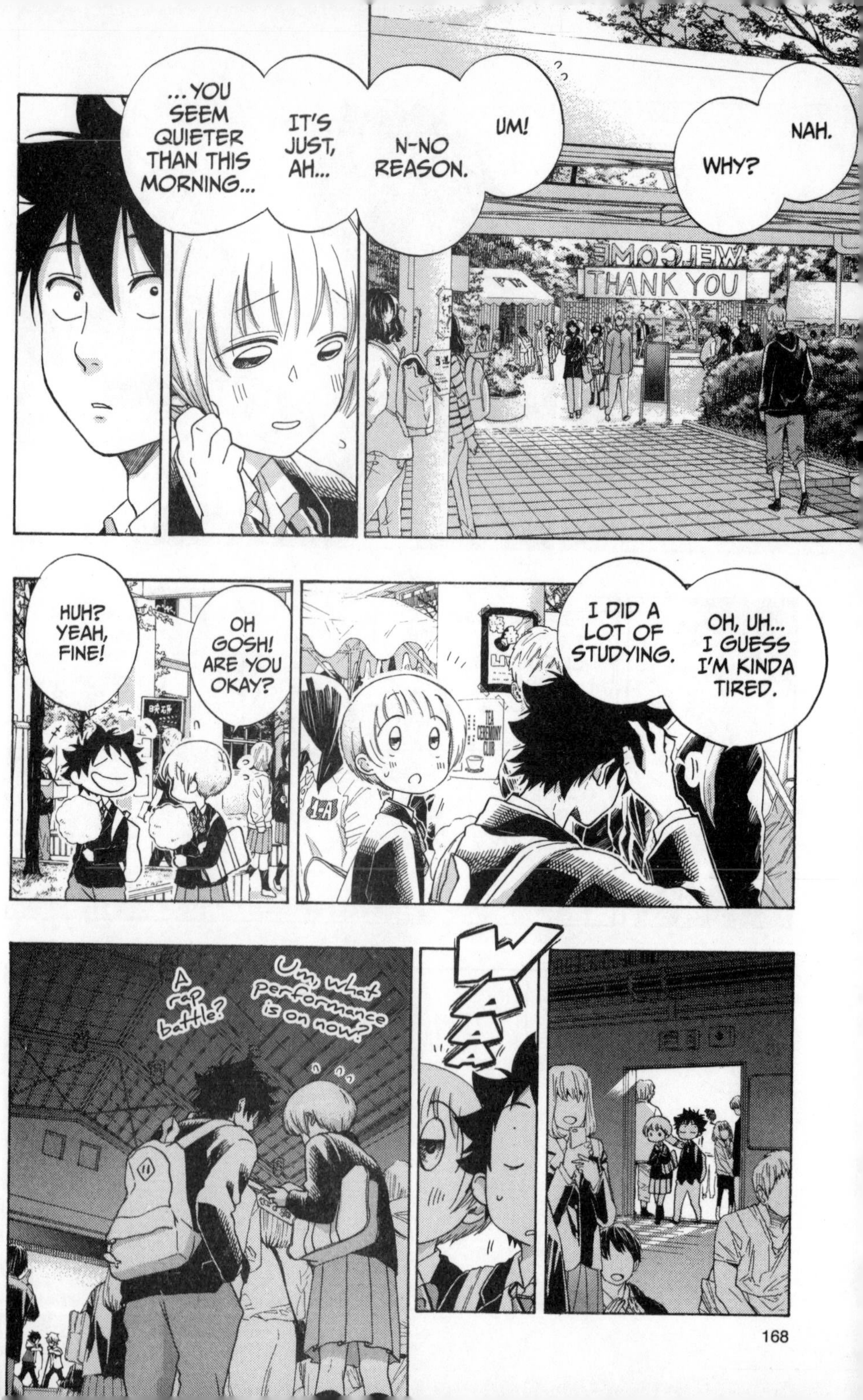
NAH.
WHY?
UM!
N-NO REASON.
IT'S JUST, AH...
...YOU SEEM QUIETER THAN THIS MORNING...
WELCOME
THANK YOU
OH, UH... I GUESS I'M KINDA TIRED.
I DID A LOT OF STUDYING.
TEA CEREMONY CLUB
OH GOSH! ARE YOU OKAY?
HUH? YEAH, FINE!
WAAA
Um, what performance is on now?
A rap battle?

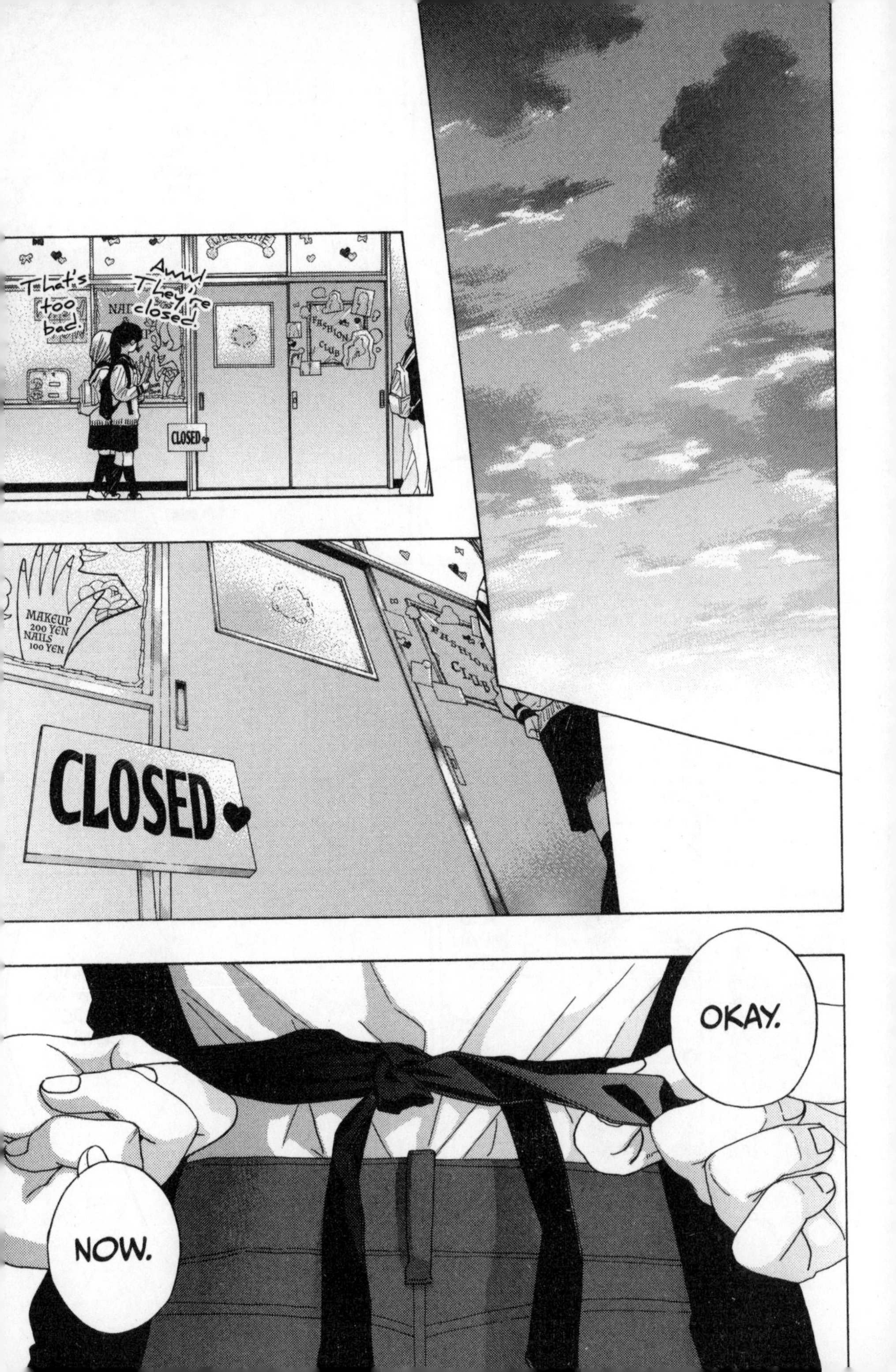
Aww! They're closed!
That's too bad.
FASHION CLUB
CLOSED
MAKEUP 200 YEN NAILS 100 YEN
FASHION CLUB
CLOSED
OKAY.
NOW.

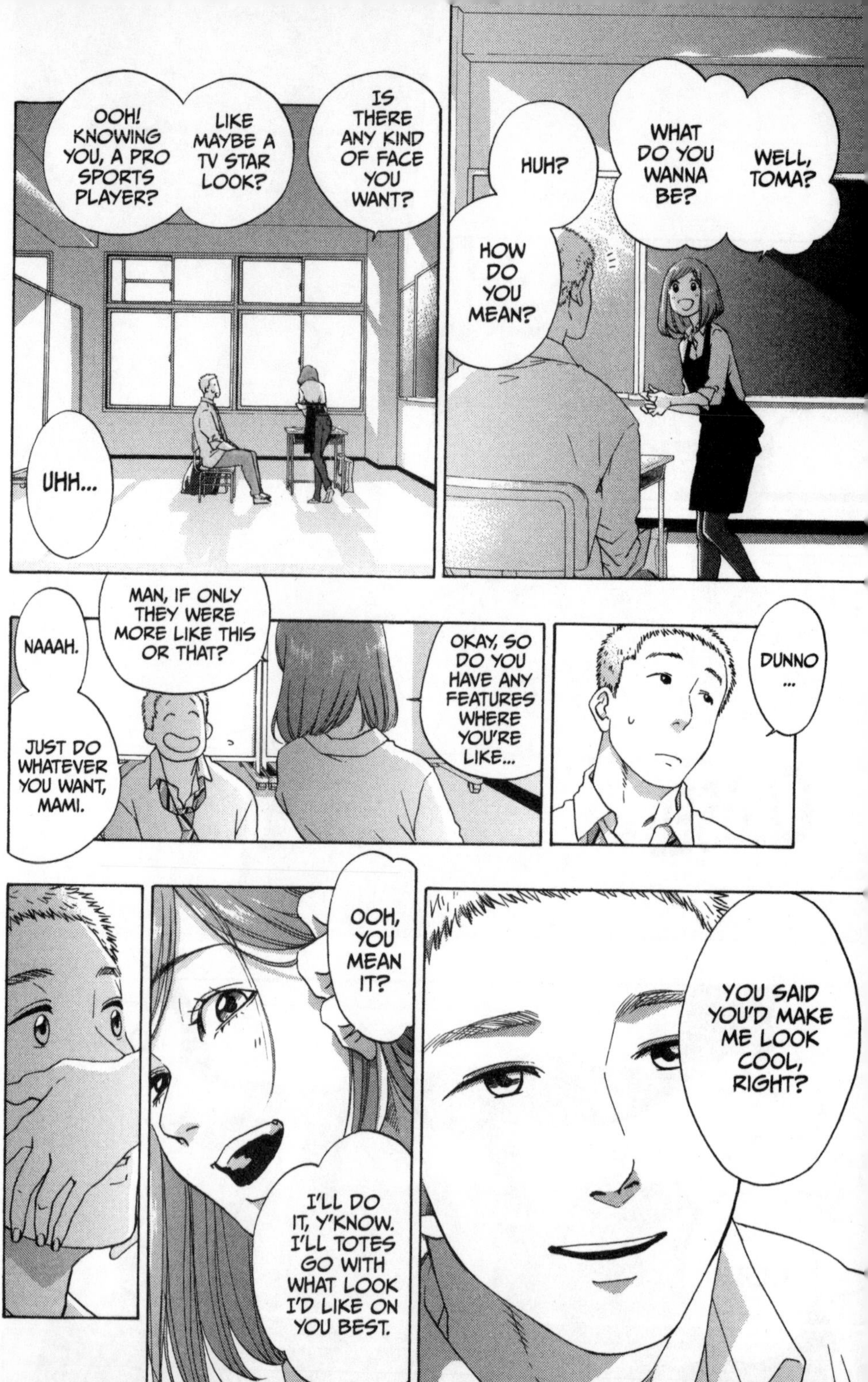
WELL, TOMA?
WHAT DO YOU WANNA BE?
HUH?
HOW DO YOU MEAN?
IS THERE ANY KIND OF FACE YOU WANT?
LIKE MAYBE A TV STAR LOOK?
OOH! KNOWING YOU, A PRO SPORTS PLAYER?
UHH...
DUNNO ...
OKAY, SO DO YOU HAVE ANY FEATURES WHERE YOU'RE LIKE...
MAN, IF ONLY THEY WERE MORE LIKE THIS OR THAT?
NAAAH.
JUST DO WHATEVER YOU WANT, MAMI.
YOU SAID YOU'D MAKE ME LOOK COOL, RIGHT?
OOH, YOU MEAN IT?
I'LL DO IT, Y'KNOW. I'LL TOTES GO WITH WHAT LOOK I'D LIKE ON YOU BEST.

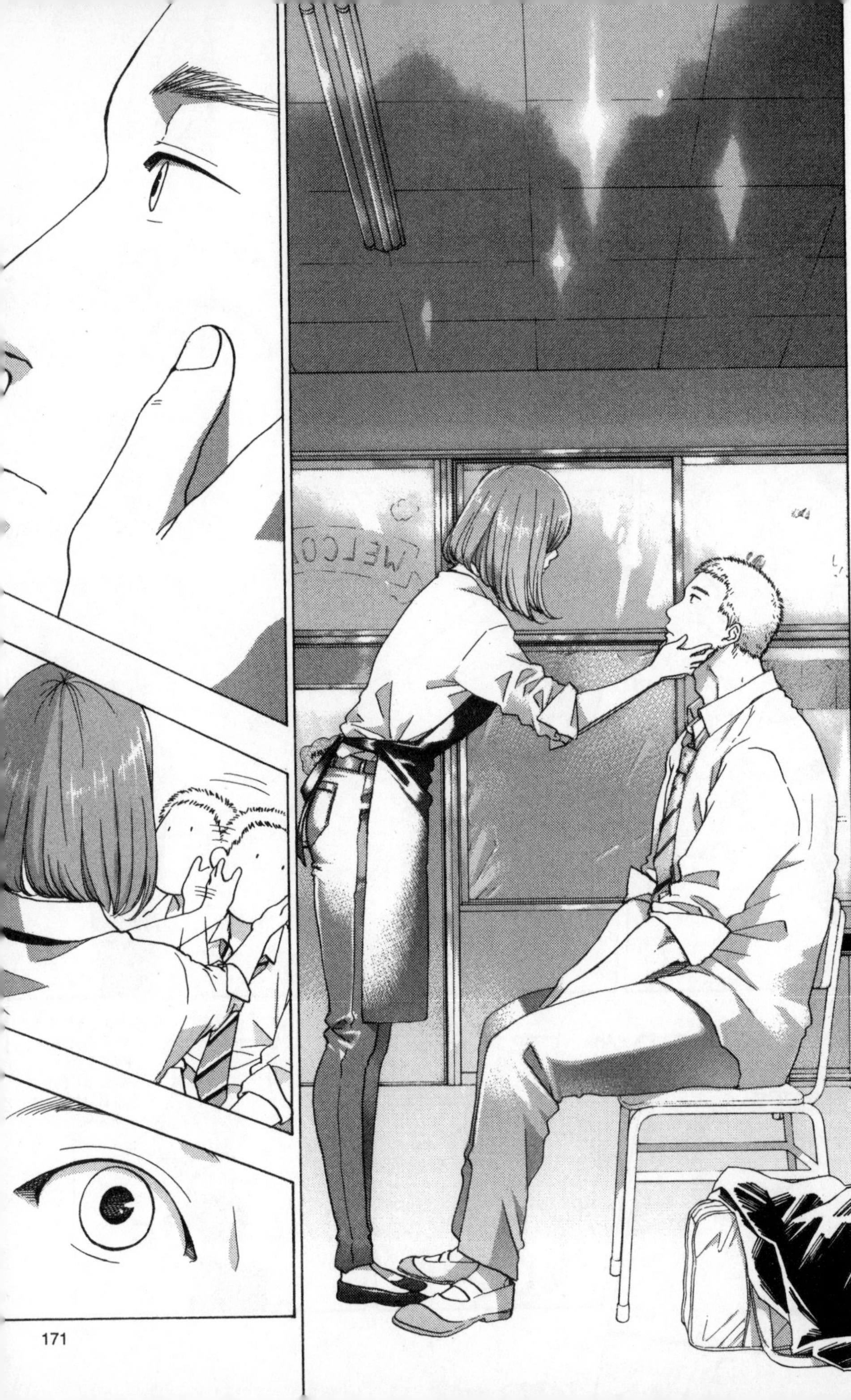

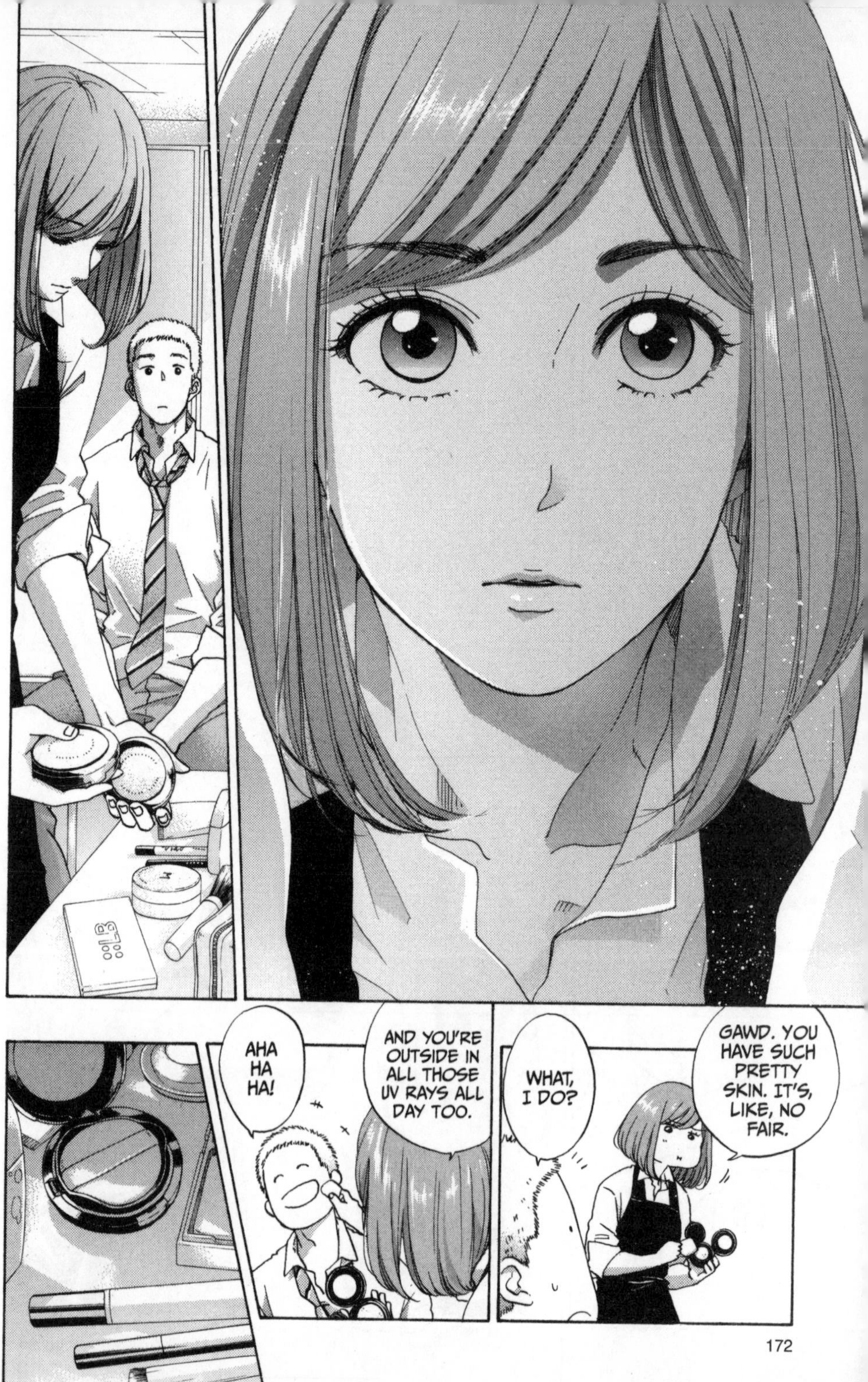
GAWD. YOU HAVE SUCH PRETTY SKIN. IT'S, LIKE, NO FAIR.
WHAT, I DO?
AND YOU'RE OUTSIDE IN ALL THOSE UV RAYS ALL DAY TOO.
AHA HA HA!

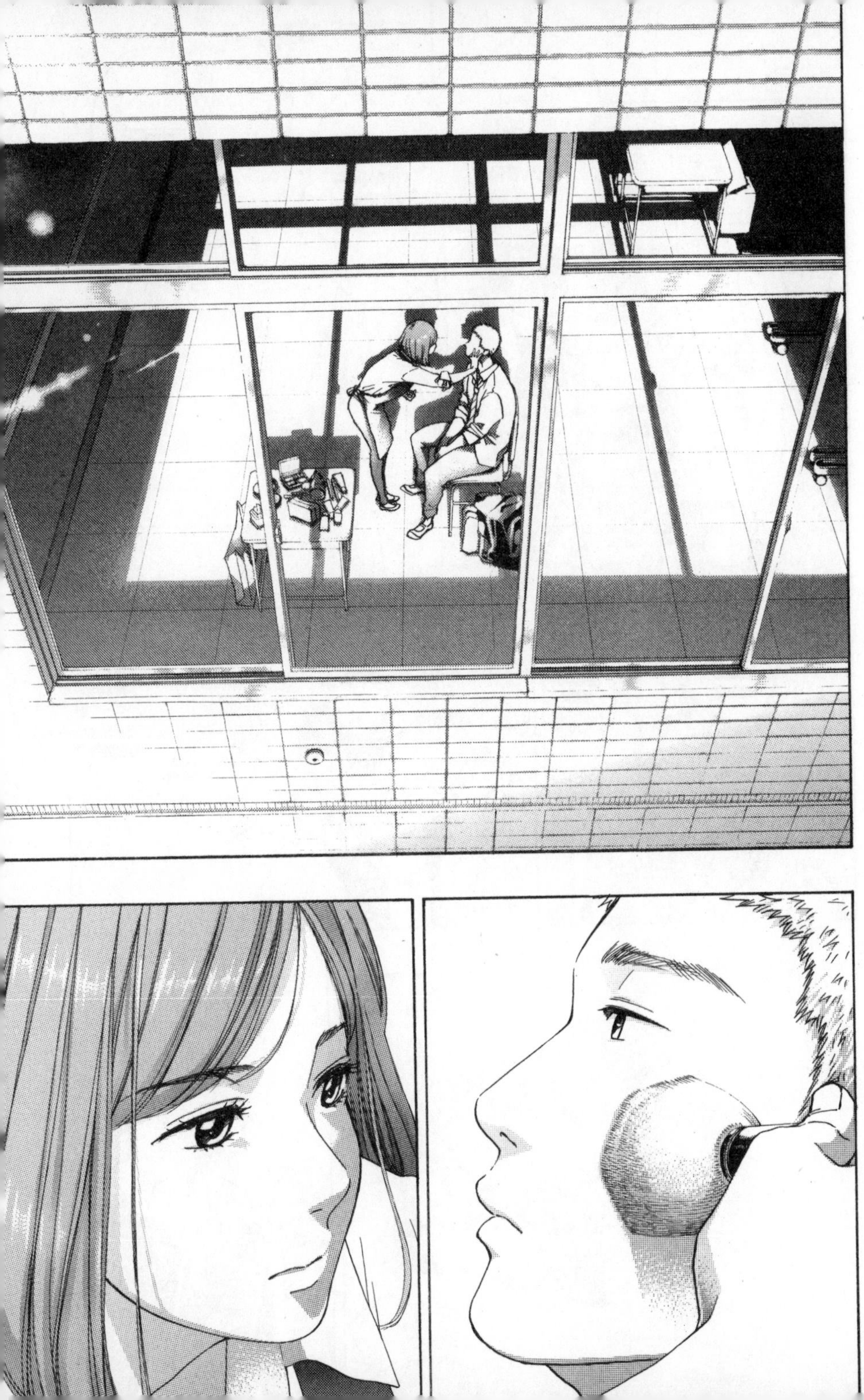

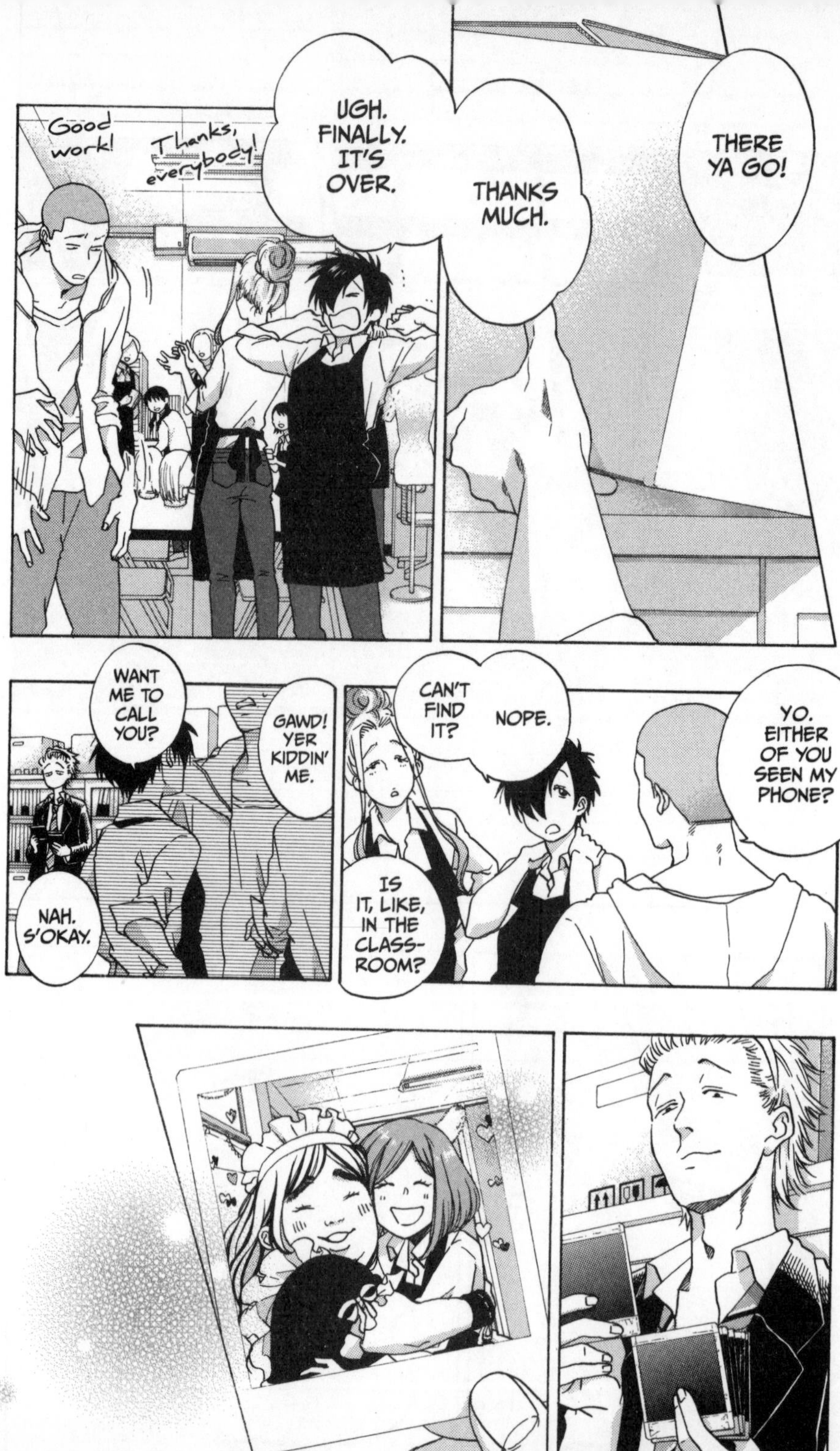
THERE YA GO!
THANKS MUCH.
UGH. FINALLY. IT'S OVER.
Thanks, everybody!
Good work!
YO. EITHER OF YOU SEEN MY PHONE?
CAN'T FIND IT?
NOPE.
IS IT, LIKE, IN THE CLASSROOM?
GAWD! YER KIDDIN' ME.
WANT ME TO CALL YOU?
NAH. S'OKAY.

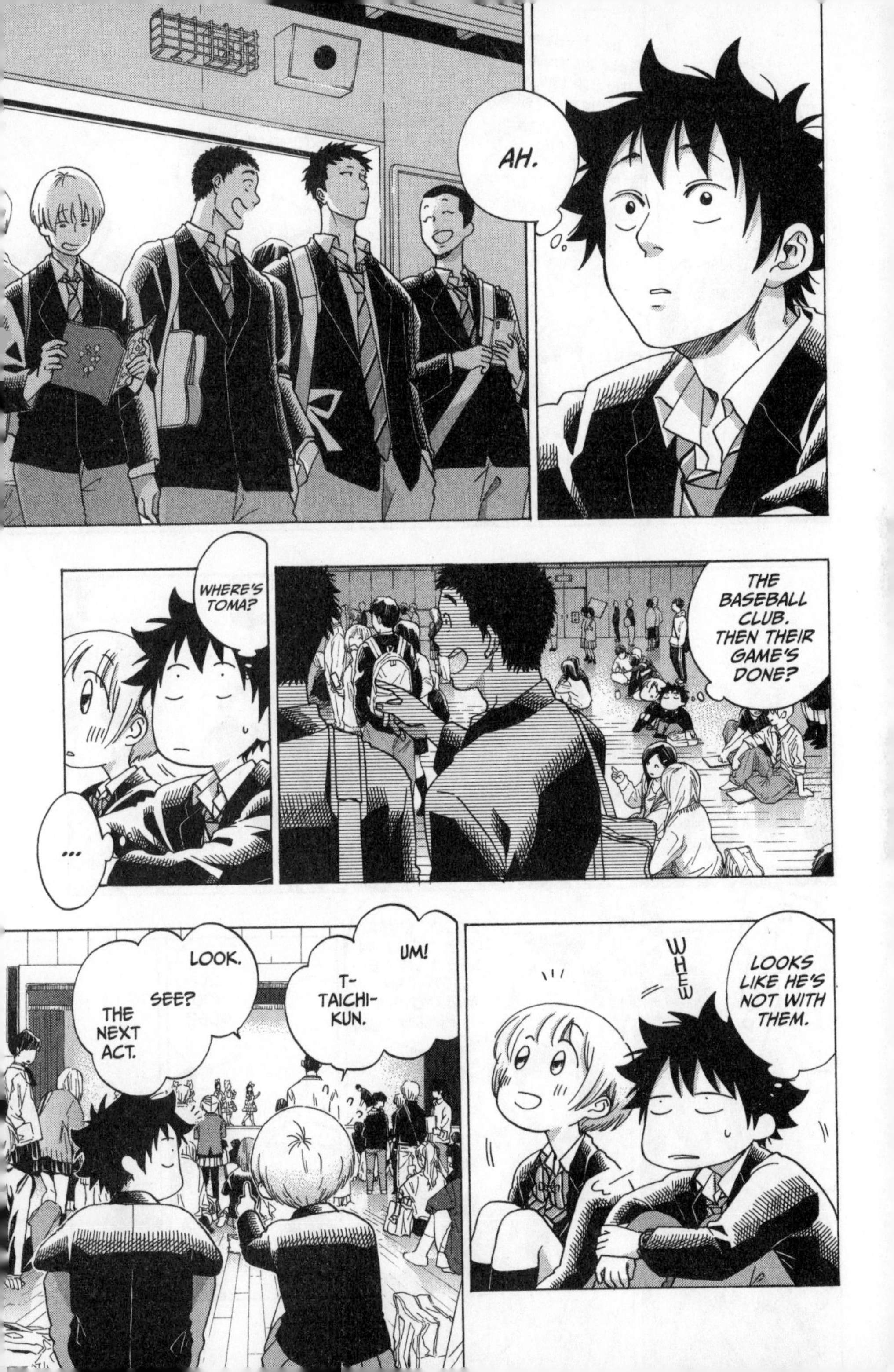
AH.
THE BASEBALL CLUB. THEN THEIR GAME'S DONE?
WHERE'S TOMA?
...
WHEW
LOOKS LIKE HE'S NOT WITH THEM.
UM!
T-TAICHI-KUN.
LOOK.
SEE?
THE NEXT ACT.

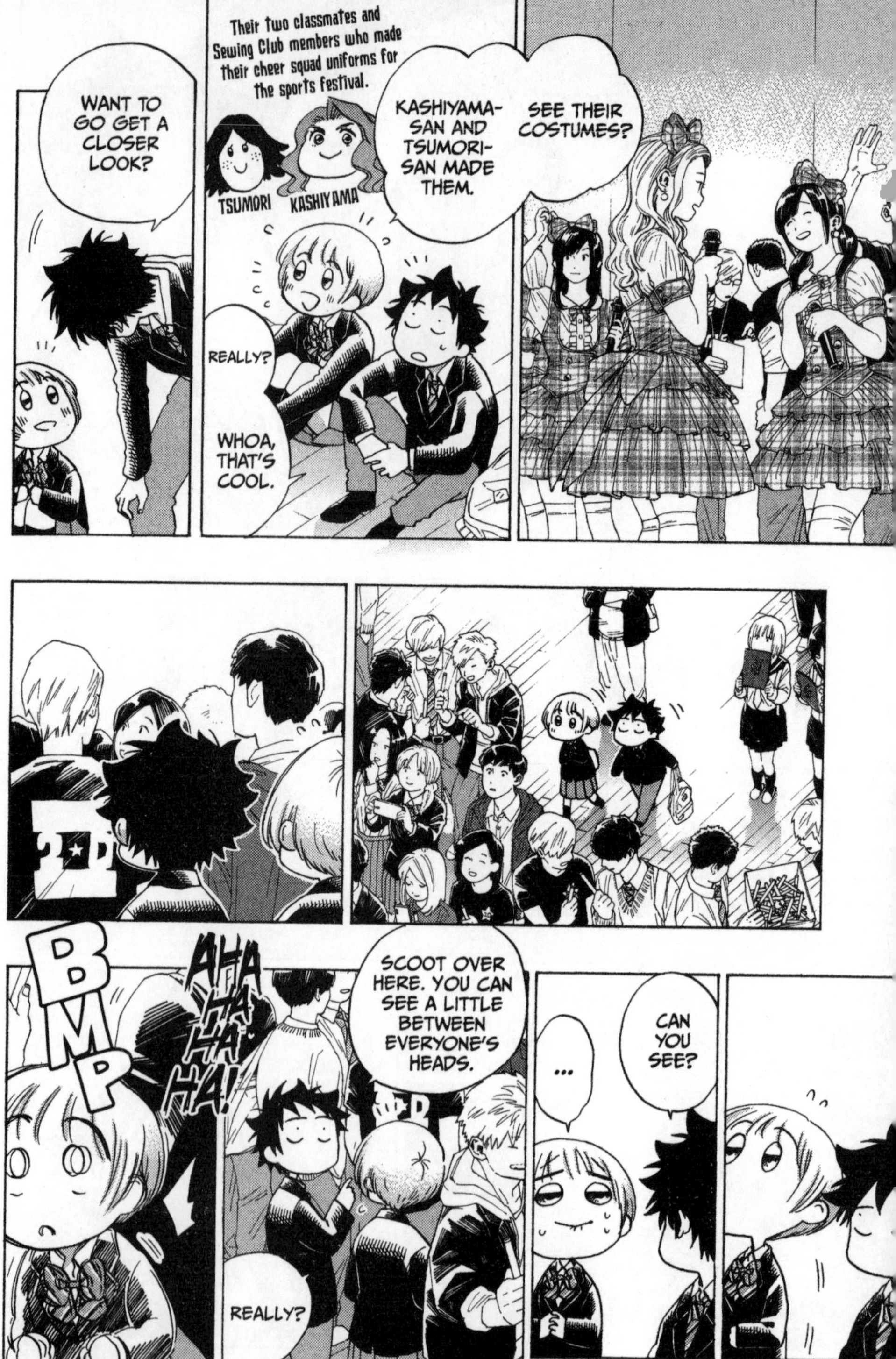
SEE THEIR COSTUMES?
KASHIYAMA-SAN AND TSUMORI-SAN MADE THEM.
Their two classmates and Sewing Club members who made their cheer squad uniforms for the sports festival.
KASHIYAMA
TSUMORI
REALLY?
WHOA, THAT'S COOL.
WANT TO GO GET A CLOSER LOOK?
CAN YOU SEE?
...
SCOOT OVER HERE. YOU CAN SEE A LITTLE BETWEEN EVERYONE'S HEADS.
AHAHAHAHA!
BMP
REALLY?

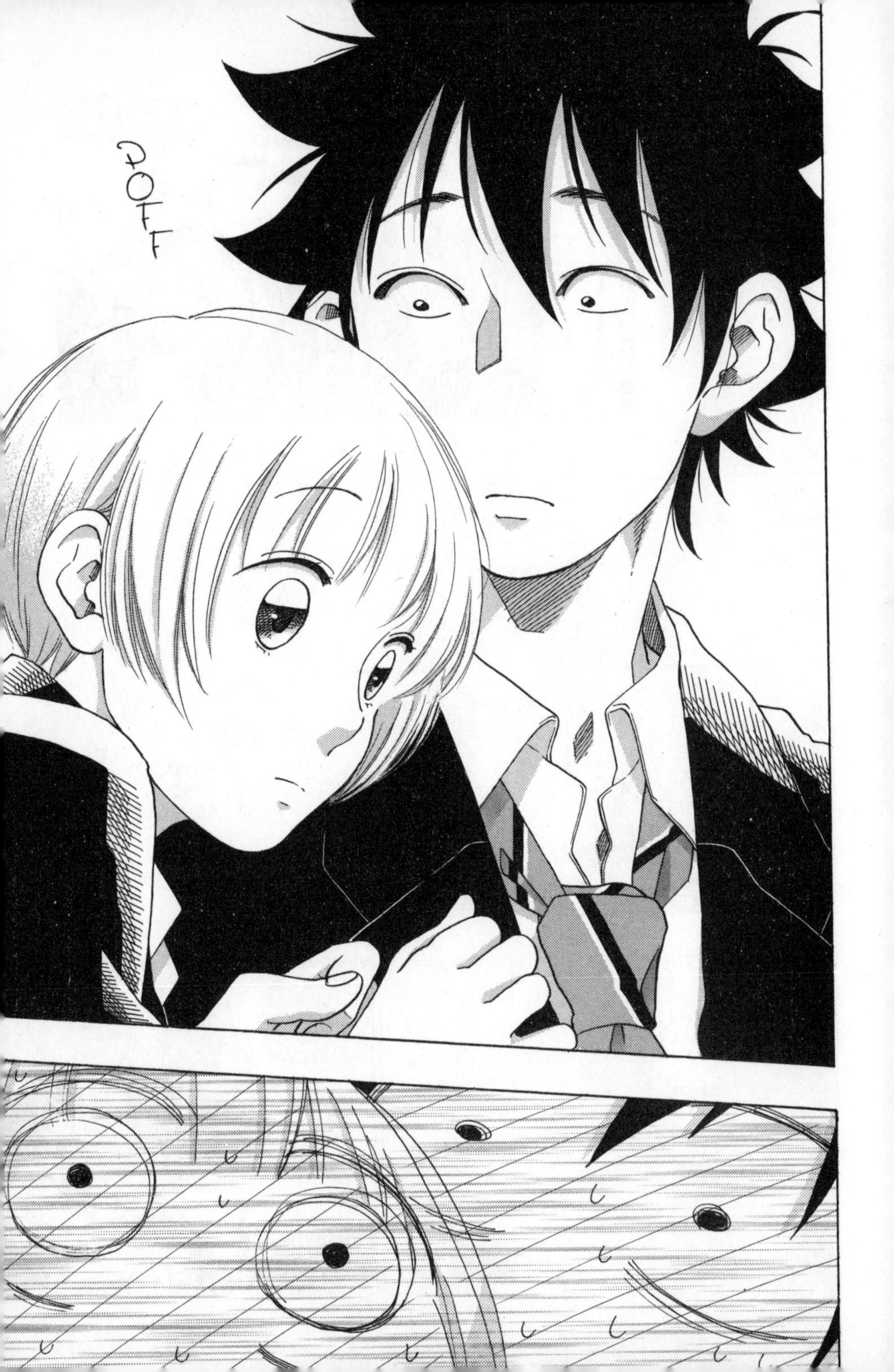
POFF

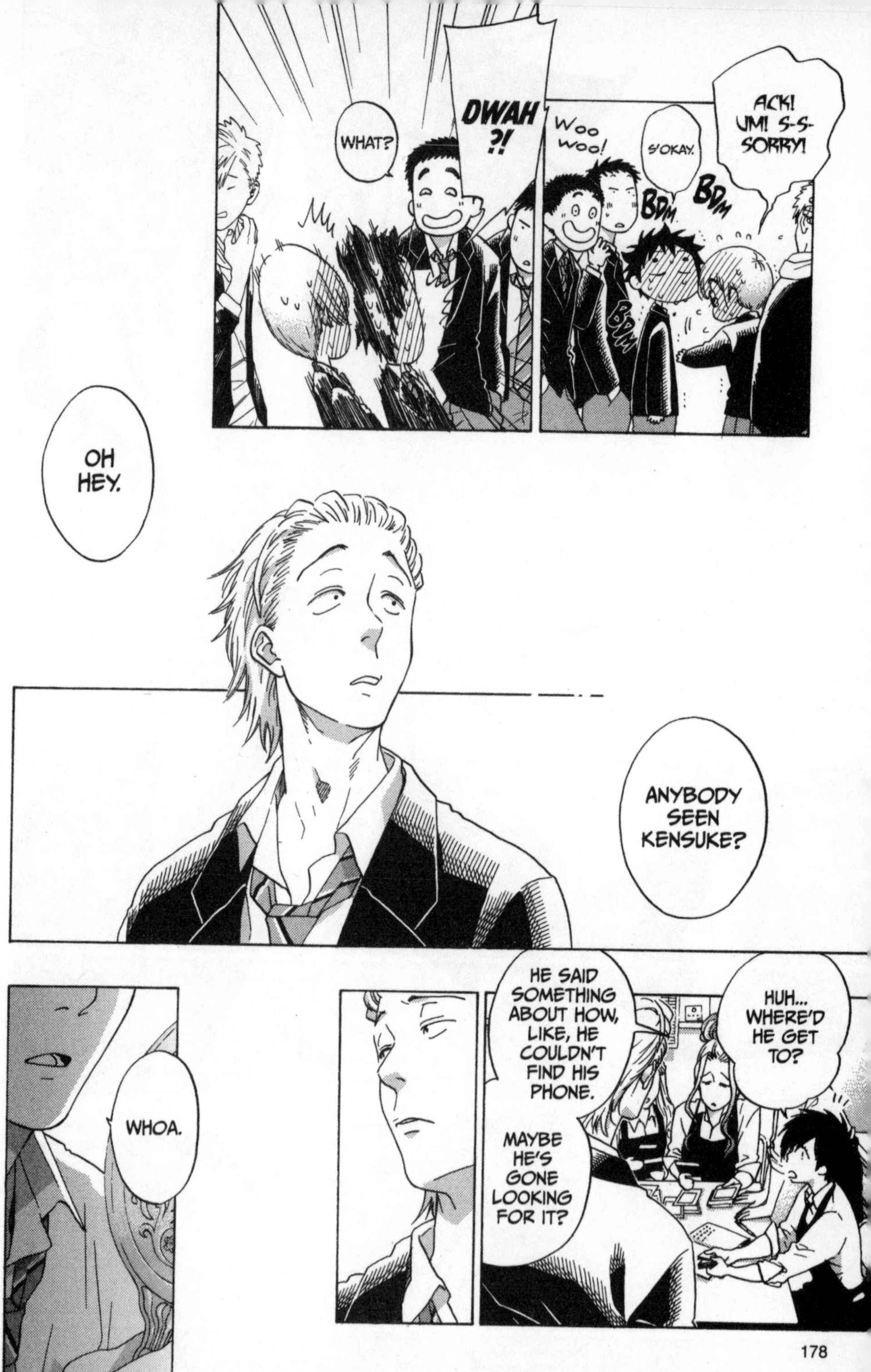
ACK! UM! S-S-SORRY!
S'OKAY.
BDM
Woo woo!
BDM
BDM
DWAH ?!
WHAT?
OH HEY.
ANYBODY SEEN KENSUKE?
HUH... WHERE'D HE GET TO?
HE SAID SOMETHING ABOUT HOW, LIKE, HE COULDN'T FIND HIS PHONE.
MAYBE HE'S GONE LOOKING FOR IT?
WHOA.

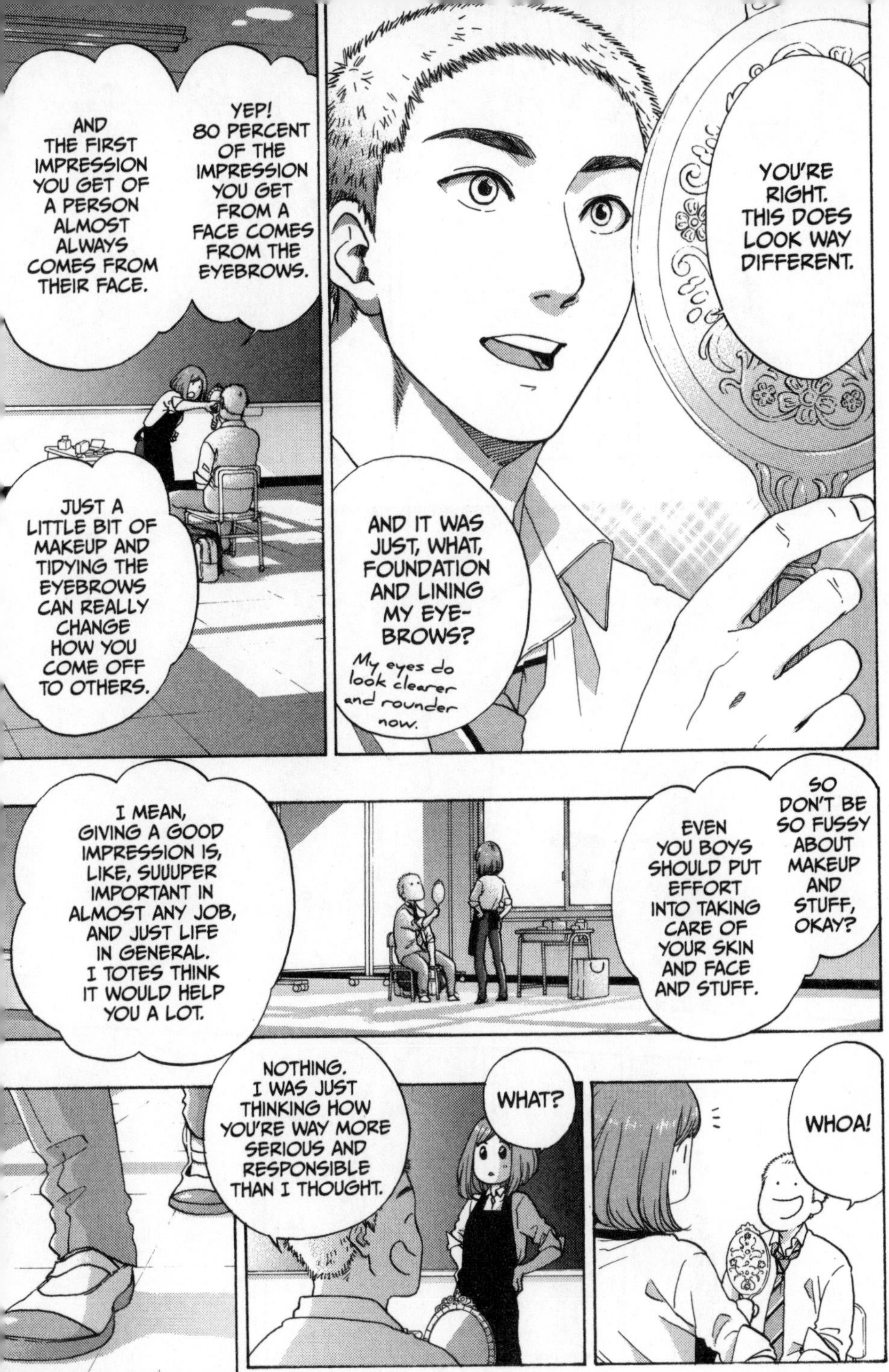
YOU'RE RIGHT. THIS DOES LOOK WAY DIFFERENT.
AND IT WAS JUST, WHAT, FOUNDATION AND LINING MY EYE-BROWS?
My eyes do look clearer and rounder now.
YEP! 80 PERCENT OF THE IMPRESSION YOU GET FROM A FACE COMES FROM THE EYEBROWS.
AND THE FIRST IMPRESSION YOU GET OF A PERSON ALMOST ALWAYS COMES FROM THEIR FACE.
JUST A LITTLE BIT OF MAKEUP AND TIDYING THE EYEBROWS CAN REALLY CHANGE HOW YOU COME OFF TO OTHERS.
SO DON'T BE SO FUSSY ABOUT MAKEUP AND STUFF, OKAY?
EVEN YOU BOYS SHOULD PUT EFFORT INTO TAKING CARE OF YOUR SKIN AND FACE AND STUFF.
I MEAN, GIVING A GOOD IMPRESSION IS, LIKE, SUUUPER IMPORTANT IN ALMOST ANY JOB, AND JUST LIFE IN GENERAL. I TOTES THINK IT WOULD HELP YOU A LOT.
WHOA!
WHAT?
NOTHING. I WAS JUST THINKING HOW YOU'RE WAY MORE SERIOUS AND RESPONSIBLE THAN I THOUGHT.

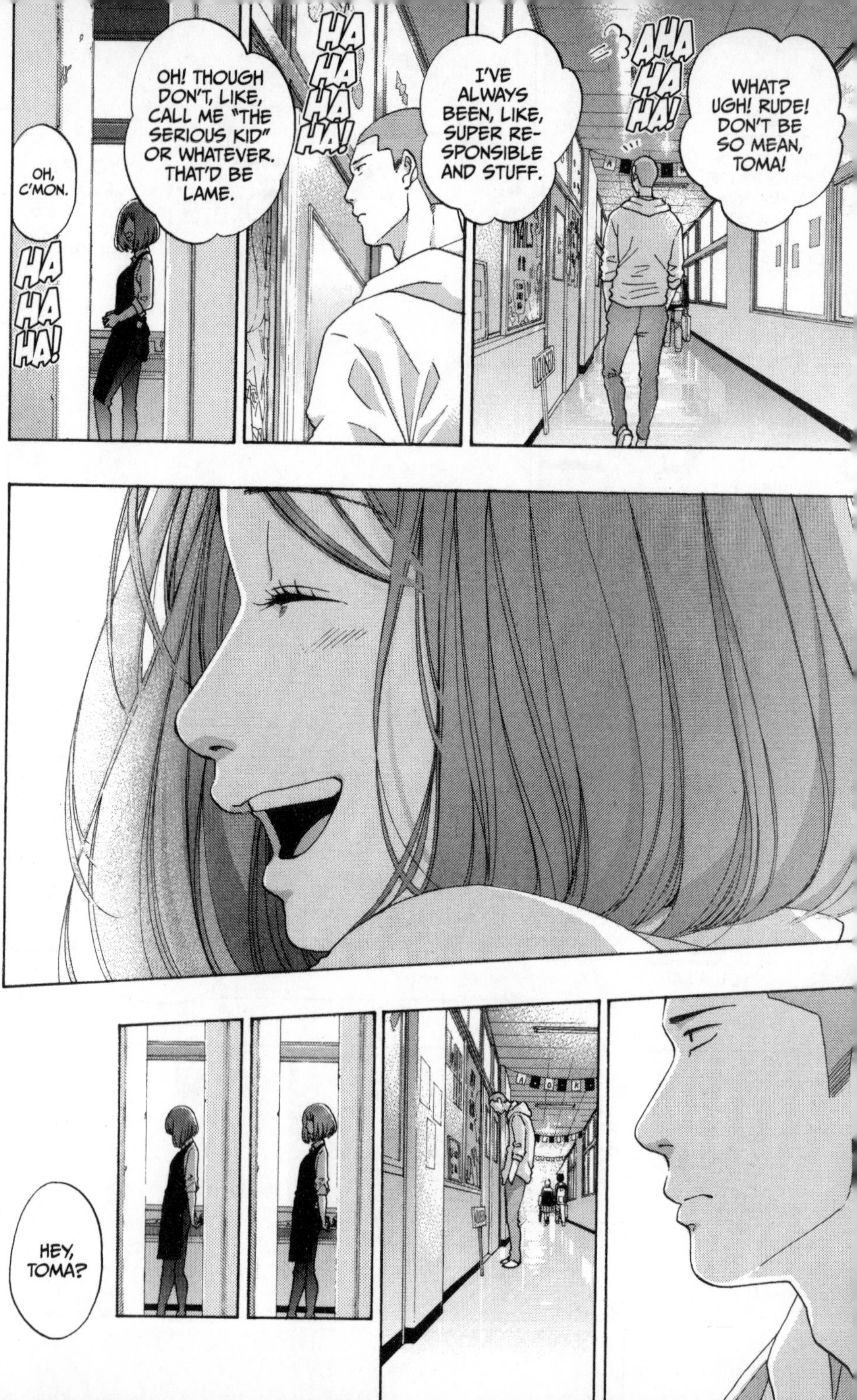
WHAT? UGH! RUDE! DON'T BE SO MEAN, TOMA!
AHA HA HA!
I'VE ALWAYS BEEN, LIKE, SUPER RE-SPONSIBLE AND STUFF.
HA HA HA HA!
OH! THOUGH DON'T, LIKE, CALL ME "THE SERIOUS KID" OR WHATEVER. THAT'D BE LAME.
OH, C'MON.
HA HA HA!
HEY, TOMA?

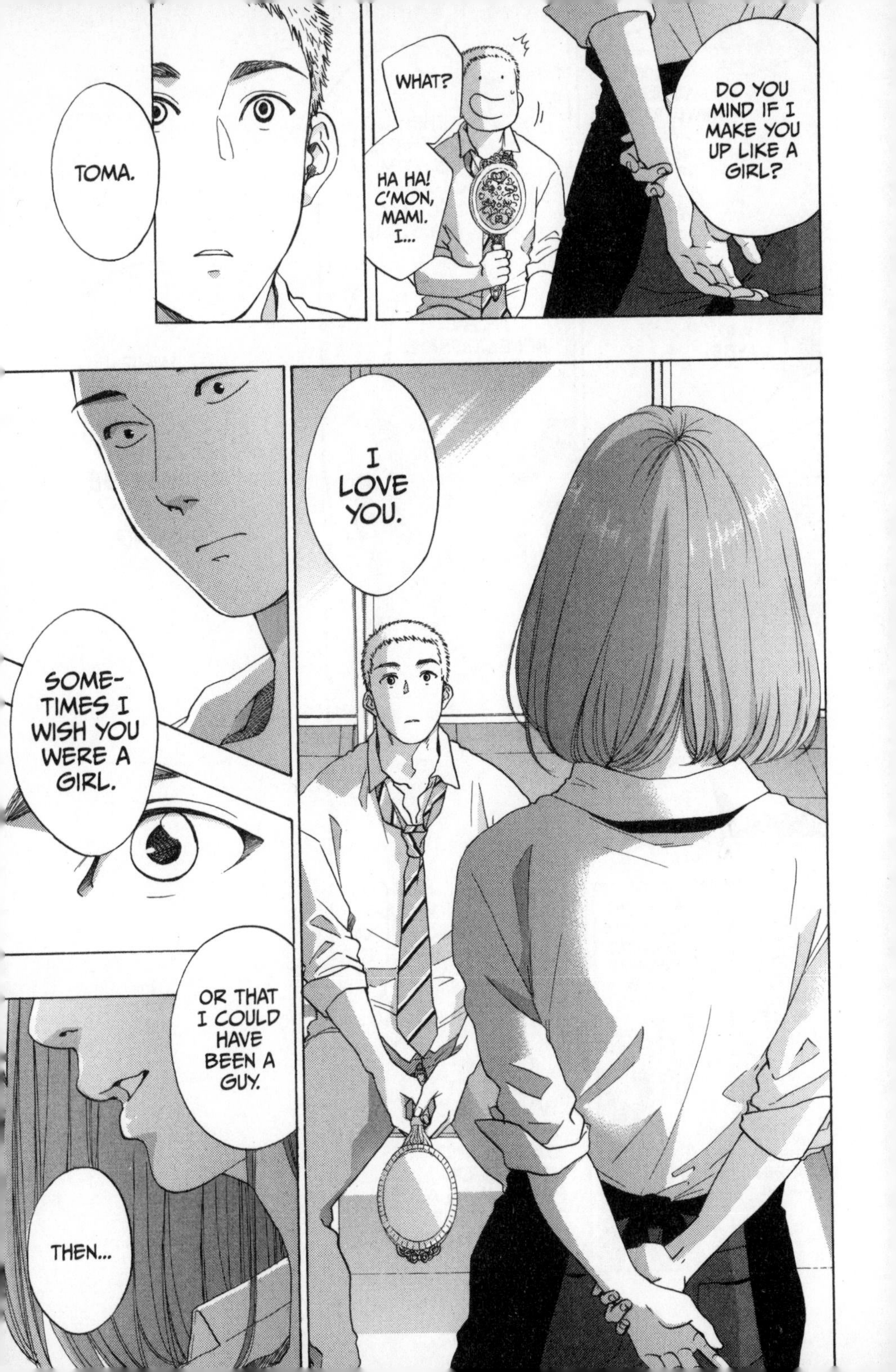
DO YOU MIND IF I MAKE YOU UP LIKE A GIRL?
WHAT?
HA HA! C'MON, MAMI. I...
TOMA.
I LOVE YOU.
SOMETIMES I WISH YOU WERE A GIRL.
OR THAT I COULD HAVE BEEN A GUY.
THEN...

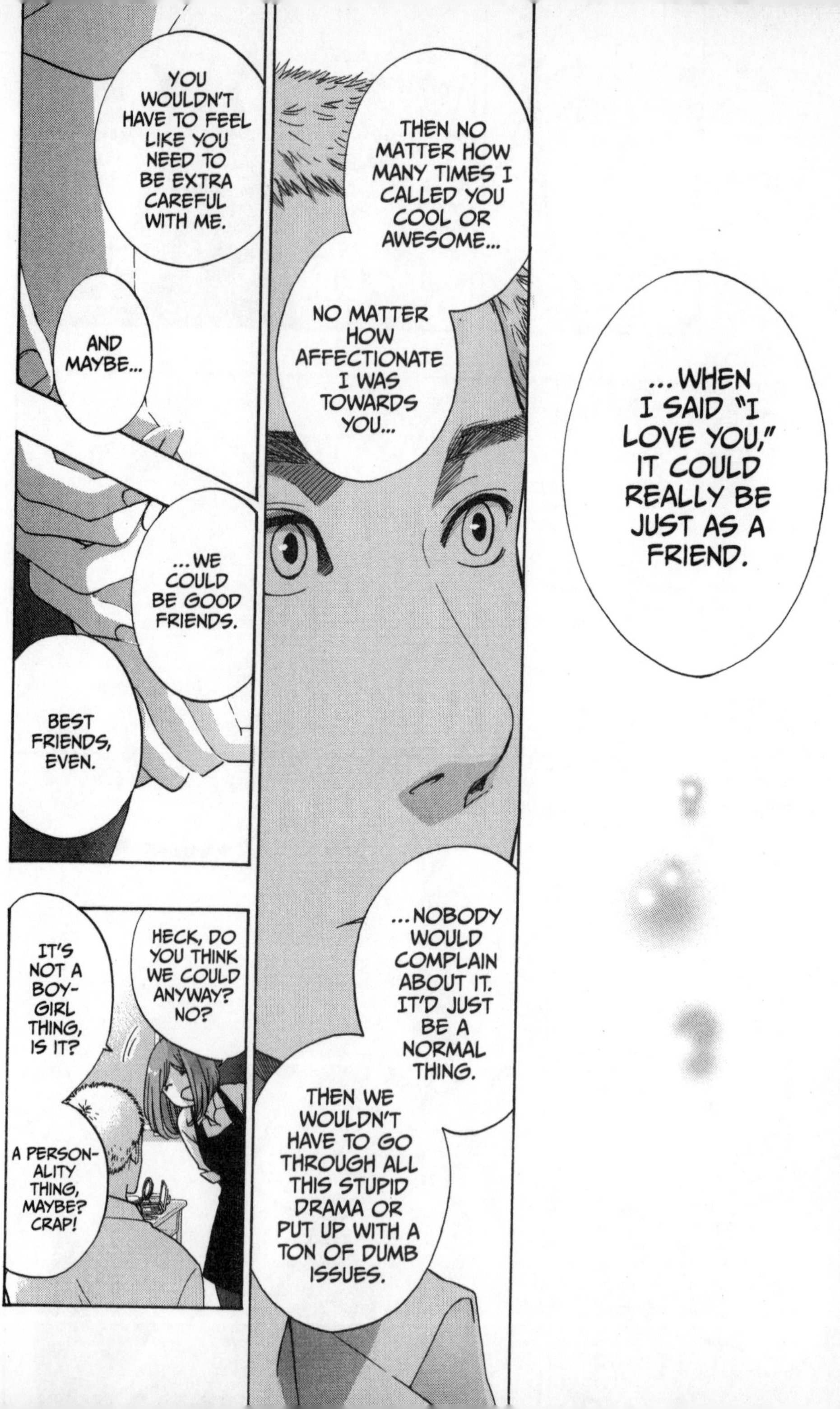
...WHEN I SAID "I LOVE YOU," IT COULD REALLY BE JUST AS A FRIEND.
THEN NO MATTER HOW MANY TIMES I CALLED YOU COOL OR AWESOME...
NO MATTER HOW AFFECTIONATE I WAS TOWARDS YOU...
...NOBODY WOULD COMPLAIN ABOUT IT. IT'D JUST BE A NORMAL THING.
THEN WE WOULDN'T HAVE TO GO THROUGH ALL THIS STUPID DRAMA OR PUT UP WITH A TON OF DUMB ISSUES.
YOU WOULDN'T HAVE TO FEEL LIKE YOU NEED TO BE EXTRA CAREFUL WITH ME.
AND MAYBE...
...WE COULD BE GOOD FRIENDS.
BEST FRIENDS, EVEN.
HECK, DO YOU THINK WE COULD ANYWAY? NO?
IT'S NOT A BOY-GIRL THING, IS IT?
A PERSONALITY THING, MAYBE? CRAP!

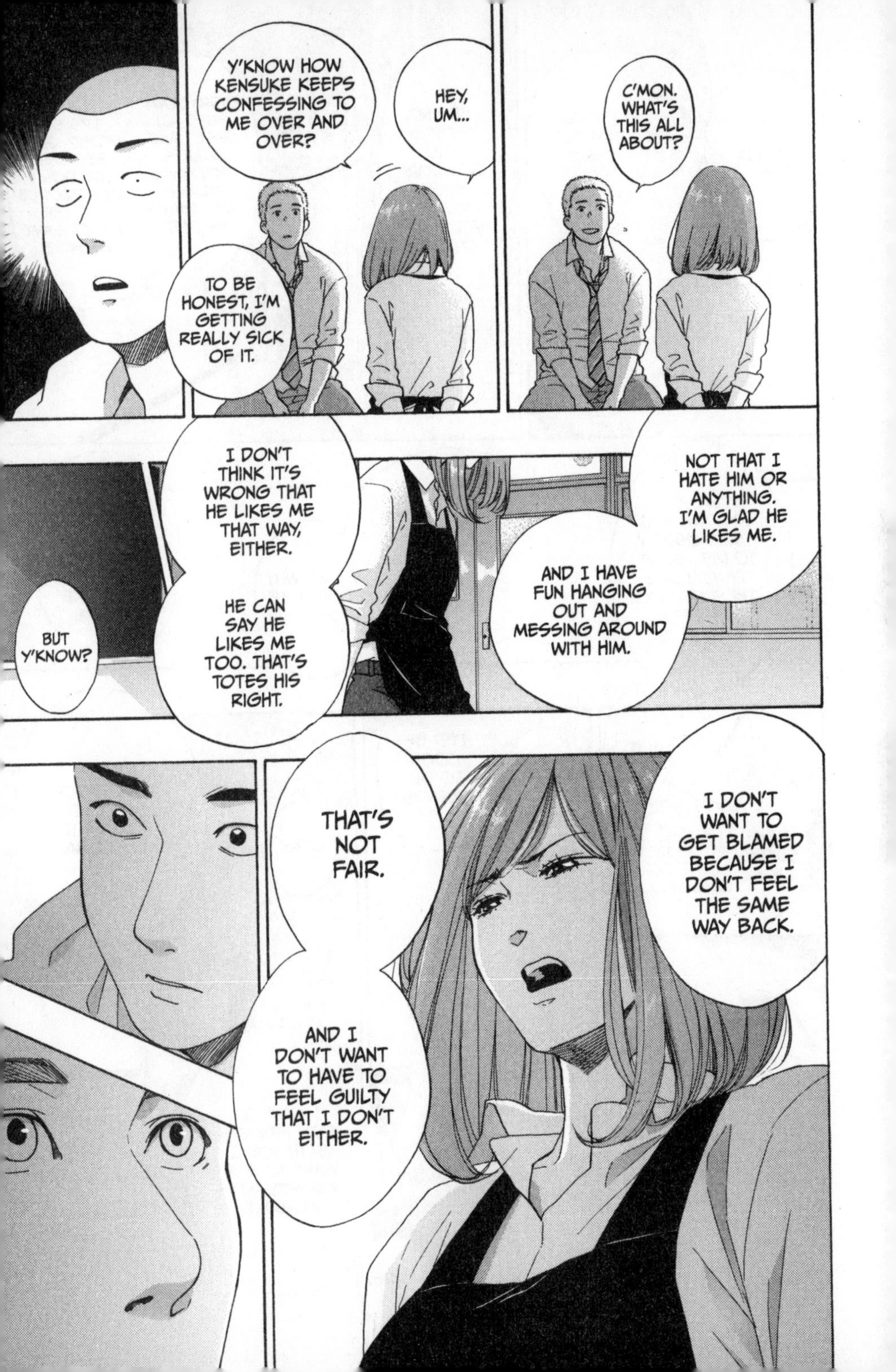
C'MON. WHAT'S THIS ALL ABOUT?
HEY, UM...
Y'KNOW HOW KENSUKE KEEPS CONFESSING TO ME OVER AND OVER?
TO BE HONEST, I'M GETTING REALLY SICK OF IT.
NOT THAT I HATE HIM OR ANYTHING. I'M GLAD HE LIKES ME.
AND I HAVE FUN HANGING OUT AND MESSING AROUND WITH HIM.
I DON'T THINK IT'S WRONG THAT HE LIKES ME THAT WAY, EITHER.
HE CAN SAY HE LIKES ME TOO. THAT'S TOTES HIS RIGHT.
BUT Y'KNOW?
I DON'T WANT TO GET BLAMED BECAUSE I DON'T FEEL THE SAME WAY BACK.
THAT'S NOT FAIR.
AND I DON'T WANT TO HAVE TO FEEL GUILTY THAT I DON'T EITHER.

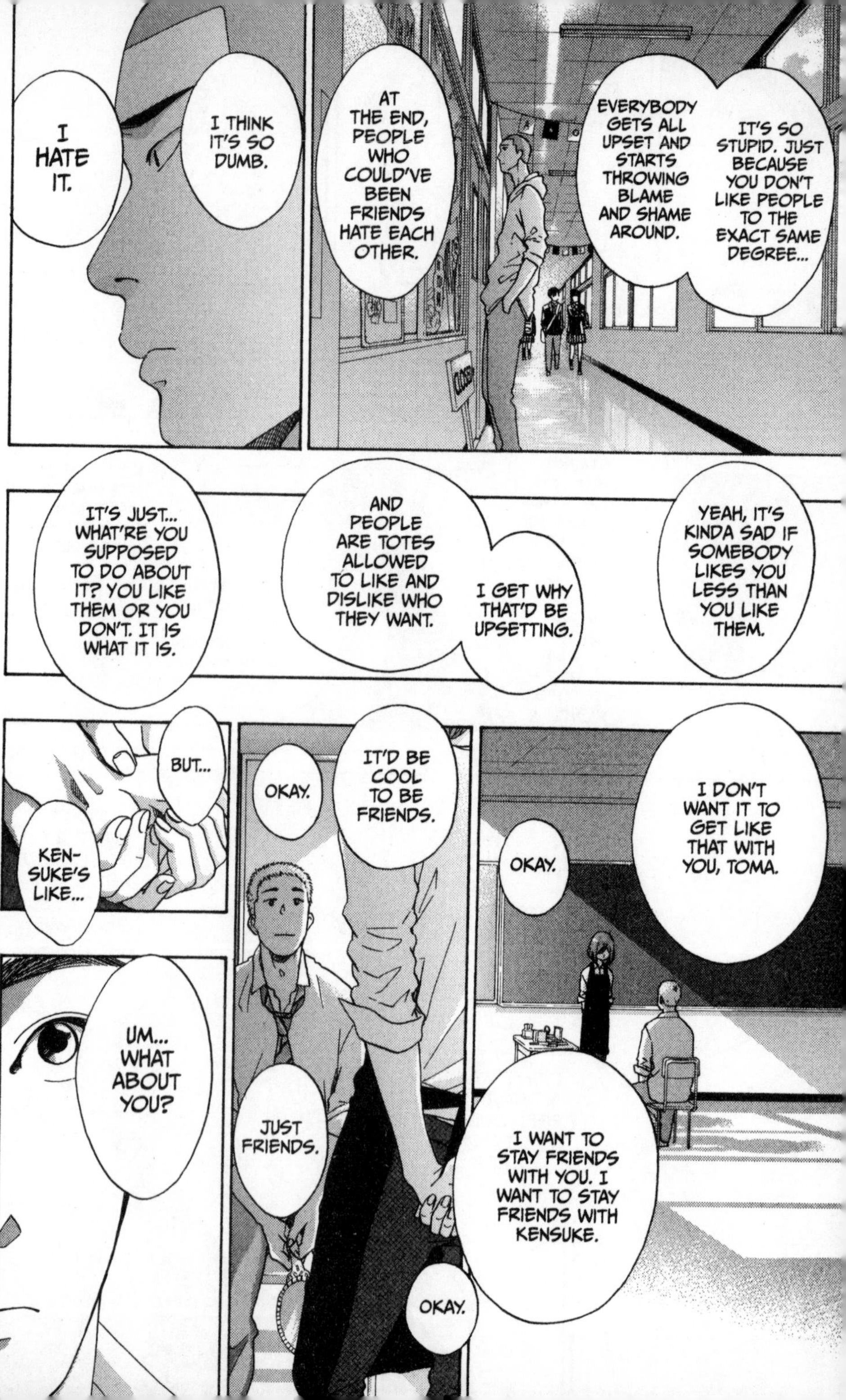
IT'S SO STUPID. JUST BECAUSE YOU DON'T LIKE PEOPLE TO THE EXACT SAME DEGREE...
EVERYBODY GETS ALL UPSET AND STARTS THROWING BLAME AND SHAME AROUND.
AT THE END, PEOPLE WHO COULD'VE BEEN FRIENDS HATE EACH OTHER.
I THINK IT'S SO DUMB.
I HATE IT.
YEAH, IT'S KINDA SAD IF SOMEBODY LIKES YOU LESS THAN YOU LIKE THEM.
I GET WHY THAT'D BE UPSETTING.
AND PEOPLE ARE TOTES ALLOWED TO LIKE AND DISLIKE WHO THEY WANT.
IT'S JUST... WHAT'RE YOU SUPPOSED TO DO ABOUT IT? YOU LIKE THEM OR YOU DON'T. IT IS WHAT IT IS.
I DON'T WANT IT TO GET LIKE THAT WITH YOU, TOMA.
OKAY.
I WANT TO STAY FRIENDS WITH YOU. I WANT TO STAY FRIENDS WITH KENSUKE.
OKAY.
IT'D BE COOL TO BE FRIENDS.
OKAY.
JUST FRIENDS.
BUT...
KEN-SUKE'S LIKE...
UM... WHAT ABOUT YOU?

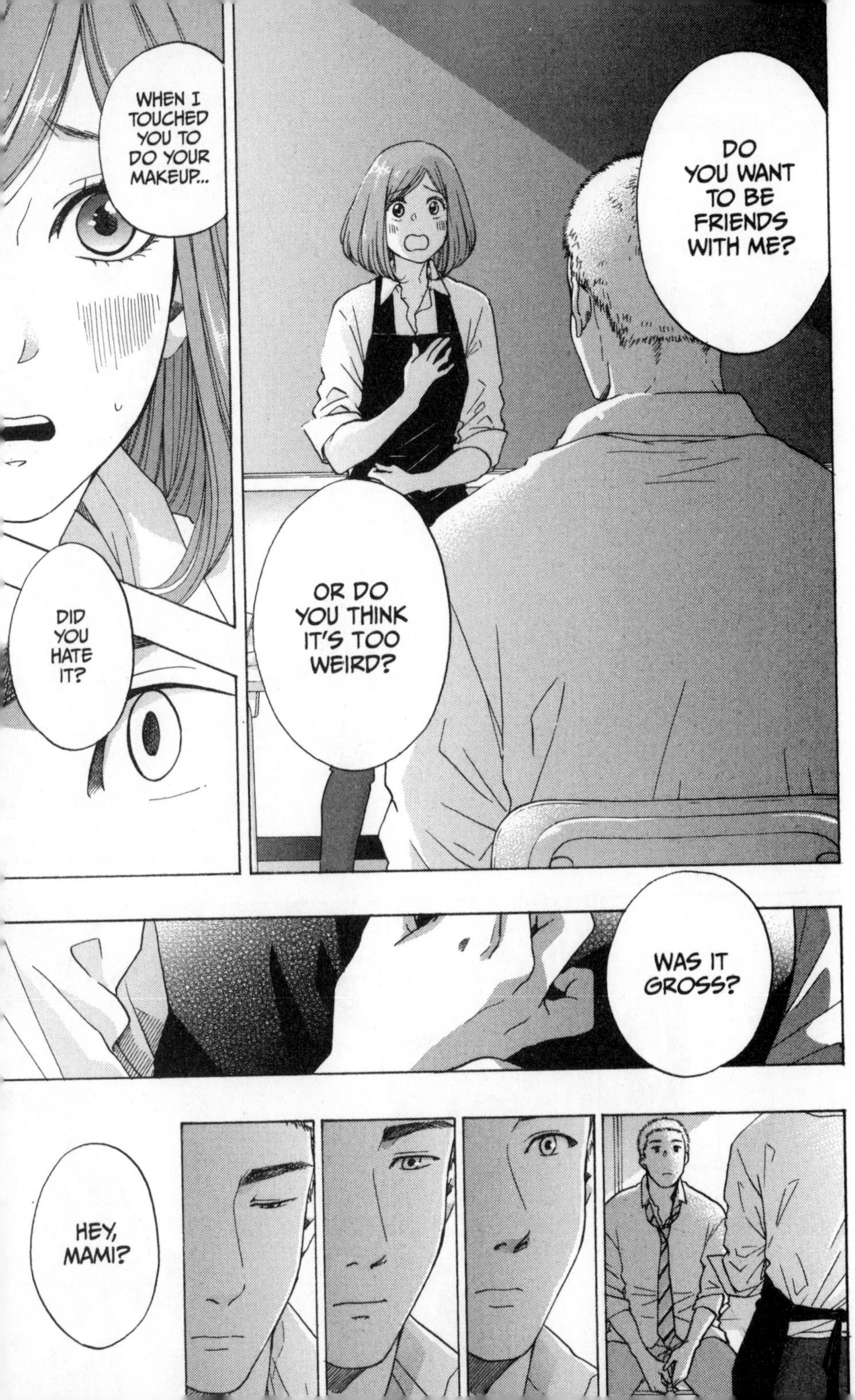
DO YOU WANT TO BE FRIENDS WITH ME?
OR DO YOU THINK IT'S TOO WEIRD?
WHEN I TOUCHED YOU TO DO YOUR MAKEUP...
DID YOU HATE IT?
WAS IT GROSS?
HEY, MAMI?

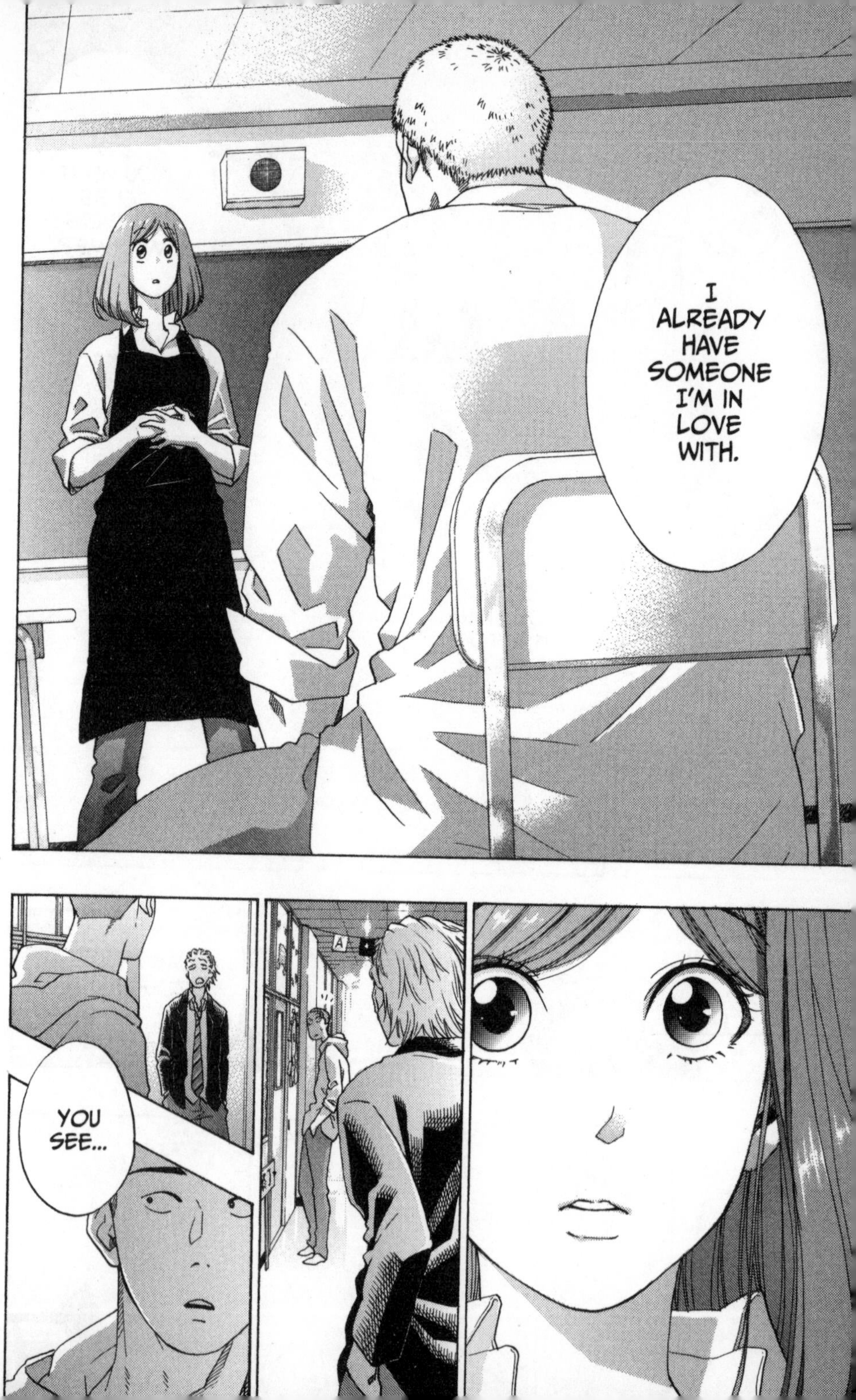
I ALREADY HAVE SOMEONE I'M IN LOVE WITH.
YOU SEE...

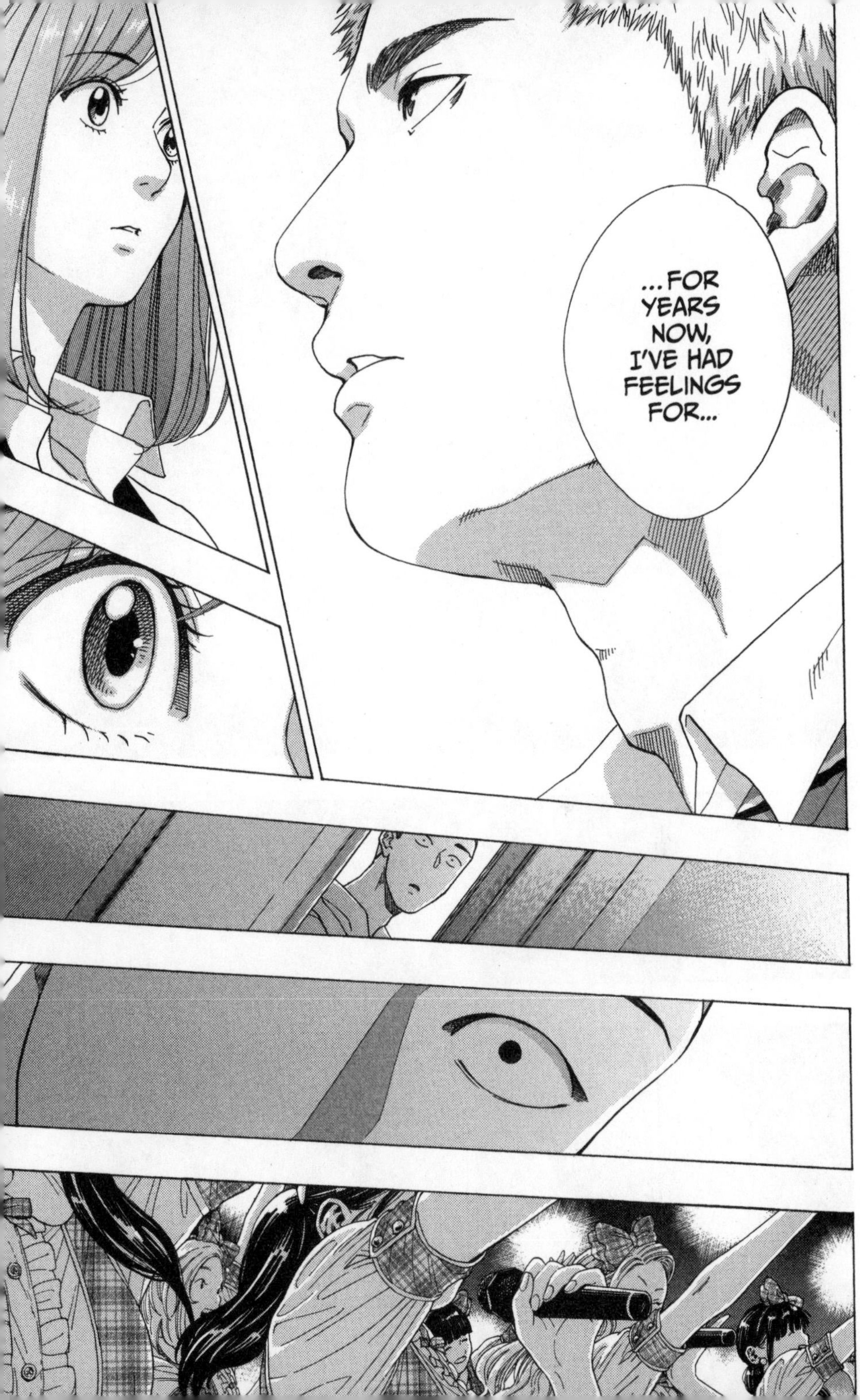
...FOR YEARS NOW, I'VE HAD FEELINGS FOR...

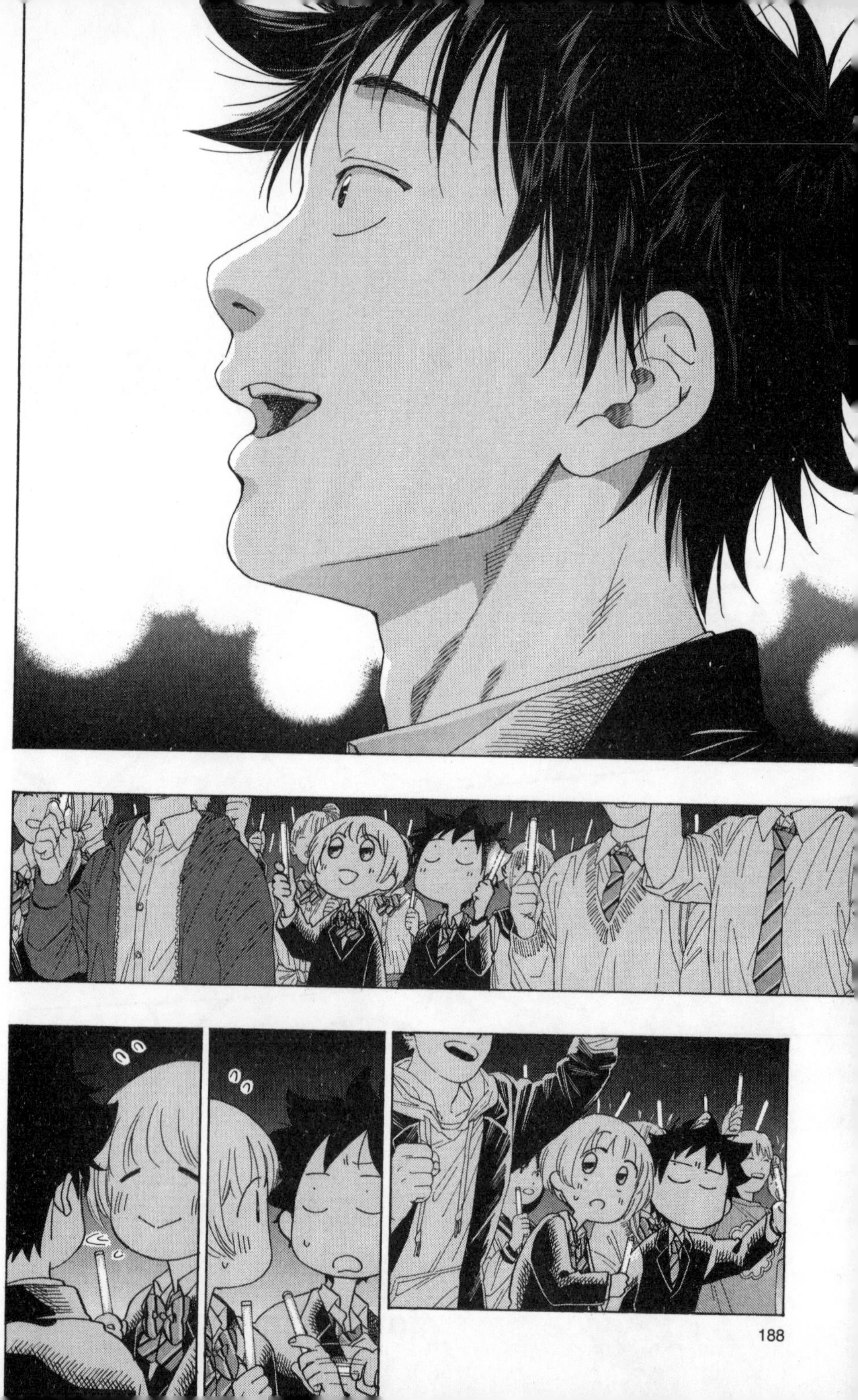

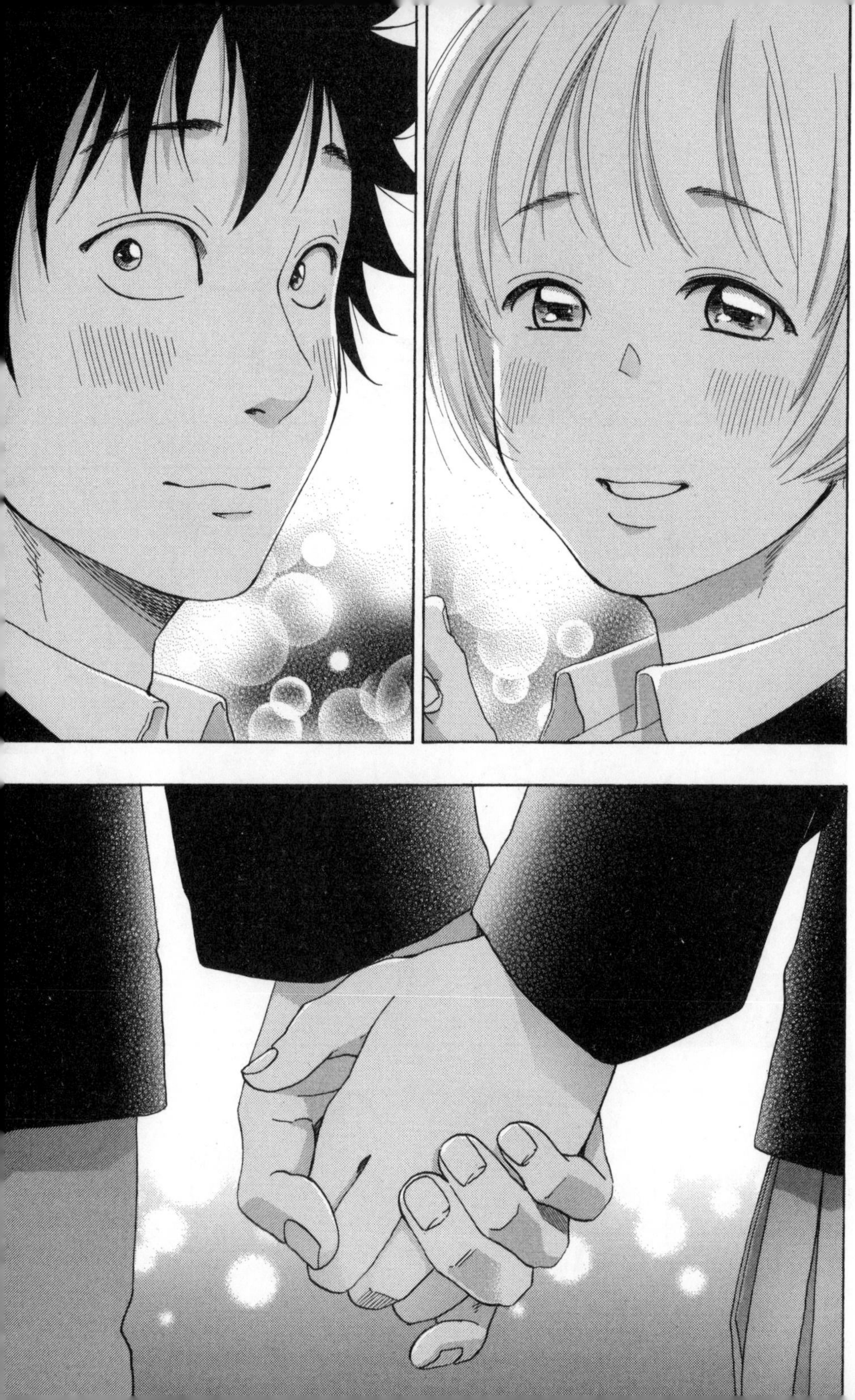

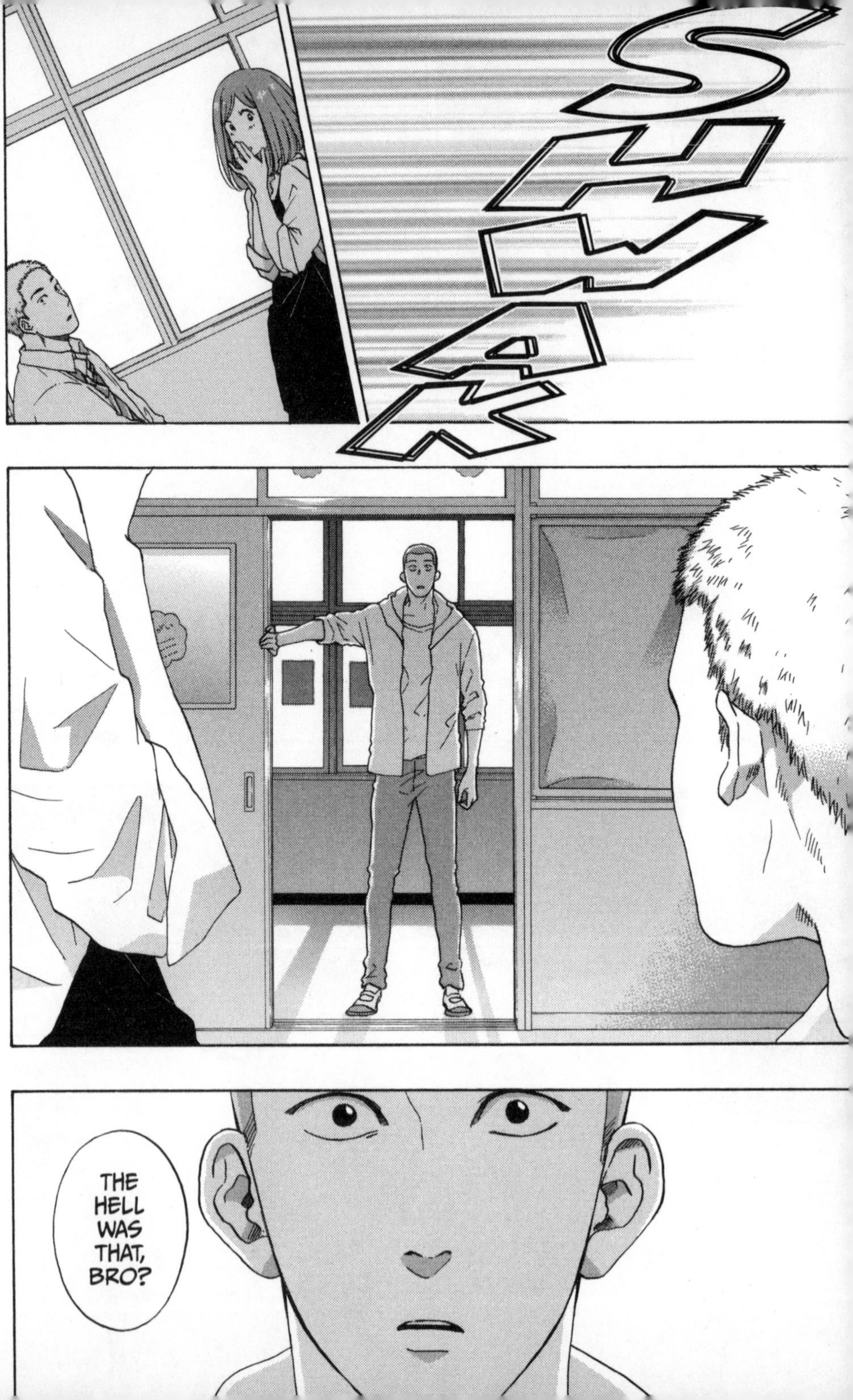
SHWACK
THE HELL WAS THAT, BRO?

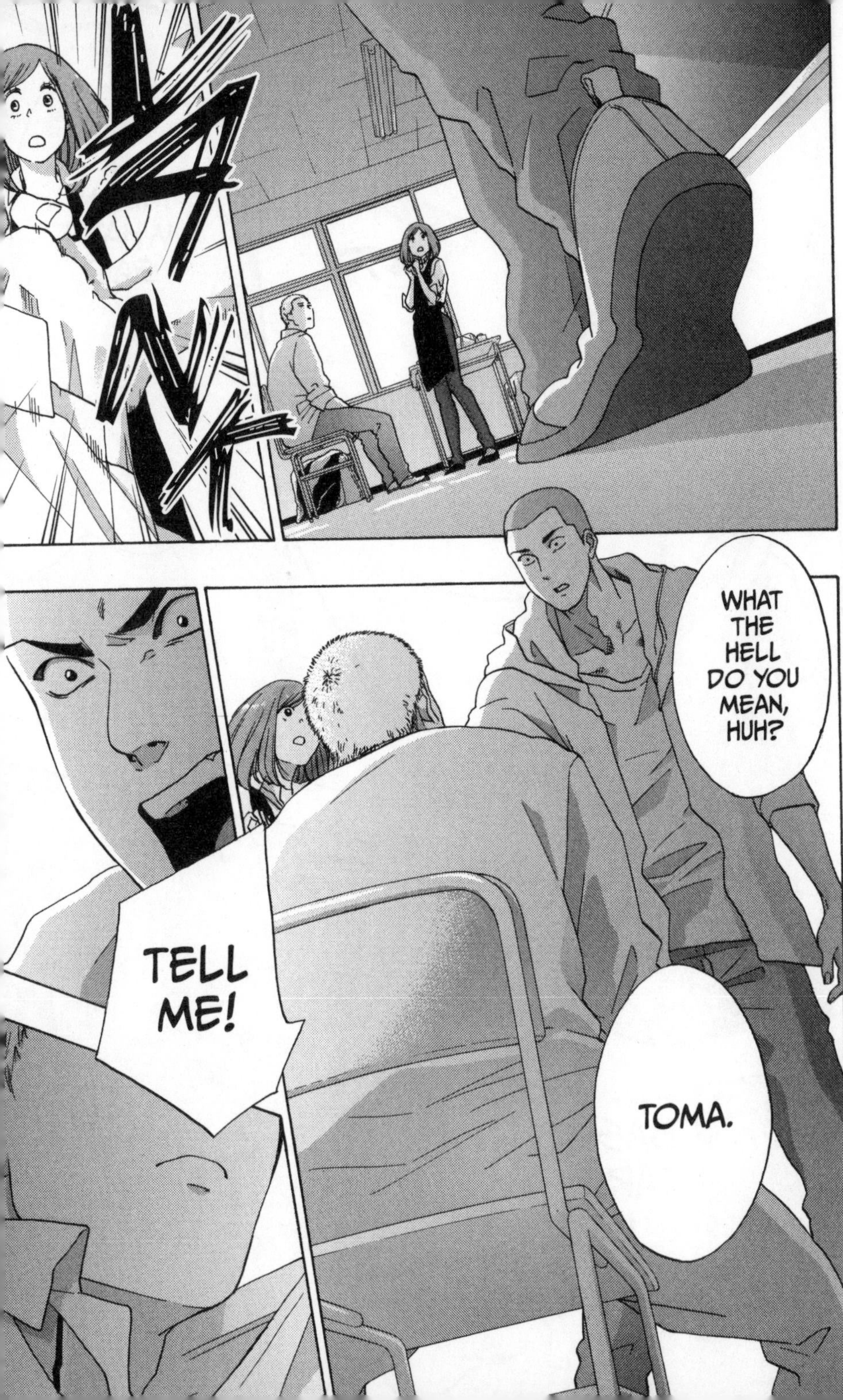
WHAT THE HELL DO YOU MEAN, HUH?
TOMA.
TELL ME!

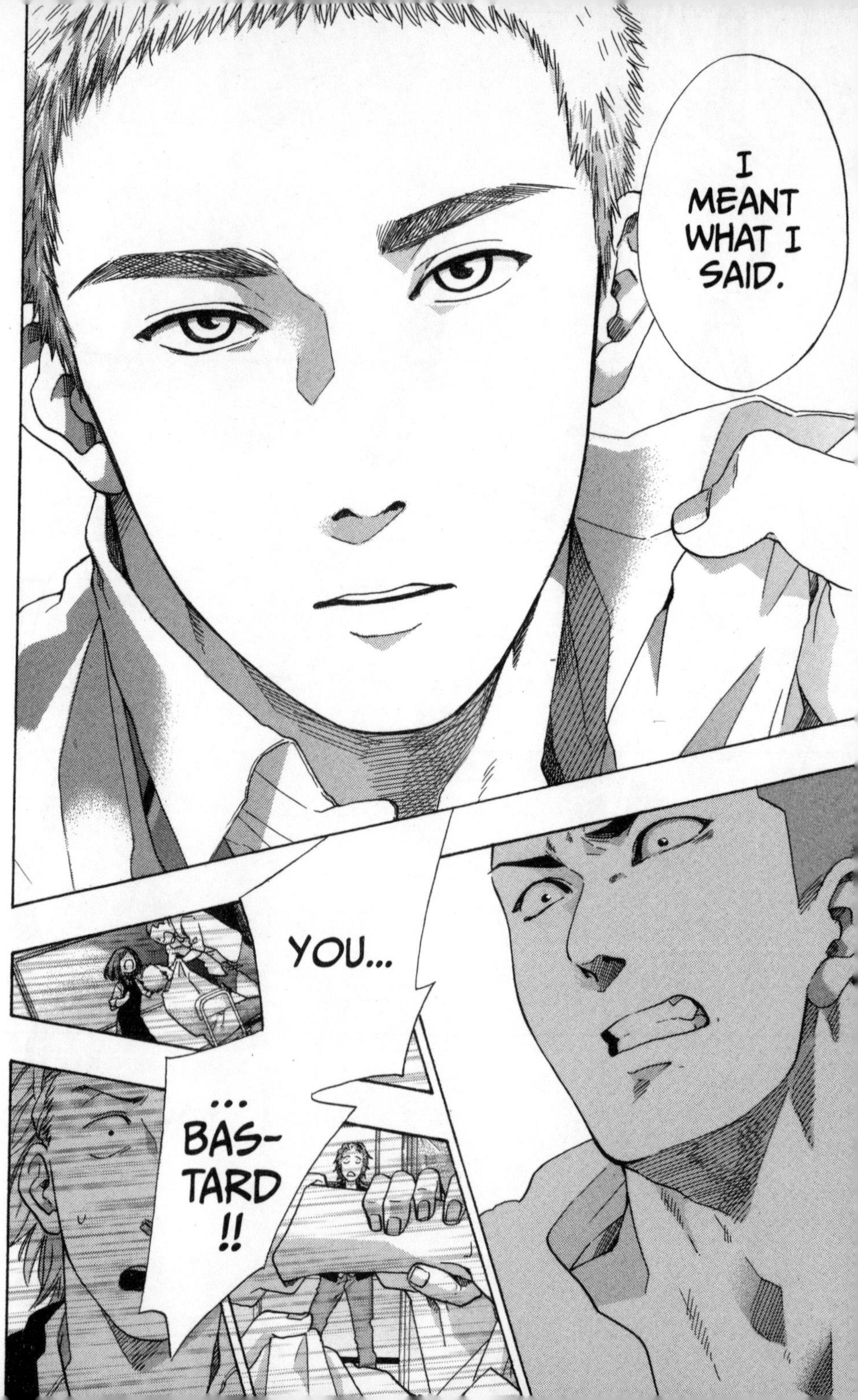
I MEANT WHAT I SAID.
YOU...
... BASTARD!!

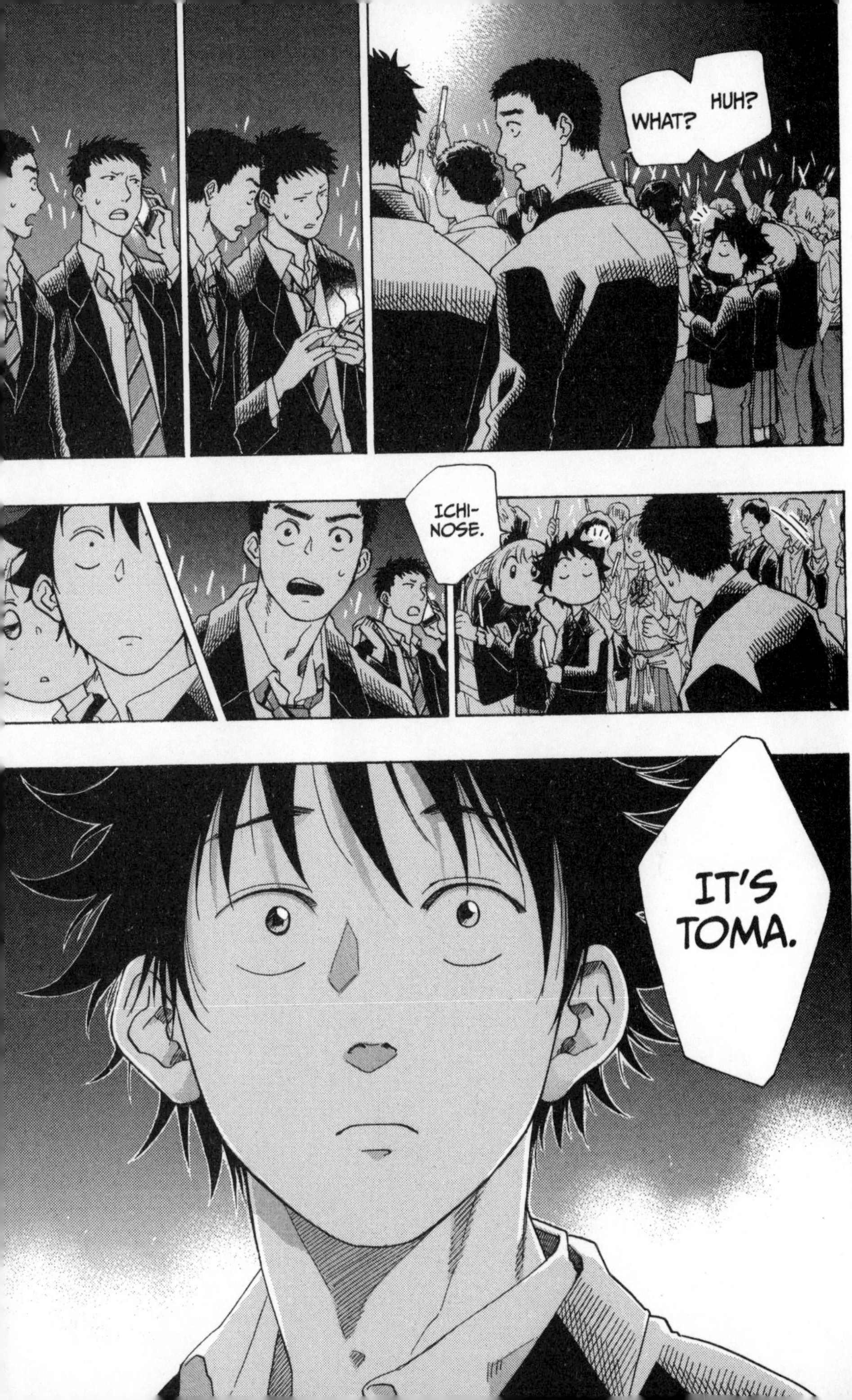
HUH?
WHAT?
ICHI-NOSE.
IT'S TOMA.

I
DON'T
LIKE
RUMORS.

CHAPTER 41

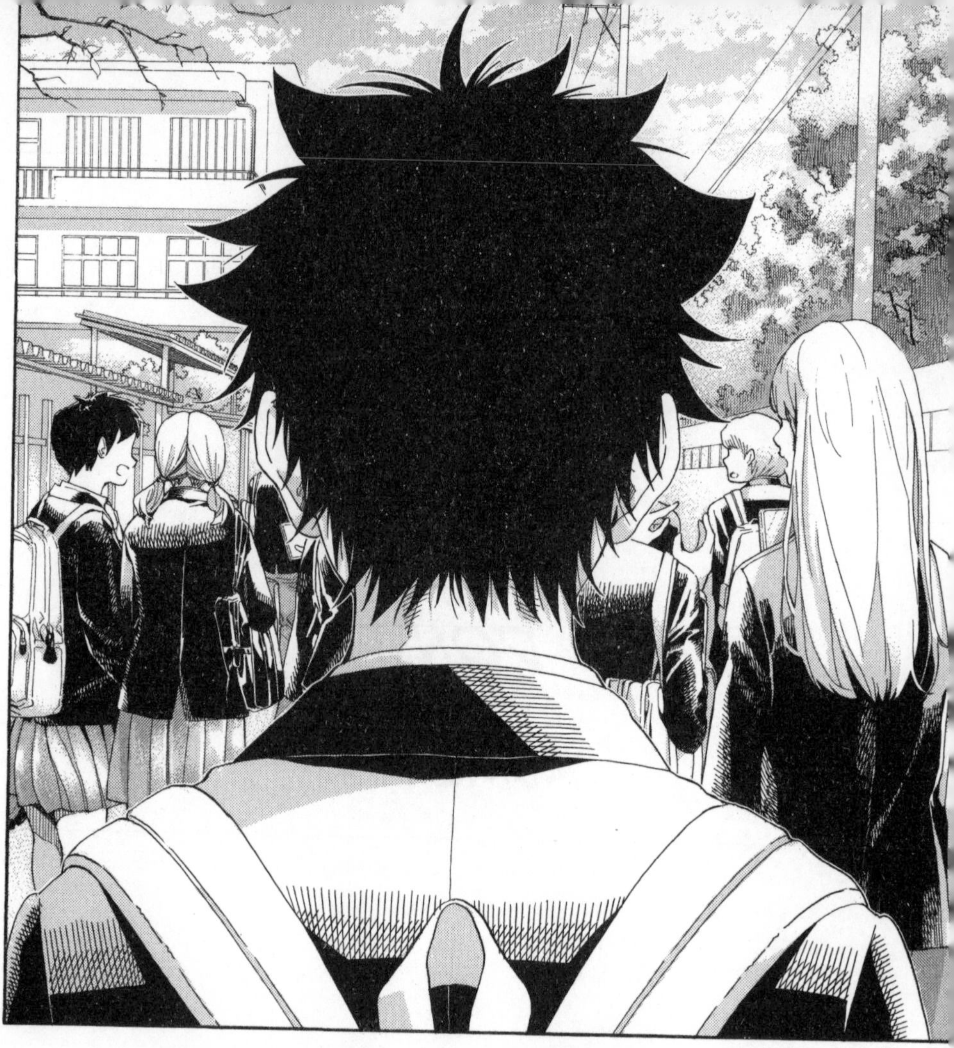

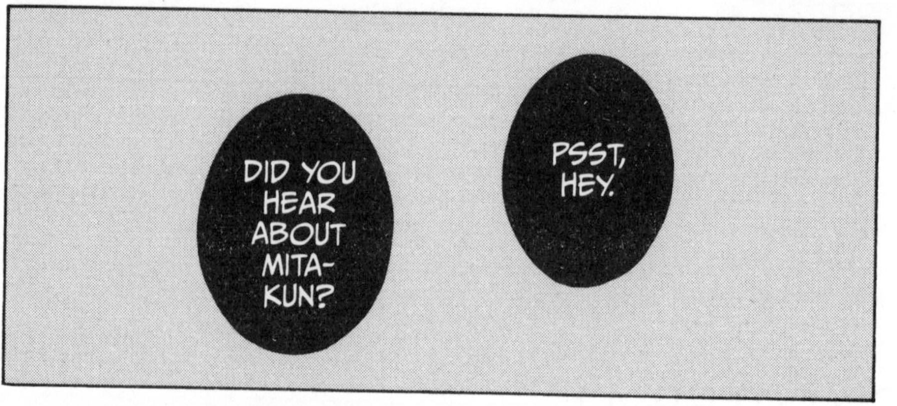
PSST, HEY.
DID YOU HEAR ABOUT MITA-KUN?

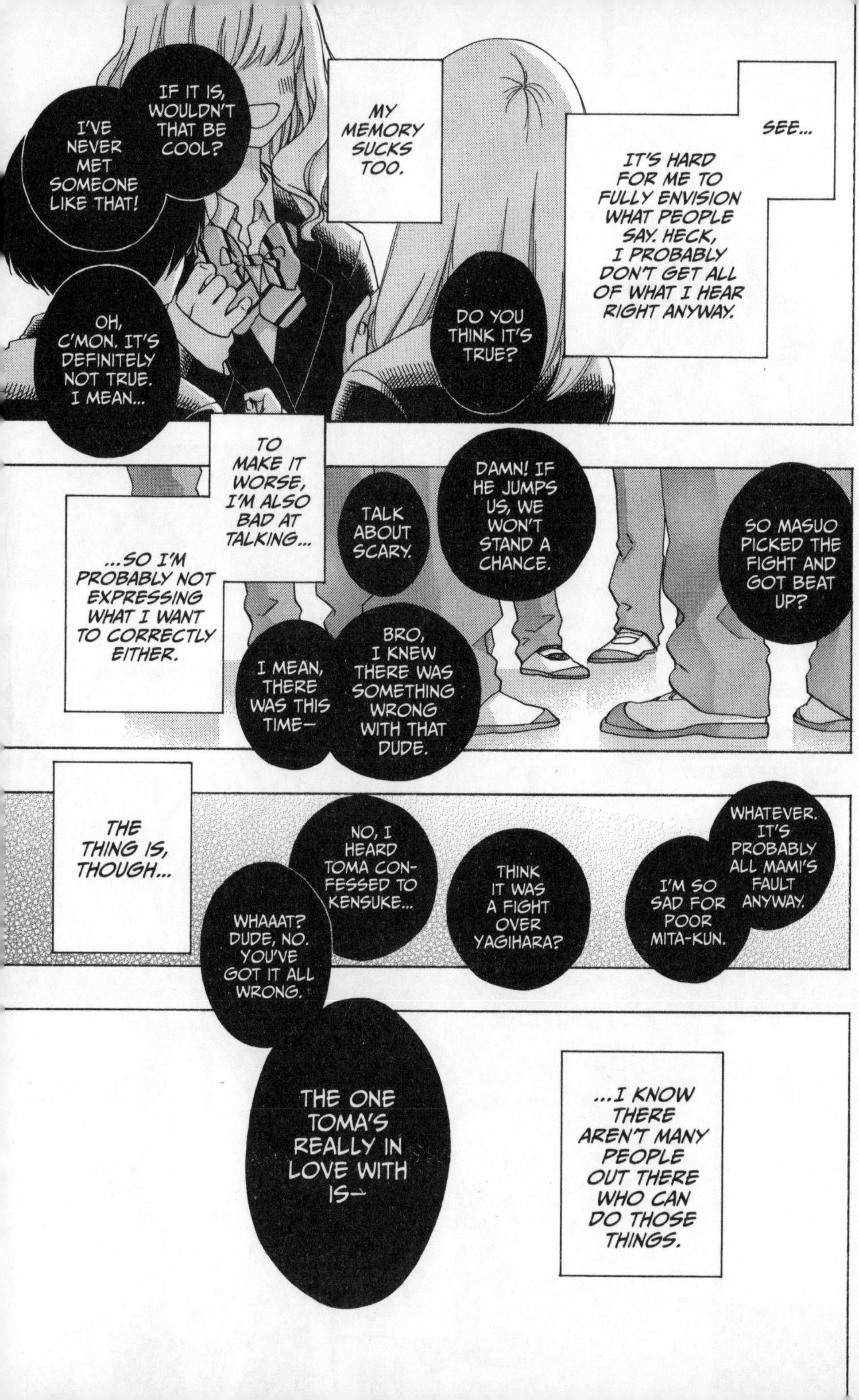
SEE... IT'S HARD FOR ME TO FULLY ENVISION WHAT PEOPLE SAY. HECK, I PROBABLY DON'T GET ALL OF WHAT I HEAR RIGHT ANYWAY.
DO YOU THINK IT'S TRUE?
MY MEMORY SUCKS TOO.
IF IT IS, WOULDN'T THAT BE COOL?
I'VE NEVER MET SOMEONE LIKE THAT!
OH, C'MON. IT'S DEFINITELY NOT TRUE. I MEAN...
SO MASUO PICKED THE FIGHT AND GOT BEAT UP?
DAMN! IF HE JUMPS US, WE WON'T STAND A CHANCE.
TALK ABOUT SCARY.
TO MAKE IT WORSE, I'M ALSO BAD AT TALKING...
BRO, I KNEW THERE WAS SOMETHING WRONG WITH THAT DUDE.
I MEAN, THERE WAS THIS TIME—
...SO I'M PROBABLY NOT EXPRESSING WHAT I WANT TO CORRECTLY EITHER.
WHATEVER. IT'S PROBABLY ALL MAMI'S FAULT ANYWAY.
I'M SO SAD FOR POOR MITA-KUN.
THINK IT WAS A FIGHT OVER YAGIHARA?
NO, I HEARD TOMA CONFESSED TO KENSUKE...
WHAAAT? DUDE, NO. YOU'VE GOT IT ALL WRONG.
THE THING IS, THOUGH...
...I KNOW THERE AREN'T MANY PEOPLE OUT THERE WHO CAN DO THOSE THINGS.
THE ONE TOMA'S REALLY IN LOVE WITH IS—

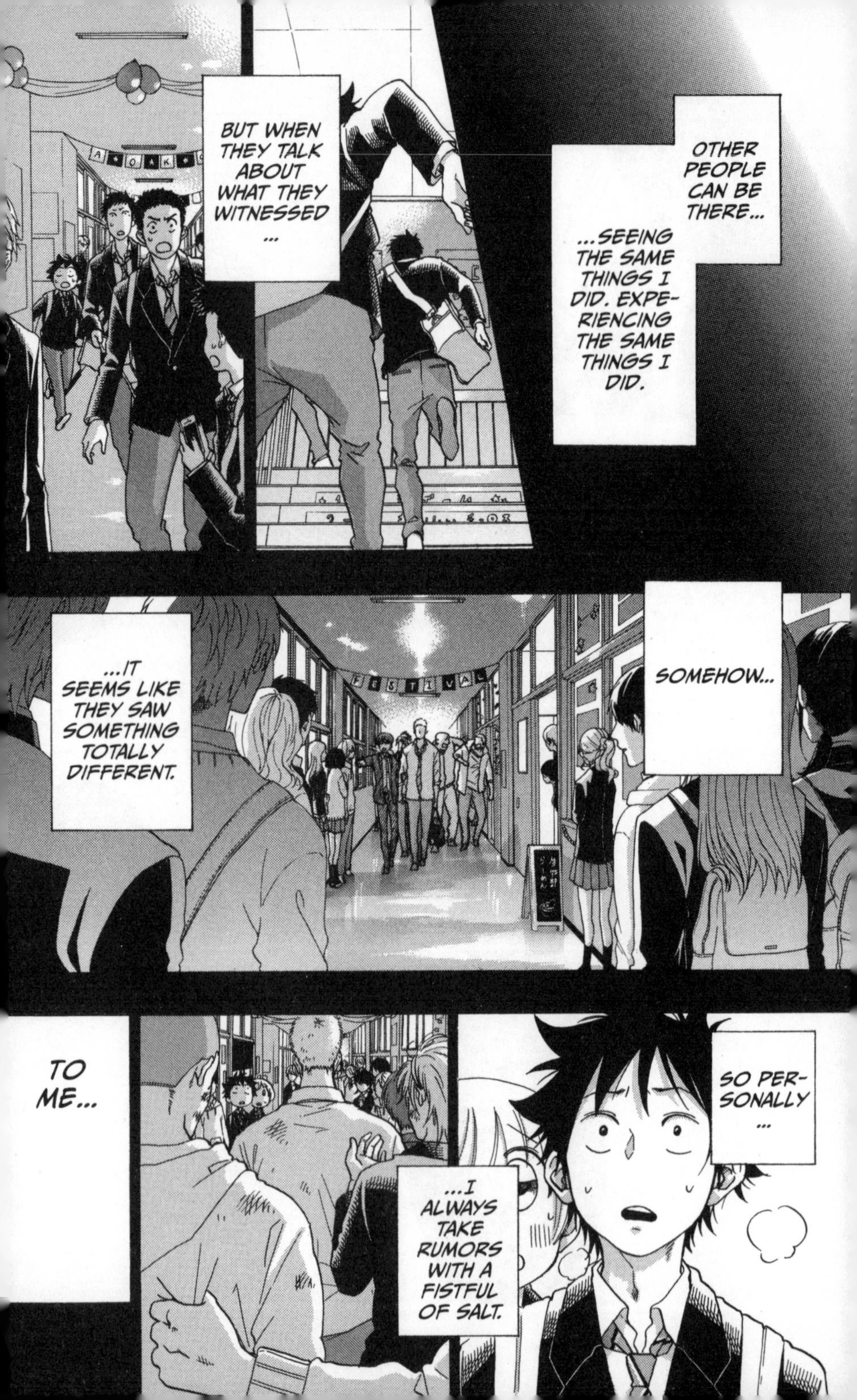
OTHER PEOPLE CAN BE THERE...
...SEEING THE SAME THINGS I DID. EXPE-RIENCING THE SAME THINGS I DID.
BUT WHEN THEY TALK ABOUT WHAT THEY WITNESSED ...
SOMEHOW...
...IT SEEMS LIKE THEY SAW SOMETHING TOTALLY DIFFERENT.
SO PER-SONALLY ...
...I ALWAYS TAKE RUMORS WITH A FISTFUL OF SALT.
TO ME...

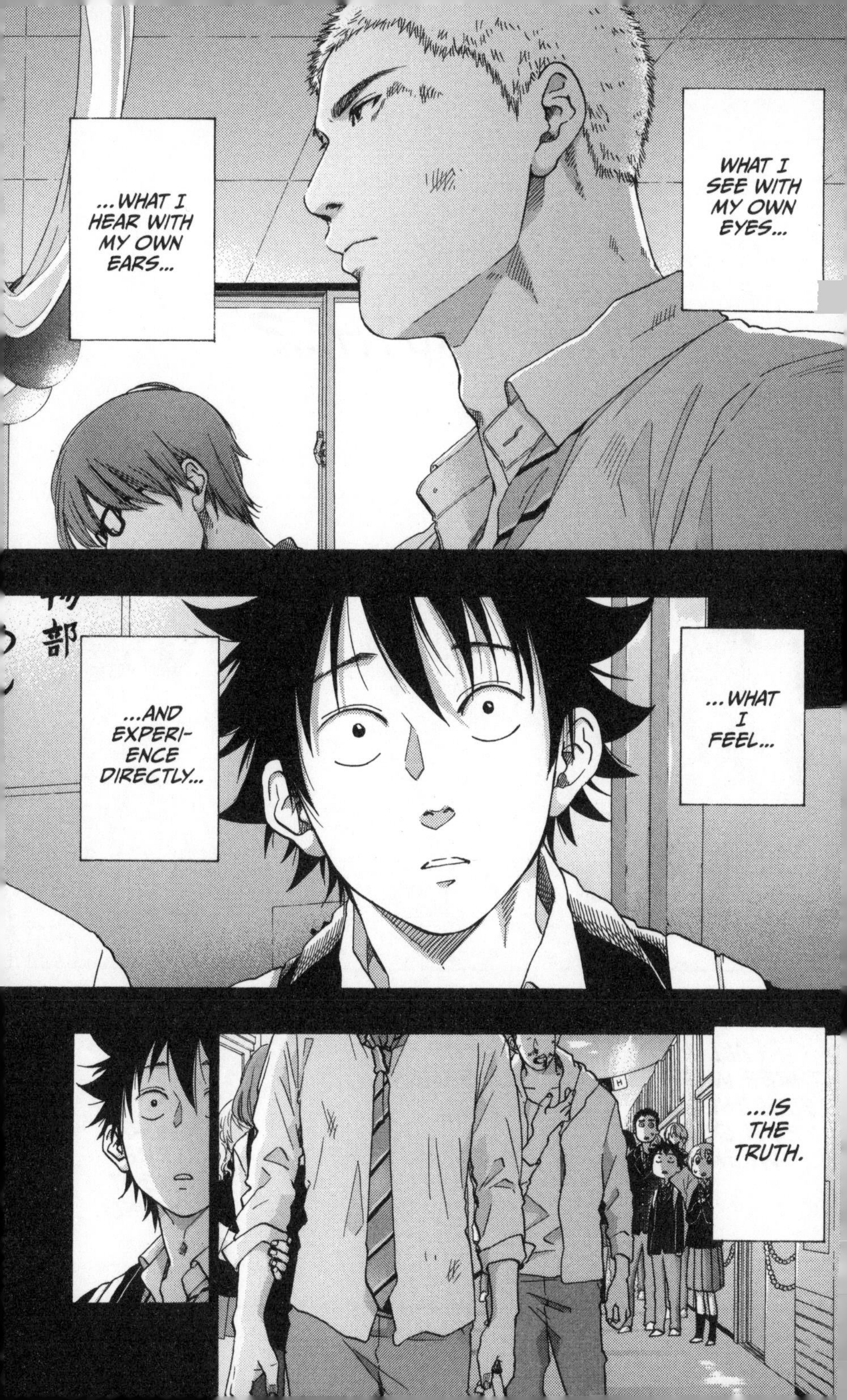
WHAT I SEE WITH MY OWN EYES...
...WHAT I HEAR WITH MY OWN EARS...
...WHAT I FEEL...
...AND EXPERIENCE DIRECTLY...
...IS THE TRUTH.

THE TRUTH...?

TOMA, MASUO AND NIMURA WERE CAUGHT FIGHTING.

AS PUNISHMENT...

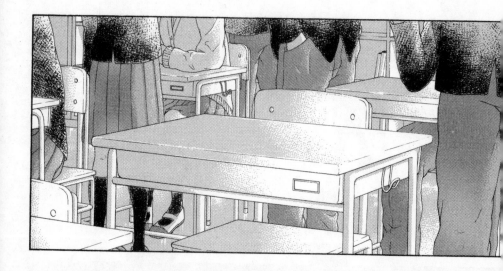

...ALL THREE WERE SUSPENDED FOR ONE WEEK.

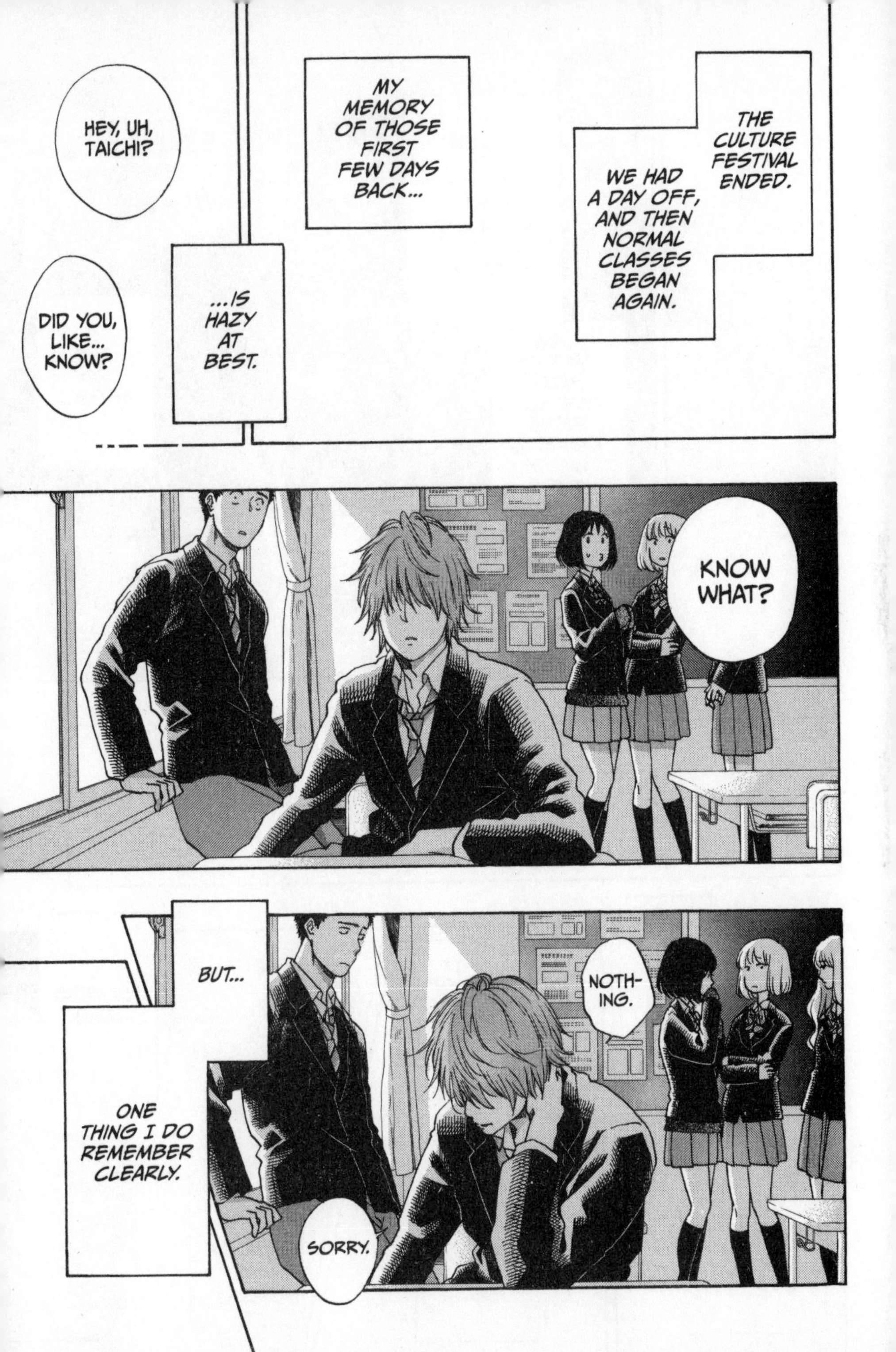
THE CULTURE FESTIVAL ENDED.
WE HAD A DAY OFF, AND THEN NORMAL CLASSES BEGAN AGAIN.
MY MEMORY OF THOSE FIRST FEW DAYS BACK...
...IS HAZY AT BEST.
HEY, UH, TAICHI?
DID YOU, LIKE... KNOW?
KNOW WHAT?
NOTH-ING.
SORRY.
BUT...
ONE THING I DO REMEMBER CLEARLY.

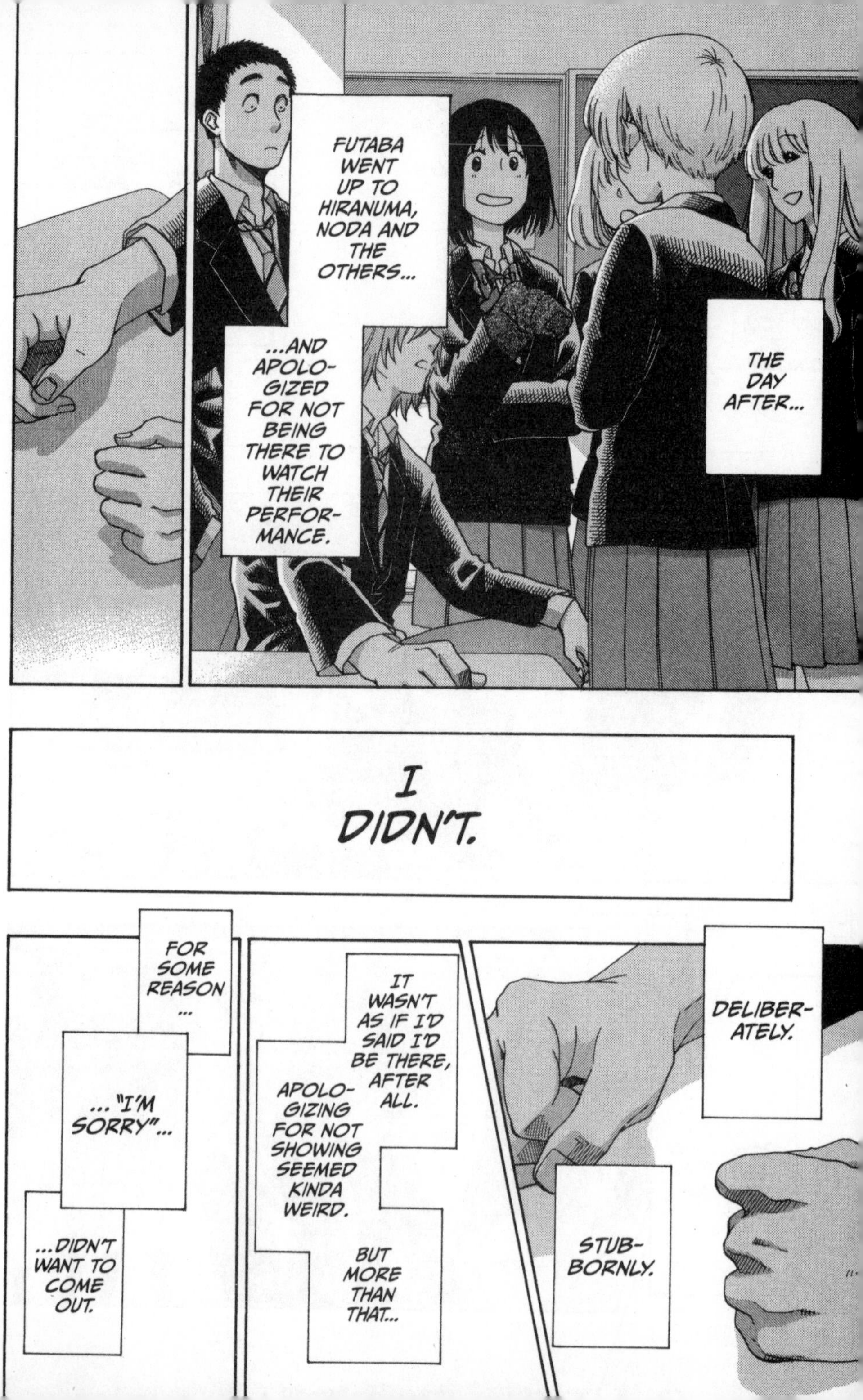
THE DAY AFTER...
FUTABA WENT UP TO HIRANUMA, NODA AND THE OTHERS...
...AND APOLOGIZED FOR NOT BEING THERE TO WATCH THEIR PERFORMANCE.
I DIDN'T.
DELIBERATELY.
STUBBORNLY.
IT WASN'T AS IF I'D SAID I'D BE THERE, AFTER ALL.
APOLOGIZING FOR NOT SHOWING SEEMED KINDA WEIRD.
BUT MORE THAN THAT...
FOR SOME REASON...
..."I'M SORRY"...
...DIDN'T WANT TO COME OUT.

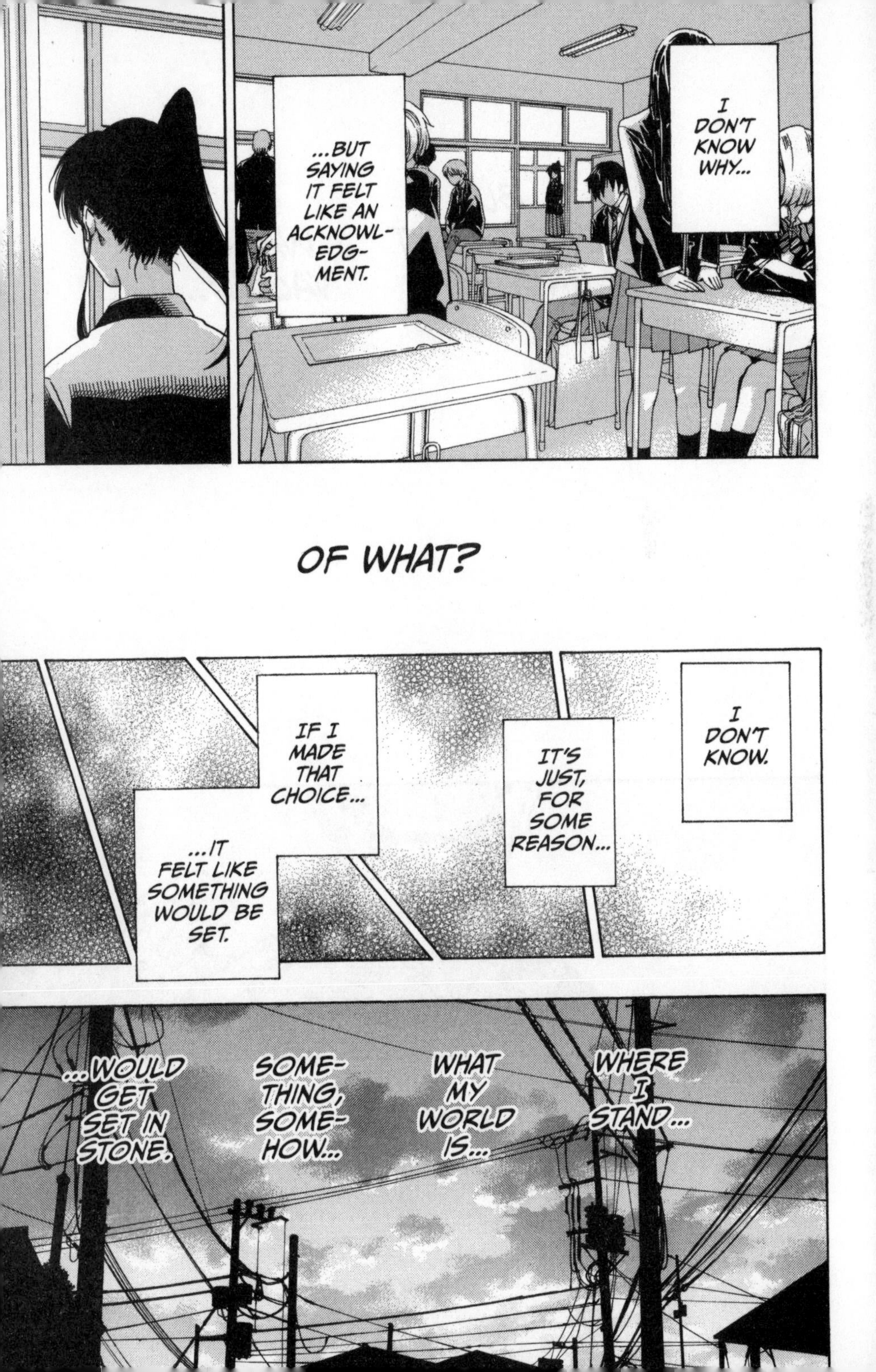
I DON'T KNOW WHY...
...BUT SAYING IT FELT LIKE AN ACKNOWL-EDG-MENT.
OF WHAT?
I DON'T KNOW.
IT'S JUST, FOR SOME REASON...
IF I MADE THAT CHOICE...
...IT FELT LIKE SOMETHING WOULD BE SET.
WHERE I STAND...
WHAT MY WORLD IS...
SOME-THING, SOME-HOW...
...WOULD GET SET IN STONE.

...BUT PERSISTENT UNEASE.

IT WAS A VAGUE...

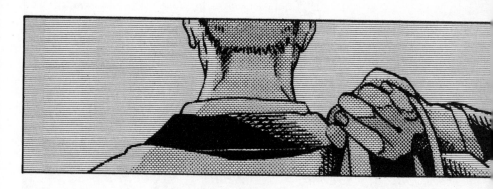

TOMA.

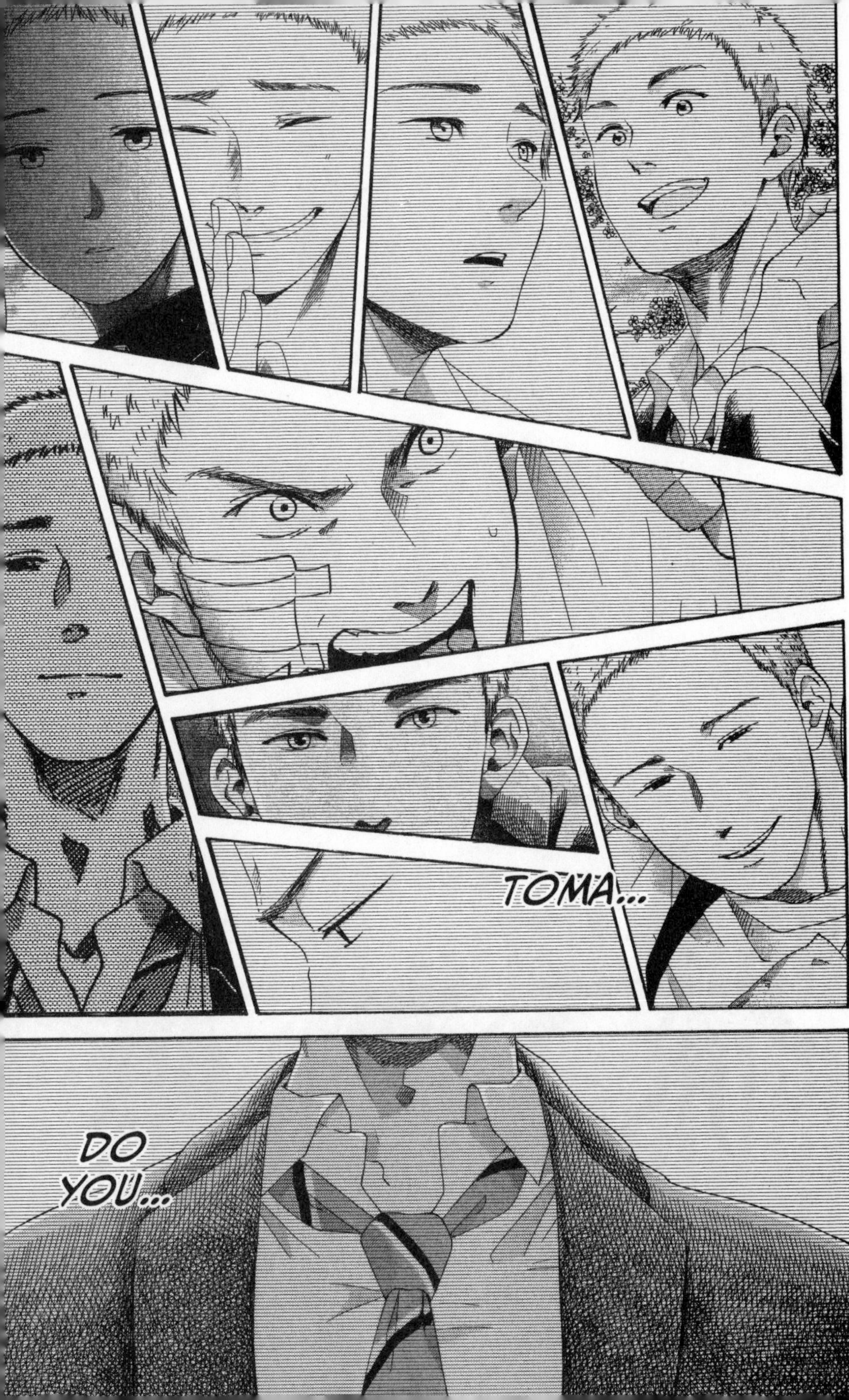
TOMA...
DO YOU...

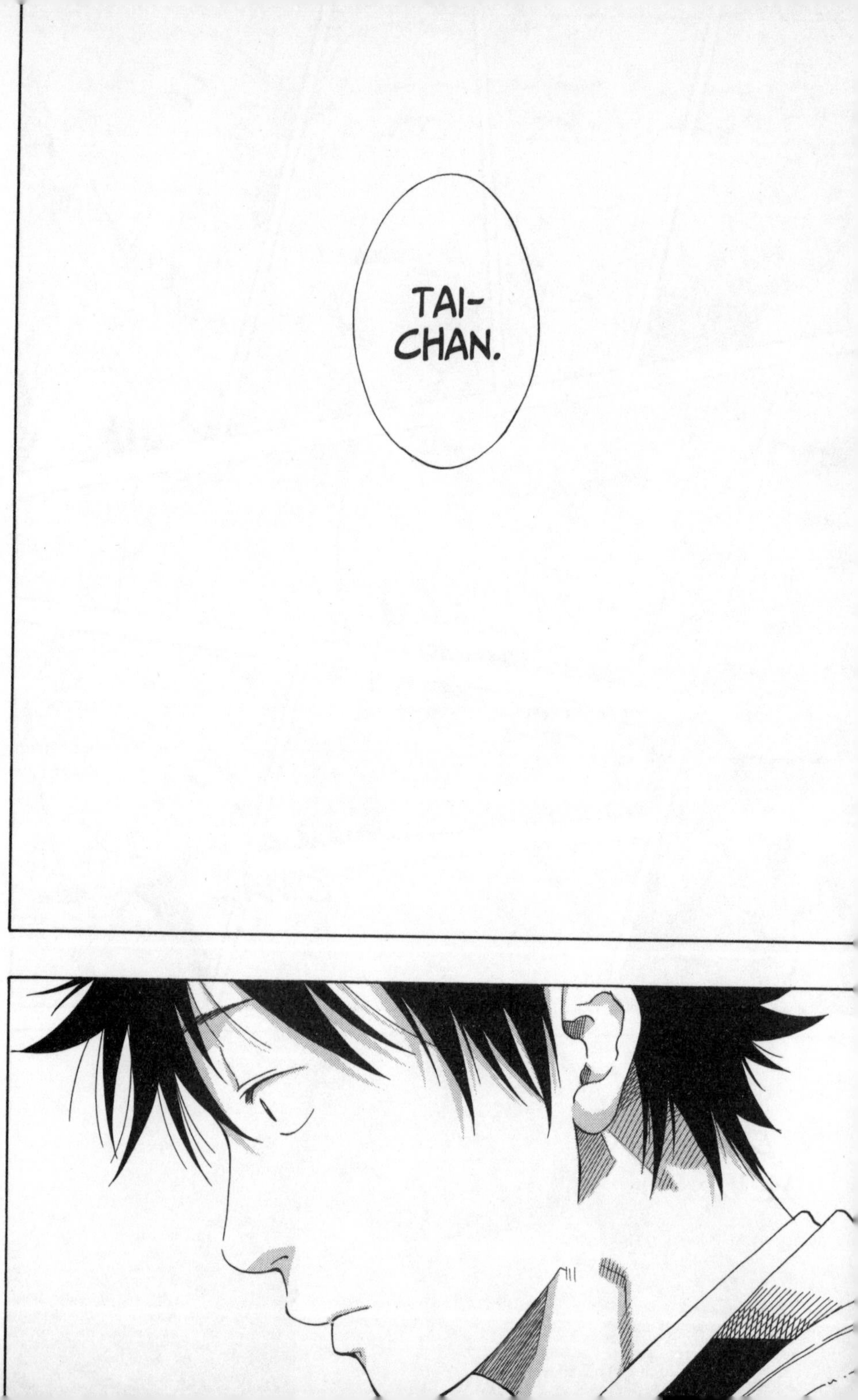
TAI-CHAN.

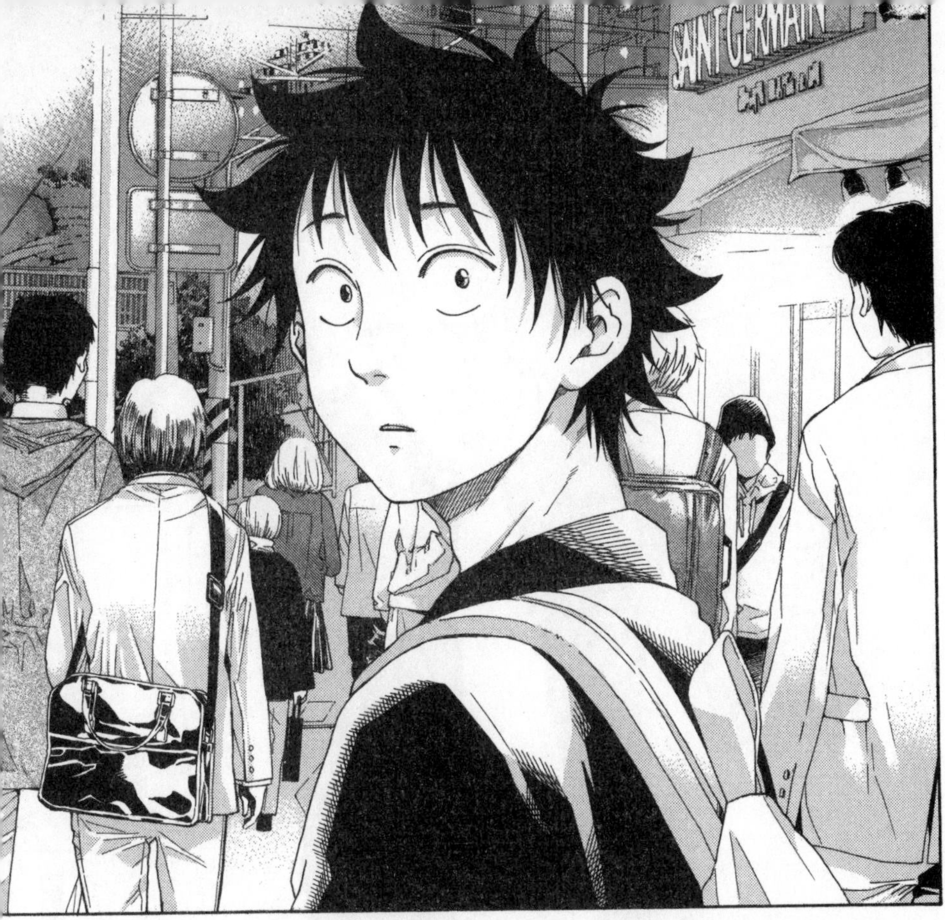
SAINT GERMAIN

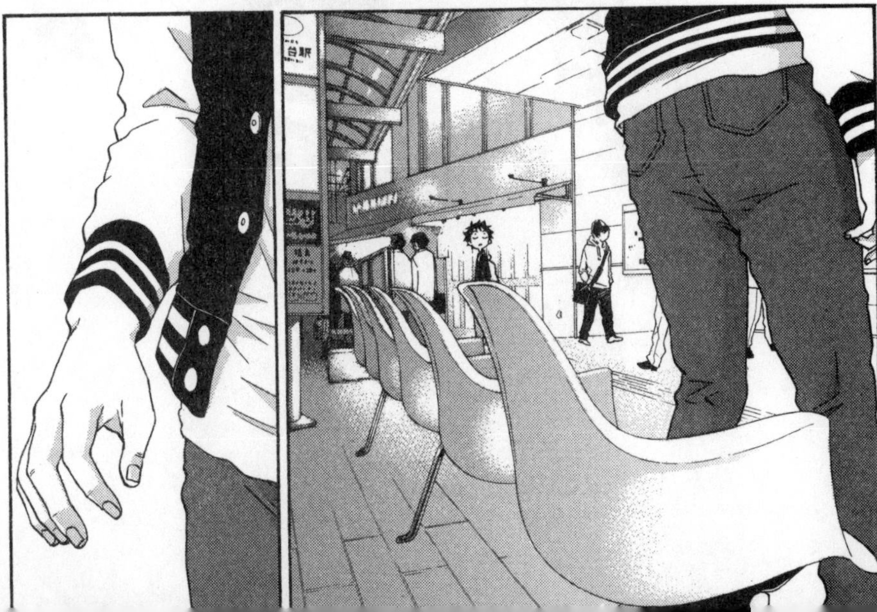

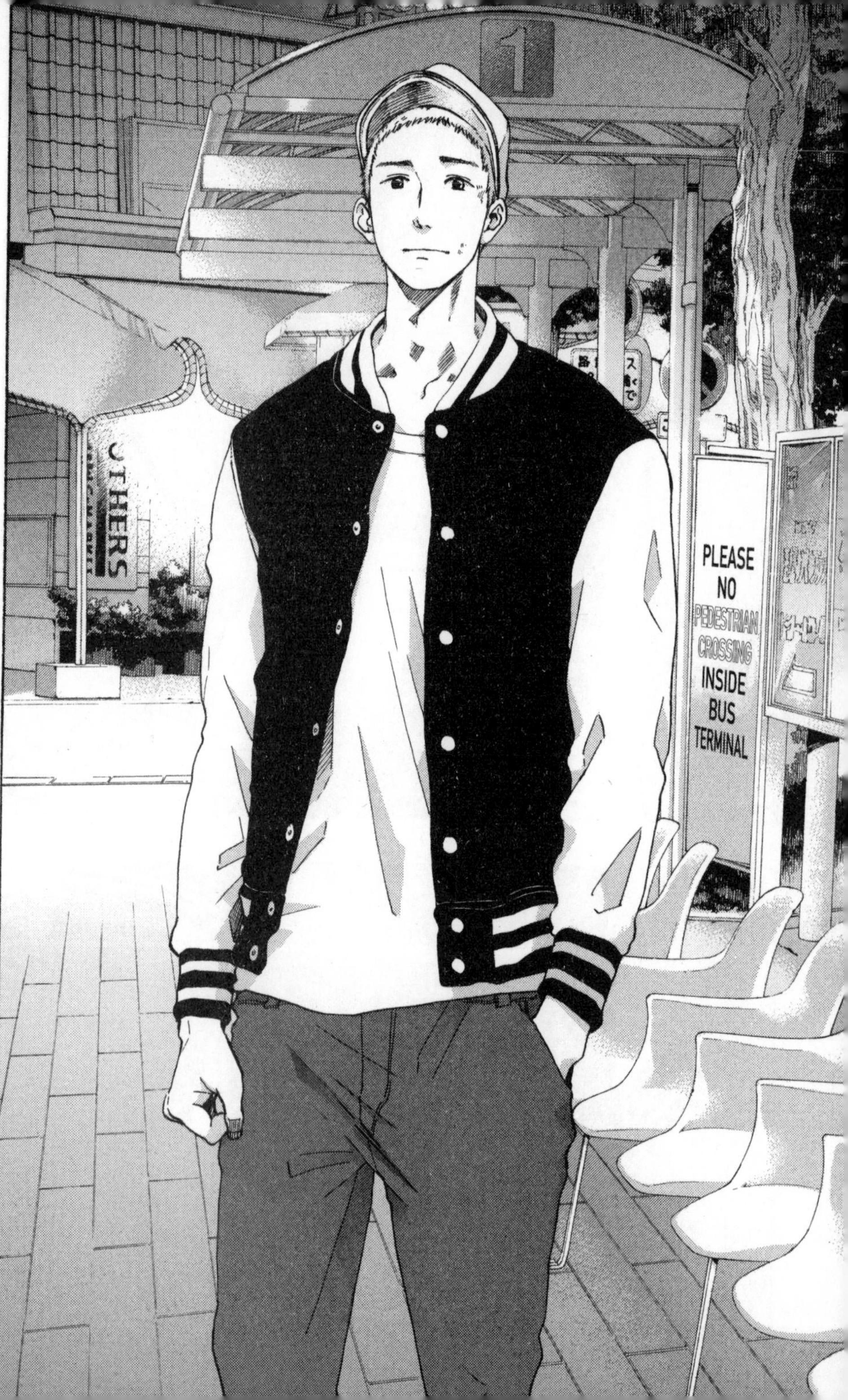
1
PLEASE NO PEDESTRIAN CROSSING INSIDE BUS TERMINAL

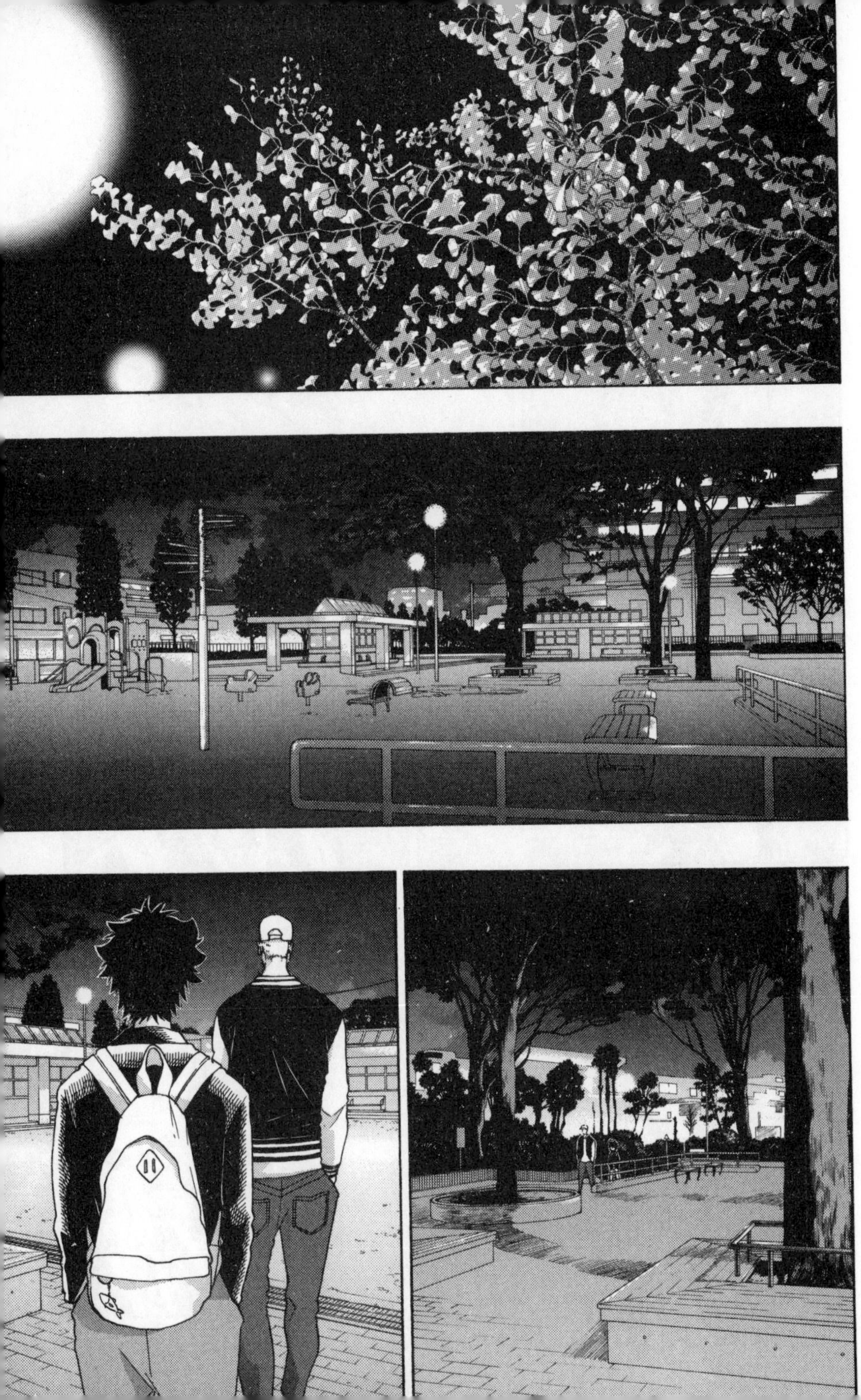

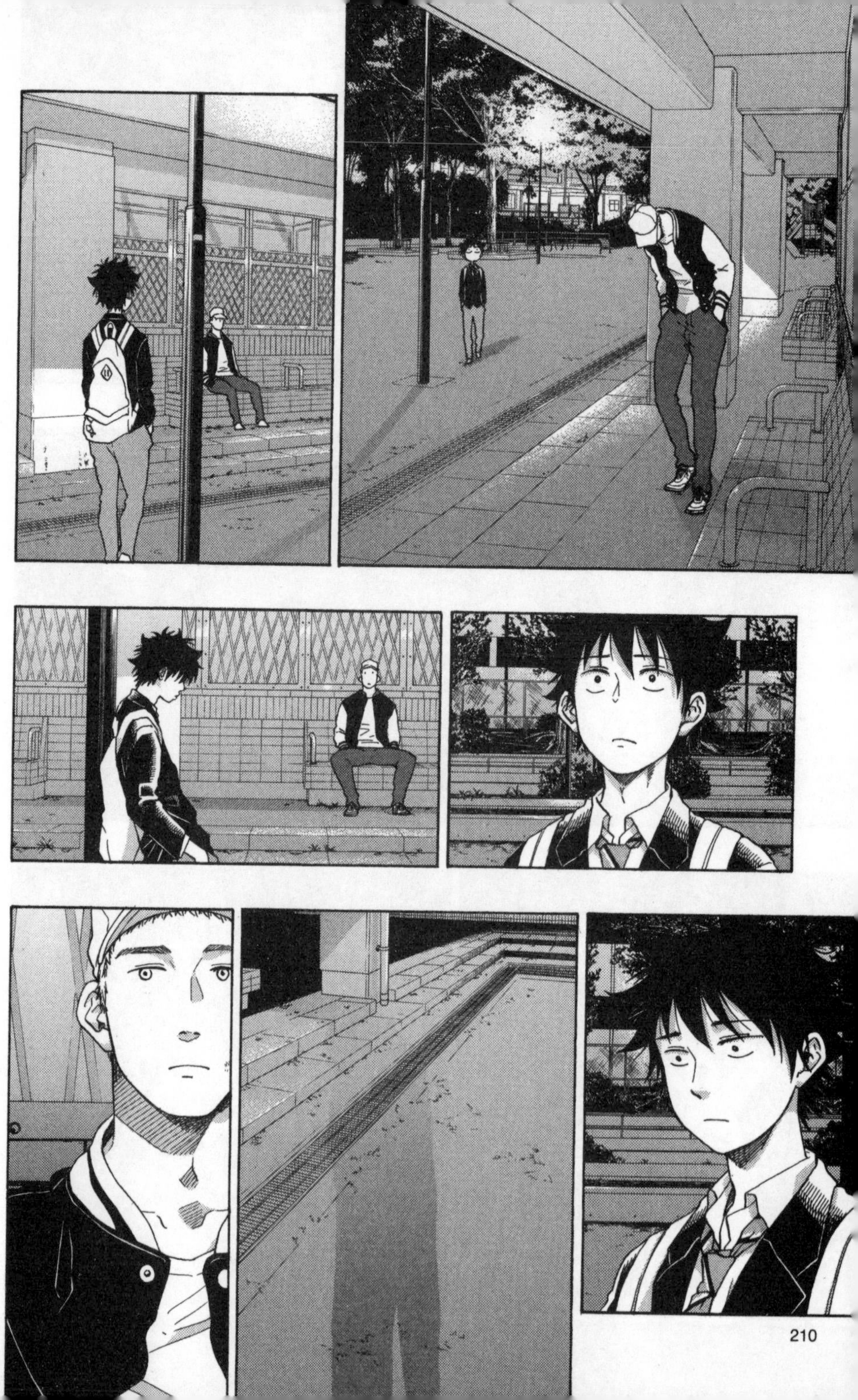

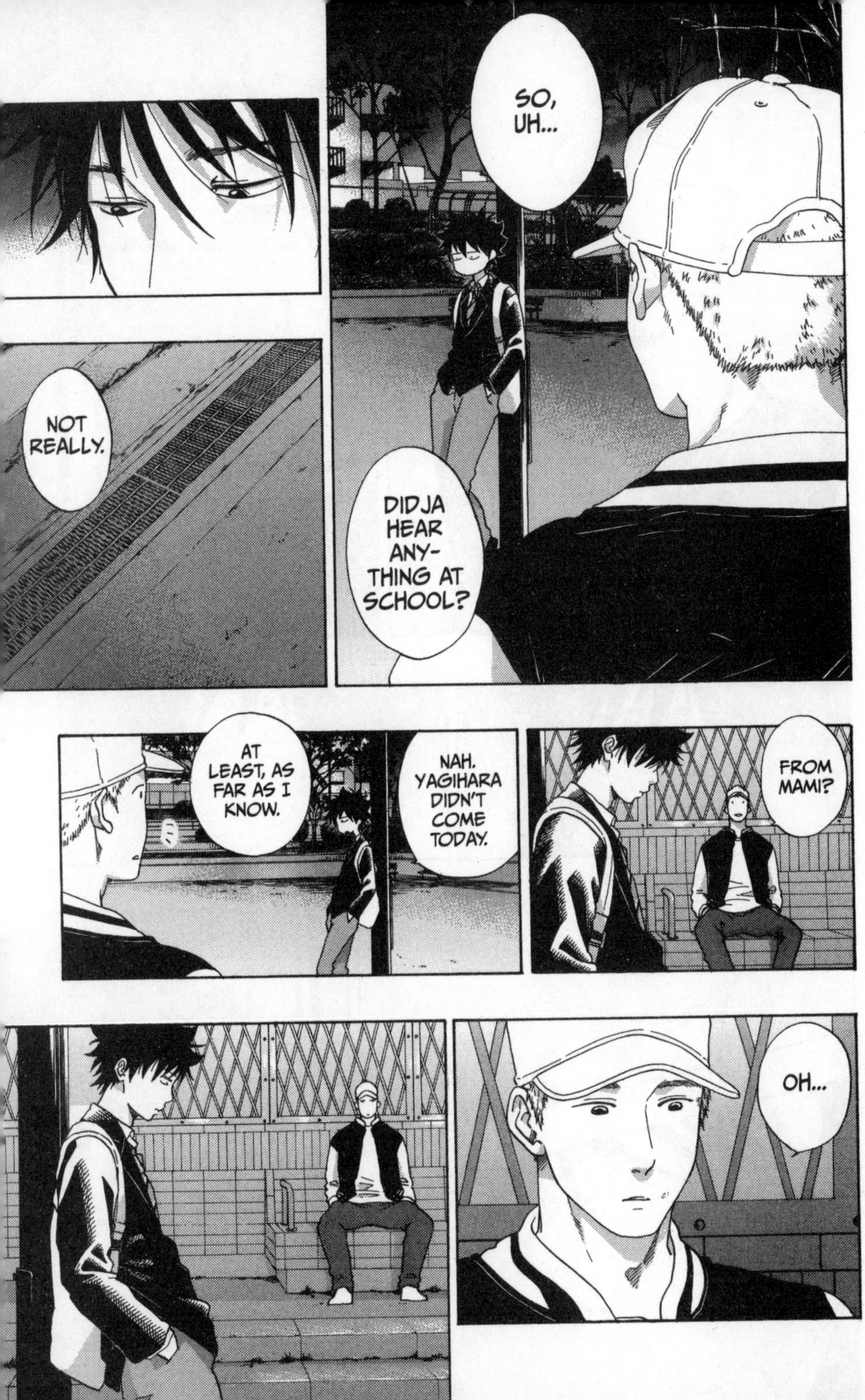
SO, UH...
DIDJA HEAR ANY-THING AT SCHOOL?
NOT REALLY.
FROM MAMI?
NAH. YAGIHARA DIDN'T COME TODAY.
AT LEAST, AS FAR AS I KNOW.
OH...

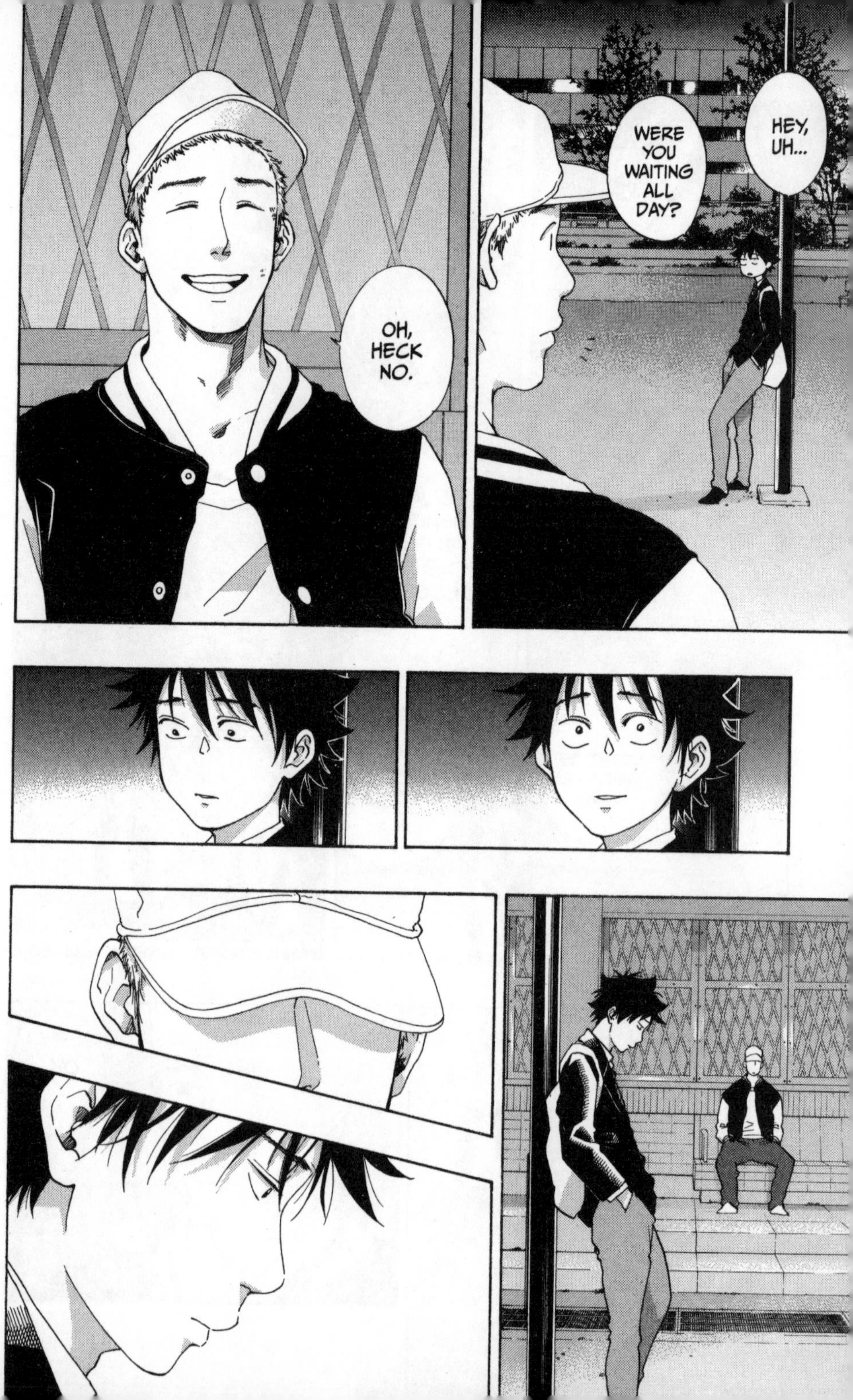
HEY, UH...
WERE YOU WAITING ALL DAY?
OH, HECK NO.

SKUF

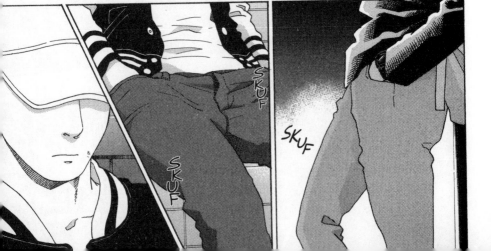

SKUF

SKUF

SKUF

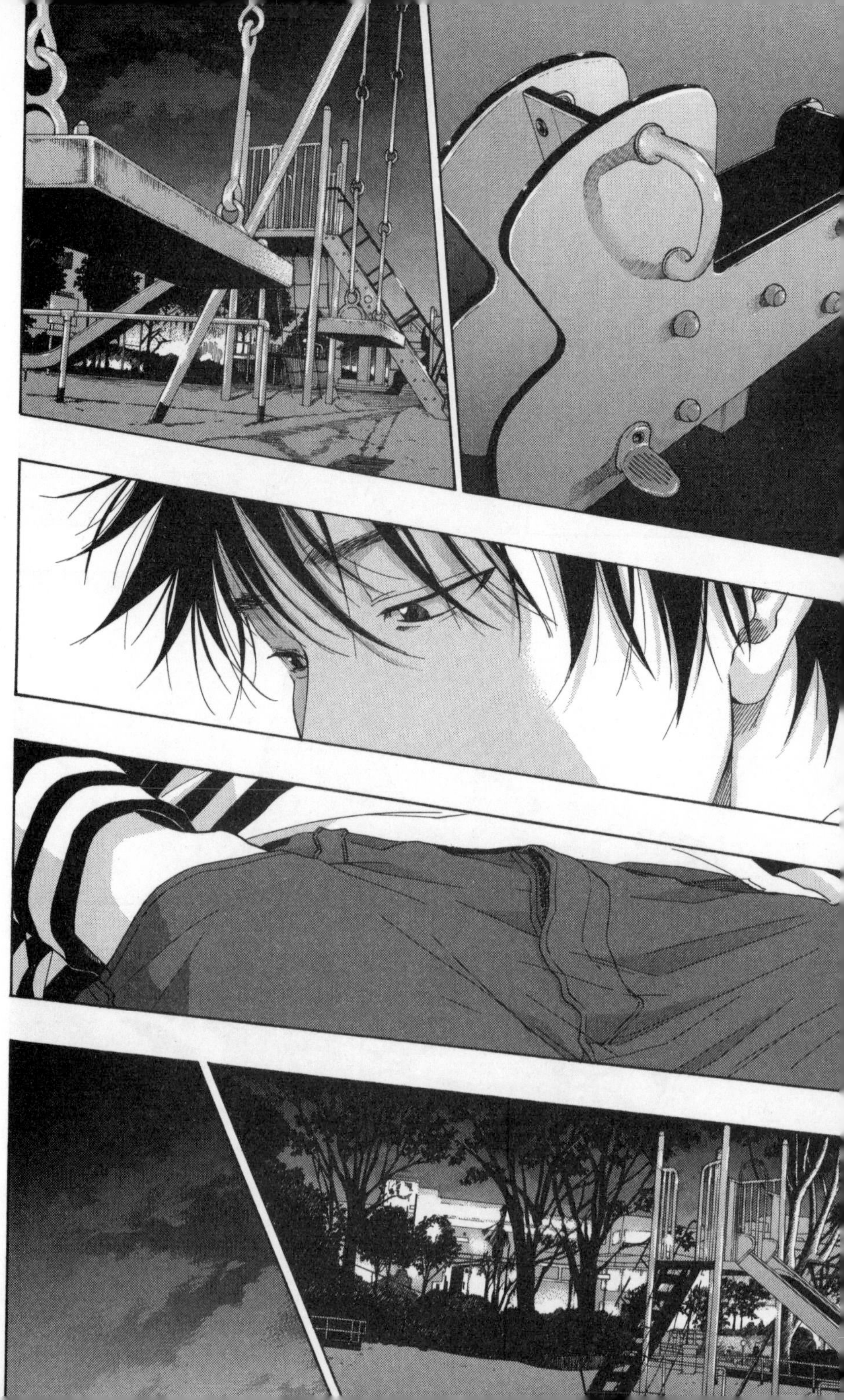

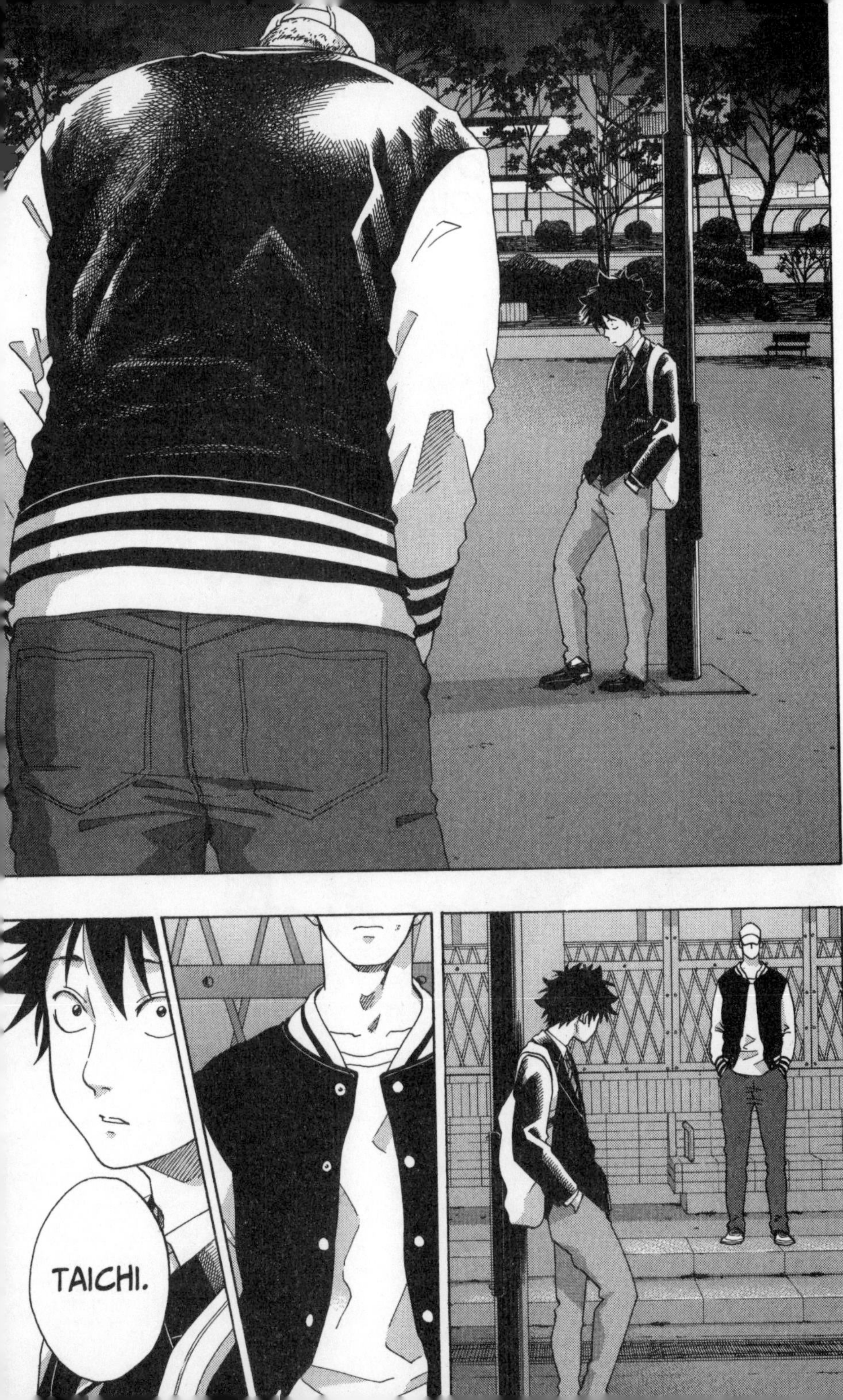
TAICHI.

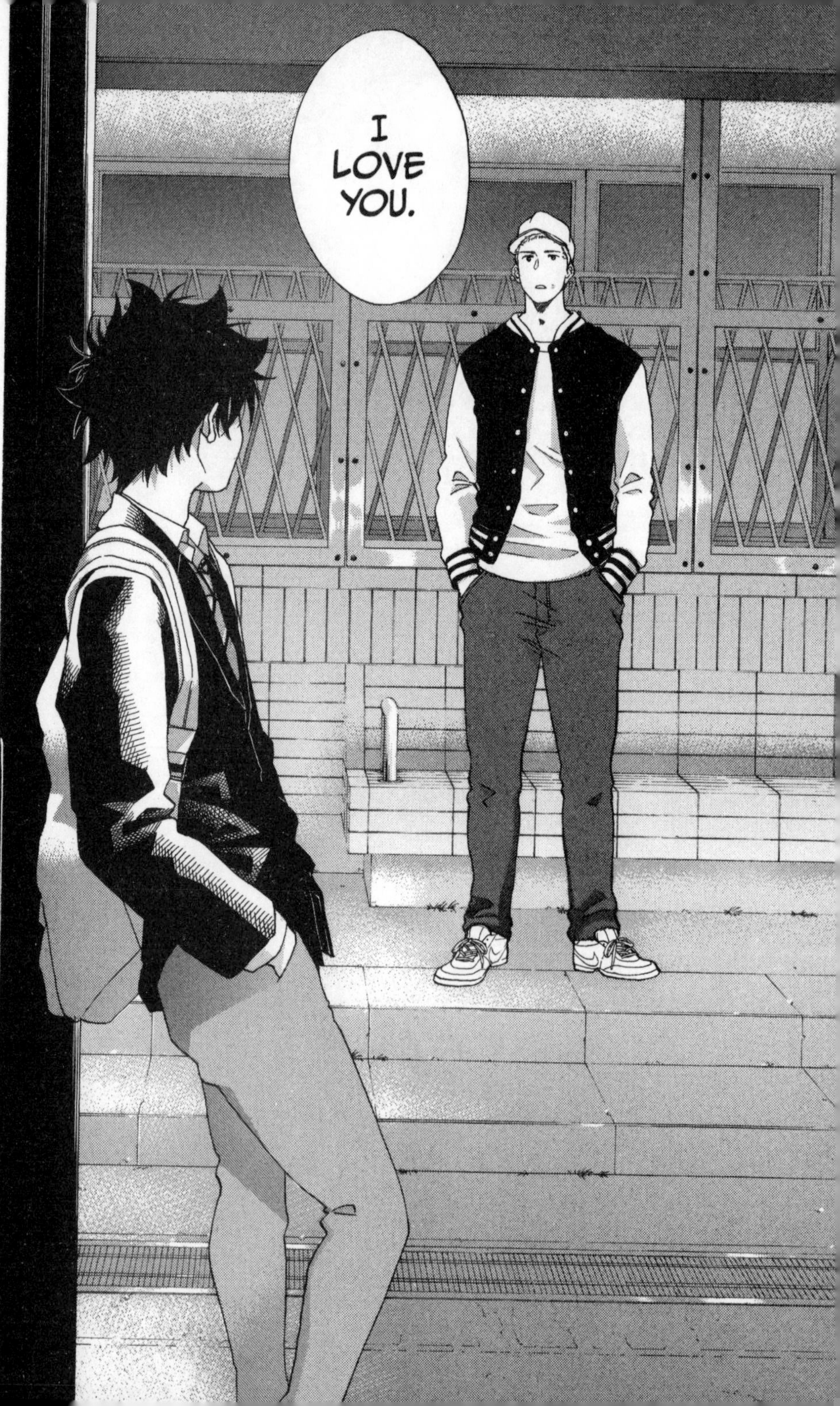
I LOVE YOU.

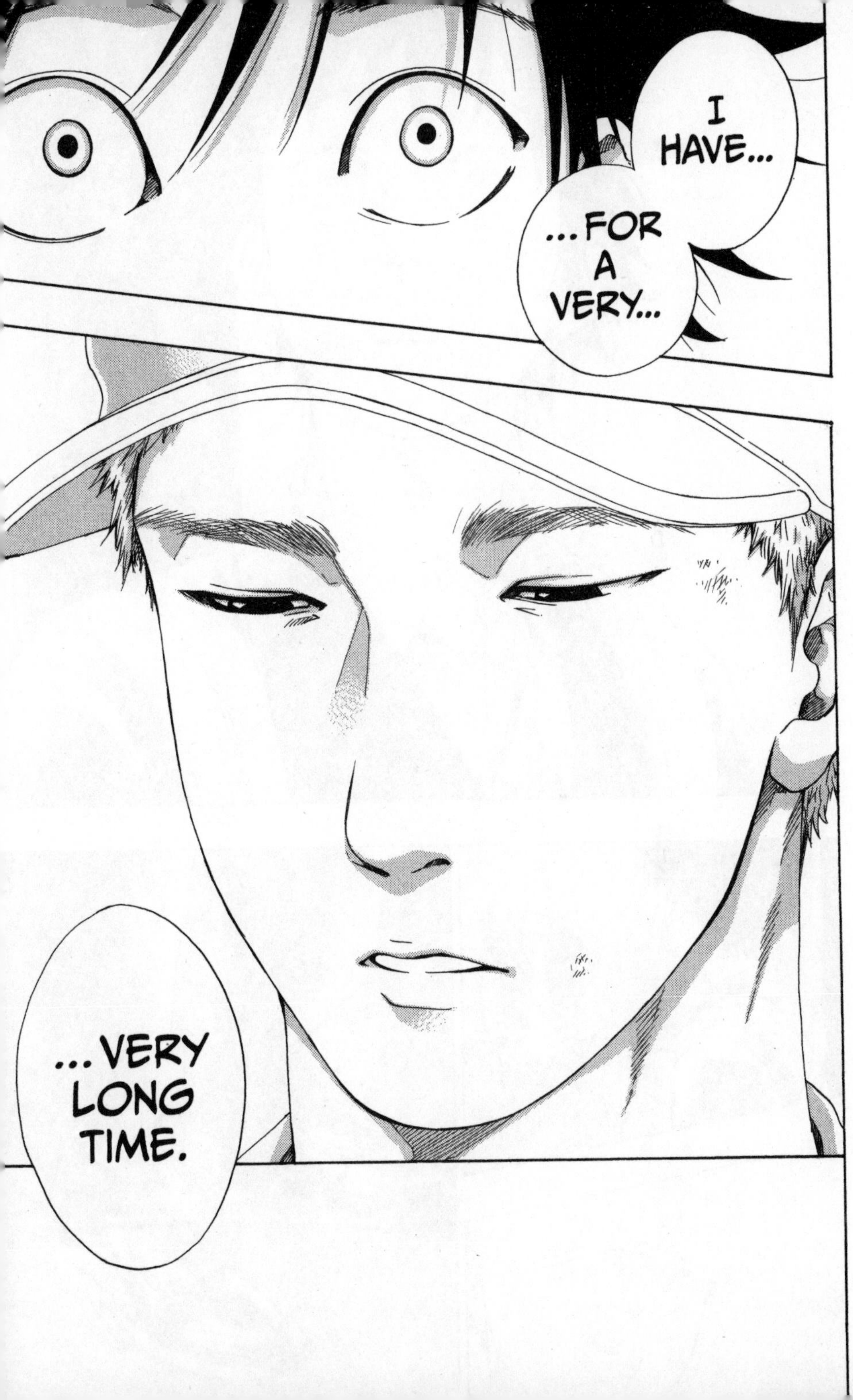
I HAVE...
...FOR A VERY...
...VERY LONG TIME.

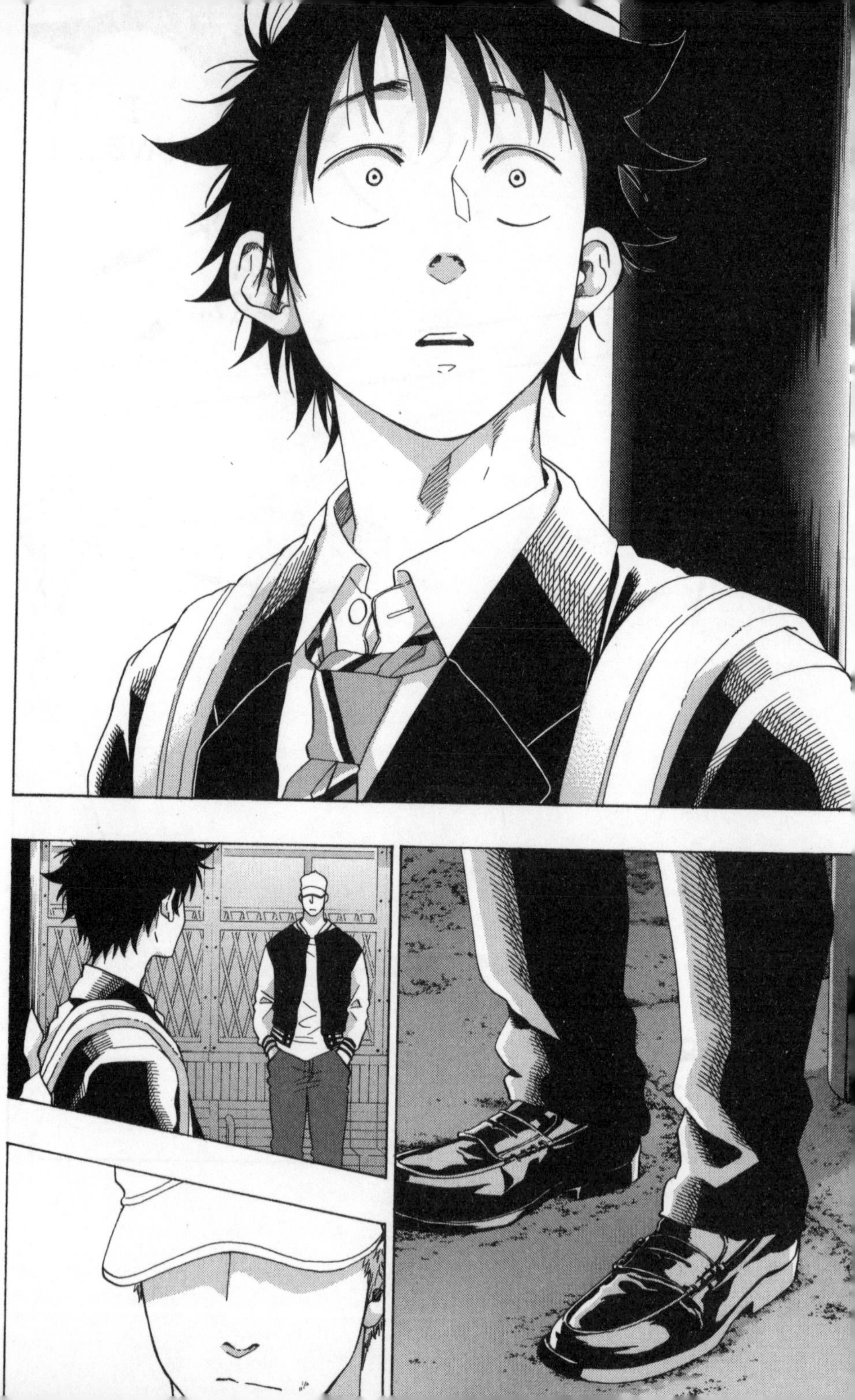

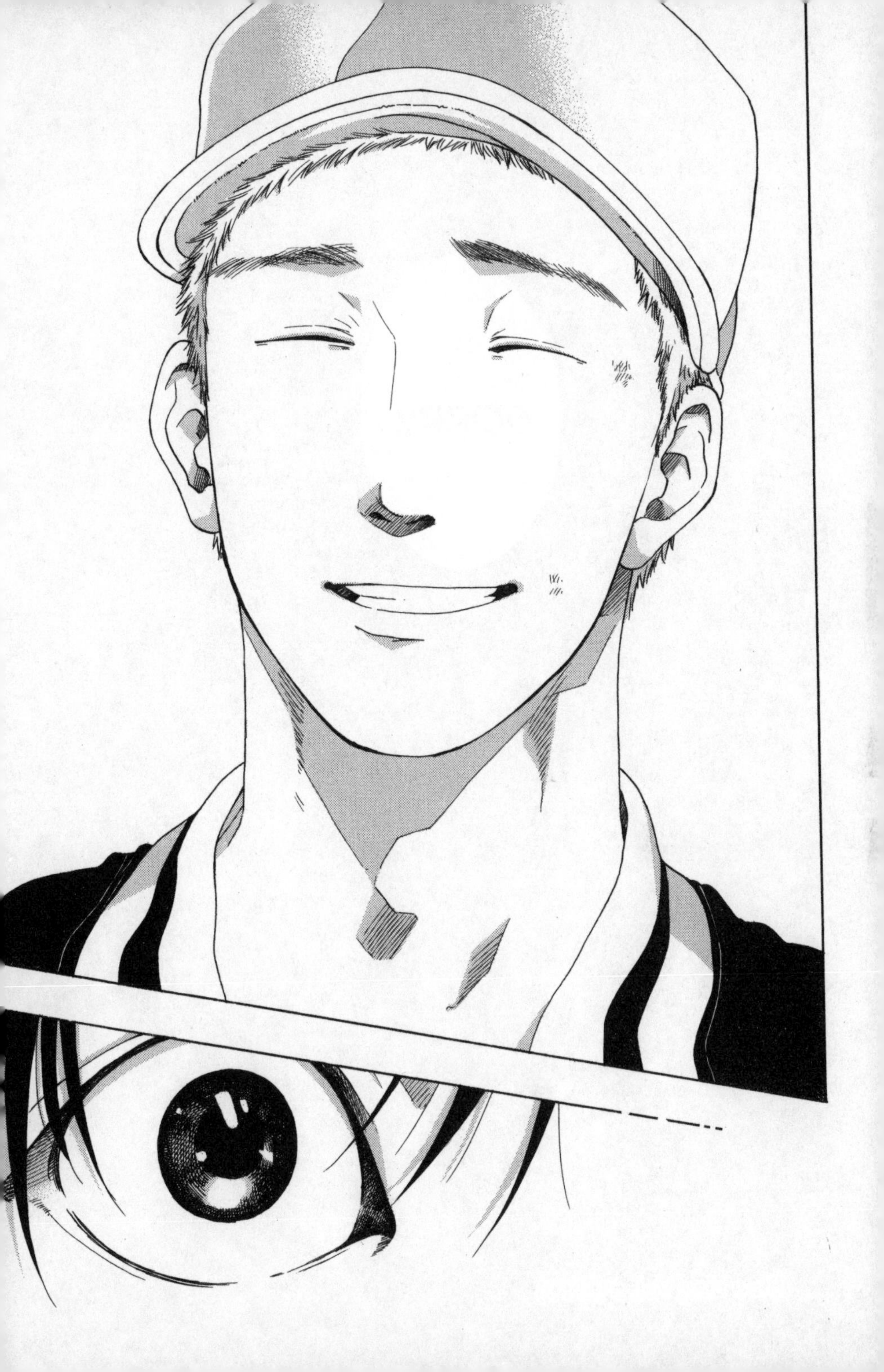

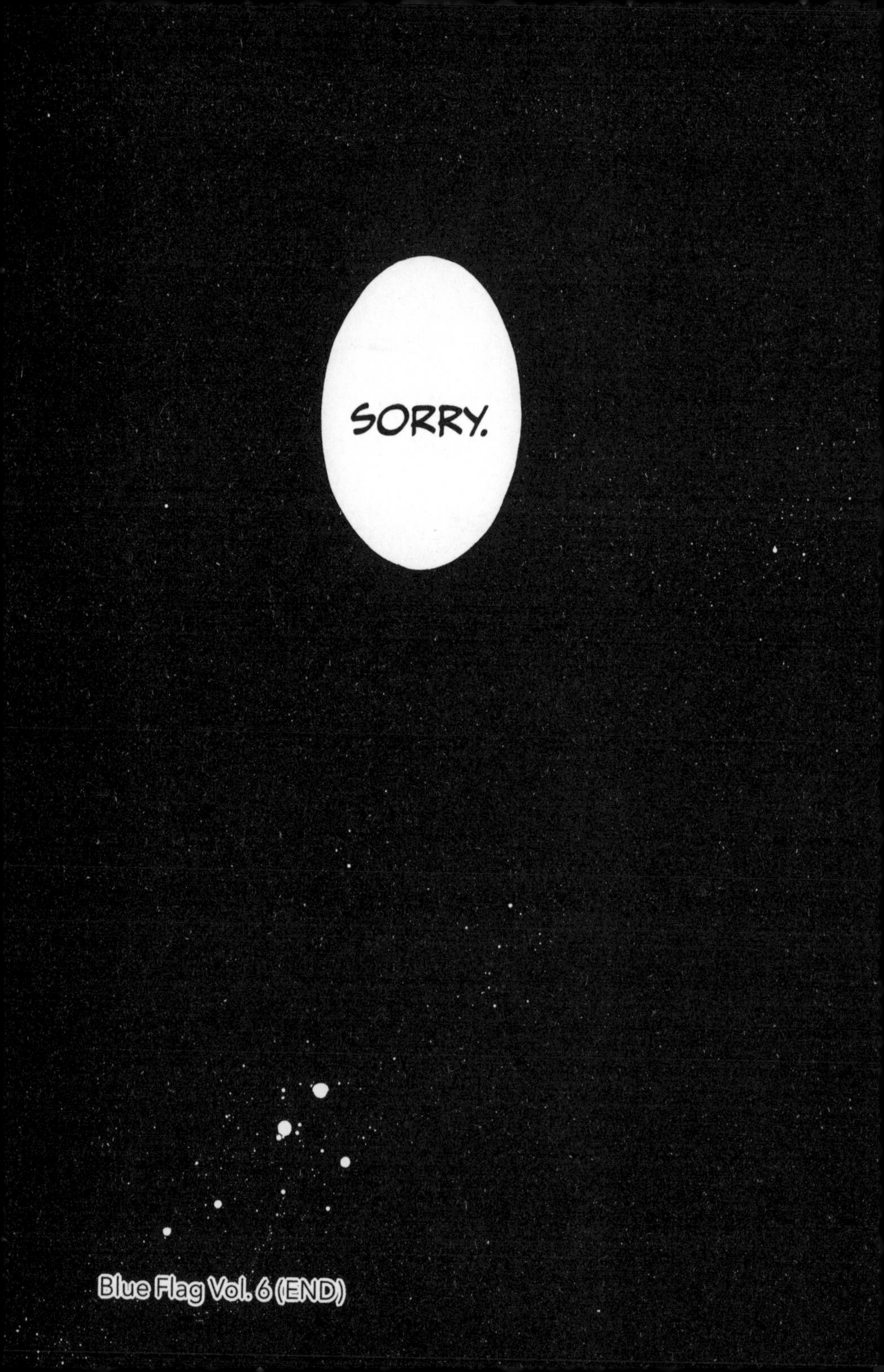
SORRY.
Blue Flag Vol. 6 (END)

BONUS 4-PANEL SHORTS

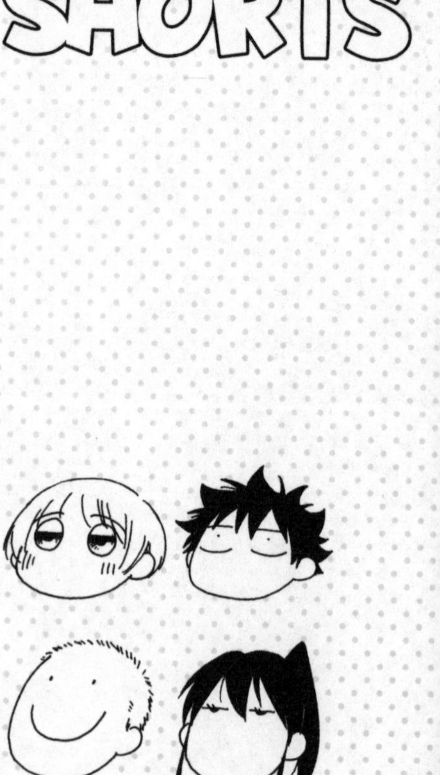

SHINGO'S MAKEUP

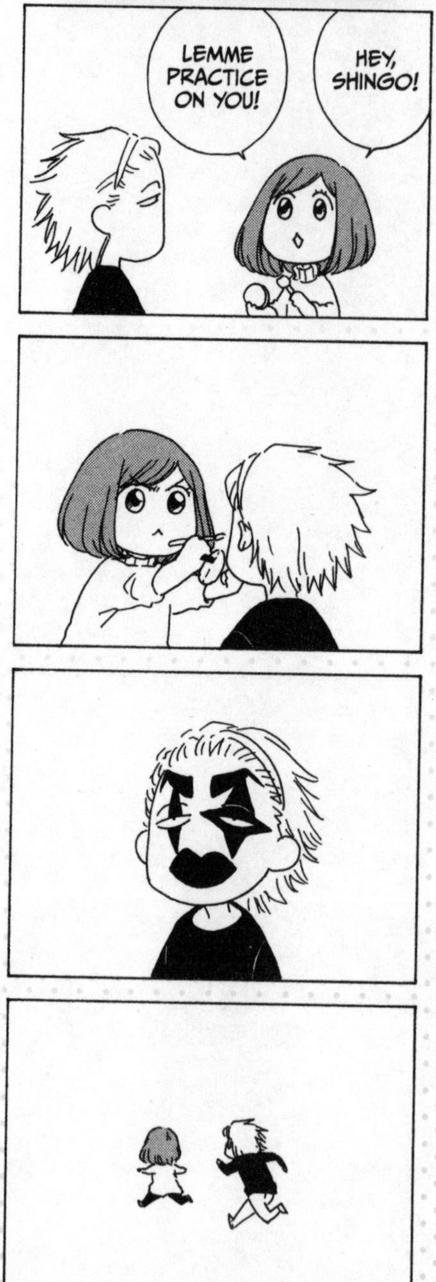
HEY, SHINGO!
LEMME PRACTICE ON YOU!

AN EXCITING CLUB VISIT

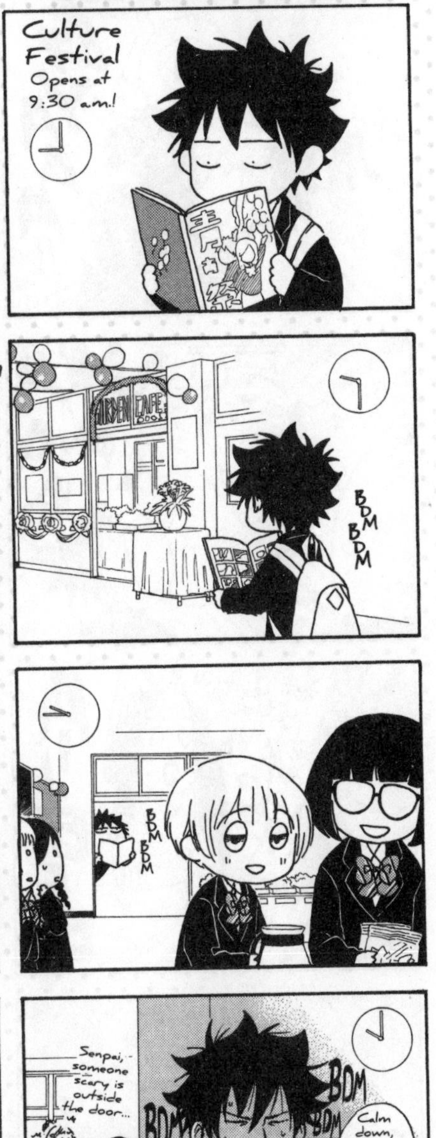
Culture Festival Opens at 9:30 a.m.!
BDM BDM
BDM BDM
BDM
Calm down, deep breaths. I'm calm caaalm caaalm caaalm...
BDM BDM BDM BDM BDM
Senpai, someone scary is outside the door...
BDM BDM

POPSICLE MAN

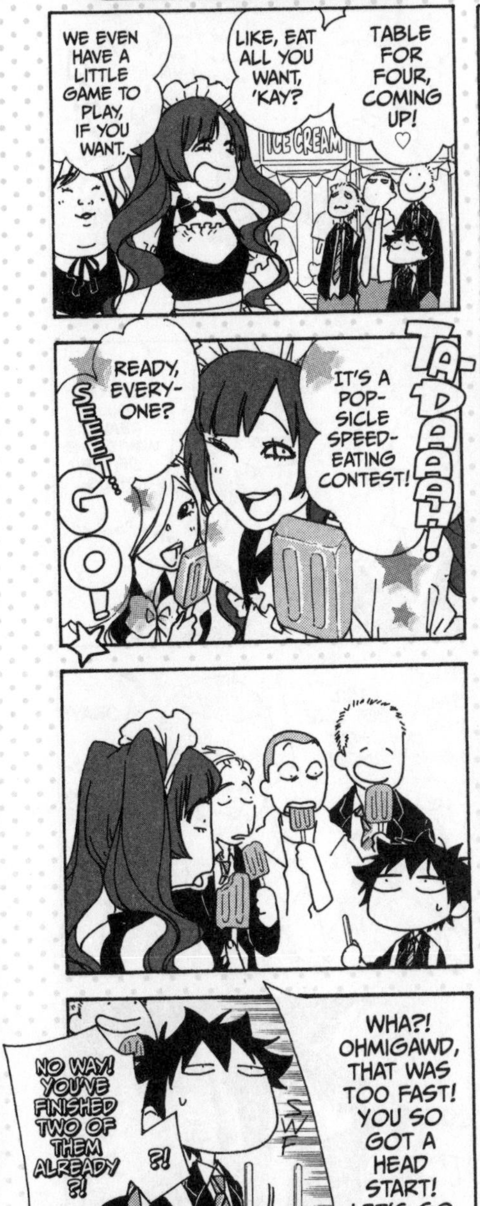
TABLE FOR FOUR, COMING UP! ♡
LIKE, EAT ALL YOU WANT, 'KAY?
WE EVEN HAVE A LITTLE GAME TO PLAY, IF YOU WANT.
ICE CREAM
TA-DAAAAH!
IT'S A POPSICLE SPEED-EATING CONTEST!
READY, EVERYONE?
SEEET...
GO!
WHA?! OHMIGAWD, THAT WAS TOO FAST! YOU SO GOT A HEAD START! LET'S GO AGA—
?!
NO WAY! YOU'VE FINISHED TWO OF THEM ALREADY?!
YO. WHY DO YOU LOOK SO PROUD BACK THERE, TOMA?

NICE GUYS

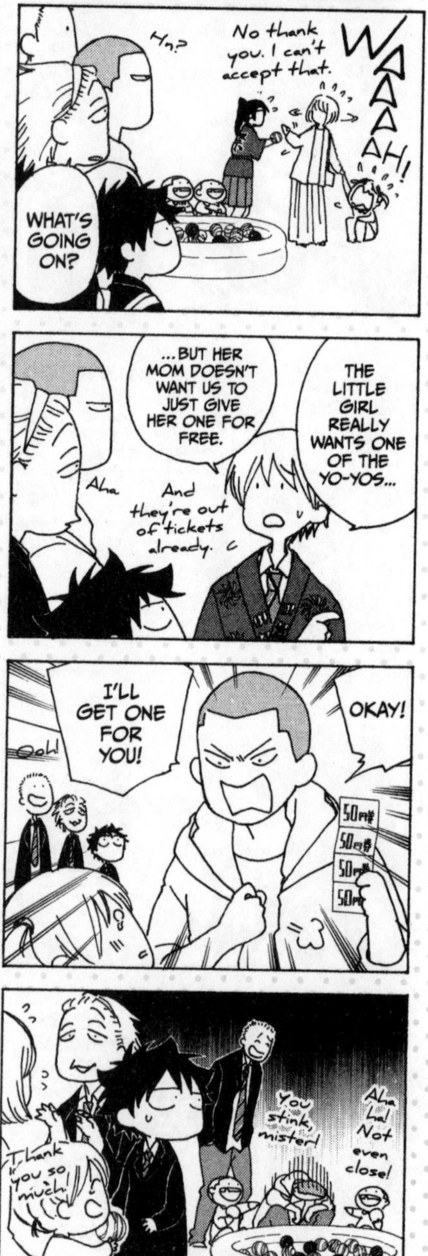
WAAAAAH!!
No thank you. I can't accept that.
Hn?
WHAT'S GOING ON?
THE LITTLE GIRL REALLY WANTS ONE OF THE YO-YOS...
...BUT HER MOM DOESN'T WANT US TO JUST GIVE HER ONE FOR FREE.
And they're out of tickets already.
Aha
OKAY!
I'LL GET ONE FOR YOU!
Ooh!
Aha ha! Not even close!
You stink, mister!
Thank you so much!

HAUNTED HOUSE OF FRIGHT

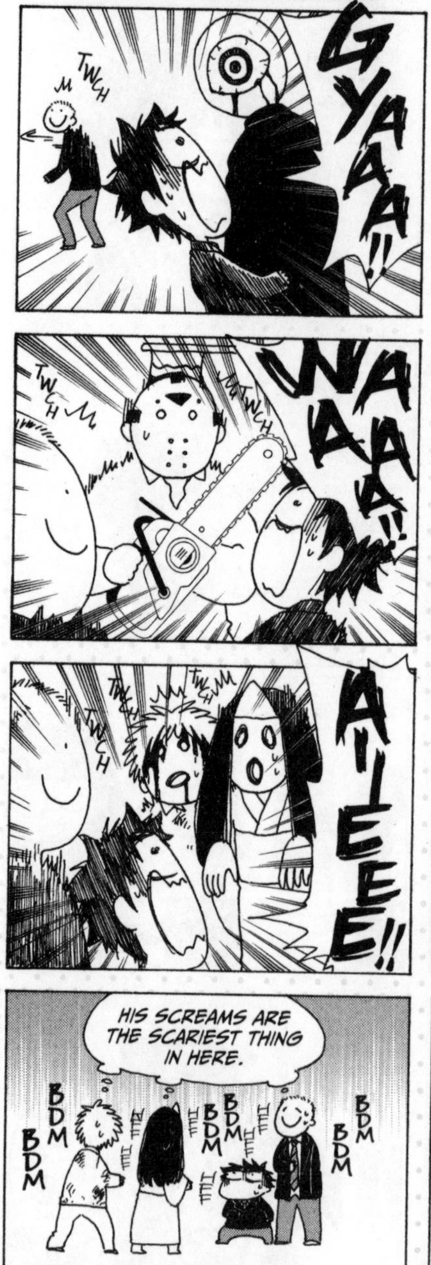
GYAAA!!
TWCH
WAAAA!!
TWCH
TWCH
AIIEEE!!
TWCH
TWCH
TWCH
HIS SCREAMS ARE THE SCARIEST THING IN HERE.
BDM BDM
BDM BDM
BDM BDM
BDM BDM

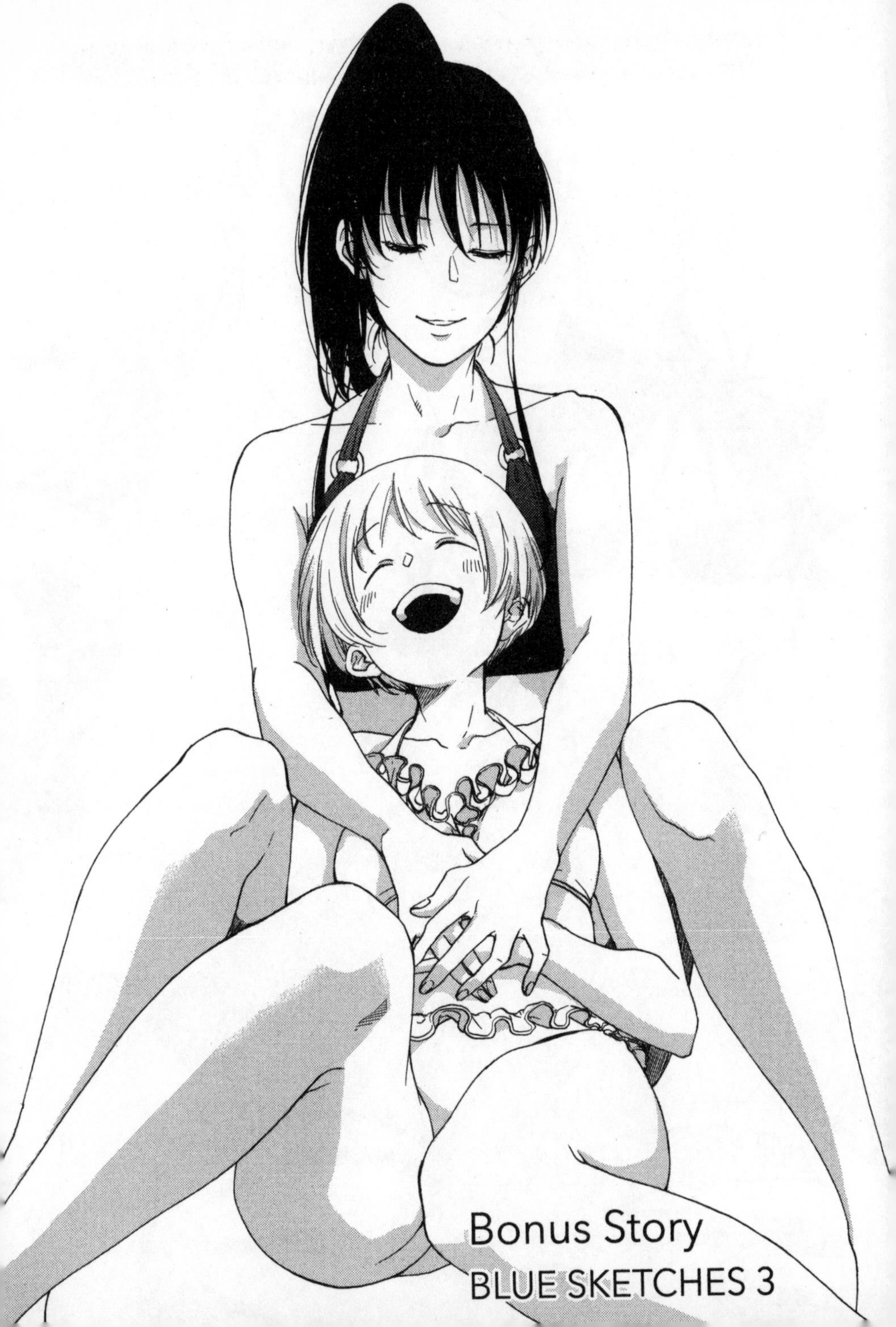

Bonus Story
BLUE SKETCHES 3

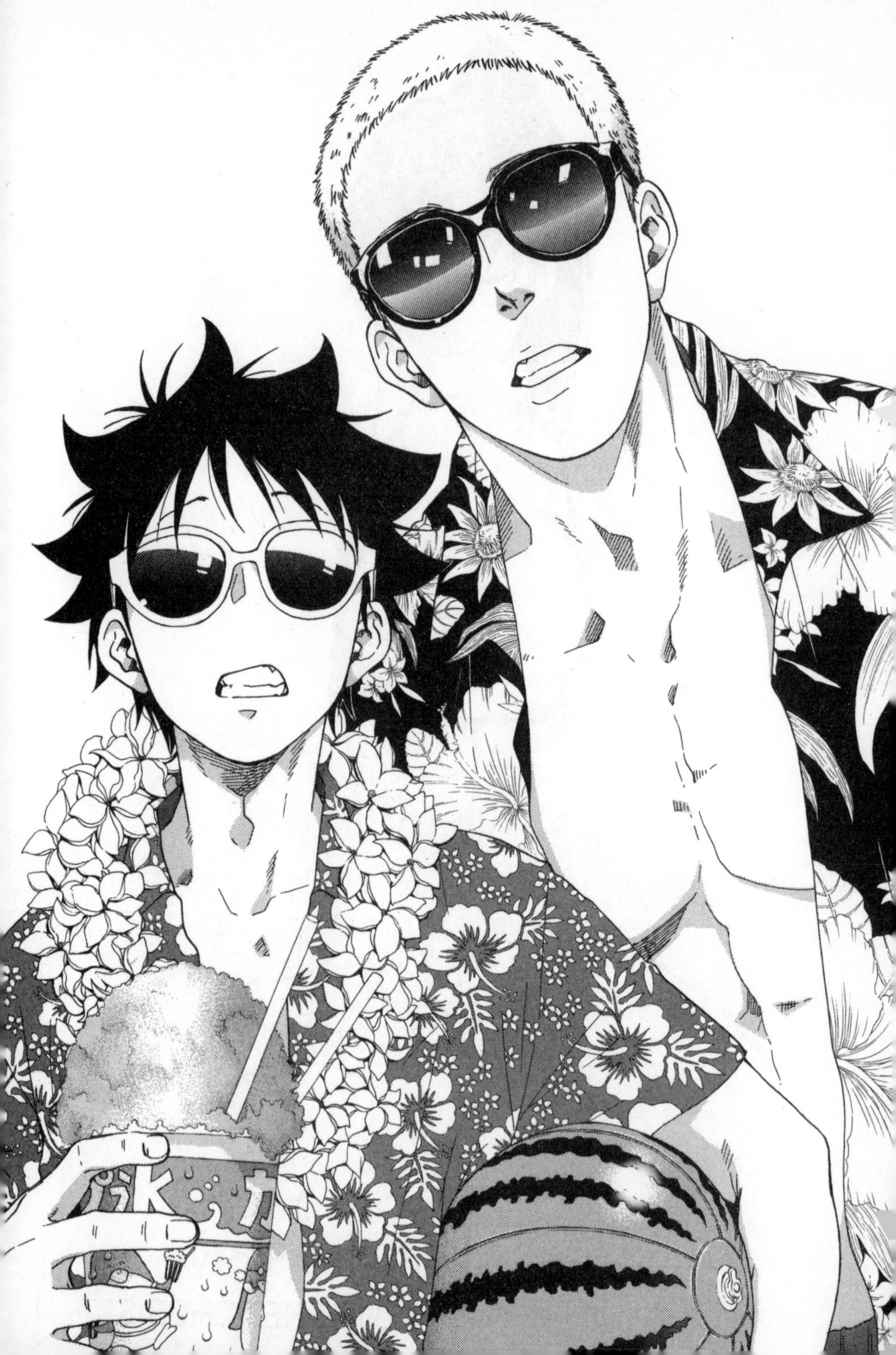

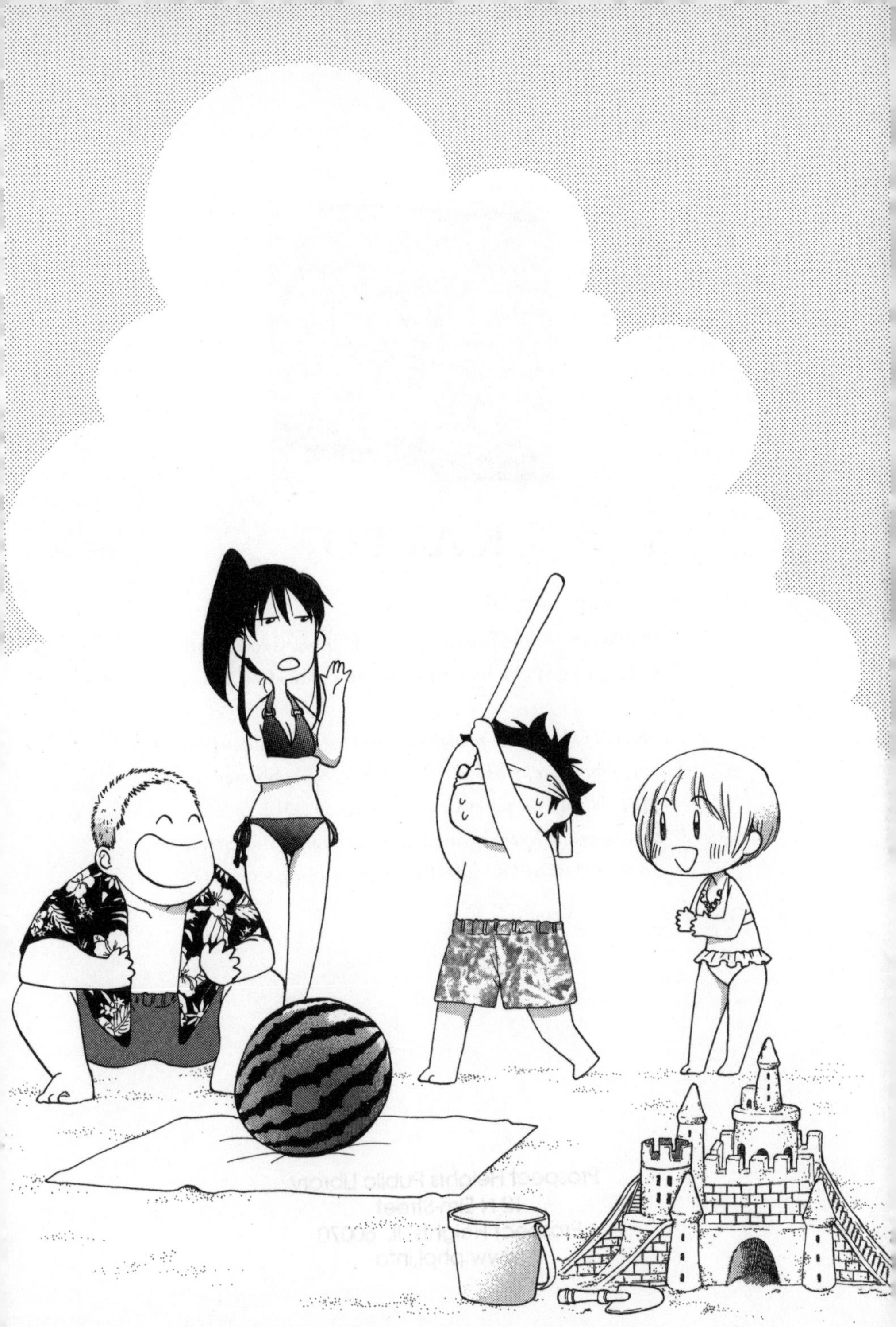

Bonus Story (END)

KAITO

Lately, one of the fun things I look forward to at work
is the game of Donjara the staff and I play after dinner.

*KAITO began his manga career at the age of 20, when
his one-shot "Happy Magi" debuted in* Weekly Shonen Jump.
He published the series Cross Manage *in 2012. In 2015,
he returned to* Weekly Shonen Jump *with* Buddy Strike.
KAITO started work on Blue Flag *in* Jump+ *in 2017.*

BLUE FLAG

VOL. 6

VIZ SIGNATURE EDITION

story and art by
KAITO

Translation / Adrienne Beck
Lettering / Annaliese "Ace" Christman
Design / Jimmy Presler
Editor / Marlene First

Printed in Italy

Published by VIZ Media, LLC
P.O. Box 77010
San Francisco, CA 94107

10 9 8 7 6 5 4 3 2
First printing, February 2021
Second printing, October 2021

VIZ MEDIA
viz.com

VIZ SIGNATURE
vizsignature.com

合格御守
合格御守

Blue Flag reads from right to left,
starting in the upper-right corner. Japanese is read
from right to left, meaning that action, sound
effects and word-balloon order are completely
reversed from English order.

YOU'RE
READING THE
WRONG WAY...